KUNDALINI JEDI WARRIOR
BOOK 1 - A NEW HOPE

JAG KALEY

Kundalini Jedi Warrior
Book 1– A New Hope

Copyright © 2021 by Jag Kaley.

All rights reserved. No part of this book may be used or reproduced in any manner whatsoever without written permission except in the case of brief quotations embodied in critical articles or reviews.

Thank you for buying an authorized edition of this book and for complying with copyright laws by not reproducing, scanning, or distributing any part of it in any form without permission. You are supporting writers and their hard work by doing this.

For information contact:

Jag Kaley at http://www.kundalinijeditraining.com/

Written by Jag Kaley.

Published in the United Kingdom.
ISBN   9781626765375

First Edition: July 2021

FOR MY ANCESTORS

YOUR ANCESTORS – JUST LIKE MINE – WERE SURVIVORS AND WARRIORS OF LOVE.

NO FAMINE, NO DROUGHT, NO NATURAL DISASTER, NO ENSLAVEMENT, NO GENOCIDE, AND NO VIRUS COULD STOP THEM FROM BRINGING YOU HERE.

TESTIMONIALS

"Jag Kaley's *'Kundalini Jedi Warrior Training Manual Part 1 of 3– A New Hope'* is a modern and fun course manual and inspirational self-development book addressing the most essential and timeless question of how to live life and become an inspired and fulfilled Jedi Yogi Warrior. Drawing from various teaching sources to illuminate the universal essence of "The Force" and its laws, the course is anchored in the Star Wars mythology and the teachings of Kundalini Yoga. It is an inspiring and efficient guide to transform one's life to more consciousness and to develop and apply the warrior spirit. Jag's witty and eloquent acumen is refreshing and infectious. An enjoyable and elevating read (and course) for awakening Star Wars lovers and yogis on the path of the Force."

Sat Siri Singh PHD - Kundalini Yoga Teacher

*

If you want to know how Star Wars can be the foundation for positive change in your life, then this is the book for you. Charismatic author Jag Kaley – real life Jedi,: martial arts blackbelt, and Kundalini Yoga teacher - reveals the secrets underpinning the success of this multi-million-dollar franchise and presents a practical contemporary training for the aspiring modern Jedi. This wonderful, starstruck, personal and practical guide is for the young hero in all of us that wants to learn to stand tall in the world without losing the magic. I double dare you to read it.

Francis Beadle AKA Fateh Singh – Buddhist and Mindfulness Teacher and Counsellor

*

"Jag Kaley offers the world a complete guide to self-empowerment and an elevated consciousness. This manual is a comprehensive and thorough guideline to becoming the best version of yourself. He has gathered so much important spiritual information in one book, that anyone who wants to be a real life Jedi now can really feel like one. A must read for any Star Wars fan."

Vero Geet Anand - Director of the Holistic Education International Association

*

"In a world that is so in need of clarity and examples of hero/warriors, I am proud to bear witness to a book that will answer the prayers of many. Like Jedi Jag, something in me was deeply activated as a boy by the mystery, magic, and spiritual connection I saw embodied by the Jedi warriors in the Star Wars movies. I wanted so badly to know how I could become as the Jedi were. Now, in this Kundalini Jedi Training Manual, Jag Kaley has given us a road map to the realization of an ideal, grounding it more deeply into this world and time. At times deeply moving and personal, Jedi Jag shows us the process by which he came to enliven and embody the Jedi archetype. At the same time, he weaves together the wisdom of many teachings as they pertain to the spiritual warrior, providing the context that makes this relevant for today's world. Astoundingly ambitious, this book also serves as a manual with powerful yogic practices that will support any aspiring padawan to take real steps along the path. The Force needed a book such as this. Many readers will be profoundly grateful that

Jedi Jag heard the call and answered by giving the world the Kundalini Jedi Training Manual." -

- Darren Hartwell Downey -Astrologer and Spiritual wellness instructor

*

"This book in your hand contains the aroma of the ancient yogic wisdom given birth by a very special man, Jag Kaley. He has carved out a path that anyone who is interested in bringing positive change in his/her life would benefit from. The book is a marriage between the Yogic Path and Star Wars. One who dives into this sacred bond, would be able to start a love affair with his/her life. It's a complete guide for self-empowerment and awakening awareness in your daily life."

Yogi Amandeep Singh – Himalayan Master-Yogi

*

"Get ready to meet the Force and awaken your inner Jedi through the powerful technology of Kundalini Yoga. Jag Kaley's book offers new insights on the ancient Warrior archetype and its qualities of fearless presence, intuitive knowing and conscious living. Witty, light hearted and yet profound, this manual is packed with valuable tools for a new generation of Jedis to face the challenges of today."

Suhab Kaur, PhD - Artist, Musician and Yoga teacher.

*

"Jag Kaley is a Therapist and KYT, and he also holds a black belt in TaeKwonDo. He uses the symbols of his early fascination with Lucas' Star Wars and ideal of Jedi to change the shadow forces driving the individual and collective human psyche and awaken the dormant Hero Archetype. He threads the timeless yogic techniques with his personal path, inquiries, and practices that can help seekers to excel on their path."

Lidija Martinovic Rekert - Yogic practitioner, Therapist and owner of the Yoga Wheel

*

"There can be little doubt that we are on the verge of an enormous shift in consciousness, and it seems that this is just the beginning of the roller coaster ride. Political, educational and health systems are no longer fit for purpose. The credibility of our leaders is at an all-time low, while anxiety and depression are at an all-time high. Many people are yearning for a connection to the sacred, the mystical. They are searching for a version of power that has integrity, honour and compassion.

There are thousands of books written on man's search for the intangible – from ancient spiritual texts to philosophy, mythology and psychology, but they all share one theme… the necessity of removing focus from the outside world and awakening the power within. Jag Kaley has skillfully woven together ideas from many of these books and produced both a guide and a tool kit to becoming empowered in the 21st century.

With the strength of mass marketing and social media stealing our focus on a daily basis, this book has never been more needed. Our era has been called the age of mass distraction, resulting in minds that are either chronically over stimulated or completely apathetic. It is a time for warriors.

Jag's desire to convey a message of optimism, particularly to a young generation, is admirable. He explains complex ideas in an accessible way. I hope he encourages an army of young Jedi to find their inner hero and to follow in his footsteps. The world is waiting to applaud them."

Eleanor O'Rourke- author of Breakdown - A Rebel's Take On Depression
The Freedom Project - How To Find Contentment In A Crazy World

*

"Whether individual or collective, this book provides an immense opportunity filled with possibilities. Rather than dwell in fatalistic hopelessness and passively watch the world go by on your screen, how about awakening your latent potential for personal triumph and service to humanity?

Jag Kaley (real life Jedi Warrior) sends out a call to the spiritual warriors of the era to arise and self-initiate. To synchronise your body, mind and spirit towards a higher purpose. Through the teachings of Kundalini Yoga, Jag provides the tools and the technology to make it real. Here is revealed the attitude that strengthens the heart and the insights you need to keep the lens of the mind clean and in clear focus. Following the path of the Jedi you will easily face the challenges of life and flourish in all circumstances.

Do you feel the sense of destiny awaiting? Are you ready transform your fears, harness your emotional charge, and align your thought patterns with the Cosmic Intelligence?

Jag describes the training, discipline, commitment, practice, and faith needed not as qualities that might put you off but that will capture your imagination and inspire you to be part of something greater. Through the beautiful interplay of the practical and mystical teachings with the archetypes as described in the Cosmic Theatre of Star Wars, Jag illustrates how our personal journey is interwoven with the Greater story of humanity. We are all part of the whole; may this book serve to guide you to play your part consciously and well.

Shiv Charan Singh - Master Kundalini Yoga teacher at Karam Kriya Consultancy

*

The Kundalini Jedi Warrior Training Manual by Jag Kaley is a brilliant work for those interested in Indian cosmology, myth and yoga. Kaley expertly intertwines these subjects into a meaningful metaphorical self study, that allows a person to align themselves into the cosmic worldview given by Kaley therein. Whether a person is a layman or expert, by reading this view they can gain many new insights. Kaley also offers psychological insights into meditation and yogic development.

- Dr Kamalroop Singh PHD (UK)- Akal Nihang Warrior

***

Jag Kaley gives us a timely training manual for the modern day Jedi with his book Kundalini Jedi Warrior training. Jag is a master at delivering the path of the Spiritual Warrior in a way that makes it accessible and meaningful. Filled with so much spiritual wisdom and deft observation of Pop culture and modern day life, his writing offers a playful and heartfelt lense to experience very profound spiritual teachings through.

- Bir Kaur Khalsa -Kundalini yoga teacher trainer

Jag's book, 'Kundalini Jedi Warrior' is a journey about self-discovery and self-empowerment, through the eyes of a Jedi Warrior. Jag shares practical, self-empowerment tools relevant to the times we are living in, with insightful quotes from the Star Wars movies. He makes the ancient teachings of Kundalini Yoga accessible to everyone and challenges us to dig deeper and question our self-beliefs: what are we doing here, how can we reach our full potential and how can we contribute to the better good of humanity and the planet. I highly recommend Jag's book to anyone who is curious to live a happier, healthier and more fulfilled life.

- Kathryn McCusker, Opera singer, Author, Kundalini Yoga teacher

ACKNOWLEDGMENTS

Firstly, I would like to thank the all-powerful Force that has guided me, inspired me, led me, and which flows through me. Without it, I could not have been a position to write and present this powerful Jedi material. I would like to thank my ancestors; without whom I would not be here today. I would like to thank my mum and my family for their support and encouragement with my book writing project. I would like to thank my teacher Dharam Kaur Khalsa for her support and grounding during moments when I was spinning out of control. A special thank you to my editor, Melissa Mitchell, who kept the ship steady and worked past the point of exhaustion to get the project finished. I'd like to thank Yogi Bhajan for bringing, and devising, these teachings for the West. I would like to thank Sat Siri Singh, who spent hours, days, and months reviewing and editing the material. I'd like to thank Veronica Leandrez for her help and support in the early drafts of the book. Thank you to Fateh Singh, Bir Kaur Khalsa and Darren Hartwell Downey for reading, reviewing, and suggesting edits for the book material.

To my feline best friend, and writing partner, Bella; whose love and cuddles got me through the frustrations of writing. I'd like to thank George Lucas for creating the best movie story ever told and for all of the creative people, and directors, that have continued to share the myth of *Star Wars* with the many generations of fans.

Finally to you all – the Jedi readers that buy and enjoy this book - I hope it has touched and inspired you to become the greatest Jedi warrior you could ever be.

*

THE STAR WARS SAGA

The terms Star Wars, Jedi, The Force, and May the Force be with You as well as several other terms from within the Star Wars film franchise which have been used in this book are the registered trademarks of Lucasfilm Entertainment Company Ltd. LLC who have not approved or endorsed this book in any way. Some of the inclusions will be encompassed of scenes, quotes, and storylines from:

- Star Wars: Episode IV – A New Hope (1977)
- Star Wars: Episode V – The Empire Strikes Back (1980)
- Star Wars: Episode VI – Return of the Jedi (1983)
- Star Wars: Episode I – The Phantom Menace (1999)
- Star Wars: Episode II – Attack of the Clones (2002)
- Star Wars: Episode III – Revenge of the Sith (2005)
- Star Wars: Episode VII – The Force Awakens (2015)
- Rogue One: A Star Wars Story (2016)
- Star Wars: Episode VIII – The Last Jedi (2017)
- Solo: A Star Wars Story (2018)
- Star Wars: Episode IX – The Rise of Skywalker (2019)

***

CONTENTS

TESTIMONIALS 5
ACKNOWLEDGMENTS 9
FOREWORD 19
FOR THE READER 21
A WORD ON KUNDALINI 23
INTRODUCTION 24

CHAPTER 1: THE DARK TIMES 28
What is The State of Our World? 29
The Masks We Wear 31
Why Even Bother? 32
Battle of Frequencies: A New Hope 34
Raising Vibrational Energy 34
    Psychological Energy 35
    Emotional Energy 35
A Fear-Based Society 37
    The Tree of Life 38
        The Meaning of the Tree of Life 39
The Return of the Jedi 39

CHAPTER 2: CYCLE OF THE AGES 41
The Four Ages 41
    Old Ways are Dying 43
    The Aquarian Age 43
This Human Experience 44
    JEDI EXERCISE: Mindfulness 45
Calling all Jedi 45

CHAPTER 3: A NEW BEGINNING 47
Am I a Padawan? 47
    Ways to Increase your Vibrational Frequency 48
    Beginner's Mind 49
        Jedi Exercise: Beginner's Mind 49
        Beginner's Mind Exercise with Daily Activities 50
Your Observing Self 51
    Jedi Exercise: Journal of the Wills 52
    Self-Inquiry 52
    Journal Entries Exercise Continued 53
Cocoon: Our Comfort Zone 54

CHAPTER 4: THE STAR WARS PHENOMENON 56
The Impact of the Franchise 56
The Inspiration of George Lucas 58
    Jedi Exercise: What Moves You? 59

CHAPTER 5: STORYTELLING 61
- The Power of Story 61
  - Jedi Exercise: Changing Your Life Story 62
- Myth Making 64
  - Joseph Campbell's Monomyth 65
- The Hero 67
  - Jedi Exercise: We Need a Hero 68

CHAPTER 6: THE HERO'S JOURNEY 69
- Hero to Warrior 69
  - The Journey 70
  - 12 Stages of the hero's Journey 71
    - The Spiritual Journey 72
    - Luke's Stages of the Journey 74
    - Jedi Exercise: Personal Hero's Journey 77
  - My Hero's Journey Story 78
    - The Awakening 83
    - The Calling 84
    - Doubt 85
    - The Mission 86
    - Canada – A New Land 87
    - Meeting the Mentors 89
    - Crossing the Threshold 93
    - Tests, Allies, and (Fr)enemies 93
    - Approach to Innermost Cave 95
    - The Ordeal 98
    - The Road Back: Summer Solstice 101
    - Resurrection: 3 Days 103
    - Return with the Elixir 105

CHAPTER 7: THE ARCHETYPES 106
- Origins of the Archetypes 107
  - The 12 Archetypes 107
  - Jedi Exercise: Archetypal Psychology 107
- The Warrior Archetype 109

CHAPTER 8: A NEED FOR WARRIORS 110
- A True Warrior 110
- Warrior Evolution 110
- Worthy Archetypes Alongside the Warrior: 111
  - The Sage 111
  - The Magician 112
- Jedi Exercise: Evolution of the Warrior 113
- Legends 113

- Sikh Warriors 114
- Warriors of Old 114
- Wars in the Name of God 117
- The Bad Reputation of the Warrior 117
- The Good Fight 118
  - Jedi Exercise: The Good Warrior 119
- Spiritual Warriors 119
  - Myths of the Spiritual Warriors 125
  - Warrior Qualities 130

CHAPTER 9: YOGA 133
- Yogis 133
  - Habits of the Yogi 134
  - Attributes of the Yogi 135
- Jedi Life 136
  - Jedi And Stoicism 137
- Kundalini Jedi Warrior 138
- Power of the Universe 140
  - Sound, Vibration & Frequency 140
    - Jedi Vibrational Exercise 141
  - Mantras 141
    - Tuning In Mantra 142
    - Sat Nam 142
    - Waheguru 142
    - Jedi Exercise: Sa Ta Na Ma Meditation 144
    - Jedi Exercise: Create your Sacred Space 145
  - My First Yoga Experience 145
- The Aims of Yoga 146
- Kundalini Jedi Warm-Up Exercises 148
- Cosmic Energy 150

CHAPTER 10: THE POWER OF KUNDALINI 151
- Kundalini 151
- What is the Force – Really? 152
  - The Force and God 153
  - The Universal Force 154
  - Protecting Your Energy 155
    - Sunia Meditation 155
  - Jedi Exercise: Hand Sensitisation 157
- Luminous Beings 158
- Knowing the Force 159
- A Way of Seeing Life 160
- Yogic Superpowers 161

- Jedi Force Abilities ... 162
- Self-Mastery ... 163
- Midi-chlorians and Prana ... 165
- Kundalini Awakening ... 166
- What Are the Benefits of Cosmic k Energy? ... 167
  - How Do I Get More Cosmic Energy? ... 167
- Kundalini Yoga Practice ... 168
  - Jedi Exercise – Sat Kriya ... 170
  - The Ten Bodies ... 171
    - 1st Body: The Soul Body ... 172
    - 2nd Body: The Negative (protective) Mind ... 172
    - 3rd Body: The Positive (expansive) Mind ... 172
    - 4th Body: The Neutral Mind ... 172
    - 5th Body: The Physical Body ... 173
    - 6th Body: the Arcline ... 173
    - 7th Body: The Aura ... 173
    - 8th Body: the Pranic Body ... 173
    - 9th Body: The Subtle Body ... 174
    - 10th Body: The Radiant Body ... 174

CHAPTER 11: A CODE TO LIVE BY ... 175

- Living the Warrior's Code ... 175
  - The Original Yoda ... 175
- The 8 Limbs of Yoga ... 176
  - The Yamas and Niyamas ... 178
    - The Yamas ... 178
    - The Niyamas ... 178
  - The Code of the Jedi ... 179
    - There is no emotion, there is peace ... 179
    - Jedi Exercise: Peace Reflection ... 180
    - There is no ignorance, there is knowledge ... 180
    - There is no passion, there is serenity ... 181
    - There is no chaos, there is harmony ... 182
    - There is no death, there is the Force ... 183
  - Be You ... 184
  - Breathe, Just Breathe ... 187
    - Pranayama ... 187
    - Vayus ... 188
    - Nadis ... 188
    - Breathing Power ... 189

CHAPTER 12: THE WILL OF THE WARRIOR 196
- Hara Centre 196
- The Dan Tien 196
- The Chakras 197
  - Navel Point 199
    - Stretch Pose 200
    - Nahbi Kriya 201

CHAPTER 13: THE DARK SIDE OF THE WARRIOR 211
- Warrior in its Negative Expression 212
  - The Dark Warrior Archetype 214
  - Hero to Warrior-Boy to Man 215
  - Warrior Evolution through Archetypal Partnership 216
    - The Sage Archetype 216
    - The Caregiver 217
    - The Magician 217
- Working with Archetypes 218
- How to Access the Warrior Archetype 218

CHAPTER 14: FEAR: PATH TO THE LIGHT SIDE 220
- Facing Our Fears 220
- Eye of the Storm 223
  - Meditation: Fear in the Now 224
- The Ghosts of Fear 225
  - Meditation: Remove Ghosts of Fear 226
- Fear of the Future 227
- Meditation: Fear of the Future 227
- Death 228
  - It is Our Greatest Fear 229

CHAPTER 15: THE POWER OF ANGER 232
- Anger 232
  - Anger isn't Good or Bad 234
  - Power through Anger 234
  - Anger as an Ally 235
    - Jedi Exercise: Gain Awareness of Your Anger 235
  - Journey With Anger 235
    - Meditation to Transcend Individual Consciousness and Anger 236
- Mind, Body, Spirit 237

CHAPTER 16: THE JEDI MIND TRICK 238
- The Mind 238
  - Thoughts 238
  - Mind over Matter 239

- No Mind 240
- Meditation 245
  - Creating your Meditation Space 247
  - Concentration Meditation 247
  - Breath Awareness Meditation 248
  - Mindfulness Meditation 248
  - Walking Meditation 248
  - Candle Meditation 249
- A Positive Mind 250
  - Jedi Exercise: Develop a Positive Attitude 251
  - The Jedi Attitude 252
  - Never Complain 253
    - Jedi Exercise: Stop complaining. 253
  - Be Grateful for the Force 253
    - Jedi Gratitude Task 254
  - Acceptance 254
- Resistance 255
- Persistence 255
- Keyboard Warriors 256

CHAPTER 17: THE BODY TEMPLE 258

- The Body 258
  - Yoga for Body Strength 259
    - Jedi Exercise: Sun Salutations - Yoga Set For Strengthening 260
    - Strengthening the Aura 262
- Martial Arts 264
  - Using the Force to Flow with our Movements 267
  - Awareness Is Everything 267
  - Conflict Begins and Ends From Within 267
  - The Journey Is What Matters 267
  - Discipline and Self-Mastery 267
- Strengthening the Nervous System 268
  - Hydrotherapy – The Power of Cold Showers 268
  - Sleep 270
  - The Jedi Diet 271
    - The Force in Food 271
    - Buying Ethical Food 272
    - Yogic Diet: Life Force Foods 272
    - Guidelines for Preparing Food 272
    - Guidelines for Good Digestion and Elimination 273
    - Dark Side Intoxicants 273
  - Body Posture and Confidence 274

- An Attitudinal Shift 276
  - The Great Cosmic Joke 277
- Jedi Mindfulness and Connecting with the Body 278
  - Grounding 279
  - Jedi Exercise: Sufi Grinds 282
  - Body Language 282
  - Jedi Exercise: Body Scan 285
  - Jedi Exercise: Gathering the Force 287

CHAPTER 18: LOVE VIBRATIONS 291

- Jedi and the Power of Love 291
  - Anakin and Padme 291
  - Han and Leia 291
  - Han and Qi'ra 292
  - Rey and Kylo Ren/Ben Solo 292
- The Need for Unconditional Love 293
- Heartbroken 294
- Meditation: Heal a Broken Heart 295
- Forgiveness 296
- Compassion 296
- The Jedi Path to Self-Love 297
  - Heart Chakra 297
  - Jedi Loving 298
  - What Self-Love Isn't 299
- Meditation for a Calm Heart 299
- Kriya for Creating Self-Love 301
- Practice Authentic Self-Love 304

CHAPTER 19: FAITH IN THE FORCE 306

- The Power of Belief 307
- A New Hope 308
- Solitude and Silence 308
  - Jedi Exercise: Silence Exercise 309
- Prayer 309
  - How to Pray 310
  - The Temple of the Jedi Order 310
- Surrender 310
  - The Serenity Prayer: Jedi Edition 311
  - Surrender vs. Control Strategies 313
  - Why Surrender is True Power 313
  - How to Practice Surrender 314
- Synchronicity 315
  - Jedi Exercise: Connect with the Force 316

CHAPTER 20: THE PHANTOM MENACE 317
- The Inner Guide: Higher Self 317
- Ego: The Phantom Menace 318
  - Characteristics of the Ego 320
  - Journaling to Explore Your Intuition 322
- Developing Your Intuition 323
  - Silence to Engage your Intuition 323
- The Golden Chain 324

CHAPTER 21: SACRIFICE 325
- Service to the Galaxy: Jedi vs. Sith 325
  - The Way of the Sith 326
  - Me-Me Generation: Rise of the Selfie & Digital Narcissism 326
  - Greek Myth: Narcissus 327
  - Apathy 328
  - The Sith Approach 328
- Selfless Service 330
  - The Power of Service 331
- Your Mission 332
  - Humility 333
  - Jedi Exercise: Solution for Apathy 334

CHAPTER 22: RISE: THE FINAL CHANGES 337
- The Ending: Change 337
- Spiritual Teachers 337
- Mentors 338
- Tipping Point 339
- Rewiring Our Habits 339
  - Unlearn What you Have Learnt 340
- Effects of Different Lengths of Meditation 341
- Meditation for Change 341

The End is the Beginning 343
Conclusion 345
Afterword 347
  EPILOGUE......BOOK 2: THE DARKSIDE 347
  An Explorative Guide Into Your Next Mission 349
Appendix 351
Jag Kaley's Bio 370
CONTACT 371
Index 371
Citations 379

FOREWORD

BY DANIEL M JONES

My journey into the light was not always an easy one. As with any Jedi, the path that lay in front of me had many trials and tribulations. At the age of 20, after being spiritually inspired by Star Wars, I opened the very first International Church of Jediism. It had come after a childhood spent studying the nature of human behaviour. I was always intrigued by the striking similarities between all religions and all cultures. Star Wars had ensnared my attention from the age of 4, and I was always fascinated by the ways in which the Saga tied all living beings together. This Force, that is so present in all cultures and religions, is what connects us all – even outside of the films. The beloved Jedi Knights who seek to uphold the ways of the light, are who we all aspire to be. We are all inherently good deep down inside, and light always tries to find its way to the surface.

When we speak about the Jedi we instantly think of Star Wars. That being said, when I hear the word Jedi, I think 'warrior'. To be a Jedi is more than just a word, a film franchise, or a TV show. A Jedi is a guardian of light - a being of pure intentions and the protector of all things good. Every one of us has the ability to be a Jedi. Not only that, but as I say, every one of us is, deep down, a Jedi at heart.

My story took a tumultuous turn in 2009, just 2 short years after I had founded the Church. What would happen in Tesco that year brought the problem of intolerance to light, and it was undoubtedly a silver lining to the entire situation. I was sadly asked to remove my headwear, a symbolic part of our Jedi ways. It came as a shock as those practicing under the principles of other religions were afforded the right to adorn their own versions of headdress.

I made mention to the store manager of the fact that it states in our Jedi doctrine that I can wear headwear. What was more upsetting was the fact that it only covered the back of my head; meaning that my face was still clearly visible on store cameras – even if that were the real problem, which I still don't believe it was. I was escorted to the front of the store where, once again, I was ordered to remove my hood. After explaining the doctrine to them once more and even going so far as to present them with a business card from our Church, they still insisted on being quite rude and pressing the matter. The matter was eventually resolved amicably, but only after it was brought to light on an international platform. This speaks to the fact that we, as aspiring Jedi, must do what is right even when others are not watching. They should have acted in a more tolerant and peaceful manner even before the spotlight was on them. I, on the other hand, understand the ignorance around the situation, but stand firm in my beliefs even when no one else is watching – even when I am simply stepping out to the store. We must stand for what is right and true at all times.

It takes me back to my point. I have seen many hours of Stars Wars, watching every little move, taking note of every little detail, and truly seeing what the Jedi bring to the table. Each and every time it forms a deeper connection to me. You see, we are all spiritual beings here in this life. However, most of us just don't know it yet.

Why don't we all know this?

The answer is complex but also simple. We have all been treated with toxic input from the world around us: game shows, video games, fast food, drugs, and entertainment. All of the above are designed to stop you in your spiritual path to enlightenment to becoming a true Jedi.

So how do we break free from this turmoil and urge ourselves as humanity towards a spiritual existence?

We submit ourselves through learning – more importantly through learning from people who have created media on this topic to help you on your journey. This book is about just that and one way you can create a connection to who you really are. Just like my heroes in the Star Wars movies taught me, so shall this book teach you.

I ask you, take your journey seriously and with an open heart and mind.

Then you will be free.

- *Daniel M. Jones, Founder of The Church Of Jediism and author of the book Power of the Force*

Nota Bene:

Daniel M. Jones is the original founder of the International Church of Jediism which has millions of followers around the globe. As someone living with Asperger Syndrome, Daniel touches people's lives through his YouTube Channel – Aspire World. He attests that the teachings of Jediism played a significant role in helping him manage his condition. Daniel has been diagnosed with Autism, Dyslexia, Obsessive Compulsive Disorder (OCD), and Attention Deficit Hyperactivity Disorder (ADHD). He uses his influence in a positive way in order to help educate people about autism. A man of many talents, Daniel has been inspiring those within his Church while still working on his chemistry degree and composing songs for his pop-punk band: Straight Jacket Legends. He is also responsible for creating the first neurodiverse panel talking about ADHD and autism at VidCon US - the largest video convention in the world.

The Jedi Masters who work alongside him at the Church are dedicated to helping others realise their full potential.

We are humbled and grateful for his support of this guide.

***

FOR THE READER

This book is also written for **you,** and for the Jedi that you always wanted to be. This is for all the dreamers; all the knights in shining armour living a plain-clothed existence. This is for anyone who never fit in, or felt they didn't belong, and that were destined for more than an ordinary life. This is for the little boy or girl within you who hoped and wished to do brave things; to save the world, or who just wanted to be an upstanding citizen of society.

Maybe you hope to use this book to become a wiser parent or more successful business person.

Maybe you wish to develop your Jedi skills to improve your grades and pursue a fulfilling and holistic career.

Maybe you are going to school and your fear of the new environment has you hoping that these Jedi skills will allow you to feel safe.

This is for all the real-life Jedi that exist out there, wherever you are in the world. This is not about becoming some fantasy character, but really about becoming more of who you already are – who you truly are. The Jedi seed of consciousness already exists within you, the tools and techniques here will help you realise your unique Jedi expression.

Becoming a Jedi is no easy thing. In today's world the temptation to the dark side is as strong as it has ever been. My hope for you is that this book will give you a new perspective on the power of the Star Wars story. I will propose practices and methods that will allow you to connect with energy within yourself as well as energy that is around you. If you've ever felt the call to be a Jedi and hoped to be so in the future, then this book will give you tools and techniques so that you may embrace your inner Jedi.

You will learn about the power of awareness and begin the practice of self-enquiry to understand who you really are. You will be encouraged to begin a formal journal practice to capture your insights and record your reflections of life and your place in the world. The beginning of the book takes a look at the current global situation and describes the dark times that we are facing. We will find that all life is a manifestation of vibration, energy and frequency. How we manage our mind and body has a great influence on the quality of life we live and how changing our frequency can lead us to a more empowered and fearless way of living.

We will look at the structure and the importance of the Star Wars myth and we will discuss how humans use traditional myths to understand the inner conflicts that shape our lives and experiences. We'll explore the "hero's journey" as described by Joseph Campbell and introduce Carl Jung, his theory of archetypes, and how they shape our personalities.

The main premise of this book is to approach life from the ***Warrior Archetype*** perspective. We'll look at the various manifestations of this archetype as well as how to re-frame and apply them in order to create the life experiences that we have always wanted. We'll also take an in-depth look at who and what the Jedi are as well as their similarities to the traditional Yogis. From here we will attempt to gain an understanding of what the Force is, as described in the Star Wars universe, and to relate it to the Yogic understanding of cosmic Energy known as the Kundalini. We'll provide an overview of what Yoga is as well as the many aspects and tools of yogic practice; giving a brief summary of the basics of practice and providing you with specific exercises and yoga sets that will develop your inner Jedi qualities.

It is in chapter 2 that we will begin the foundational work of change to develop the different aspects of your humanity - developing the mind, body, spirit - with various yogic exercises to develop strength and resilience. We'll explore the 3rd chakra, where a warrior's strength comes from, and then begin developing the will of the Warrior Archetype. I strongly suggest adopting a yogic lifestyle to support and increase your access to The Force. These shifts will allow you to implement small changes to your life that will encourage the development of warriorship. Warriors must master their fear and channel the energy of anger for the greater good of all.

We will, therefore, explore the power of sound and mantra as a tool to quieten the mind and increase your vibrational frequency; looking at the development of Siddhas as well as how these yogic superpowers can be experienced and used in practical life. We develop our intuition as our inner teacher to guide us through the vicissitudes of life. You will come to see that as you inhabit more of the qualities and traits of the Jedi, you will be able to slowly increase your vibrational frequency and experience greater states of power, presence, peace and happiness.

Towards the end of the book, you will become acquainted with the Jedi's most powerful weapon and how reclaiming this aspect of yourself will help you fulfil your destiny in becoming a warrior. Then you will be able to decide how you will use your new warrior's powers to create a positive change in the world. You have the option of reading the book in its entirety – from cover to cover – or perusing a few chapters that appeal to your own personal plight. I do encourage you all to complete the exercises in order of appearance only once you have read the entire guide as they will systematically develop your mind and body in a progressive manner.

Writing this book has been its own hero's journey for me . This is the first book I have ever written and I had no idea what a challenge and endeavour it would be. My own challenges with dyslexia have meant the process of writing at times became the metaphorical dragon I had to overcome . The completion of this book ends a long 3 year journey which began in October of 2018. Whilst reading you may find some errors , mistakes or passages that may confuse you , I would ask for your patience and understanding and hope that you would contact me (contact details are at the back of the book) and let me know what you find so that I may amend things for the future revised version of this manual. Thank you for being part of this writing journey with me .

Good luck, and may the Force be with you.

***

A WORD ON KUNDALINI

Kundalini Yoga is sort of its own insular community - there are teachers and practitioners all over the world. I would make an approximate guess of around 30,000 people worldwide practice and teach this form of yoga and outside of this there are almost 100,000 yoga teachers worldwide

Known as the Yoga of Awareness, Kundalini is an exceptionally powerful tool which harnesses the power of one's soul; allowing you to truly experience it. We exert our will over all of our energy – both physical and mental. We combine the use of breath, mantra, postures, body-locks, mudra, and eye-focus to balance the body's glandular system and purify the blood, as well as to give one nerves of steel and the lung capacity of the greatest free diver.

It is a universal practice that the everyday man – and woman – can partake in. It allows us to reign in our thoughts and manage the stresses of the outside world with the calm composure of a leaf floating atop the water. Brought to us by Yogi Bhajan, Kundalini has been openly taught for the last half a century. It was brought to light in order to help us navigate the transition from the Piscean Age to the Aquarian Age.

Kundalini is a powerful energy that once awoken can have a great many benefits on the mind and body as well as connecting us to the source of all creation. There are instances when the energy rises in some people that they may experience some uncomfortable sensations and strange experiences .These cases are rare but do happen. If you are worried or if you are experiencing adverse effects from the awakening energy you may contact us for guidance and support. (Contact details can be found at the back of this book).

This book is aimed at a new generation of people who are becoming spiritually awakened. It is a solution to the challenges of the current times. It is for Star Wars fans who want to develop, or deepen, their understanding of the Star Wars themes and mythology. It is an opportunity for people to develop Jedi attributes and apply them to real life living. It is for new, beginner, intermediate, and possibly, advanced students of yoga. This book is intended to be a light-hearted, self-help manual whose principles and practices applied would transform their relationship with themselves and life in general.

DISCLAIMER:

The information provided in this book is designed to provide helpful information on the subjects discussed herein. This book is not meant to be used, nor should it be used, to diagnose or treat any medical condition. For diagnosis or treatment of any medical problem, consult your own physician.

***

INTRODUCTION

For as long as I can remember, I have always wanted to be a Jedi. It's one of the earliest and most fundamental memories that I have. All I really remember about my childhood was Star Wars. Growing up, and maybe even helping me to grow, Star Wars saturated my early formative years with magic and fun. The films came with the promise of adventure and hope for the future. Everything good about being young and finding my way in life was connected to Star Wars. The franchise got me through some very dark days and difficult times when I was growing up. As someone who was immersed in a troubled home-life – with no small thanks to my alcoholic father who literally was my own Darth Vader and, in my opinion, the personification of evil – Star Wars felt like a beacon of hope. However, the former is a story for another time. I would even go so far as to say Star Wars saved my life. It was my light in the dark; the place that I could retreat to in order to escape when it all became too much to bear. It has been my guiding light; reminding me of the long journey we all embark on from the moment we are born.

It reminds me that we all experience trials and tribulations.

It solidifies my belief in the power of the human spirit to overcome evil and save the day.

For me, these films are like a childhood sweetheart. Watching them was undoubtedly the first time that I fell in love with something completely. This book is my love letter to the Star Wars world that I grew up with. Perhaps the blank canvas of a naïve, young, fresh mind just waiting to be filled with magic and spectacle meant that I was in the right place at the right time.

I had no choice but to fall in love with Star Wars.

Maybe it was a biological drive.

Maybe it was the fulfilment of fantasy.

Maybe the story called to some deep longing within me.

Maybe it was destiny.

Watching the movies was only the beginning. The toys and figures provided a connection to my heroes and their adventures. To me these were sacred objects that were more important than food, sleep, and school – definitely more important than school.

These 3.75-inch plastic characters made the galaxy that was far, far away seem nearer and oh so real. They were something tangible and they allowed my creativity to flow as I came up with new stories and adventures for the heroes that I had only seen on screen. My first ever Star Wars figure was a stormtrooper. I took him - it could've been a her - everywhere with me. I made him a small house made of cardboard; cut some windows out and fashioned a bed out of tissues for him. He was my buddy during the ordeal of growing up in a dysfunctional home environment and navigating the growing pains of childhood.

I can remember so vividly how I longed to have a lightsaber - and more toy figures - but money was tight, and my parents did the best that they could which made me desire for my favourite toy heroes even more. A deep longing and ache to have, and own, a part of this fantastical universe sparked some eventful play time with friends from down the street. This was where neighbourhood friends became allies, and vast adventures could be created if we could all just play along nicely with each other – after all, we never had a better incentive. Having the opportunity to see and touch the toys the other kids had; recreating whole scenes and chapters from the films together was enough to make even sworn enemies get along. It was a chance for our imaginations to once again run wild. We laughed, played and fought and every now and then. A figure would meet its end as a fun game turned into an all-out battle; the cardinal sin was damaging someone's toy in the process.

Then the tears and arguments would start.

As the sun went down, we would all be called to come inside for the day and there would be a moment of sadness as we waved goodbye to each other, yet a glimmer of hope knowing that we would return to begin a new adventure together the very next day.

I remember playing for hours when I was alone; mostly pretending to be a Jedi Knight. I had already had a fascination for comic book heroes like Superman and Spiderman at that point, but Jedi were different.

They were human.

I was human.

I believed wholeheartedly that it was possible for me to become a Jedi. I would run around the garden pretending that I was on a mission to save the world. I pretended that I could use the force and make people do things by waving my hand or looking at them. I believed that my body was stronger and more powerful than the other kids on the block. With my family, I would speak slowly and I would try to sound wise "this is not the broccoli I am looking for " much to my mums disdain.

The franchise meant so much more to me that just posing as a bit of escapism from the real world. The Jedi masters taught me about honour, bravery, facing your greatest fears, and how one person could make a difference in the world. They taught me that the light side could overcome the darkness.

That good can prevail.

That I could make a difference.

That I had a mission and purpose in life..

As I write this, I know I am not alone. Generations of children have been inspired by this galactic story beyond the stars. What is it about this particular story and characters that have endured for so long? I believe that there is something universal about the themes and language of the Star Wars universe. The Star Wars myth of heroes and villains makes it easily relatable and touches on some of our deeper hidden motivations. Perhaps as children we felt young and helpless, and the films allowed us to live a life or bravery vicariously through these heroes. Maybe there is a hero in all of us who also wishes to be brave and make a difference in the world.

*

In 1986, when the Star Wars story concluded with return of the Jedi, the evil empire had been defeated and balance had been restored to the universe. As the years went by and the toys got put away, new interests took over. The dream to be a Jedi faded like an over-watched VHS video of Star Wars.

For a moment, the dream had been put back up on the shelf with the rest of the figurines.

*

THE FORCE AWAKENS

The news of George Lucas selling the rights to Disney was frightening: "Oh no," I thought, "This big money-making machine is going to ruin this precious thing and ruin my beautiful childhood memories," but in 2017 something amazing happened.

Something magical.

There was a calling.

An awakening .

When the release of "The Force Awakens" was announced something old and sacred awoke within me. Memories of the past flooded my mind and my stomach fluttered with excitement for what was to come. In that moment I was a kid again and I remembered just how much I loved these stories. It made me reflect on how I had always wanted to be a Jedi.

I realised that my life path and current career was very similar in nature to what the Jedi do - in theory, at least. I reflected on my life journey and where I was. Up until that point, my life had taken many twists and turns that saw me leave university with a business degree, and begin a corporate career only to realise that I was not happy. I started to feel that there had to be more to life than that path. I was searching for something deeper. Searching for some meaning and purpose, and so a period of self-discovery began. During this time I fell into a dark depression that led to a spontaneous spiritual awakening. This profound experience inspired me to begin my own hero's journey. I quit my job and left the life I knew behind; relocated to Canada, and found myself becoming a yoga teacher. This road would eventually lead to my training as an integrative transpersonal psychotherapist.

I locked on to the deeper meaning that I had always taken from the films once more, and I think this deeper meaning, which many of us experience, is the power of these films. The fans have a profound connection to these stories – bordering on obsession. We bring our own sense of personal meaning to the entire experience; and that is exactly what the franchise is – an experience. Star Wars fans are not just ordinary fans, these are not just movies for us.

I believe the reason that we loved these films as children were because they spoke to the hero which exists within all of us; to the inner battle of light versus dark and good versus bad that we all struggle with and hope to overcome. It was then that I had this crazy idea: what if it was possible to be a real-life Jedi?

What would a real-life Jedi look like?

How would they act in this modern world?

Were the films alluding to something deeper that lay within?

So as the Force awakened in me again, it really got me thinking; are the ancient yogis really just the modern version of the Jedi? There were many parallels. They both work with unseen forces and energy; achieving what many people believe to be superhuman feats. They've both had to train and refine their senses through years of practice. They both use the practice of meditation to hone these senses. They've both been historically aware of an energy that existed in all things. They are protectors and guardians of the universe.

With the enthusiasm that I had last experienced in my childhood, I was once again falling in love with Star Wars. I started looking into the history of the movie and where George Lucas got his inspiration from. An old interview by Bill Moyers called *The Mythology of Star Wars'* sees Lucas explain that what these films deal with is the fact that we all have good and evil inside of us and that we can choose which way we want that balance to go. The Star Wars movies touch upon the many themes of life. They explore issues of friendship and our obligation to a group or a cause as well as how our family's lineage and generational trauma are passed down to the next generation. Classic ideas of good versus evil fall at the centre of the films' themes and there is an incredible amount of importance placed on the responsibility to your fellow man as well as the responsibility to uphold the virtues of honesty, integrity and doing the right thing. He speaks about how we can influence our life journey and that from the many paths which we walk down, we may discover that we have a great destiny to fulfil. He wraps up by stating how being wrongly influenced can take us on a path that leads to dark places. [1]

The films, however, also explore our relationship with machines and technology and how these can lead to great acts of good or destruction. If one was to wake up spiritually and listen to their inner feelings, they would come to the realisation of what it is that they have a particular talent for and what contributions they could make to society. I discovered that Lucas had been influenced by other eastern religions and traditions; taking inspiration from the legends of King Arthur, the Knights of the Round Table, and the Japanese culture of the Samurai. Lucas stated that he wished to give children a language for spirituality and another way to understand God. He wanted to inspire the younger generation to understand that there are good and bad ways to live life and that if you follow the good things, life can turn out better for you. His creation of The Force is rooted in such basic concept because he wished it to be universally appealing; a religion for the secular age, if you will. Something that is so well suited to our time precisely because it is so bereft of detail that everyone gets to add their own layers of meaning. Lucas, through a long process of trial and error, seems to have deliberately encouraged viewers' unique interpretations. I think that the reason that these films and stories have had such a deep, lasting impression and universal appeal is because they speak deeply to our souls. Could the advent of these new films be a calling to reach for some unrealised potential within us?

Are we being called to connect with a higher power?
Are we being asked to follow the hero journey?

***

CHAPTER 1: THE DARK TIMES

> *For over a thousand generations, the Jedi Knights were the guardians of peace and justice in the Old Republic. Before the dark times, before the Empire."*
>
> *- Obi Wan Kenobi, Star Wars: Episode IV – A New Hope*

A LONG TIME AGO IN A GALAXY FAR, FAR AWAY...
THE WORLD IS IN CHAOS.
POLITICAL AND MEDIA SCANDALS ARE BEING EXPOSED EVERYDAY. WE HAVE BEEN DISTRACTED AND CAUGHT IN THE MATRIX OF CONSUMERISM AND EGO IDENTIFICATION.
WE HAVE BECOME SEPARATED FROM EACH OTHER AND OURSELVES; WALKING AROUND HALF-DEAD.
WE HAVE BEEN CONSUMING INFORMATION THROUGH SCREENS AND TECHNOLOGY. THE KALI YUGA, ALSO KNOWN AS THE DARK AGE, IS FULLY UPON US.
THERE IS A GREAT DISTURBANCE IN THE FORCE BUT SMALL GROUPS AND INDIVIDUALS ARE STARTING TO TAKE THEIR POWER BACK, REALISING THAT THE ONLY WAY TO CHANGE THE WORLD, IS TO CHANGE THEMSELVES.
THE TRAINING HAS BEGUN. MORE ARE AWAKENING.
MANY ARE NOW WORKING HARD TO DEVELOP THE SKILLS AND QUALITIES THAT WILL ALLOW THEM TO BECOME AGENTS OF CHANGE; BRINGING IN A TIME OF PEACE, BROTHERHOOD, AND UNITY.
WE ARE USHERING IN THE GOLDEN AGE...
TO BECOME THE NEW JEDI...

*

In a Galaxy not so far, far away... all Star Wars movies open with a dramatic opening scroll, also known as the opening crawl, which describes the current state of the universe, the current state of affairs, and the struggles and challenges that behold the universe.

How did you respond to the opening scroll?
Is it something you can relate to?
Can you feel a disturbance in the Force?
Are you currently living a happy and fulfilled life?
Does your existence have meaning and purpose for you?
Do you feel as though there is something wrong with the world?
Would you like to see things happening differently?
Maybe you are angry or depressed with what's been happening in the world or maybe even worse; you feel that everything is actually OK. Are you aware of what's happening right now? Do you ever sit and ponder the world's current condition?

The manual that you hold in your hands could be a solution to these times if you are willing to answer the call of reaching and fulfilling your potential; of fulfilling your spiritual destiny.

*

WHAT IS THE STATE OF OUR WORLD?

Are we heading towards the extinction of our species?

Has the over-mining of oils and minerals depleted our natural resources and left us with no sustainable future?

Is global warming a real thing or just some government initiative?

Have we gone too far to even have a chance to save the world?

Human beings in our current age are at war with the world and at war with themselves. We have a "war on terrorism" and "the war on drugs", but what about the war on the harmful status quo? There are as many as 40 wars and conflict areas around the world at any given time. Many of the conflicts don't get the media or policy attention such as the wars in Iraq, Syria, Afghanistan or Ukraine, but the toll of decades-long conflict – from Colombia to the Ogaden, from Kashmir to Western Sahara - leaves a devastating legacy for the people who have been impacted by them. We are facing issues around social inequality and the distribution of wealth.

Earth is abundant and we have all of the resources that we need to satisfy all the people of the world. Yet, even in these abundant times, we still have nearly half of the world's population - more than 3 billion people - living on less than £2 a day. More than 1.3 billion people live in extreme poverty with less than £1 a day. Of all the heartbreaking statistics, the worst one for me is that 1 billion children worldwide are living in poverty.

We have lost faith in our leaders and governments, and rightfully so as stories of scandals emerge. These scandals involve politicians across political parties and from the highest reaches of government. There have been widespread reports of staggering amounts of bribes, and money laundering of epic proportions.

Hollywood and the entertainment industry have a history of abuse and misuse of power as well as subtle manipulation of the masses; and these are just a few of the secrets that they have tried to keep quiet. The recent prosecution of Harvey Weinstein and other Hollywood stars like Kevin Spacey, R Kelly and the likes, has brought to light the nasty underbelly of abuse, corruption, and the connection to satanism amongst other occult practices.

We've seen things like "MK ultra-mind-control programming" – a top secret CIA project centred around the use of LSD and mind control drugs – as well as mandatory sexual assault, horrific cases of pedophilia and child molestation, as well as rampant drug use and alcoholism. There are unhealthy influences by older persons directed toward younger persons and powerful persons having absolute influence over the entire careers of actors and actresses.

Powerful groups and individuals have had complete control of mainstream media narratives. Productions pushing junk-science propaganda through popular programs has come to the fore. The then election of America's 45th president had shown a rise in hate crimes, rampant racism, greed, and the polarisation of countries' peoples around the issues that matter.

The 2020 coronavirus pandemic stopped the world in its tracks and there will be no going back to the world we knew. There is no normal to go back to, and to be quite frank, none of us should want to go back to that normal anyway. Human beings perpetually used the world and its resources for their own selfish needs. We wish to be entertained; we want everything now, and fast, as we continue to over-consume with just the click of a mouse. A society of living for instant gratification and the quick pace of life has increased physical health issues, and mental health issues due to stress and burnout. Our lifestyles, the pollution of our environments – both physical and spiritual – has led us to the precipice of destruction.

Men and women everywhere are beginning to despair as the old, uncomfortable world is falling apart. With escalating violent crimes and a declining global economic situation, the deterioration of ethical standards, as well as the deterioration of relationships - in particular the family unit – coupled with the disinformation and propaganda has forced humanity into a desperate corner. The unscrupulous actions of the media complex; working towards wholly political interests for all of those who profit from withholding the truth must be addressed. We have our back firmly up against the wall; no longer knowing who to trust and who to listen to. People everywhere are becoming desperate enough to rise up and fight for their freedoms.

"What you know you can't explain, but you feel it. You've felt it your entire life, that there's something wrong with the world. You don't know what it is, but it's there, like a splinter in your mind, driving you mad." (2)

- Morpheus, The Matrix

Are we ready to believe that there is an Evil Empire - a group of people ruling the world for their own selfish gains? Are we ready to believe that the things that are happening are orchestrated - or are they just a response from Mother Earth as nature responds to all of our past actions? Are they merely repercussions for the way that we treat the planet; the destruction of the rainforests, wild forest fires, species extinctions, over-farming, polluting our seas, and the hunting trade of animals? Are we not being held accountable for the fruitless and frivolous wars over oil and other natural resources? What are we to make of the 5G networks that are being set up in cities across the globe? Is this really for our benefit, or is there something else going on? Are we to believe the conspiracy theories, or are we to believe the mainstream media's information? What about all of the people saying that we are being guided by aliens and other inter-dimensional beings?

It's enough to make one's head spin.

We are constantly being bombarded with information that is cold and lifeless. Technology and social media are overstimulating people's minds with information, data, and opinions; causing cognitive dissonance in our natural biorhythms. When was the last time you read a book for pleasure? Have you noticed any changes in your ability to concentrate and focus? How is your memory lately?

*

THE MASKS WE WEAR

Every day we put on an act, doing our best to be normal and conform to society's rules. We put on a mask everyday as we get dressed to go to a job that we don't like, to make money, and to buy stuff that we don't really want, in order to impress people that we don't really like.

We struggle to find the energy to get up and go to work or to handle seemingly difficult situations with our bosses. We find reasons to have specific colleagues that we don't like and going to work makes us feel that the act in and of itself is literally sucking the life, soul and Force energy right out of us. In many ways, we are fighting metaphorical demons and dragons every day.

Managing your bills and finances has become an extreme sport on its own as you find that things are costlier than they were last week; and it always seems to be that way, every single week. Dealing with the stress of upcoming exams and worrying if all the studying and student debt that you're racking up will actually lead to a job that fulfils you - or is at least good enough to pay your bills. Mental health struggles with increased pressure seem to be mounting, as well as not being able to concentrate and using social media to distract ourselves from what is really important; deteriorating health, or new and unsolved health conditions.

Wondering if you are doing enough or if there is more you can do? That's just one of the signs of the times that we find ourselves in. Nothing we do ever seems to be good enough – or at least that's what we tell ourselves. We live in a perpetual cycle of resting to make up for the stress that we go through and feeling stressed about taking that time to make up for the initial stress. We're like dogs chasing our own proverbial tails. So we struggle to find meaning in our lives, and we beat ourselves up for being human and needing downtime because we've been programmed to work harder and longer – "smash those goals", and be a go-getter. We believe that we have to "win at life", as if it were some sort of game; telling ourselves that we need to be more and get more in order to be deemed worthy or successful.

Finding satisfaction from life, knowing that you have relevance, contributing and feeling that your life matters in the greater scheme of things is what we all want – and deserve. Managing time is becoming increasingly difficult in today's life. Be it travel, work or studies; there's constant distraction in everything that we do. Blame it on WhatsApp, Facebook, Twitter, Instagram, or any other of the latest apps on the market, but the distraction is there all the same.

The biggest problem that people face every day is just handling themselves. These days the enemy is not present in another country or in another family. The enemy is present inside us. So we are our own enemy. We need to be steady in thought, word, and deed. We need to be able to silence the bad wolf and feed the good wolf. We need to be able to draw back, take perspective and look at our problems from above. We need to be able to pull ourselves out of the doldrums and focus on what is truly important – our vitality, our relationships, and our environment.

We seem to think that we are productive members of this society if we pay our bills on time, have mortgages, and increase our debts. People are finding that they do not need to go out to create relationships as all their needs are taken care of online - shopping, relationships, sex, food delivery, Netflix and box sets to binge on; it's all there. Society is now set up in such a way to encourage separation, isolation, and individualism. We are walking around like zombies staring at our phone screens with our Bluetooth and wireless headsets plugged in and the world blocked out.

We have a lot of noise competing for our attention and this overwhelm is causing us to lose connection to our true potential. By masking the useful information with a hideous noise, our potential is drained out of us. While life is easier in terms of survival and work, societal norms have changed drastically; making it more difficult for our health. Based on the research, this change is affecting everyone, and especially today's children, which doesn't bode well for the future of humanity.

We have lost connection with what is real and what is important. We obviously can't continue living the way that we are.

It isn't sustainable.

The amount of suffering is way beyond obscene.

*

WHY EVEN BOTHER?

The world is facing an unseen problem. People have defaulted to apathy. There are no more heroes. We live in a frequency and vibration which is fear-based. This book is a call to embrace your inner Jedi and be a solution to the problem. Apathy is the feeling that we can't do anything about our situation and no one else can either. It revolves around two big H-words:

Hopelessness & helplessness.

When we feel apathetic we are operating from a place of victimhood. Have the conditions and experiences of the world caused you to stop caring completely? Have we all become so apathetic to the current state of the world and our place in it? Apathy could be seen as the greatest disease the world has ever experienced. While true apathy is a feeling, it's also an attitude, and sadly, that attitude is one of indifference, unconcern, unresponsiveness, detachment, and dispassion. Such an attitude zaps you of so much energy that you end up constantly feeling lethargic, listless, and enervated — almost too "paralysed" to act — and certainly without the will to do so. This is why apathetic individuals are easily identified by their passivity. Their interest in confronting life's challenges is seriously compromised. They just don't care enough, and frankly, they don't care that they don't care. All states hold an energetic frequency and apathy holds one of the lowest forms of vibration.

That low frequency state then begins to have an impact on your own emotions and wellbeing. To put it plainly, not caring is detrimental to your experience of life.

Everyone is looking for someone to blame. Although some people are actively getting out there by voting, carrying out demonstrations and charity work, or simply volunteering and wanting to make a difference, we have come to a time in our history where very little of these efforts actually work. What is needed is to take back our power and our sovereignty? This requires inner work and inner transformation; it's not enough to simply want to change our external conditions. The next revolution will not be televised, it will occur within. As we change our inner world we will directly impact and influence the outer world.

In the past, you would go search out a guru, a teacher, or some other form of wise person to answer some of life's most challenging questions, but now there is so much information that we don't know what to do with it. We are becoming less and less able to process and integrate information because there is just so much of it and most of it contradicts itself. This in itself leads to a sort of "analysis- paralysis"— to not knowing what to believe.

I think that one of the biggest questions that we are all facing right now is; *Can there be a new hope?* We are all desperate to see a change in the world. We are witnessing all of the pain and chaos around us and yet we do not actually know what to do with the overload of information. We end up feeling powerless and become apathetic when in actuality, it's a gift. It's only when we are up against the wall, in the way that we are right now, that we can finally make the shift and start to become the change that we wish to see in the world. My challenge to you as the reader is this: Ask yourself the difficult questions and actually seek out the answers. What are you prepared to do? Are you prepared to forego the life of bondage and claim your power? Are you willing to be a victor instead of a victim? Are you willing to stand up and be counted instead of only being a number? Are you willing to live instead of merely existing? Are you willing to take charge of your own life or would you prefer to keep handing your power over to those who misuse it? Are you willing to believe in yourself? Are you willing to believe that you, as an individual, have the power?

Your power is your birthright.

Peace and prosperity are your birthright.

Good health and vitality are your birthright.

You are a sovereign being.

I have one more question for you all; are you willing to change your actions, to stop practicing separateness, and to join hands with those who strive for the freedom of all? Every person has something to offer no matter how small it may seem, and at this time, I can assure you that every little bit counts. Every person is needed and therefore the opportunity for all is quite unprecedented in this respect. It is not the sky that is the limit, but your belief in yourself that will set the bar. This is not about being anti-establishment or about taking up military arms. I am challenging you to take part in de-conditioning yourself and to arm yourself with the courage and spirit of the Kundalini Jedi Warrior. It's not another world war that is needed, but a global revolution of our way of life and our belief structures.

*

BATTLE OF FREQUENCIES: A NEW HOPE

How do you feel about the current situation here on earth? Are you afraid of the future and what it might bring? I know it may seem like I've asked an exponential amount of questions at this point, but it's all for a good reason. You need to be able to think critically for yourself once more. You need to be able to look outside of the box that you've been conditioned to live in. The world is in trouble. We are locked in a battle of the ages as the world that we live in today is in a state of chaos, but the enemy is no longer viable and "out there". There is no one to attack, because the real enemy is the enemy within. This manual is all about change; about our inner change, and the battle with its phantom menace.

The battle that we face now is one of energetic frequencies. They, whoever they are, let's call them "the evil empire"— or rather, anyone who vibrates at the level of fear, disconnection, apathy and blame — are the new polarity to the light side of our Force. The Jedi's challenge in this modern era is to raise our frequency - to be able to change our vibration at will. We must learn to manage our vibrational frequency because we are spiritual beings, or rather spiritual energies, residing in a physical form and whatever we vibrate within broadcasts out and manifests in the world.

RAISING VIBRATIONAL ENERGY

Our state of being is the ultimate tool of health and wellness. In *Power Versus. Force: The Hidden Determinants of Human Behaviour*, psychiatrist David Hawkins, MD, PhD, studied the nature of pure consciousness (3). He quantified the power of a positive thought and the power of a negative thought; developing a logarithmic scale of levels of consciousness in the process. Dr. Hawkins came to his conclusions through research and kinesiology testing. Both your inner and outer musings will affect change over your being. These alterations to your vibrational field or calibration come in the form of psychological energy, behavioural energy, emotional energy and physical energy. Psychological energy is the power of thought, behavioural energy is your level of consciousness, emotional energy is encompassed by anger, fear, grief, love and other emotions, and physical energy is the power you wield from physical strength, flexibility and endurance.

The very core of your cells is filled with energy as it seeps through you, flowing around you and into you before making its way back into the universe. This is why our tissues can be plied and pulled into various states. It must be noted that Western medicine has always acknowledged the usefulness of ancient Chinese and Ayurvedic medicine. The mind-body connection is undeniably powerful in healing physical health.

Let's explore some of the varying energy fields now.

PSYCHOLOGICAL ENERGY

Your psyche is said to be the embodiment of the soul. This energy stems from your thoughts and what you think is therefore incredibly important. What you think eventually comes to be reality. In other words, thought takes on form. These thoughts that you harbour all carry this creative Force. They can change unpredictably and create varying emotional states. We relay external experiences into internal thoughts which then alters our state of being. When we react unconsciously instead of taking conscious control of our thoughts, we allow external events to control us. When we act consciously, we control our experiences instead of being victims of circumstance. Think about what you would rather be – a cause or an effect?

As noted by Dr. Rappa of Baylor University Medical Center; "Emotions are really energy in motion, or e-motion. After thought becomes emotion, emotion is transduced or expressed in a physical form to be experienced. The effects of our thought-forms and emotional states occur in distinct physiological terms: i.e., illness or disease. A high state of stress can lead to the expression of endorphins and cortisol; the cascade is easy to follow. Chronic stress and anxiety, grief, and anger are even more powerful, acting through the neuroendocrine system to produce physical states like hypertension, ulcers, and even cancers." [4]

We live in a cycle whereby we create these states of angst and ill health. This then becomes the focus of our thoughts and we evolve into these beings that are perpetually mentally and physically ill. It is thus no surprise that when we begin feeding our minds with the thoughts we wish to manifest out in the world, this is what comes to pass. We have to actively control our minds if we wish to succeed in becoming a centred Kundalini Jedi Warrior.

EMOTIONAL ENERGY

If we wish to know our truth, we must go within and become incredibly introspective. Look at your relationships, belief systems and attitudes in order to analyse what emotions come up for you in each of those different areas.

When you become aware of your unresolved traumas and emotional conflicts, you can begin seeing where your responsibility in the fray falls. Nothing happens to you, but happens for you and with you. Therefore, you must take responsibility for everything in your life to some degree. Many of the physical ailments that we face today are merely outward manifestations of an internal emotional embattlement.

Dr Peter Rappa goes on to elaborate that "Dr. Carolyn Myss has pioneered research into the organisation of emotional energy within the human energy system. She has identified seven major specialised energy centers (or "chakras")—tribal power or group forces, the power of individual relationships, the power of personal honour, the power of heart, the power of will, the power of the mind, and our spiritual connector—each resonating according to emotional experience." [5] The energy of all these centers is directly related to a specific organ and can thus be used to access said organs. They are intricately linked via the glandular system and neural pathways. Deep internal stress and feelings of being disempowered will often likely come before an ailment. The following illustrates the power levels that are associated with states of consciousness and their corresponding emotions. Have a look and see how your emotions might be affecting your level of consciousness and vice versa.

LEVEL	LOG	EMOTION
Enlightenment	700-100	Ineffable
Peace	600	Bliss
Joy	540	Serenity
Love	500	Reverence
Reason	400	Understanding
Acceptance	350	Forgiveness
Willingness	310	Optimism
Neutrality	250	Trust
Courage	200	Affirmation
Pride	175	Scorn
Anger	150	Hate
Desire	125	Craving
Fear	100	Anxiety
Apathy	50	Despair
Guilt	30	Blame
Shame	20	Humiliation

(6) Dr. Hawkins Power Vs. Force: The Hidden Determinants of Human Behavior. Carlsbad, CA: Hay House; 2002

This is not a process. It's not one of those things that you have to work at. As soon as you adopt a higher state of being, you become it. It is instant. In order to remove the ailment from our lives – physical or mental – we can shift our paradigms instantly by changing our emotional responses; especially where we've become ill due to disempowerment. By increasing your vibrational energy, you will release yourself from the chains of a negative psyche.

Although changing your frequency will also benefit you in many ways - including feeling happier and being more in alignment with yourself and your natural rhythms - you can also connect to the flow of the Force which will allow you to manifest and create more seamlessly.

*

A FEAR-BASED SOCIETY

"I must not fear. Fear is the mind-killer. Fear is the little-death that brings total obliteration. I will face my fear. I will permit it to pass over me and through me. And when it has gone past I will turn the inner eye to see its path. Where the fear has gone there will be nothing. Only I will remain."

— **Frank Herbert, Dune**

We live in a climate of fear, fuelled by disinformation due to media companies peddling political and financial agendas in order to keep the masses asleep with fake news. The political system has become our latest form of entertainment as people vote and support personalities that they hope will ease their existential angst.

We are encouraged to buy and consume, to keep the economies and false structures in place as people live with insurmountable debt locked into our very own self-made prisons. Human beings crave comfort, peace, and safety and we will give anything to gain this, including giving away our power and sovereignty for the illusion of safety. This fear is created by the media and the false narrative imposed on them in order to keep us in a fear-loop. Fear is not created from outside situations but created in the mind, as all feelings and emotions are, but external narratives and pressures can worsen this. As we struggle to create change in a world that so desperately needs it, we must resist many temptations. Temptations are a path to the dark side. One of the most pressing temptations that we must resist is the temptation to remain silent when witnessing injustice. When experiencing adversity, we must resist the temptation to become cynical. As we strive to solve our human problems, we must resist the temptation to settle for easy answers that do not address the root cause. When obstacles seem to block our progress towards peace, we must resist the temptation to give up and give in to fear. If we start to see and experience things from the perspective that there exists a Force greater and higher than our limited sense of self, understanding that there are greater things at play in our universe, we begin to touch the edges of magic and fantasy where anything is possible. It is possible to become a real-life Jedi and impact our world. It is possible to embrace the light of our inner essence; to bring in new hope and a new dawn for humanity and defeat the dark side. This journey that you are about to undertake is one of moving from the head to the heart - which holds your greatest superpower. You will make the move towards being guided by a pearl of higher wisdom and intelligence as you reclaim your inherent power and create the change that we need in the world.

May the force be with you, and may you be the force.

"Fear of life is really fear of emotions. It is not the facts we fear but our feelings about them. Once we have mastery over our feelings, our fear of life diminishes."
- David Hawkins, Letting Go: The Pathway of Surrender

THE TREE OF LIFE
"What we do in life echoes for eternity" –
- **Maximus Decimus Meridius, Gladiator**

Everything and everyone around you are connected to one another in the same way, shape or form. We are part of what is known as the natural and social web of life. We are connected to nature and dependent on it for everything that we need. It sustains us all – family, friends, and loved ones alike – thus connecting us to each other. Sometimes the connections are obvious and sometimes they aren't, but these immeasurable connections are always there; silently affecting the way we engage ourselves and each other.

Buddhism views that everything in the world is interconnected. When Buddha gained enlightenment, it was achieved through the realisation that interconnectedness is the true nature of all beings. We are not only connected to other people, but to the air through our breathing and to the universe through light. Therefore, these interconnected relationships should be symbiotic. Earth is home to millions of specie, and because they all compete for the same resources and share this one space, they interact and move around one another in a collective pattern more commonly known as symbiosis.

In essence, all life is connected to other life because we all exist in the same space. We share the air we breathe, the sources of food we eat - or make - ourselves, and we share the space that we live in. The tree of life is an ideology that is widespread across many belief systems. We come to know another tree of life in the Star Wars franchise.

In Star Wars: The Last Jedi, we see Rey discover the Jedi library in a tree while attempting to bring Skywalker out of his exile to aid the Resistance. The tree is actually called an Uneti; a Force-sensitive organism that has long been revered by the Jedi Order. The one that grows on Ahch-To is obviously ancient; most likely stretching back to some of the earliest days of the Jedi. We then see another powerful moment in the franchise when the tree is destroyed by Yoda. It is done to show young Luke that the past is not the future and that the Jedi can be something of purpose again, even if not by the ways of old. This in itself is similar to the Tree of Knowledge which connects the heavens to the underworld. It is also believed to connect all of creation to one another.

No matter the creed, culture, or religion, there will be some form of text which depicts a tree as something sacred. Even Christianity proposes the tree as the plane upon which the ways of the modern world were built as can be seen in the Garden of Eden with Adam and Eve. It is a sacred symbol which stands as a metaphor for the evolution of life; exploring the relationship between all creatures in existence.

THE MEANING OF THE TREE OF LIFE

The Tree of Life, as we know, represents how we are all interconnected. It is a symbol for our togetherness and is a beacon of hope in that we are not alone. As the roots grow deeper into the soil, they absorb all that they need from the earth; stretching out towards the sky to embrace the gifts of the sun and moon.

In Buddhism, the Tree of Life is known as the Bodhi-tree and it is believed to be the Tree of Enlightenment. It was under this tree that Buddha reached enlightenment so it is seen as a very sacred symbol. The spiritual meaning of the Tree of Life is symbolic of personal growth, strength and beauty. The symbol itself represents our development as one of the many species on the planet. Just as the branches grow towards the sky, so do we grow and develop as individuals, but also as a collective.

The greatest sages, philosophers, and spiritual masters have always understood the interconnection of the universe. People also have this sense of connection with everyone and science is finally catching up with the innate knowledge of the greatest thinkers.

Quantum physics has taught us that once a particle is joined, it is always connected regardless of distance. Some of the most decorated scientists have conducted experiments with almost 100-percent certainty that when splitting photons, even at great distances, they act as if they are still connected and communicating with each other. Other noteworthy experiments have involved taking a swab of human DNA and sending the sample hundreds of miles away. With the use of electronic messages, the DNA would react to the originator's emotions - which were being intentionally stimulated for the experiment.

We are breathing the same air that people inhaled and exhaled thousands of years ago. The air we breathe is composed mainly of nitrogen and oxygen gas. Very little is lost in space and only occasionally is there a new source of carbon or oxygen introduced into this planet. So, every breath that you take has atoms that have been here for billions of years.

The Big Bang Theory is the most accurate explanation for the beginning of the universe which states that we all came from the same source – hence, we were once connected, and therefore, we will always be connected. What we do, think, and feel affects the people, places, and wider world around us. As we change the world changes.

*

THE RETURN OF THE JEDI

The Kundalini Jedi Warrior's approach is that everything that happens in life is a spiritual lesson. As a Jedi, situations are offering us an opportunity for growth and we are being asked to expand all aspects of ourselves. Taking on this perspective allows us to develop our nature through the higher powers that exist. We then can begin to approach life from a place of personal power and self-mastery. Keeping our "bubble of protection" up allows us to remain happy and compassionate whether we experience loss or profit, joy or sadness, victory or defeat, and praise or criticism.

The only enemies are the ones that exist within our minds. The historical idea of the warrior going into battle with swords drawn or guns blazing, ready to destroy the enemy at any cost, will not work in the Aquarian age that we are entering. The warrior energy has been used to gain material wealth and status, as well as to overcome and dominate everyone around us. The true energy of the warrior has been hi-jacked. Even with all of its advancements and progress, the world has seen humanity thrive at a great cost. The environmental changes are a direct result of the greed from our need to conquer and dominate. To turn this ship around will require a type of warrior energy directed and focused in a new way. We must inhabit the qualities of warriors with the Jedi approach to the sacredness of life. As Jedi, we develop spiritual discernment in order to see through the dark forces and the nature of the negative ego. Fear feeds off the negative ego and creates separation within ourselves, which leads to a general distrust of our fellow human beings. It is this disconnection which then causes us to also disconnect from the Life Force energy itself. The Jedi slay fear with spiritual vigilance and a connection to the Force that is greater than themselves. This allows them to have steadiness. A Jedi works on himself through self-inquiry, attitudinal healing, adjustment-making, and denying negative, egoistic thoughts from entering the mind; transcending duality. Maintaining one's faith, trust, and hope in an all-powerful Force allows one to be in their power and to remain even-minded. Being a Jedi Master means not being a victim. Jedi work on the mastery of the spiritual, psychological, and physical planes of existence; keeping their focus on those places where evil dwells and allowing light and love to restore balance to the Force.

***

CHAPTER 2: CYCLE OF THE AGES

> *This is the fourth age, the Kali Yuga, and it's a time of great darkness. At the end of this age, there's supposed to be a cosmic dissolution and then life begins anew. It's a wonderful cycle of rebirth."*
>
> *- Frederick Lenz*

THE FOUR AGES

In the previous chapter, we described a world in chaos. According to the Vedic scriptures, our current age, known as Kali Yuga, is one of spiritual darkness, violence, and hypocrisy. This age is full of corruption as political leadership falls into the hands of unprincipled rogues, criminals, and terrorists, who use their power to exploit the people. Entire populations are enslaved and put to death. The saints and sages of ancient India describe the people of this age as greedy, ill-behaved, and merciless. Severe droughts and plagues are everywhere. Slovenliness, illness, hunger and fear spread. Nations are continually at war with one another. The number of princes and farmers are in decline. Heroes are assassinated. The working classes want to claim regal power and enjoy royal wealth.

Kings have since become thieves. Civilisation lacks any kind of divine guidance. The sacred books are no longer revered. False doctrines and misleading religions spread across the globe. The men of Kali Yuga seek only money. Only the richest have power and those without money are their slaves. The leaders of the state no longer protect the people, but plunder the citizenry through excessive taxation. Men will become averse from religious rites, without restraint, maddened with pride, ever given over to sinful acts, lustful, gluttonous, cruel, heartless, and harsh of speech. Some reflection on our current world situation mirrors these ancient prophecies, and they have been foretold as the end times. Things are always darkest before the dawn and yogic teachings tell us of the dawning of a new age.

Time and life move in cycles of birth, transformation, and death. Cycles are part of the natural world. It is now common knowledge that the earth doesn't rotate perfectly around its axis but that it has a wobble to it. This wobble isn't constant, it only occurs every 26,00 years. This 26,000-year cycle is divided into 12 phases, which are related to the 12 astrological signs. Depending on which constellation the earth is 'wobbling' towards at any given point will determine the astrological sign we will be dominated by.

The cultures of the past such as the Ancient Egyptians, Mayans, Hopi, Laika, and Incas were of the understanding that the sun served as an energy portal. As the biggest star in our galaxy, it has the ability to redirect energy from our galactic centre. With advanced knowledge of astronomy and astrology, these ancient cultures noted a perfect alignment of the Sun and Earth every 26,000 years. From around 2000 B.C. to 0 A.D. we were in the Age of Aries. From 0 A.D. to the present, we have been in the Age of Pisces and we are now transitioning into the golden age and have been since 2012. The last big cycle to begin was on December 21, 2012. "According to the ancients the dawning of the final 2,100-year

Zodiac Age, the Age of Aquarius, on December 21st, 2012, heralds the arrival of the Golden Age signifying the completion of one full cycle of our entire galaxy, which marks the end of all cycles of time." (7)

The Hindus, on the other hand, divided this cycle into what they called the Four Yugas; namely, Kali, Dvapara, Treta and Satya. If we look towards the Greeks, we can see these four ages spanning the Iron, Bronze, Silver, and Golden ages. We'll explore these in greater depth below.

THE GOLDEN AGE OR SATYUG (THE SPRING)

This is known as the dawn of humanity. It is notably a time when there existed a paradise on earth. The world was united under one kingdom whereby there was an air of peace and happiness amongst all of humankind. Pain, suffering, sorrow, and sadness was not known to man.

THE SILVER AGE OR TRETAYUG (THE SUMMER)

While this remained as close to a paradise as the prior age, the purity of the soul was beginning to dissipate. Although suffering and sadness were still relatively unknown, things would begin to shift with the coming of the copper age.

THE COPPER AGE OR DWAPARYUG (THE AUTUMN)

Spiritual awareness has now been completely lost in this age. Humanity has moved from a higher realm of spiritual being to a lower realm of physical consciousness; giving into their vices. There is no longer unity under one kingdom, and conflict brings with it the first signs of suffering and sorrow. Ego is now the ruler of humanity.

THE IRON AGE OR KALIYUGA (THE WINTER)

This is undeniably the darkest period of humanity. The soul has lost all enlightenment and evil runs rampant around the world. Greed, sorrow, war, lust, hatred, suffering, and pain are commonplace at levels. It is known as the dark night of humanity.

Just as we wake up at dawn and fall asleep at night, each 26,000 years is a cycle of falling asleep and waking up anew. We transition from these dark ages back into the light and in so doing, pass through to a new age. It doesn't take much to see that we are in the dying stages of our very own Kaliyuga. Instead of acting as one, as the Force and the Tree of Life determine, we move away from each other; doing our level best to slash away at the ties that bind us. We are no longer working together but have become shards of a once united humanity. We have our own agendas and desperately seek ways to enrich our own households at the expense of others – both materialistically and spiritually. Petty fights separate us, leaving some feeling triumphant while others feel lost.

OLD WAYS ARE DYING

"It is the nature of the Kali Yuga that most human beings are now held back from spiritual liberation due to the gravity of inertia, apathy and laziness, (known in Sanskrit as the quality of tapas) that overwhelms this age. Despite this seemingly gloomy prognosis, there is a way out of this predicament for those with the will and stamina to awaken from the rampant lethargy, within and outside of themselves, to take action."
- Zeena Schreck, **Demons of the Flesh: The Complete Guide to Left Hand Path Sex Magic**

Each age comes with its theme and vibe. The Piscean Age has been dominated by hierarchical power. The key to this phase was that all power was on the outside. You needed an outside authority to tell you who you are. To have a successful and happy life, you need to resolve this question. The key to the astrological sign of Pisces is "I believe." During this age, in order for you "to be," you needed to find someone or something to believe in. When you found that thing, you attached yourself to that thing and were guided on how to live. This could have been a religion, a political ideology, a charismatic leader, work, etc. The keys to life were hidden and the secrets remained in the halls of power, in the monasteries, or in the ashrams. However, during this time, you didn't need to know these secrets, only to follow leaders and guides who did. As a result, this created pyramidal social hierarchies, and it was essential to find your place in the pecking order.

The Age of Pisces, which was primarily about authority and power, is not letting go of its hold on human consciousness so easily. Religious extremism, political extremism, social prejudice, and economic disempowerment are Piscean tools of war that are still being waged to keep humans divided and afraid of one another. As a result, we are, therefore, more likely to surrender our personal power to government leaders.

Fear is the primary weapon being used by controlling Piscean leaders to stop the advent of Aquarian principles. It is not the first time in history that this has happened. Jesus, one of the first Aquarian teachers, was crucified by a cabal of religious and political leaders. Look closely, and you will see the same thing happening today. This has been the foundation for human consciousness for the past 2,000 years. Everything that you have learned from your parents, and they from their parents, going back generations and generations, has been coloured by this Piscean frame of reference - and now that is all suddenly changing.

THE AQUARIAN AGE

"We have been in the transition from the Piscean Age to the Aquarian Age for the last 50 or so years. The official beginning of the Aquarian Age is November 11, 2011, or 11/11/11. Considering that this is a 2,000-year cycle, no matter which date you accept, we are in for lots of changes." [8]

Throughout the history books and in almost all cultures, religions, and belief systems across the world, there is always talk of a time when there was peace on earth – a harmonious time when everyone got along and no one sought to outdo the other. There is talk of living in harmony with nature; with everything being perfectly balanced. They all seem to place this period at roughly five thousand years ago; claiming that there was Heaven on earth.

The consensus is that by some wrongdoing of our ancestors, we fell from an age of soul purity and peace towards body-consciousness. We then gave in to our vices, being attachment, ego, lust, greed, and anger.

According to Confluence Media; "It is told that after the change in the human way of life and the fall of the human consciousness all the tragic global calamities started to take place on Earth, whose geological, climatic, and mental impact managed to erase that Golden Age from history almost completely." (9)

In our upcoming Golden Age – or Aquarian Age – we will be dominated by networks and information and our key phrase shall become "Be to Be". You see the essence of the sign of Aquarius is I know and therefore we will know things. Everything will come to light in this Age of Information. There will no longer be the vertical hierarchies of the Piscean Age, but a horizontal air of equality. This is how we come to own this vertical dimension; when ***me and the Force are one***. The focus can now shift from our identity and existence ("to be or not to") towards accepting ourselves as a whole ("be to be"). We will no longer need to have beliefs in the external but will find infinite wisdom within ourselves.

"With this understanding, it is easier to comprehend what has been happening in the world over the last 50 years. On an inner level, since the 1960s, there has been a huge movement towards personal transformation: self-awareness, self-improvement, yoga, meditation, tai-chi, alternative healing methods, natural foods, etc. There has also been a major increase in depression, suicide, anxiety, stress, and drug use, both pharmaceutical and recreational." (10) While this shift continues to bring out the best and worst of us as human beings, we see how civil rights movements are being taken seriously, but how some members of society push back and seek to remove our freedoms even further. It shows two opposite ends of the spectrum. Some people are embracing the change with arms wide open and others are shunning it; refusing to embrace anyone other than those who are just like them.

*

THIS HUMAN EXPERIENCE

It feels like the world is spinning and life is moving faster. We have progressed more in the last 50 years than we have in the previous 1,000 years but, have we really progressed? We still have war, racism, violence and, in many ways, we have not psychologically changed that much. But there are signs and prophecies which talk of a great cataclysmic unfolding that will change and upgrade us and ultimately be the next great leap in our evolution as a species. This evolutionary jump - or upgrade - will be one that deeply affects our consciousness as we embrace our identity as spiritual beings. We are witnessing a shift from one type of consciousness to another. The duality that has been at the core of philosophy, religion, politics, and human relationships for the past 2,500 years is radically shifting to one of unity and convergence. We are leaving the Age of Pisces and entering the Age of Aquarius and everything is changing. We are spiritual beings having a human experience, after all; we are not our minds and our beliefs.

JEDI EXERCISE: MINDFULNESS

Take a moment to witness.

Sit down somewhere quiet, make yourself comfortable, and close your eyes; allowing yourself to experience each of your senses. Hear the sounds around you. Smell the air as you inhale through your nose. Become aware of the taste in your mouth and the feeling of the clothes against your skin as well as the pressure of your body on the furniture. Feel your feet on the floor. Realise that all the sensations come to you via your physical body and that you are not your body. Now, concentrate on your mind. Watch your thoughts as if they are playing on a television screen in front of you. Allow your thoughts to meander by themselves, but realise that because you can observe them, that you are not your thoughts. They are simply a product of your mind. Now, actively and consciously change your thoughts as many times as you want and realise that through your ability to do this you can control your mind and therefore you are not your mind. If you are not your body or your mind then, ask yourself -what are you? You will not find an answer. Only some more thoughts, but behind those thoughts is your intelligence; observing silently. It is an intelligence which is not your body nor your mind, so you are not a physical entity. Then this life cannot possibly be what you have believed it to be. Your name, your circumstances, your career, your social standing, your marital status - in fact everything - is dependent upon you having a physical body that is controlled by a mind. It is your physical body that has a name and an age. It is a physical body which gives you social standing and which makes it possible to be married and have children. Behind all of that - beyond your body and mind - there is an indwelling intelligence.

*

CALLING ALL JEDI

When we recognise the precise and exact nature of cyclic time, we can also joyfully expect and work for a new dawning of the Golden Age. For this to happen, great changes must take place in human affairs. It is a process of change that can only begin from inside the individual. When we understand that all change is from soul to mind, then from mind to body - or matter - we realise that it is our spiritual awakening and purification which can change the world.

"When we change, the world changes. The world will not become a better place through more resistance or conflict; this only adds to the total sum of fear and anger in the world. To fight for peace is a false belief in itself. To think that peace comes from conflict, or that conflict is necessary to achieve peace, is to think right comes from wrong. Deep change is an incognito process within each soul. Through meditation or yoga – union - we awaken and restore our true, peaceful selves; we absorb the light of truth and love from the Supreme Force and we are spiritually empowered so we can then share it with others." [11]

As we radiate our spiritual energy and reflect the Force into the world in gentle and humble ways, the effects of our inner change reach out to other souls with an invitation to do the same. We begin to ask those spiritually confounding questions "why me" and so on because we want to connect with our souls at that deeper level. This is the reason why centering ourselves and sitting in peaceful meditation can help us to heal the world and those in it; including ourselves. The primary responsibility for the modern Jedi is to assist the Force in this task of bringing about the Golden Age, to defeat the dark side.

We are steadily evolving thanks to the immense amount of pressure that the internet has placed on our nervous systems. We process more information in a day than people had to process in their entire lifetimes during the 1600s. However, evolution is a tricky process and not everyone will be capable of making the change. What worked in the past will no longer work in the future. Those who cannot make the shift will need help. The tools and technology are here and you will learn these in this manual.

Transformation is never a painless process. Just like when you decide to fast, the first few times that you cleanse your system you are going to feel like a train wreck. You'll experience headaches and nausea because all of the toxins in your body are being stirred up to be eliminated. What is happening right now is that we are all collectively going through this shift. The entire planet! Mother earth herself! We are heading into a time of radical change. It is a time of great potential growth and expansion, but it is also a time of great potential pain and suffering. In order to maintain your stability in this shift, you need to fully understand what is happening around you.

Welcome to the Aquarian Age!

CHAPTER 3: A NEW BEGINNING

> "*You have much to learn, young Padawan.*"
>
> *- Grand master Yoda*

AM I A PADAWAN?

Life teaches us a great many lessons. Some lessons we choose and others are thrust upon us. We are never too old to learn. Learning and growing is a part of life.

Padawan is a term used in the Star War movies to describe a beginning student; a new person training to become a Jedi Knight. A Padawan is required to pass some basic tests by the Jedi council that allows them access if they possess a strong enough connection to the Force to be accepted. A Padawan is usually an inexperienced person who has little or no understanding about the mysteries of the Force. Historically, Padawan training would commence during the formative years of a being's life, and they would become proteges under a Knight or Master. Jedi training was best suited to someone who lacked experience in a Jedi classroom environment and had little experience of life. Slowly - with guidance - the young student begins to understand, philosophically, the nature of reality and the unique contribution that they could make to the Force. They eventually move on to one-on-one training with a Jedi Master. They begin to learn by watching and accompanying him/her on missions all around the galaxy.

Jedi Padawans are paired with more experienced Jedi who, like them, would have also trained with a Master. The Jedi trainer would have had to go through many trials, and as part of their training to become a Master they must have mentored and trained a new student. This ethic of passing on what you have learnt is a very important aspect of the Jedi nature and it allows them to mature as well as to develop compassion and patience as they find ways to shape the student's temperament.

You may have been walking your own path to awakening for many years or you may be new to this journey. Whether you have many experiences and have developed considerable skill there is always more to learn and master.

My Jedi journey has been a long and arduous one; filled with trials and tribulations. I will share my experiences as well as some of the techniques that I have learned from my own journey. This will help you to avoid unnecessary setbacks along your own journey. My role is to guide you and mentor you in becoming a real-life Jedi. There will be exercises and tasks, much like the mindfulness exercise that you've completed, which will help you to set reasonable and achievable targets - targets that will test and stretch you. In the next chapter we will take our first steps in training. The following exercises of journaling, self-inquiry, and approaching this work with a beginner's mind will aid you greatly in developing awareness. That awareness will be the foundation up which your journey to become a Jedi will be built. When we become aware of our blind spots, we are in a greater position to do something about them which allows us to be more effective and powerful.

Our life circumstances and experiences shape us and make us who we are. Understanding who we are and how we got here holds important information for our future happiness and success. As Jedi we take the approach that we will always be students of life and its mysteries. This approach allows us the greatest opportunity for growth and expansion.

WAYS TO INCREASE YOUR VIBRATIONAL FREQUENCY

"Know thyself."

- Plato, Athenian Philosopher

There are several ways that we can alter our vibrational frequency. Having practices and actions that can uplift our vibration is of vital importance during this time.

When you have a higher vibrational frequency, your body will feel lighter, but not just your physical body. Your spiritual and emotional bodies will also feel lighter. You will come to experience greater personal power as well as peace, clarity, and joy. Your levels of discomfort will be eradicated and your energy as well as your zest for life will soar. You will feel less sleepy during the day; cutting back on your nap time, if you have any. It puts you on a different energy plane. Self-help guru, Bob Proctor, comments on the fact that the law of vibration is one of the fundamental laws within all of the universe. Nothing is ever at full rest, as we are in constant vibrational motion. Just think about the fact that in order to move a body part, you had to activate your brain cells into motion as well.

There are many things that we can do externally to raise our vibration; such as being in beautiful, scenic places, being in nature, being around animals, eating good food, surrounding ourselves with others who possess a high vibration, creating an uplifting environment at home, and engaging in these Kundalini Jedi Warrior works on shifting and enhancing your inner world and overall attitude. Let's have a look at some action steps below:

1. **Be open minded**. An open, positive mindset improves your overall happiness.
2. **Learn something new every day**. Cherish all the different aspects of life that exist.
3. **Do something you've been afraid of.** Courage gives you a real high and positive confidence for the future. Taking smaller steps until you are ready to face your biggest fears is a good strategy but please take precaution to not put your life in danger.
4. **Stay hungry for more.** Set ambitious but achievable goals. You're happiest when you're growing and learning new things
5. **Take things lightly.** When you take things less seriously, you're bound to have much more fun.
6. **Remain curious - Always.** You'll find that you'll discover a whole new, and exciting world behind curiosity.
7. **Reflect on what's happening in your life.** Knowing how you feel helps you make future decisions that will boost your happiness.

8. **Adopt the mindset of a life-long learner.** Life-long learning is the 'ongoing, voluntary, and self-motivated' pursuit of knowledge for either personal or professional reasons.

BEGINNER'S MIND

"In the beginner's mind there are many possibilities, in the expert's mind there are few."

- Shunryu Suzuki, The Professor and the Zen Master

Have you ever heard the story about the Zen monk and his cup of tea? If you haven't yet, allow me to tell it to you:

Once, a long time ago, there was a wise Zen master. People from far and near would seek his counsel and ask for his wisdom. Many would come and ask him to teach them, enlighten them in the way of Zen. He seldom turned any away. One day an important man, a man used to command and obedience came to visit the master.

"I have come today to ask you to teach me about Zen. Open my mind to enlightenment." The tone of the important man's voice was one used to getting his own way.

The Zen master smiled and said that they should discuss the matter over a cup of tea. When the tea was served the master poured his visitor a cup. He poured and he poured and the tea rose to the rim and began to spill over the table and finally onto the robes of the wealthy man.

Finally, the visitor shouted, "Enough. You are spilling the tea all over. Can't you see the cup is full?"

The master stopped pouring and smiled at his guest. "You are like this tea cup, so full that nothing more can be added. Come back to me when the cup is empty. Come back to me with an empty mind."

"Shoshin" is a word from Zen Buddhism meaning 'beginner's mind.' It refers to having an attitude of openness, eagerness, and lack of preconceptions when studying a subject, even when studying at an advanced level, just as a beginner would. As a padawan learner we adopt this approach so we develop humility knowing there is always more to learn. "Beginner's mind" means dropping our expectations and preconceived ideas about something, and seeing things just like a beginner would. If you've ever learned something new, you can remember what that's like: you're confused, you don't know how to do whatever it is you're learning, but you're also looking at everything with curiosity and wonder. That's beginner's mind." (12)

JEDI EXERCISE: BEGINNER'S MIND

Before we begin, I'd like you to inhabit a beginner's mind. Approach this information as if it is the first time you are understanding these concepts. Allow yourself to be free; suspend disbelief and fall into this adventure with the same naivety that Luke Skywalker did when he began his own hero's journey. Allow the unexpected and suspend judgment based on old beliefs.

Go back and watch the Star Wars movies - or at least your favourite one - and use a beginner's mind to review it. You could also try watching one that you have seen the least amount of times and imagine that it's the first time you are watching them. The point of this exercise is for you to drop all of the ideas and preconceived notions that you have surrounding the plot and storyline. Take note of your experience and record your reflections in a journal.

1. What new details did you notice?
2. Were you able to detach and view it as a new film?
3. What was your takeaway message from the viewing?

**Complete this exercise before moving on with the rest of the guide.

The beginner's mind is an approach that allows us to become mindful and aware of the present moment; heightening our senses and becoming aware of the liveness of the Force energy which flows through us. Now that you have tried the exercise in relation to something that you're a fan of, I would like you to try it with something more mundane. Try the exercises below for the next 7 days; journaling your insights and experiences as you do.

BEGINNER'S MIND EXERCISE WITH DAILY ACTIVITIES

Take any daily activity - breakfast, showering, brushing your teeth - and imagine that this is the first time you have ever done these things. In doing so, note your experience.

1. You start by reviewing the activity of eating with fresh eyes; as if you don't know what to expect, and as if you hadn't done it thousands of times already.
2. You really look at the food, the bowl, the spoon, and try to see the details that you might not normally notice.
3. You truly notice the textures, tastes, smells, and sights of the food; paying close attention as if you don't already know how the food will taste.
4. Everything seems new; perhaps even full of wonder.
5. You don't take anything for granted, and appreciate every bite as a gift. It's temporary, fleeting, and precious.

*

YOUR OBSERVING SELF

"Be mindful of your thoughts, Anakin, they betray you. You've made a commitment to the Jedi order, a commitment not easily broken."
           - Obi-Wan Kenobi, Star Wars: Episode II – Attack of the Clones

The past we cannot change. We cannot control the future either. Being present is connecting to the reality of the moment. Being present is about being here; right **now**. The more you are in touch with your feelings, senses, and experiences, the more you can regulate your behaviours and regulate your approach to life.

Being present requires focus. When you are lost in your thoughts, you are not present. The Thinking-Self and the Observing-Self are the two major aspects of your mind. The Observing-Self is not a thought or a feeling but more of an awareness — it's a perspective from which you observe your experiences objectively almost like seeing them from a distance. Your thoughts are constantly changing and the same is true for your feelings.

The Observing-Self is the part of you that does not change, but that experiences. Whereas the Thinking-Self is the part of you that judges, the Observing-Self helps you to become aware of what you are doing. The Observing-Self is like the sky. Your thoughts and emotions are like the weather. No matter how strong the storms are, they can't damage the sky.

A great way to tap into your observing-self is through journaling. Journaling can be an invaluable tool for the Jedi in training. It can help you record observations and insights as you become more self-aware. Journaling is a creative technique that will encourage you to pour your thoughts onto paper, instead of holding them in or letting them burst out at the wrong time or place. Sometimes, we believe that what we feel and think is not worth sharing – so we either hide them or reject them and release the energy erratically through any other distracting method or behaviour.

I started my first diary in the year 2000 as a way to capture the events of my life during this big transformative year. I had never really been a big writer and always preferred images as a way of communicating or understanding my inner process, and I think that this is why films have spoken to me on such a deep level. So, when I began to journal, I really just recorded the events of the day; things that I did or eventful happenings. Over time, I began to write about things that were upsetting for me and exploring the "why" and meaning of things occurring in my day-to-day living. I found that my journaling was acting as a place where I could really express all that was too strange or difficult to understand. My journal was almost like a friend that I could tell anything and everything to, without fear of reprisal. As I continued the practice, I noticed that the habit of writing began to feel like a conversation. The simple act of writing seemed to give me answers and understanding about things that would happen to me, and this clarity is the primary objective behind my urge to write to this very day.

Journaling is one of the most widely used self-reflective tools at our disposal. It is a powerful tool because it actually involves dealing with our thoughts and emotions in the present moment; without judgment. If judgment comes while writing, it stays there so we can later read it in order to understand how and when we tend to judge our emotions and thoughts. As it is a creative tool there is no right way to do it. Just write or even draw; doodle what you think and how you feel in that very moment. The most important element of the entire process is being true to yourself. Don't just write down what you feel and what you think; write down what you think about how you feel. If writing or doodling doesn't work for you, you can tear pages out of magazines, print images off the net, and stick in articles that inspire you. Everything that you write down in your journal is yours so do not be afraid of it.

JEDI EXERCISE: JOURNAL OF THE WILLS

Let's practice an easy journal entry that can be done anytime. Write down whatever comes to mind. Don't worry about typos. and forget about coherence. Just pay attention to what you are thinking about and put it down on paper. Whenever you get a negative emotion, feeling, or sensation, just write it all down; almost as if you were ranting to a friend. The more that comes out, the lighter you will feel.

You can imagine your journal as your own 24-hour personal therapist that is open and ready to listen! If you cannot come up with anything to write, you can draw something. Here are some journaling prompts that are likely to get you going. There is no time limit and no rush, so just be curious about what comes up. Just free flow and record whatever you hear in your mind or, if you would prefer a bit more structure, you can choose one topic that you want to look at.

The following prompts can help to get things going.
1. What is the real issue?
2. What is it that I'm really feeling (Physically & Emotionally)?
3. What am I feeling and experiencing in my body right now?
4. What is my aim/goal or life's purpose?
5. Is this relationship healthy for me?
6. What are the next steps I have to take to accomplish my goal?
7. What are my favourite movies or books and why?
8. What was the best place I've eaten out at?

Then go on to make some bullet points around the following:
1. List your successes.
2. List the personality traits that you admire (Check how or where are those traits present in yourself If they are not present, how could you incorporate them?) Your Jedi journal can also be used to collect your thoughts , experiences and observations as your progress through your Jedi training.

SELF-INQUIRY

We develop greater awareness when we take the time to reflect and inquire about what we are learning. This is why it is absolutely crucial for you to create time and space for reflection and inquiry in your daily life. It will provide you with the opportunity to notice the impact of what you are learning and practicing. These practice/reflection cycles provide us with self-insight that helps us learn how to make corrections in the moment. It provides us with a map of our progress and allows us to clearly see any patterns that emerge.

Journaling brings you into a state of mindfulness — past frustrations and future anxieties lose their edge in the present moment. There's a strong connection between happiness and mindfulness. It calls a wandering mind to attention. You go from passivity to actively engaging with your thoughts. The act of just writing can be a bit like clearing out all the channels of your mind by flushing your mind system out so that you can uncover what's really happening underneath all that mind noise.

I want you to understand that you're not just scribbling words down and expecting them to change your life; no, that would be ridiculous. However, I do want you to acknowledge the fact that even the most astute construction team needs a written or drawn blueprint before they can commence with the immense task before them. Emotional intelligence is incredibly important and journaling allows you to manage those emotions as well as to be aware of the emotions of others. Becoming self-aware builds a bridge for empathy; giving you the intuition to better understand those around you.

When you are able to get on the same page as others, despite varying beliefs, you will have successfully cultivated your emotional intelligence. Be disciplined in setting aside time to write in your journal. The more you practice, the more fluent in the ways of intuition you will become. It will eventually snowball into other areas of your life, providing you with the discipline that you need to get things done. You will free yourself from becoming mentally entangled in simple traumas.

"Studies have also shown that the emotional release from journaling lowers anxiety, stress, and induces better sleep." [13] Journaling about positive experiences can boost your mood, while journaling about negative experiences can help you to understand them. As our memories work off of remembering the last time that we remembered an event, not the memory of the actual event itself, journaling is a way for you to create positive imprints in your mind around certain events in your life. Take it one step at a time. Be patient with your processes and become aware that patience and consistency are crucial in forming new habits. Write first thing in the morning or the last thing before bed, so that you can create this habit. You can put pen to paper or you can use an app; the possibilities are limitless and the choice is yours.

JOURNAL ENTRIES EXERCISE CONTINUED

Journaling should become a habit. Here are more prompts to get you thinking and reflecting for continuing your journaling practice. Choose any one subject for a journal entry:
1. When do I feel the most alive?
2. What am I passionate about?
3. What are my best memories?
4. What makes me sad?

5. What makes me frustrated or indignant?
6. When do I lose control of my emotions?
7. What daily activities bring pain and suffering to my life?
8. What daily activities add value to my life?
9. Who brings joy and positivity to my life?
10. Who brings strife and negativity?

You may also want to record interactions with friends, family members, and others where places of conflict or upset arise; this will also give you insight into areas of your development that need work.

*

COCOON: OUR COMFORT ZONE

"One can choose to go back toward safety or forward toward growth. Growth must be chosen again and again; fear must be overcome again and again."

- Abraham Maslow

In the book *Shambhala: The Sacred Path of the Warrior* by Chögyam Trungpa Riponche, Riponche lets us in on teachings that can take us down the path to becoming a warrior. It speaks of the fact that we currently live in these artificial cocoons; created with the artificial comforts around us. We are enclosed in these cocoons; shielding us away from the beauty of the world which is unraveling as a result of the Aquarian Age. It is like trying to go back into the womb and remain there forever without being born; oh but we must be born. We must face the world outside. This is known as creating a shield from the Great Eastern Sun.

When we hide away from the world, we feel secure. We haven't quieted our fear, we have made ourselves numb with it. We take this cocoon as an inheritance; passing it down after us to those within our inner circles. It is familiar, comfortable, and sleepy. We remain in this place of comfort; irrespective of the fact that it may not be good for us. It's easy to remain here because there is little to no risk – there is no anxiety. However, it stops you from achieving all of the things that you are capable of and it leaves you in misery. Your brain's learning centers have effectively shut down because you are so used to the repetition of the mundane, the known, and the safe.

As the saying goes, you will learn more about yourself when you take the road less traveled. So, veer away from the darkened, dampened, cocoon. Stay away from the comfort foods, the porn, the drugs. Leap out of that comfort zone, and dedicate yourself to something purer of spirit because whether you like to believe it or not, you are paying a huge price for your comfort zone. Do things that make you feel uncomfortable. Walk into unfamiliar places, internally and externally.

Now, this book may push and even make you feel slightly uncomfortable at times, but you will undoubtedly gain something from the journey. I congratulate you for taking your first steps!

"You have taken your first steps into a wider world."
- **Obi-Wan Kenobi, Star Wars Episode IV: A New Hope**

***

CHAPTER 4: THE STAR WARS PHENOMENON

> *"I thought Star Wars was too whacky for the general public."*
>
> - George Lucas

THE IMPACT OF THE FRANCHISE

In this chapter we will explore the impact of the Star Wars Saga, and why this sprawling space opera became the pop culture phenomenon that is today.

There has been no other film series like it. Expanding four decades; this space opera that has captured the hearts and imaginations of generations of movie-goers has grown from strength to strength. The first film, *A New Hope*, premiered in 1977. 42 years and 9 films later we see the saga come to an end on December 19th 2019. Many of us have grown up with the sounds, sights, and sayings from the movie; having had it form a part of our everyday language. Phrases like "evil empire", "May the Force be with you", and "Luke, I am your father" have become part of pop culture.

The film franchise has grossed more than $10 billion worldwide and this figure hasn't even taken inflation into account nor does it include re-releases and special editions. Whilst also holding the Guinness World Record for highest grossing box-office film within the science-fiction film niche.

The films have spawned toys, games, animated movies, as well as theme parks and they continue to capture the imaginations of fans around the world. The main characters of Star Wars - Luke Skywalker, Princess Leia, Han Solo, Chewbacca, R2-D2, and C-3PO - have all become household names with people even naming their children after their favourite Star Wars characters.

The Star Wars franchise appeals to all ages and genders, and it could be described as an event movie that unites people from many walks of life. People have even had Star Wars themed weddings!

Star Wars fans could be described as being obsessed at times and have become legends in their own rights. There have been a number of groups and organizations formed that support this deep passion for this cinematic universe. They have taken cosplay to a whole other level and have even starred in the films themselves. The *501st Legion* is an international fan-based organisation dedicated to the construction and wearing of screen-accurate replicas of Imperial Stormtrooper armour, Sith Lords, Clone Troopers, bounty hunters, and other villains from the Star Wars universe. There are dedicated fans who spend hundreds of hours and thousands of dollars to create functioning replica lightsabers and R2-D2 units for the love of the film.

"The members of the *R2 Builders Club* -a group of techies devoted to fashioning working versions of R2-D2; the garbage-can-size droid - definitely spend time in their basements—and garages and workrooms. It has paid off: J.J. Abrams, the director of the forthcoming "Star Wars: Episode VII," has hired a pair of them to work on the film. And don't forget about Chris Bartlett, whose C-3PO costume was so good and human-cyborg patois so perfect that Lucasfilm has sent him around the world—and into Barack Obama's White House—to serve as an ambassador for the brand." (14)

People used to queue all the way down the block to buy a movie ticket for Star Wars' latest release. This was, of course, before the advent of internet sales. This waiting in line became the hallmark of the franchise; showcasing how fans would go to great lengths to be the first of the lot to view the films. Some would cosplay, and camp out for a whopping 3 weeks!

Now there are fan films which are made in honour of our beloved franchise, and Lucasfilm has even gone so far as to create an entire annual contest and award ceremony for Star Wars fan films. In 2002 The official Star Wars Fan Film Awards began and it got an overhaul to be named the Star Wars Fan Movie Challenge in 2007.

If you have not seen or heard of Star Wars before then you just might be from another planet. We have provided a brief synopsis of each movie in the Appendix but we would recommend you invest some quality time into the process and actually watch them. Trust me, you will not be disappointed! Perhaps after you finish reading the manual you will be inspired to check them out. Nevertheless, we hold no judgement if you have not seen the movies, but we encourage you to watch them if you wish to understand the many references in this book.

The Star Wars narrative spans galaxies and strange new worlds. It introduces us to fantastical aliens and strange beings where an epic battle of good and evil are played out through the lineage of the Skywalker family. Star Wars is about knighthood, war, glory, revenge, redemption, and never forgetting your roots. It explores the themes of love, hate, service, balance and fulfilling one's destiny.

At its core, Star Wars is about an ancient religion versus the evils of modern technology. It is the classic story of good versus evil; where the light meets the dark and is encompassed by all the elements of a battle of this nature. It tells the story of a young orphan boy's humble beginnings and how he became one of the greatest Jedi to have ever existed; only to be tricked and turned to the dark side - to become one of the most famous villains of all time.

As the story progresses through the movies, we get to meet his son and how he is challenged to face his deepest darkest fears and redeem his lost father. The prequels explore how it all began and the most recent movies invite us to share the journey of the new generation of Jedi and heroes.

"The cultural influence of the six Star Wars films - plus the novels, comics, television shows, games, toys, spoofs, and documentaries - is such that, in the 2001 United Kingdom census, some 390,000 people stated their religion as Jedi, making it the fourth largest religion surveyed. shows, games, toys, spoofs, and documentaries - is such that, in the 2001 United Kingdom census, some 390,000 people stated their religion as Jedi, making it the fourth largest religion surveyed. In the foreword you may have read how in 2007 Daniel

Morgan Jones became world famous for founding The Church of Jediism at the age of 20 and it now has over 500,000 members around the world. Just last month, members of the performance art group *ImprovEverywhere* filmed themselves re-enacting Princess Leia's capture by Darth Vader in the New York subway, and the automotive navigation systems company TomTom recently made "Star Wars" voices an option for its GPS devices.

Star Wars also has had more-subtle influences on Hollywood. It pioneered the modern special effects blockbuster as well as the modern movie trilogy, leading the way for *Lord of the Rings* and *The Matrix*, among others. It also showed that merchandising can make even more money than the movies do? The deal that *Star Wars* creator George Lucas made with Pepsi co over merchandising rights for the prequel films was estimated to be worth roughly $2 billion. Changed special effects, toys and marketing, changed the fortunes of Hollywood." [15]

*

THE INSPIRATION OF GEORGE LUCAS

Lucas explained how, as he was growing up, he was impacted by countless early cinematic influences like the classic spaghetti westerns of the past and modern sci-fi movies like Flash Gordon. He adored Flash Gordon as a child and had even requested the rights to recreate the film. In a strange twist of fate which he was refused the film rights and went on to create Star Wars instead - close one!

George Lucas set out to make a sci-fi movie of a different caliber; something that even teenagers would enjoy. He was quoted as saying that he had wanted to give the youth of the time some faraway and exotic place for their imagination to run wild in. While Watching the Star Wars movies, it is easy to recognise the many sources that influenced the themes and narratives of the films. The films draw heavily from philosophical concepts of death, balance, and redemption.

The Star Wars saga includes elements of classical mythology - the heroic epic journey - making reference to ancient traditions and ideas which we will explore in this book. *Star Wars* is ultimately about the journey of life we all take and touches on the very human experience we all live. Some of the topics it explores include: sins of the father, redemption, coming of age, leaving an ordinary life in search of something much greater, and the idea of a purpose in life as well as achieving our true destiny.

Star Wars takes inspiration from powerful elements that are present in other cultures and wise old traditions from around the world including Confucianism, Shinto Qigong, Zoroastrianism, and Taoism as well as other strong eastern influences including those from within the Southern and Eastern Asian religions. It even touches upon Christianity and parts of the Abrahamic religions.

Star Wars creator, George Lucas has also admitted that Hinduism and eastern spirituality inspired some of the concepts in the *Star Wars* movies like the energy of the force and, most notably the Jedi religion. He wanted to explore and give young children a connection to God and higher power as a way of understanding classic religions.

"I put the Force into the movie in order to try to awaken a certain kind of spirituality in young people— more a belief in God than a belief in any particular religious system. I wanted to make it so that young people would begin to ask questions about the mystery. Not having enough interest in the mysteries of life to ask the question, 'Is there a God or is there not a God?' That is for me the worst thing that can happen. I think you should have an opinion about that. Or you should be saying, 'I'm looking. I'm very curious about this, and I am going to continue to look until I can find an answer, and if I can't find an answer, then I'll die trying.' I think it's important to have a belief system and to have faith."

- George Lucas

Lucas went on to explain that most of the spiritual essence of the movies were a depiction of all religions; like a synthesis of the lot. It showed how man has dealt with spiritual dilemmas throughout history.

In an interview, Lucas has specifically cited the fact that he became acquainted with the term "jidaigeki" (period drama, the Japanese genre of samurai films) while in Japan. It is widely assumed that Lucas took inspiration for the term Jedi from this. The Samurai warriors of Japan are somewhat parallel to the concept of the Jedi as an elite warrior class specialised in combat and swordsmanship techniques charged with protecting their respective societies.

The knights of old have a strong influence or theme within the movies as we can see the inspiration being taken from Arthurian legends and Celtic folklore. We begin to see quite early on in the franchise, the strong sense of courage, chivalry and knighthood amongst our protagonists.

"The legendary King Arthur Myth has a significant parallel to Luke Skywalker as a young orphaned hero embarking on a journey to restore peace and justice to his society. Arthur's use of his sword Excalibur as a tool of achieving objectives is reflected by Luke's use of his lightsaber in the same manner. The life and character development of Luke Skywalker also resembles that of the legendary King Arthur. Both are orphans who later become heroes in their early adulthood. Both also have mentors who are much older and provide them with guidance and/or training. Arthur was mentored by Merlin and Luke was mentored and trained by Obi-Wan Kenobi prior to continuing his training and mentorship with Yoda. The role of Anakin Skywalker, as Luke's father, mirrors that of Uther Pendragon as King Arthur's father as well." [16]

JEDI EXERCISE: WHAT MOVES YOU?

Take a moment to reflect on the things that inspire you. What types of stories do you resonate with? What are you naturally drawn to? Are there world cultures that invoke a sense of mystery and interest in you? Using you Jedi training journal write an entry on this:
- Who influences you?
- Who guides your direction?

- Who improves your life?
- Who inspires you?
- What characteristics do you admire in these individuals?
- What characteristics inspire your own behaviour as a result?

Note all these different aspects and see how they are part of your life and even your identity as a person. Record your findings in your Jedi journal.

***

CHAPTER 5: THE IMPORTANCE OF STORYTELLING

" *Tell me the facts and I'll learn. Tell me the truth and I'll believe. But tell me a story and it will live in heart forever."*

- Native American Proverb

THE POWER OF STORY

Are you sitting comfortably? Then, I'll begin...Once upon a time... Does that simple opening line take you back to your childhood? Perhaps it's a line you've read night after night, in book after book, to your own children. As humans we love stories, reading them, watching them, acting them out, and creating them. They serve as lessons we wish to teach our kids - to understand our place in the universe and everything in between. Humans make up stories, tell real truths through stories, and get lost in stories. Great stories bring people together in a sense of commonality, and nothing beats the great joy of sitting around a campfire, sharing a story under the stars. *Star Wars* could be argued to be one of the greatest stories to ever grace the big screen. The ultimate story of good versus evil and the triumph of light over dark. Storytelling is what connects us to our humanity. It is what links us to our past, and provides a glimpse into our future. Since humans first walked the earth, they have told stories; long before even the written word or oral language. They told stories through cave drawings and then around fires. We have always told stories as a way to shape our existence. Things happen to us - the elements of a story - but as humans, we have unique perspectives, which shape how a story is relayed.

The Ancient Greeks were serious about their entertainment. They used drama as a way of discussing the world around them. They pondered on what it meant to be human and we need these stories to explore our humanity now more than ever. They give us a sense of community and help us to face the challenges laid out in front of us; including some of the darkest aspects of our humanity. If we look back to the 5th century Athenians, we see how they lived through almost an entire century of wars. They lived through the plague and they came out anew. Sophocles Theban Plays, for example, make these experiences central to all. It then becomes a burden that we all carry instead of just those who have lived through it.

"Star Wars is ultimately a modern way to tell ancient stories. It uses modern techniques and visuals to distill some of the oldest lessons from our collective mythology. It reaches deep into our collective history as social beings, but at the same time it never ends up being too heavy. It spices up these lessons with thrilling adventure, heartfelt camaraderie, and above all, an effervescent energy that makes it accessible to all ages"

- Pablo Hidalgo, Studying Skywalkers

Let it be known that these plays weren't there simply as a means of entertainment, but as a medium for the collective suffering of humanity. When played before the right audience these plays still have the same effect in delivering an impactful message. They act as a reflection of ourselves, no matter how hard it may be to look at it. Just like a history lesson, it shows us how far we have come and how not to go back to where we came from. It gives us the courage to forge new ways forward. It gives our lives meaning, because when we are a part of that collective, we are able to feel as though our existence has meant something. Even if someone remembers us only in the slightest, we will have left our mark as the protagonists of our own story. This is the very reason why we create stories. This is why we need storytellers. They are what make us human.

JEDI EXERCISE: CHANGING YOUR LIFE STORY

Our lives are a compilation of stories that we tell ourselves - stories of what we've done, how we've done it, and what we want to do. Stories about who we are and who we are not. These stories create our reality, but they're not always real. They're interpretations of the truth, filtered through our perceptions, expectations, hopes and fears. Sometimes these stories don't work for us. They don't lead to what we have envisioned for our lives and they may even hold us back. We wind up stuck, unhappy, disappointed, or worse. However, the stories of our life are malleable. We can rewrite them as often as we want. In doing so, we can create a new reality for ourselves. If you feel your life story could use a rewrite, here are a few ways to start…

1. CHANGE YOUR VILLAIN.

Maybe it's a person, maybe it's a condition, maybe it's something within you that holds you back.

Whatever the enemy is in your life story — the thing you think is responsible for preventing you from getting what you want — you have the power to change it.

You may not be able to make it disappear -though sometimes you can - but you can shift how you see the role that it plays in your life.

Imagine this:
What if the villain in your story isn't actually what's held you back?
What if you've battled the wrong enemy all along?

2. CHANGE YOUR ORIGIN STORY.

Every hero has an origin story, but it's possible that you've chosen the wrong story to define how you came to be the person that you are.

Think back on the choices that you've made, the path that led to where you are today, and recognise that other circumstances may have been just as influential to your development in better ways. Maybe your origin story isn't one of somebody who suffered misfortune in your youth, but rather one of somebody who overcame incredible challenges.

This may sound like splitting hairs or arguing semantics, but semantics matter in storytelling.

3. CHANGE YOUR LOCATION.

If you move across the world, your life story will be rewritten, but you don't have to make that drastic of a location shift to alter your story. Think about the locations where you spend the majority of your time and consider how things might change if you altered those locations: a different neighbourhood, a new workplace, an alternate hang-out spot with friends. What if you took the five places you spend most of your time and replaced three of them with new places where you did new things with new people?

Sitcoms typically set all their scenes in the same couple of locations because those are the situations in which the show is based. If they change those locations, they change the show.

The same is true for your life.

4. GIVE YOURSELF NEW POWERS.

Your life story up to this point has been based largely on the abilities you've developed — your powers - but you can always learn new skills and these newfound powers can drastically change the course of your life.

They can be career-related, a hobby, or a passion, but stretching yourself and learning new things will change the story of your life.

5. CHANGE YOUR SUPPORTING CAST.

Who are the supporting characters in your life? What friends, family, and co-workers occupy the most space in your story?

Think about the influence they have on your life and how they make you feel.

Are they positive? Negative? Distracting? Inspiring?

Switching up the supporting cast in your life — or the ways that you interact with them — can drastically change your story.

6. END THE CHAPTER YOU'RE IN.

Most stories are told in chapters and every chapter has an end.

If your story isn't heading in a direction that you want, consider which chapters you can end.

7. CHANGE YOUR GENRE.

If you had to pick a genre for your life story, what would it be?

Action? Comedy? Tragedy?

It's a tough question to answer, but it reveals your perspective on the life story you've told yourself.

What would happen if you looked at your life through the prism of a different genre?

What would happen if you made a conscious decision to change your tragic outlook to a comic one - or if you chose to focus on romance over drama?

A lot might change.

8. MAKE YOUR END YOUR MIDPOINT

As we get older, we settle into our lives, careers, and relationships. We begin to feel that our story has been written. If you don't like how it's come together, that can be a problem. However, there's a simple thing that you can do to reframe your perspective and rewrite your story.

Remember that wherever you are in your life right now is just the midpoint of the story — not the ending.

In screenwriting, the story's midpoint is where everything the hero thinks is happening in the story gets turned upside down and the hero realises that their story has actually only just begun.

That's not a bad way to think about the story of your life — no matter where you happen to be in it.

*

MYTH MAKING

"We need myths that will identify the individual not with his local group but with the planet."

- **Joseph Campbell, The Power of Myth**

A myth will usually explain the reasons for a cultural practice or phenomenon. It is a traditional story; passed down through generations. While it can contain some traces of historical fact, it is most often based in the supernatural in order to give it the desired impactful effect. The ancient Greek word "mythos", means myth and it can also mean 'sacred story', 'traditional narrative' or 'tale of the Gods'. These stories were used to create an understanding of right and wrong in ancient times. Wisdom, after all, can always be found in the consequences of the action of the characters within the myth.

Steve Sansweet gave his perspective on the significance of Star Wars, the great modern mythology. "Certainly there are movies that people talk about — and even watch year after year — decades after they've been released, such as The Wizard of Oz. But for the Star Wars saga films to still be front-of-mind, soul-deep, and much beloved nearly 40 years after the first movie was released, puts them in a category all by themselves. We've just commemorated the 400th anniversary of William Shakespeare's death, and while I can hardly predict the future, it wouldn't surprise me if people worldwide still remember the cultural phenomenon that Star Wars has become hundreds of years from now. And a large part of that can be attributed to the ancient myths, some thousands of years old, that underlie many of the characters and storylines of the Star Wars films. The Skywalker family story, based on the hero's journey, the choices we all make in life, the chance for someone's final redemption despite never-ceasing hostilities in the world — these have contributed to Star Wars becoming a touchstone across cultures, borders, and all the other barriers we confront on a daily basis." (17)

The strength of mythology also lay in the ease with which people could identify with the characters in the tales, as these were always individuals with their faults and shortcomings. Ultimately these characters helped them to understand the complexities and contradictions of life, but myths are more than mere stories and they serve a more profound purpose in both ancient and modern cultures. Myths are sacred tales that explain the world and man's experiences within that world. Myths are as relevant to us today as they were to the ancients.

Myths answer timeless questions and serve as a compass to each generation. They showcase the consequences of our actions and encourage us to act with wisdom. They are cautionary tales that highlight how following the Dark Path can garner catastrophic results. When we take heed of these tales, they can help us to avoid similar consequences. Armed with this wisdom, we are primed to make the right decisions.

When it comes to religious tales of old, they serve as the ultimate truth with which we can interpret our own inner workings and lives. Through them people have, historically, found their purpose in life. They, therefore, connect us to these sacred realities.

The reason why myths are still around in this day and age is because their lessons can still be applied to modern day issues. Their powerful symbolism is still relevant and they still serve a purpose for us; providing us with much needed insight. We would never have come as far as we have as the human race had it not been for myth. Star Wars provides us with the modern myth that we need to face our own social dilemmas. The films touch something deep within us; going past the point of pure entertainment and calling our souls back to their true nature.

"Star Wars is the first myth we all embraced as a global culture. What that culture has done with the story is remarkable. It is emergent behaviour: fans continue to fashion all kinds of memes, fictions, and behaviours out of its raw materials, far beyond anything its creators anticipated. The myth is evolving. What that means for the future is anyone's guess, but I think it's instructive to look at the history of fairy tales in Europe. Stories like Red Riding Hood have thrived in evolving forms for hundreds if not thousands of years. Star Wars is universally applicable, enough for it to potentially last as long."
- Chris Taylor - Author of How Star Wars Conquered the Universe

JOSEPH CAMPBELL'S MONOMYTH

American author, Joseph Campbell, examined the functions of myths on a universal level; assessing how they have the power to transcend creed and culture. He explored the myth as an ideal in various literature and came up with the notion that the myth always follows the same pattern. It is said that Lucas was inspired by his book, *The Hero with a Thousand Faces* when he was creating Star Wars. It has been told that they even met up and worked together; with Campbell helping Lucas create the modern myth that we now know as Star Wars.

Campbell highlighted that human cultures' mythologies usually include a cosmogonical, or creation myth, concerning the origins of the world, or how the world came to exist. The active beings in myths are generally Gods and Goddesses, heroes and heroines, or animals and plants. The Star Wars myth is set in a timeless past before recorded time or the beginning of critical history. The inclusion of the Force in the Star Wars myth establishes a sacred narrative because it holds religious and spiritual significance.

Joseph Campbell's main literary contribution was his recognition of the way in which the same story structure was used in all myths from around the world. He, for the very first time, exposed the pattern that lies behind every story ever told. He was able to gather all these different ideas and elements of the storytelling together so as to recognise the inherent pattern in all of them and to articulate them into what is now known as, The Monomyth. The following depicts an outline of *The Hero's Journey* by Joseph Campbell:

Campbell discovered that all of the world's hero myths were basically all the same story retold endlessly in infinite variations. He found that all storytelling, consciously or not, follows the ancient patterns of myth and that all stories, from the crudest jokes to the highest flights of literature, can be understood in terms of the hero myth; which he named the "monomyth" and whose principles he lays out in his book 'Hero with a Thousand Faces'.

The theme of the hero myth is universal, occurring in every culture, in every time; it is as infinitely varied as the human race itself; and yet its basic form remains the same, an incredibly tenacious set of elements that spring in endless repetition from the deepest reaches of the mind of man. Campbell's thinking runs parallel to that of Swiss psychologist Carl Jung, who wrote of the "archetypes: -- constantly repeating characters who occur in the dreams of all people and the myths of all cultures. (we will meet master Jung Jedi in the next chapter). Jung suggested that these archetypes are reflections of aspects of the human mind – that our personalities divide themselves into these characters to play out the drama of our lives. He noticed a strong correspondence between his patients' dream or fantasy figures and the common archetypes of mythology; he suggested that both were coming from a deeper source, in the "collective unconscious" of the human race. (18)

According to *The Hero with a Thousand Faces* there are characters which are commonly repeated throughout mythical tales across all cultures. These characters are replicas of the archetypes of the human mind and usually revolve around a young hero, a wise old guide, a shifty antagonist, and a shape-shifting being. Any myths which follow this construct play on our own inner archetypes and thus feel true to us. This is one of the primary reasons why Star Wars connects so deeply across multiple generations of fans. (19)

They are like maps of our own psyche and as such we deem them as realistic even when they seem to be the workings of fantasy. They appeal to everyone because no matter what religion we prescribe to or what language we speak, they reflect our human nature. They stem from our collective unconscious and thus this also bolsters the idea that we are all connected via one true source – or Force. These myths can be used to understand and explore any manner of human problems.

THE HERO

I have always been fascinated by heroes. Maybe deep down all I ever wanted to be was a hero; to be brave and strong, or to rescue a damsel in distress and save the world. Growing up, my room was littered with comic books and movie posters reflecting my favourite heroes. I always gravitated towards heroes that were closer to reality; heroes that were more plausible and that could actually exist in real life. To me, these were heroes like Batman, Captain America or Daredevil, as they were essentially an everyday person grounded in the real world and their superpowers were gained mostly by training and refinement of their human abilities. I think growing up with my challenging early history, I was longing for someone to come and rescue me, and it was a long time until I realised that no one was coming to save me. I had to become the hero of my own life.

According to Webster's Dictionary definition, a hero is *"a mythological or legendary figure often of divine descent endowed with great strength or ability, an illustrious warrior, a man admired for his achievements and noble qualities, one who shows great courage, the principal male character in a literary or dramatic work, the central figure in an event, period, or movement, or an object of extreme admiration and devotion."* [20]

Everyone knew what a hero was in ancient times. Some of the most well-known heroes of old include Achilles, Perseus, and Hercules. More often than not they were believed to have qualities of a God and were, therefore, worshipped as such. There are also our modern-day heroes such as Jesus Christ, Lorenzo de Medici, Leonardo da Vinci, Martin Luther King, William Shakespeare, and Sir Francis Bacon. The younger generation of the 20th century now see football players like Leonel Messi, Cristiano Ronaldo, and David Beckham as their personal heroes, while others look up to popular characters like captain jack sparrow, The Rock, Willy Wonka and - in this modern age of social media - even several stars from YouTube and Instagram. You'll have children who look outwards to find their own version of a superhero while some children will see their own mum as their number one hero.

"For we have not even to risk the adventure alone, for the heroes of all time have gone before us."

- Joseph Campbell, The Power of Myth

According to Campbell's definition of a hero, "A hero is someone who has given his or her life to something bigger than oneself." It is said that almost anyone can become a hero whether by choice or happenstance. However, the evolution to hero is usually a painful one and will require them to fight many battles both internally and externally. It's almost as if greatness cannot be achieved without prior strife, struggling, and good deeds.

There are notably two types of deeds that the hero can engage in. There is the iconic heroic deed, whereby the hero gives of himself and sacrifices himself for others, and there is the other whereby he returns with the spiritual knowledge needed to help others on their path. Whichever of the two the hero undertakes; this process is cyclical and often marked by a lengthy journey.

JEDI EXERCISE: WE NEED A HERO

I have so many heroes and heroines that I look up to for inspiration, guidance, and their overall approach to the heroic journey of life as well as the soul gifts they have left for the world. Some of these include:

JORDAN PETERSON - Psychology professor; Thought provoker
BRUCE LEE - Martial arts master Jeet Kun Do;
GAUTAMA BUDDA - Leader teacher of the Buddhist dharmic faith;
CARL JUNG - Swiss psychologist;
KING LEONIDAS - General of the legendary 300 Spartans;
THE SILVER SURFER - Cosmic superhero from the Marvel universe.
JULIAN ASANGE -Whistleblower /truth seeker
GRETA THUNBURG- Environmentalist
JOAN OF ARC - French patron saint
LUKE SKYWALKER- Jedi knight
RUSSEL BRAND - Master of the addictive personality
JESUS CHRIST- Son of the Force
GURU NANAK DEV JI -Religious innovator

Take some time to ask yourself some pertinent questions regarding your own heroes.
- Who are your personal favourite heroes?
- Reflect on their qualities?
- Are these aspects which you already embody or qualities that you wish to have?
- Do you see a pattern in your choices?
- Do your hero's follow a similar theme or story for you?

Write your reflections in your Jedi journal under self-enquiry.

***

CHAPTER 6: THE HERO'S JOURNEY

"A hero is someone who, in spite of weakness, doubt or not always knowing the answers, goes ahead and overcomes anyway."

— *Christopher Reeve - Superman*

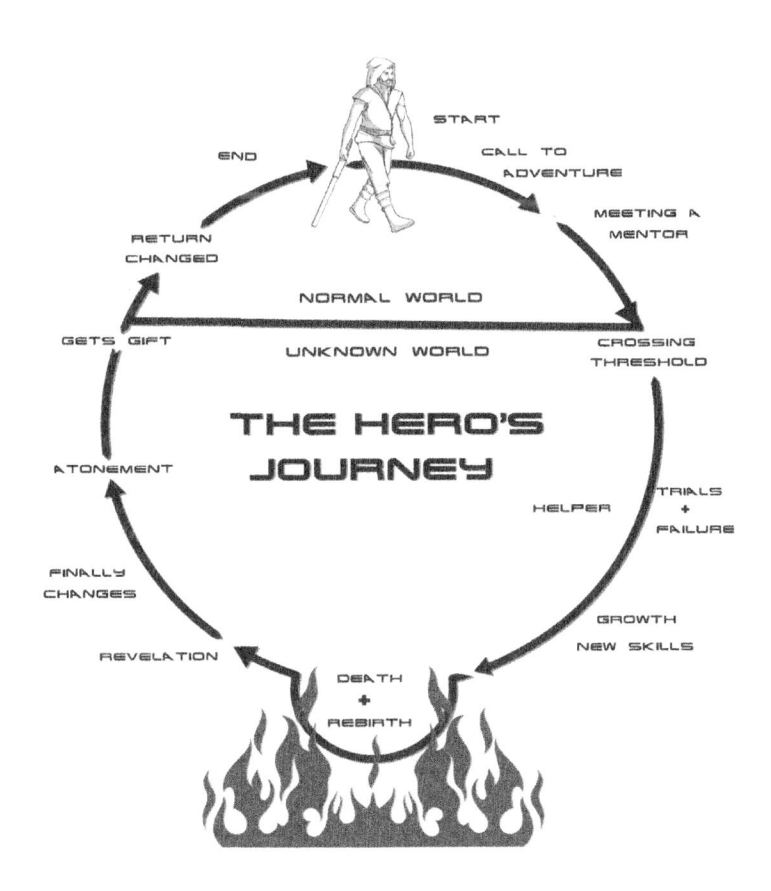

DIAGRAM OF THE STAGES OF THE HERO JOURNEY

HERO TO WARRIOR

The Hero is the boyhood/girlhood archetype which matures into the Warrior Archetype. Part of this maturation process centres on a shift in a man's loyalties. "The Hero's main motivation is to be the hero and to receive all of the acclaim that goes with being a hero, a reward, fame and sometimes the hand of the princess but selfishly it is really about himself– his motives are for impressing himself with himself and to impressing others.

The Warrior's motives, on the other hand, are geared towards something greater than himself and his concerns." The Warrior's loyalty centres on a cause, a God, a people, a task, or a nation – it's always something much larger than the individuals themselves. The Warrior has a "central commitment" around which he organises his life. His life's purpose is rooted in ideals and principles, which naturally strips away superfluities and pettiness and brings his life great meaning.

Jedi offer themselves to the service and protection of the universe and to keeping the force in balance within themselves. They never fight or battle for themselves but for the greatest good of all.

THE JOURNEY
"We must let go of the life we have planned, to accept the one that is waiting for us."

- Joseph Campbell, The Power of Myth

The hero's journey isn't just for classical heroes, but for all of us. It is, essentially, a path of maturation that all evolving humans are invited to follow. We have many hero's journeys throughout our lives; from small journeys and stages in our daily life to larger heroes' journeys like changing careers, marriage, and having children or deciding to follow a totally new path of life that is unknown and undiscovered.

Unbeknownst to yourself you have already achieved one of life's greatest heroic adventures for you are - here alive and reading this book. In an article by Greg Twemlow called *'There's a Hero in All of Us'* he shares a great passage from Otto Rank in his short book called *"The Myth of the Birth of the Hero"*. In it, he says that *"[everyone] is a hero in his birth. He has undergone a tremendous transformation from a little, you might say, water creature, living in a realm of the amniotic fluid and so forth, then coming out, becoming an air-breathing mammal that ultimately will be self-standing and so forth. This is an enormous transformation and it is a heroic act, and it's a heroic act on the mother's part to bring it about. It's the primary hero form, you might say.* (21)

He goes on to describe his version of what a hero is and how they become the hero. Greg Twemlow paraphrases it most eloquently:

"Life in the village has been peaceful and happy until one day when that suddenly changes. The villagers have been challenged/attacked/killed by an evil creature, a dragon, a group of bandits — an evil force.
Our hero at first seeks solace and protection and awaits someone to step forward to take a stand and provide protection for the village.
Nobody steps forward and without notice, there's a second attack, much worse than the first. It's clear that unless someone steps forward, the village and everyone in it will perish. A hero is born. She now knows that unless there's firm action, the village will be destroyed.

Our hero accepts her mission to leave the village and head into unknown territory to find and destroy the evil force.
On this heroic journey, she will be challenged and her life threatened. As she overcomes challenge after challenge, she comes to the ultimate obstacle; the one that could literally take her life. Our hero does not pause to consider her safety, but she confronts the evil force and strikes it down with her sword.
Now she can return to the village to be proclaimed a hero and forever after be worshipped." (22)

12 STAGES OF THE HERO'S JOURNEY

Campbell best defined the 12 steps of the hero's journey and we will explore them below. Firstly, a hero always begins his journey with a quest. This hero is often just an ordinary person out in the world like the rest of us and it is because of that that they are initially hesitant to embark on the quest that they have been called to go on. We'll then see them receive the inspiration that they need through the help of a mentor or perhaps even an ancient scroll which will guide them. Once they have overcome their misgivings and committed to the journey that lays ahead of them, they will be met with friends, foes, and tests along the way. This will often lead to a showdown of some sort; bringing them face to face with their deepest fears. Only through surviving this ordeal do they get the reward of spiritual knowledge and insight. They will then journey back home; completely transformed by their experiences in order to share what they have learned.

No matter who you are, you will receive a call to the unknown at some point in your life. Many of you will not have answered a prior call due to it being far too uncomfortable and daunting of a task. These calls are often disregarded because they are not things which are presented with facts. They are strange sensations within you, urging you to take a leap of faith. The decision that you have to make in order to answer the call will seem irrational, illogical, and just plain insane, but it will persist even when you try to ignore it. In fact, the more you try to ignore it, the more it will persist. This is your intuition guiding you, and you need to listen. It is only the uncertainty of the matter which preys on your fears, but you will not be at peace within yourself unless you heed the call. You will only look back on the missed opportunity to fulfil your life's purpose with resentment one day.

You must learn to be faithful to yourself and to your intuition if you want to truly embark on your own hero's journey towards becoming a Kundalini Jedi Warrior. A many number of things could be trying to prevent you from crossing that threshold to your journey. These could be friends, parents, partners, or even just your day-to-day responsibilities. Once you set off and find yourself in the unknown in spite of those who advised against it, you will begin to search within yourself for the answers instead of looking towards external sources. You shed the fears of your past and embrace your future; becoming exceedingly aware of the dangers that lurk out in the world. However, the fear of these dangers will no longer have a stranglehold on you; accepting them for what they are and not attempting to control them.

You will then face your own series of trials and tribulations which will require the highest level of mental resilience and patience from you. They will pull at your inner fears and self-doubts. You must hold fast to a belief within yourself and trust your intuition. Each trial will give you new knowledge which in turn will prepare you for the next trial, and so on and so forth. You will eventually emerge triumphant after years of toiling, and it is then that you must return home to share what you have learned.

While Campbell's monomyth is open to interpretation, it is something that can be applied to your own journey as we transition into the Aquarian age. Always follow your intuition and embrace the beauty of the unknown.

THE SPIRITUAL JOURNEY

"My advice to you is not to undertake the spiritual path. It is too difficult, too long, and is too demanding. I suggest you ask for your money back, and go home. This is not a picnic. It is really going to ask everything of you. So, it is best not to begin. However, if you do begin, it is best to finish."

- **Chogyam Trungpa**

Maps and guides can help us to successfully reach our goals that lay in wait at our final destination. The hero's journey could also be seen as stages on the spiritual journey. People have felt a pull toward something greater than themselves since the beginning of time. Ancient cultures had many stories that served to illustrate the journey to fulfilling one's destiny and experiencing 'wholeness' or 'enlightenment'. These journeys, as mythologist Joseph Campbell described, were the "Calls to Adventure." A call to adventure is something we all experience at least once in life. When we embark on this adventure, we begin the process of gaining self-understanding and reclaiming our precious soul gifts.

The archetype of the hero/heroine discovering their true spiritual nature goes back thousands of years. The Greek's told the story of Orpheus who descended into the underworld to rescue his bride Eurydice from Hades. The Nordic people had their hero-warrior Beowulf, and the Sumerians wrote of Inanna who battled her sister in the dark world. Throughout history, there have been so many stories of individuals who have struggled through hardship to find themselves, but of what importance are they to our path?

Essentially, these heroes and heroines symbolise our spiritual journeys: of leaving everything familiar behind, entering the unknown, encountering numerous unconscious monsters, and finally returning back home with a sense of renewed fulfilment and wisdom. Here are the 12 signs that you're being called to walk the spiritual journey of awakening:

1. You feel lost in life;
2. You long for a place that feels like your 'true home';
3. You keep wondering what your meaning or purpose is;
4. You feel like you have a big destiny to fulfil (which is yet to be revealed);
5. You sense that there's much more to life than meets the eye;
6. You're experiencing strange synchronicities, signs, and omens;

7. You're shedding your old self and are transforming, but you don't know who you truly are yet;
8. There's a sense of nostalgia and nagging longing for something you can't pinpoint;
9. You experience bouts of melancholy, depression, and existential crisis;
10. You feel extra sensitive and fragile;
11. A lot of what you once valued seems meaningless and empty; and,
12. It feels like the rug has been pulled out from underneath you, and you're falling.

The spiritual journey is one of evolution. You transition from the ego to the soul, and then from the soul to the spirit. What most of us fail to see is that the journey is not linear, but circular. We are merely completing the circle by returning to the state from whence we came. All we are doing in walking the spiritual journey is waking up from the dreamlike state that we have been in all of our lives. As Melody Larson states, we are "opening our eyes to both our multidimensional nature and our singular state of Oneness."

We begin moving from a state of negativity to a state of positivity – from suffering to acceptance, from powerlessness to empowerment, from fear to love. Larson has created a road map for this journey to awakening. She explains how the 12 steps of the road map coincide with the 12 chakras, the 12 signs of the zodiac, and Jung's 12 archetypes. All spiritual paths are ultimately about this journey. They then also fall into 3 stages which coincide with the trinity of ego, soul, and spirit as well as the creation triangle of intention, action, and manifestation, and to the Hero's Journey of preparation, adventure, and return.

While the road map demarcates the terrain of the general journey, it will be unique to you. How one person traverses the valleys and mountains is not necessarily the way that you will traverse them. I invite you to have a look at Larson's 12 steps and 3 stages below, as laid out on *Trans4Mind*. They will help you pinpoint where you are on your journey and what to do in order to move on to the next step:

STAGE ONE – PREPARATION. STRENGTHENING THE EGO.

1. **SEPARATION** - Just trying to survive and thrive. "I am alone."
2. **BELONGING** - Wanting to fit in and be loved. "I'm part of a tribe."
3. **SELFHOOD** - Rebelling and making personal changes. "I want to be free."
4. **COMMUNION** - Shifting beliefs and finding compassion. "I accept myself and others."

STAGE TWO – THE ADVENTURE. HEALING THE SOUL.

5. **SOVEREIGNTY** - Enjoying authenticity and success. "I am secure."
6. **SEARCHING** - Lost, in crisis, seeking meaning. "There must be more than this."
7. **SURRENDER** - Cultivating faith, seeking aid. "Not my will, but thy will be done."
8. **HEALING** - Embracing the shadow, healing karmic wounds. "I am whole."

STAGE THREE - THE RETURN. MERGING SOUL WITH SPIRIT.
9. **GUIDANCE** - Opening intuition, finding Soul purpose. "I know my soul contract."
10. **CO-CREATION** - On purpose, serving. "I use my gifts for the highest good."
11. **TRANSMUTATION** - Mastering Laws and Forces. "I create multiple realities."
12. **UNITY** - Awakening, Enlightenment. "All is one. I am THAT." (23)

You could traverse all 12 steps in this lifetime or take many lifetimes to do so. You will go back and forth between steps, and the journey will not be simple and linear as one might expect it to be. Just embrace wherever you are on your path to awakening. Embrace it without judgment; knowing that all steps are equally important. Everything is as it should be.

LUKE'S STAGES OF THE JOURNEY
Let's explore these now through the lens of Luke Skywalker's journey in the Star Wars universe. We see the hero's journey being played out by three of the characters across the 9 movies. We see the story arc of Anakin Skywalker in films 1-3, then we're introduced to the story of his son, Luke Skywalker, in films 3-6. Finally, we are made privy to the journey of Rey Skywalker in films 7-9. Here, we will focus on what is known as the original trilogy. If you are getting a little lost at this point, check the Appendix for the **"Stages in the Journey"** breakdown.

1. ORDINARY WORLD.
This is the current world and state that we find our hero in. In Star Wars, we have Luke, a bored and frustrated farm boy living out his days working on his uncle's farm. Luke longs for adventure, maybe being a space pilot, but, alas, he has responsibilities and cannot leave. He likes to stare at the sunset and dreams of what may lay out there. Our hero is uneasy, uncomfortable, even unaware - an experience we can identify with. Luke wishes he could join his friends in the space academy and feels his life is pulling in different directions and causing stress.

2. THE CALL TO ADVENTURE.
In this stage, something usually happens that shakes up the status quo, either from external pressures or rising from deep within. Either way, it is here that the hero begins to experience the beginning of change. In Star Wars, two new droids are bought to help Luke's uncle work on the farm and this serves as an early introduction to new allies that will join him on his journey. R2-D2 gives Luke a message of distress from Princess Leia, who needs someone to transport the droid to planet Alderaan, and so he sets off on his journey.

3. REFUSAL OF THE CALL.

The hero feels the fear of the unknown and tries to turn away from the adventure. Luke isn't thrilled about leaving his home planet and getting into trouble with his uncle for going on a wild goose chase. Luke meets Obi-Wan "Ben" Kenobi and delivers the message. Obi-Wan then has the following conversation with Luke.

Luke Skywalker: Alderaan? I'm not going to Alderaan, I've gotta get *home*, it's late, I'm in for it as it is!
Obi-Wan "Ben" Kenobi: I need your help, Luke. She needs your help. I'm getting too old for this sort of thing.
Luke Skywalker: Look, I can't get involved. I've got work to do. It's not that I like the Empire; I hate it, but there's nothing I can do about it right now... It's all such a long way from here.
Obi-Wan "Ben" Kenobi: That's your uncle talking.

- **Star Wars: Episode IV – A New Hope**

When Luke returns home, he finds his uncle and aunt have been murdered. He is shaken awake and the world he once knew has fallen apart. The hero is almost pushed into a new world and reality.

4. MEETING WITH THE MENTOR.

The hero comes across a seasoned traveller, a wise old man, a wizard, or finds some sacred scrolls or teachings that show him the ways of the world. This character – or piece of information - acts as a mentor of the world who gives the hero or heroine the training, equipment, or advice that will help them on their journey. The hero also reaches within a source of courage and wisdom. Obi-Wan Kenobi convinces Luke to follow his heart by showing him his father's lightsaber. Obi-Wan Kenobi [to Luke]: *"You must learn the ways of the Force if you're to come with me to Alderaan."*

Luke finds out things about his allusive past and is given a sacred object in the form of a lightsaber. Mentors not only pass on knowledge and information but also provide gifts and tools that will aid them in the upcoming journey.

5. CROSSING THE THRESHOLD.

The hero commits to leaving the world he once knew and enters a new condition with unfamiliar rules and values. The Hero might be discombobulated by this unfamiliar reality and its new rules. Luke finds himself in a bar fight; upsetting someone and this could be seen as Luke crossing the first threshold away from his small safe world into a larger, unknown and more unpredictable place - or what is termed the "Special World". Luke and Obi-Wan leave Mos Eisley for Alderaan.

6. TESTS, ALLIES, AND ENEMIES.

The hero faces trials and tribulations. The hero is tested and sorts out allegiances in the Special World. Luke encounters enemies and Obi-Wan has to step in as they try to elude the stormtroopers who are searching for them. Luke meets his first allies in Han Solo and Chewbacca and they set off to encounter the galactic federation. Obi-Wan begins to train Luke in the ways of the force.

7. APPROACH.

The story now shifts as the hero and his companions begin their approach into the innermost cave; a fearsome lair of dread and villainy manifesting as the death star. Here there are more tests for the hero.

Luke takes an active approach to find the princess who had sent the original message which brought them here. Luke and his newfound allies prepare for the major challenge against the Dark Side.

8. ORDEAL.

Near the middle of the story, the hero enters a central space in the "Special World" and confronts death. Alternatively, this can be seen as them facing their greatest fears. Out of the moment of death comes a new life.

Leia's rescue from the Death Star, and later, Luke using the Force to destroy the Death Star is a prime example of this. In the journey this leads us to the hero's great ordeal. After rescuing the princess, he witnesses the death of his mentor at the hands of the story's villain; evil personified as Darth Vader. Although he rescues the princess, it is a low point in the hero journey and he hits rock bottom; feeling more lost than ever without his guide – his teacher. It is here that he must confront his greatest fears and if successful can transform into the hero.

9. THE REWARD.

The hero takes possession of the treasure won by facing death. There may be a celebration, but there is also the danger of losing the treasure again. This stage of the journey is the reward for all the hard work and sacrifice the hero has made, although there was a great loss in the previous stage, here there is once again a glimmer of hope.

Luke has emerged as a hero; saving the princess and obtaining the plans for the Death Star that could defeat the empire and his now arch-enemy Darth Vader.

10. THE ROAD BACK.

About three-fourths of the way through the story, the hero is driven to complete the adventure, leaving the "Special World" to ensure that the treasure is brought home. Often a chase scene signals the urgency and danger of the mission. The next stage of the journey is the road back, and the story is not over for the hero. It now includes the hero having to take responsibility for his previous actions.

Luke cannot return to the ordinary world just yet. His actions have angered the Empire and they are now on a march to destroy him as well as his newfound family and friends. He must now face down the enemy one more time.

11. THE RESURRECTION.

At the climax, the hero is severely tested once more on the threshold of home. He or she is purified by one last sacrifice; another moment of death and rebirth, but on a higher and more complete level. By the hero's action, the polarities that conflicted at the beginning are finally resolved. Then comes the stage of resurrection. This is his last and final test; the true climax to his hero's journey. Everything he has endured, faced, and learned all comes together as the dark side attempts to destroy the hero once and for all.

The odds are stacked against him and his allies as they prepare for the final battle. The battle is intense and the rebels are seconds away from the death star being in a position to destroy them once and for all, until there is only one-star fighter remaining. Luke hurtles down the blast shaft to hit a target only 2 meters wide. It is here that Luke, once again, hears the inner voice of his mentor - Obi-Wan - telling him to let go and trust the force. Luke takes his final step of believing in something greater than himself and turns off his targeting computer with little help from Han Solo. He reinforces the importance of allies on the hero's journey. He shoots and destroys the Death Star.

12. RETURN WITH THE ELIXIR.

The hero returns home or continues the journey at this point, bearing some element of the treasure that has the power to transform the world as the hero has been transformed. Luke receives a hero's welcome as they return to the rebel base with the elixir. He has overcome his inner demons and has grown from a mere naive and innocent farm boy to becoming a young man who successfully defeated the dark side and brought peace for the rebels. He is awarded a medal, bestowed upon him by royalty, signifying his favour with the Gods and higher power. Luke joins the rebels and decides to become a Jedi. A new journey can now begin.

JEDI EXERCISE: PERSONAL HERO'S JOURNEY

The heroes' journey is a storyline that has resonated with us on an almost cellular level throughout time and it is still the basis for so many novels and movies. I know that there is a hero in each and every one of us. There'll be times in our lives when we courageously make a stand to protect others or defend our family. In fact, it's something that many people do on an almost daily basis - though perhaps not consciously. There's a very strong chance that you are a hero, yet you may not think of yourself in those terms. Take some time to reflect on your own journey.

1. Take a moment to reflect on how you've lived your life.
2. Think of those times when you bravely stepped forward.
3. What is the most heroic thing you feel you have ever done?

4. Who were your personal hero's when growing up?
5. Have your heroes changed over time?
6. Who are your heroes now?
7. Have you ever taken a hero's journey?

Write your story in your Jedi training journal and reflect on the major themes of your story.

MY HERO'S JOURNEY STORY

My story begins in the summer of 1999.
A three-year journey was nearing its completion – the journey to obtain my business degree. A failed accounting module meant that I had to complete an extra 6 months before I passed. I scraped through, but I had done it; I had finished and won a hard-fought battle.

I never did exceptionally well at school. I had mostly been distracted in class and ordinarily disruptive; most usually involved in trouble of some sort. My teachers referred to me as an effort minimiser who was not suited to academia. If I was not in some classroom brawl then I was in trouble for disrupting the other students and I was labelled a problem student. I spent a lot of time with the teacher but not because I was the teacher's pet. Oh no. I was there to be kept under close supervision so that they could make sure that I didn't break something or start a fight with the other kids. Most of my school reports had a common theme:

"We hope that he can one day fulfil his potential."

My degree success was as much of a surprise to me as it was for my friends and family. Due to my rebellious nature, and not following the rules, they presumed that I would never amount to much and that I would probably end up following the same path as my father. It wasn't that my friends and family harboured some form of ill will towards me or anything of the sort.

It was just that it was against my projected trajectory.

Now that I was armed with a degree, I could enter the workplace and finally be seen as a productive and successful member of society. I could prove all the haters wrong.

I would prove that I had not turned out like my father.

But upon completing it, I really had no idea what to do next, or what type of career I should follow. I had no interest in being a doctor, accountant, or any other profession that would satisfy my parent's dreams. I wasn't really interested in anything. Growing up I thought that it would be cool to be a ghost hunter or something unusual, and off the beaten path. I always had the feeling that I had some great destiny to fulfil. I was really good at art but probably not good enough to make a career out of it. I was always good at selling things when I was young. I had the gift of the gab, as they say. I liked to wheel and deal and I guess my goal was to become a millionaire.

That seemed like a worthy and achievable goal for life.

My girlfriend, at the time, had just finished her law degree a year before I had graduated and had just begun working. Her dad was a doctor, and she had started employment as a medical representative. The job was pretty easy by her accounts. She would go out to visit doctors; selling them the latest product, and only had to work half-day. She suggested I try pharmaceutical sales as it was a field-based job that paid well, didn't have a manager breathing down my neck, and would give me a company car with many other added benefits. After the financial struggles of university life, this seemed like a pretty good deal.

When I look back now, it was almost blind luck that I landed the role that I did. It was as if fate had a hand in what transpired. I ended up working for one of the largest pharmaceutical companies in the world.

I felt like I had finally made it.

My parents could now be proud of me, because I had proved that I was not a failure.

Somehow, I became one of the top-performing sales representatives in the company, which was confusing as I never really went to work. You see, I had struggled to shake off the habits of university life; so party on it was. The job mostly entailed going around to medical surgeries and talking about our latest respiratory machine or something of the sort. The goal was to persuade them to use our products and thus increase our sales. Most of my work involved inviting them out to dinner meetings to establish greater rapport and build trust. The doctors loved being wined and dined. What I lost in discipline and going to work during the day I made up for with personality and showing the doctors a good time. It seemed this was more than enough to achieve high sales and within a year I had become a member of the company's prestigious sales academy; being officially recognized as their top performer. I was lavished with trips abroad, stays at The Savoy and other top London hotels. I received a company expense account and every month they would send me gifts; even sending my mother flowers on her birthday - solidifying my position as a successful son. Every evening I was either out at a restaurant, hosting guests, or partying in a London nightclub; drinking way too much and using drugs on a daily basis.

I was living the high life.

I became confident – no; arrogant - with my newfound success. I was the best in the biz. I could do no wrong. I purchased my first property soon after starting up with that company. It was a 3-bedroom semi-detached house and shortly after that my company car was upgraded from a VW Golf to a brand-new Mercedes CLK. They even allowed me to have my own private license plate that read "Big Jag".

I was 26, and I had it all.

Then a few years later came the breakdown - or the breakthrough?

It was during the company's annual sales conference that my bubble burst. The company had taken all 1500 sales staff to Walt Disney World Resort in Orlando Florida to celebrate the launch of their next blockbuster drug. We were 'wined and dined' and treated to all access at the Disney theme park. I mean they actually shut down the whole park so that we would have sole use. All the shops and bars were open for us to use and you could go on any ride as many times as you would like as there were no queues. On the third day, we visited the water parks which had also been closed for that evening so that we would have sole use of the whole park to party.

I have no idea how much it would cost to close an entire park down but I'm guessing it would be a lot. As 1500 other individuals and I descended into the park for another night of drinking and partying, I remember seeing a family with 2 children being asked by security guards to exit the park. As they walked by, I heard the young girl ask her mummy:

"Why do we have to leave? I really wanted to see the killer whale."

The mum - not even looking down at her daughter - replied, "Well darling they get to stay because they have more money than us"

As she walked by, I caught her eye contact and the dejected young girl just sadly looked down towards the ground as they were being escorted out of the park. BAMM! It just hit me in the stomach. I became sober very quickly; shocked at the impact of our fun and games. I desperately wanted to tell the family that they could come and stay; sneak them in as one of the groups, but as I looked back to find them, they had disappeared beyond the view of our crowd.

I felt sick for the rest of the evening. I felt sick for all the money that was being spent and wasted as well as how this whole trip was orchestrated to manipulate us into working harder so that we would achieve higher sales. There was something wrong with this picture. It didn't seem fair or right. Maybe there was something wrong with me. I think I must have spent the next few days in a haze as if I'd been hit by a car. I was walking around dazed and confused. After dinner I avoided the champagne reception that was planned for the high achievers and went straight to my room where I sat with my head in my hands; confused and bemused. The same question kept going round and round in my head:

What is the meaning of life?

And more importantly, what is the meaning of **my** *life?*

Was this a breakdown or a breakthrough?

Once I returned home from the literal Disney World of life, the haze of my world seemed more and more artificial. This was a world where some had a lot and others had very little. Life was unbalanced. Life was not fair and only the most ruthless progressed. Like Disney World this whole world is a created illusion that covers up the truth of reality.

I was having an existential crisis. my life went from being happy to being plunged into a sphere of doubt and questioning. I had achieved my long hoped for desires; received everything I had ever wished for and yet I felt a deep, and desperate sadness - an emptiness.

I felt cold.

The rug had been pulled from underneath my feet, and there was nothing beneath me; nothing to hold onto. My house, car, and career success felt meaningless. This identity I had created felt unreal. I was a fake. Nothing felt real anymore and that sudden realisation haunted me moment by moment in everything that I did. The curtain had been pulled back and I realised that the great and powerful Wizard of Oz was just a silly old man, shamefully hiding behind a curtain.

I tried to ignore the feelings but no matter what I did, or what I bought, nothing seemed to fill this empty void I was experiencing. Once again, the same question would repeatedly enter my consciousness, "is this all there was to life"?

I could not turn off this voice in my head. From the moment I woke up to the moment I went to sleep; more and more questions arose.

Surely there must be more to life than this?
What is happiness?
Is there something else I should be doing?
Do we have free will?
Is everything predetermined?

My days became filled with existential angst, and the questions as well as unanswered thoughts plagued me like a virus demanding an antidote. I had gone from being a high-flying, party-happy, sales rep to a depressed old man looking for answers. I had achieved all that I ever thought I would need to be happy, and yet here I was - lost and confused with my understanding of life. I tried to talk to some friends and work colleagues who all thought that I was either pulling their leg or that the solution to my misery was to simply settle down and get married. Days became weeks, and weeks turned into months as I continued to spiral down into a dark pit of despair; not knowing how to get myself out. As dark as it became, I thought that there had to be a way out of it.

I did my best to keep busy; throwing myself into work but as the day ended, I became scared to come home. I was scared of the unending stream of unanswered questions. There were days when I was too tired to fight, and the feelings would overwhelm me to the point that I would just be laying on the ground in a catatonic state, staring at the blank ceiling for more hours than I would like to remember. The fading of the sun and the coming of the darkness of night became my only reference that change was happening in my immediate environment and that the day was passing.

I did my best to hide my current reality from everyone. I became an actor in my own life. I had decided to break up with my girlfriend prior to this and I had begun to believe that the demise of my relationship may have been the cause for my low feelings. I just needed to be alone. I needed some time to make sense of all this.

As this dark night of the soul continued, I decided that it might be time to get help. I spoke to my doctor who had become a close friend due to my company role and all the evening meetings as well as frequent visits I paid him. He offered me a lot of care and support as I described my situation. He seemed surprised by that downtrend in my mood as I hid them so well with my social mask. I did such a good job of presenting this happy-go-lucky personality. He suggested that I take antidepressants to help elevate my mood; suggesting that my recent break up was the primary cause of my current condition. I struggled to express that something inside of me felt entirely wrong and that I didn't know what was happening to me. It was like no one understood what was happening to me.

He also arranged a psychiatric assessment with the local mental health team to help assess if there were any deeper, underlying problems. For some reason, I felt happy and optimistic that I would finally get some answers and explanations for my current state. It gave me hope that I could get back to enjoying life. I asked them if they knew what the meaning of life was and how one could remain happy. The assessment was brief. Maybe it *didn't help that I was smiling most of the time; looking at the consultants as Gods who would heal me and bring me out of this unknown, unnamed dark space. They asked questions, and I gave responses. They looked bemused with my presentation, a look that confirmed they had no idea what I was talking about. After about an hour the consultants concluded that there was nothing wrong with me and suggested that I make some changes to my diet.*

I left feeling more confused than ever.

My job allowed me ample time for thinking and creating more questions. The previous benefit of only having to work half a day became a disadvantage; leaving me time to scramble for answers. I resorted to spending my afternoons in the local shopping centre bookshop. I didn't know what I was looking for as I scanned the small self-help chapter of WH Smith's bookstore. The internet had not fully become the thing it is today, and finding information was done the old-fashioned way - via libraries or by finding someone who knew about these things. I would try to act cool; doing my best to pretend that I was not looking for books to help myself. I felt embarrassed.

Wasn't self-help for losers who couldn't get their shit together?

I did my best to avoid the pregnant ladies and others who were also cruising the self-help section - avoiding eye contact at all costs. I shuddered to think what anyone would think if they caught me looking here. I bought my first book on how to be happy. Within a month I had amassed a range of titles including The Way of the Peaceful Warrior, the Celeste Prophecy, Conversations with God, as well as some Buddhist books by Jack Cornfield. These were my entry points into a new world. They spoke about the unknown; the unseen worlds of spirit and a calling to fulfil one's destiny. These books were lifelines for me. I began to hope again. I felt alive and hungry for more information. See there were other weirdos out there who must have questioned the same thing. I'm not alone. Others had experienced something similar to myself and from their experiences were now offering insights and potential solutions. I found a book on meditation and began to practice meditation which literally lasted all of 15 minutes as I just couldn't get into it. As I sat there and tried to focus - without success - I realised that this was not going to help me.

In my mind I needed quick, direct answers – an immediate remedy to stop feeling this constant discomfort.

It was around this time that a movie called The Matrix came out. Looking back now this film was a catalyst for my spiritual awakening. The cool sunglasses, superhero leather-wearing characters of Neo, Trinity, and Morpheus as well as the state-of-the-art special effects literally blew my mind. But there was a deeper aspect to the film. It questioned our reality. It spoke of claiming the power of who you are and, for the first time in ages, I felt alive. The Matrix movie questioned everything.

Are we just power supplies for an artificial reality for a system that controls us?

The words of Morpheus rung through my being.

"What you know you can't explain, but you feel it. You've felt it your entire life, that there's something wrong with the world. You don't know what it is, but it's there, like a splinter in your mind, driving you mad."

- **Morpheus, The Matrix**

Inspired by the philosophical musings from the movie, I decided on joining an evening course in philosophy. It was a 9-part weekly course, and meetings consisted of discussions around the nature of reality, the meaning of life, and the structure of thought. This is what I had been searching for. All the answers were here, nothing was wrong with me, I was walking a new path.

I felt like I had entered a different reality; an unseen world. A world of magic. A world where anything was possible. I had found my place in the world. Then one night in April of 2003 an unexplained event would change my life-path forever.

THE AWAKENING

It had been a fairly routine day. I had gone to work and, on the way, home bought some food from the supermarket. It was an ordinary evening involving some mindless tv and I had finished my dinner around 9pm. I decided to go to bed early to start reading a new book I had found on Buddhism and nodded off around midnight. What happened then would change my life forever. It was around the early hours of the morning maybe 2am or 3am. I was awoken by loud noises downstairs. It sounded like the sofas and furniture in the living room were being moved and dragged around. I could hear loud banging and scratching sounds; coupled with the sound of plates smashing. I lay in my bed frozen but wide awake; eyes bulging with fear, total shock, and confusion as to what was happening. I thought that maybe the house had been broken into, but I knew that that was not possible as the house alarm was set and had not gone off. I noticed my breath had become very shallow and fast; almost hyperventilating from panic. I felt my body temperature drop and I broke out into a cold sweat as I listened intently to the noises; hoping to perceive what was happening downstairs. I hoped that it may be coming from next door and not something inside my house. The smashing and dragging of furniture across the floor continued for what felt like an eternity. For some reason, I tried to hide under my covers in some vain attempt that this would protect me in any eventuality.

And then everything stopped.

Silence.

Like a stillness after a storm - an eerie silence.

A foreboding silence.

The noises stopped, and my hearing became sharp and more focused. I felt my mouth had gone dry, and I was feeling hot like I had a fever. Then I heard what sounded like chains being dragged on the floor and I heard a heavy thump as if someone had taken the first step on the staircase leading up to my bedroom. I was now rigid and could not move. I thought about getting up and jumping out of the window, but I was frozen stiff. The footsteps became louder as each thump brought the sound and threat closer. I was sure that it was some sort of spirit, or entity. I imagined a black-cloaked figure edging closer and closer to my door.

Death was coming for me.

The thuds grew louder as they edged up the stairs and the presence stopped outside my bedroom door. Once again there was a deathly silence. At this point, I noticed that the bed had started shaking. My body started to move slowly at first, then as a shudder, and then as my panic grew, my whole body started shaking like I had been touched with an electric current – like a lightning bolt. I tried to scream, but my teeth were clenched tight as my body convulsed and shook. This continued for over a minute, and then it slowed down. My body was burning up, and I was sweating profusely as images flashed through my mind's eye. I felt like I was in a time tunnel. Images and noises whirred past me as I flew through time and space. I was in the midst of a lucid dream.

I was transported to another time and space , I saw my beloved with another man.

I did not recognize this man, and a deep anger arose up within me - a hatred born of betrayal. The young man greeted me with a smile and attempted to embrace me as my beloved looked on. What had happened here? I became wild with rage. I drew my sword and with a blow severed the young man in half and continued to strike him down again and again. I turned to my beloved with tears of rage and pain streaming down my face. In my drunken fury I turned to her as I took the blade and cut her in two. Her body fell and I struck her again and again until my face, hair, and body were covered with her blood.

I stood there soaked and stunned as I tasted the bitter sharpness of the blood as it reached my tongue and lips. I slowly came back to waking consciousness. The room felt charged with a stillness and silence that I had never felt before. I was in a void of no space or time. I thought that I was having an out of body experience.

I felt horrified and afraid.

My heart rate slowed down, and my sweat had turned cold, causing my body to shudder in the cold sweat. I still couldn't move and so I lay there - frozen, and speechless. At some point, I drifted off into a deep sleep. The next morning, I woke up with dread and fear running through me. I knew that I could not stay there again that night; especially not on my own. I timidly got out of the bed; my body feeling weak and beaten. I tiptoed downstairs to find everything in its place. I noticed my neighbour outside his house and it was a relief beyond belief. I opened the door and wished him good morning. I made small talk and asked him if he had heard anything loud and strange the night before. I half-joked that it felt like there might have been a mini earthquake. He looked at me with a puzzled look on his face and, after some back and forth, he wished me a good day. I stayed at my parents' house for the next few nights; too frightened to return home. I took a few days off of work to try and understand my experience.

THE CALLING

One evening shortly after that encounter I began hearing a voice - not from outside but from within. It was almost like a stern whisperer telling me:

"Leave everything behind and make your way to Canada."

It reminded me of the scene in Star Wars: Episode V – The Empire Strikes Back when Luke is left for dead in an icy wasteland after his encounter with the Wampa. It was as though Obi-Wan was speaking to me through the power of the Force just as he had instructed Luke to go to Dagobah and find the Jedi Master Yoda to complete his Jedi training.

"Great," I thought, "Now I'm hearing voices from Jedi Masters!"

I tried to ignore it and put it down to a figment of my imagination. Over the next few weeks though, the voice kept returning until it was almost the only thing I would hear in moments of quiet or stillness. Like the books I had been reading, this was a message from higher realms:

"Go to Canada. Find your soul. Fulfil your destiny."

DOUBT

Over the coming weeks, I tried to forget about the experience. I kept myself busy with working and distracting myself. It mostly worked during the day. In the evening, however, the voices within started coming back stronger.

"Leave. You must leave now."

It kept going round and round in my head. I also found myself repeating a word that I had never heard before. I kept repeating the word 'Kundalini' and I had no idea what that meant. I found myself laughing every time I thought of it. Where had I heard this word, and what was it? Perhaps I read it in one of the Buddhist books I had been reading.

It was during this time that I was headhunted by a rival company. I had been doing so well with my sales that the only strategy the rival company had was to employ me. They offered me a larger salary with many benefits and gave me a chance to work for the new number 1 pharmaceutical company in the world. This would be a great career move. I considered the offer; thinking that if I took the job, I could buy another property and perhaps buy a second car, but what would be the point?

Would I be any happier if I did this?

My ex-girlfriend suggested that we should get married and settle down; that we should start thinking about a family. I started to feel torn; conflicted with this inner voice telling me to leave the life that I knew behind and my common sense fighting back and telling me to stay.

This calling over the weeks continued to get stronger, and it was driving me mad. Then one morning I woke up and made the decision that I would go!

The voices stopped.

I felt at peace.

There was an inner calmness.

A stillness.

I knew deep down inside that I had to do this.

I was taking a significant risk by going to Canada. I didn't have a plan, and I didn't even have any savings. I didn't really know anyone that lived there, and yet something within me guided me to just get there. This intuition – if I can call it that – told me that things would all work out fine. All I knew was that I was about to go on an adventure of a lifetime.

THE MISSION

Within weeks I had told close family and friends about my decision to leave. The reception was mixed. People were mostly confused about my plans and did not understand my decision.

"Why are you leaving everything you have built?"
Your career is going great, you'll be promoted to a manager soon."
"Just settle down and marry that good girl." -

By good my parents meant that she was also Indian and that she would be an ideal fit for "us". A few friends were excited and thought it was a brave decision. They supported my adventure - with the small disclaimer that maybe I shouldn't actually sell my house and all my belongings just in case it didn't work out. However, I felt so sure that this was the right thing to do. Actually, in some ways I had never felt so sure of anything in my whole life before.

I planned to start a new life, a new job, and to have a new beginning – to just see where fate would take me. Looking back, it seems quite reckless, but at the time I had full confidence in this inner Jedi voice. I suppose I was also strongly influenced by all the books I had been reading. I felt that this move would relieve my deep dissatisfaction and would provide answers to the meaning of life. The month before I was scheduled to leave, I attended the Euro 2004 football finals in Portugal when I broke my arm in a jet skiing accident. Hospital trips and an early flight home threatened to call off my destiny. Everyone thought that I would cancel the flight and perhaps only leave once my arm had healed, but I was determined not to let the accident stop me. I didn't change the date and I was adamant I had to leave. I would travel with my broken arm; nothing was going to stop me. For someone that had generally just floated through life and who had gone with the path of least resistance, I was now like a man on a mission. It was almost as if the accident itself had prompted me forward with even more fervour than before. So, I packed up all my things, sold all my furniture and belongings, handed in my resignation, and handed back the keys to the Mercedes. I felt like Luke selling his landspeeder and thinking; "Take it. There's nothing left here for me now," as they drove my pride and joy off down the road. For me, I had received a calling from my soul and I was willing to sacrifice everything in order to fulfil that calling.

It was my destiny.

The reality of my situation didn't really hit me until I was sitting on the plane. I could see all the faces of friends and family as they waved me goodbye. Flashbacks and memories of my old job, as well as my girlfriend, came rushing towards me and then the tears started to flow.

July 15th, 2004, at 7pm in Heathrow airport, I left behind the life that I had known to find the life of new.

"Fuck! What have I done!?"

This was the point of no return. The engines roared as we lifted off. The warrior in me was scared but willing to take the leap of faith without any guarantee of success. If I retreated now, I would continue to retreat for the rest of my life.

This inner voice that told me to go was so strong - so powerful - that I almost became blinded to anything but this mission. Anxious questions raced through my mind.

Had I made a big mistake?

Why was I going to Canada of all places?

Growing up I absolutely loved drawing, and it was one of the few subjects that I actually passed with good grades at secondary school. I had been drawing mountains with a city backdrop throughout my youth; with my final year art project themed on this very scene but from the perspective of past, present, and future. It was this image of a large city with a backdrop of snow-capped mountains that had inspired this lifelong obsession with Canada.

Had I always known that I would one day come to Canada?

CANADA - A NEW LAND

My first few weeks in Canada were busy as I attended my cousin's wedding and had planned a driving holiday with a friend. After the wedding in Calgary, I had spent the month travelling the US west coast in a Ford Mustang fulfilling one of my dreams of driving across America and going to Hollywood. I had arranged to meet a friend in LA and to spend a few more weeks thereafter travelling to San Diego ,California ,San Fransisco and Sin city. Most of the journey I had spent in a semi-conscious state as I tried to comprehend exactly what it was that I was doing. My friend was supportive, suggesting that I have a trial run in Canada and return home after a few weeks. This felt like a cowardly route. The inner voice was quiet and no more guidance was being offered. It was too late - I had to go all in. After my 4-week driving trip, I flew back to Canada and I found an apartment in the downtown area of Vancouver.

A few years before the move, I had travelled to Canada to visit family and they had taken me around the city as well as parts of the mainland. On the trip I remember seeing a building that had a huge mural painted on the wall - a huge killer whale jumping out of the water. I remember looking at it and saying that I would move to the building if I ever came here again, and - yes you guessed it - the apartment that I had found through the classifieds ads was in the very same building. I took this as a sign - in the Celestine Prophecy story it mentioned that these types of synchronistic happenings guide us and give us the confidence to know that we are on the right path in our search. I knew that I was in the right place and at the right time.

However, I was feeling a little lost. I had no idea what to do next. I thought maybe I could get a job and start off slowly and that this would be a good way to meet new people. Luckily my resume was good and I had great success with a top blue-chip company; securing an interview fairly quickly. The preliminary interview was a success and the recruiter said that he had 5 other companies that were interested — that was right up until the question of a working permit and visa came up.

I did not have one.

I had filled in a visa application for a working permit whilst in England; collecting all the documents and submitting all my medical paperwork only to decide at the last minute that it was not worth bothering with it. I hadn't planned the work side of things and I hadn't thought it out correctly. I thought the universe would sort everything out. I walked home depressed with no idea what I was doing there; the heavy Vancouver rain began to fall, I was demoralised walking alone like an alien in a strange land.

"Maybe I should just go back home and plead with her to take me back. Maybe I could get a new job."

I felt like I was out in the middle of the ocean; lost and adrift with nothing to hold onto. I fell back into the experiences that I would have back in my house in England. I found myself stuck in my new apartment most days. My arm had healed and allowed me to use the gym downstairs but it was usually empty. I could go days without speaking to anyone. Occasionally I would see the doorman to the apartment, but I couldn't find anything to say except 'hello'. I would wander the streets aimlessly; losing track of time.

What was happening here?

I felt that I was all alone and I was kind of freaking out as I had no plan or idea as to what to do. I seemed invisible; as if no one noticed I existed. It was as if I was in one long waking dream that I could not wake up from. I felt like I was losing the plot. Thoughts rushed through my head of returning home but to what? I felt like after making all that change, to go home with my tail between my legs at that point would have been shameful. The days turned into weeks and I began to worry about my length of stay. My visa was only valid for 6 months, and if things didn't change, I would have to go back.

One day, whilst I was out aimlessly walking, I stumbled upon an old bookshop and decided that I would go in and perhaps find a book that offered me some inspiration or guidance. This bookshop was huge; floor to ceiling with old books on 3 different levels. It was almost like this bookshop had been here since the beginning of time and after asking about it, I found out that it was indeed one of the oldest - started in 1967. Sadly, it closed in 2012, but while I was there, it served as a good source of inspiration and somewhere that I could retreat to try and find clarity. As I scanned the self-help and new age section in peace - no new mothers or strange looks here - I started to find books of a different caliber; or rather these books found me. I continued to scan the shelves and that voice within returned saying;

"Yes, that one, pick that one, and this one."

Before I knew it, I had a pile of books in my arms. Being a second-hand shop, they were very cost effective and I found that my spirits were lifted once more. I felt excited and eager to read as if these books held the answers to what I should do next. I devoured the books. I would read literally from morning until night - or at least until my eyes went heavy and the words on the page began to blur. I was reading a wide variety of topics; from self-

help, to self-development, esoteric knowledge, Buddhist books, the Kabbalah, Christian inspiration, books on meditation, and even books on witchcraft. I made copious amounts of notes as I read. My apartment had turned into a study laboratory with paper, notes, and books all over the place. From all my reading, I began to make auto-suggested lifestyle changes that would help me connect with a deeper part of myself. I stopped eating meat and drinking alcohol. I realised back home that I had become accustomed to drinking when entertaining and had been consuming at least a couple of bottles of Jack Daniels a week; especially during those dark periods of being catatonic. "Yes," I thought, "This is why I came here. To find myself and to realise my soul." I was reading almost a book a day depending on the size, which surprised me as I had not been studious or a big reader growing up. Superhero comics were my go-to read. Yet here I was and I couldn't stop reading. The more input I received, the more input I soaked up, I felt like Johny 5 from the movie Short Circuit as I desired more input. I absorbed all of these teachings and perspectives. I felt like if I read enough, I would find answers to what the soul was and how I could achieve enlightenment.

The books all spoke about the power and need for meditation if we wish to access the answers we have long searched for. The answers I was searching for could not be found in books alone. I began to practice meditation again. I mean, it wasn't like I had anything better to do. Each day, I would increase the amount of time that I sat for. I started with 5 mins and then 10mins and over those long cold months built up to practicing for several hours at a time.

Each week there would be a local downtown newspaper that was delivered to all of the apartments called 'The Insider'. One week, the paper arrived with 2 Sikh people on the front cover which was nothing unusual except they were white Sikhs. Growing up in a Sikh family, I had never really connected with my faith or religion. Maybe it was due to early experiences of having to go to the temple and sit for hours and hours with my mum listening to things I couldn't understand. I had not ever really felt like a Sikh, and if anything, growing up in a white area, I had done my best to pretend I was white. There was an interesting article about this early morning meditation that they were conducting at a yoga centre in Kits.

I was intrigued.

Something told me that I should go there. I thought that maybe I would visit this studio which also had a Gurdwara – or Sikh temple of worship - and the newspaper article mentioned there was a library of teachings. I felt that it may be good to go. To bow and pray. Perhaps it would change my luck and that my visit to Canada would receive a higher blessing. Worst case scenario; I might pick up some books which may give me more information about spirituality.

MEETING THE MENTORS

I decided on a day that I would pay the studio a visit and planned my mini adventure. I walked across the main bridge that linked downtown to the upper city area. Bridge crossing is also a spiritual metaphor for crossing over into another world. I walked until I came to what seemed like a very small shop amongst a parade of shops. As I walked in, it was as if time had stopped. I have never experienced silence or a space like it. It seemed that all the noises, and thoughts - all forms of thinking, in fact - had stopped. I stood for a moment as the wind chime at the door echoed throughout my whole being. A pleasant smiling lady dressed in all white at the counter greeted me and welcomed me, asking if there was anything she could help with. I told her that I had come to check the place out as I had seen the newspaper article. She smiled and told me that the featured teacher on the cover would be conducting the 7 PM class if I was interested in joining. I was feeling tired from the long walk and told her that I had to get home and that I would come back another day. She smiled once more and offered me some tea; encouraging me to walk around. She pointed out where the studio entrance was as well as the toilets. The place had a small bookshop selling spiritual paraphernalia, mantra CDs, and all-white clothing – which was somewhat strange to me. There was another door which had a sign over it. It read 'Gurdwara'. This is not what I was expecting at all. It wasn't bigger than a room. Growing up and visiting the Gurdwara on a Sunday, I was accustomed to a temple being a huge venue with a huge kitchen and loud prayers being broadcast on the Tannoy, but this was just a small room.

There was no one in the room.

There was a small box outside with some rumāl - or head coverings - and I picked one up. I asked the lady if it was alright to go inside, and she replied; "Yes, of course. Take as much time as you need."

I entered this very beautiful, clean, pure space. This was not like any Gurdwara I had ever visited. It was peaceful and serene. It felt very sacred.

Bani - or sacred music - was playing gently in the background and I took a deep breath; feeling all of my tension leave my body. I noticed that my shoulders dropped and my body became very relaxed. All my thoughts, worries, and anxieties of being here in Canada - of being lost - all vanished. This might sound cheesy, but I don't know any other way to describe it. It reminded me of Han Solo's words in Star Wars: The Force Awakens.

"Chewie, we're home."

I found myself smiling as if I had been dipped into a pool of nectar. It was as if a heavy load had been taken off me. I felt like I was shining – all brand new. The room became brighter as if it was filled with light.

I was blissing out.

I stood in front of the guru and, with my hands together in prayer-pose, closed my eyes and prayed like I have never prayed before. I prayed as if God was actually there and listening. My usual prayers included reading out a wish list of things that I wanted and how if God could, would He please get me all of those things ASAP. As I prayed in that little room I started to feel different. I prayed with thanks for God guiding me to this place. I found that I had no desires and found myself saying; "Please let me serve you for the highest good of all." I heard my mind saying; "Good of all!? You better ask for some help, or guidance mate, because you are lost!" I ignored this internal dialogue; feeling this deep sense of gratitude

- almost as if I were being coddled in a huge puffy cotton duvet. I was warm and snuggly; a sense of completeness coming over me as I bowed and touched my forehead to the ground in a slow and deliberate manner. I remember stepping back, sitting down, and enjoying this sacred space.

What was happening here?

I was sitting here feeling so alert and so alive. I was so full. This had not been in the realm of my experiences before. Growing up I didn't really connect to my religion. I would dread the times when my mum would inform us that we would be visiting the Gurdwara. I remember it always being such a boring thing - having to sit and listen to hours of sayings and prayer. I didn't understand it and found that the Granthi - or priests - were always scary looking, grumpy, and mostly would be telling the kids off for running either here or there. I just couldn't wait for it to be over every time we went. I had always felt different coming to the Gurdwara growing up. My parents had decided to cut my hair in my youth, but according to Sikh tradition we are not meant to cut our hair; being instructed instead to wear a turban. This formed part of the reason why I always felt judged and out of place - like I didn't belong. As I sat and reflected, it dawned on me that I have always felt a bit different; not quite fitting in. I was a bit of an outcast - maybe even a little weird - but here I was and I felt totally at home. I came out of the Gurdwara space feeling great and as I came out the lady at the desk introduced me to the teacher for the evening class "Hari Singh, there is someone who was thinking about joining your class this evening." Slightly surprised as I came out, I met my first ever Kundalini Yoga teacher. He was big and tall, like a big cuddly bear - although I'm not sure he would appreciate that. He was wearing all white and he welcomed me with a smile and greeted me, 'Sat Nam'; going on to ask if I had ever taken a class before to which I replied that I hadn't. He recognized my accent and asked if I was from England. When I responded that I was, he commented that that evening's class would be especially for people from England.

I laughed as he suggested that I leave my things in the cloakroom area and come in as we would start soon. I didn't know what to expect as I had never done yoga before and I was not even sure that I wanted to go, but then I remembered that I would only be going home to an empty apartment. The warmth and pleasantness as other people started to arrive - all in good spirits – made me think that it might be nice to stay and meet some people. I was excited at the possibility of actually getting to talk to people who were interested in the world of spirituality just as I was. I sat near the back; mostly watching others to see what the protocol was. I wasn't sure of what I was supposed to be doing, but it was a good class. We had our eyes closed for most of the class and as Hari spoke it seemed like all his comments and phrases were aimed directly at me. He spoke about us being spiritual beings having a human experience, and how we all come from faraway lands. He spoke of how we can feel quite alien at times and it all rung true. During relaxation time, I felt myself leave my body and travel through some sort of space portal like a black hole. I felt like I was falling into the pits of eternity. There was no end, and no beginning. It was only when I heard Hari bringing us back around that I realised that I was still there in that room. It felt like I had been asleep for hours. The whole atmosphere of the class and the people in it was so peaceful and relaxing - like we were in another dimension, away from all things. It was like I almost forgot where I was. After class a few students sat and had tea. Some sat quietly while others talked in hushed tones to one another. It seemed that these people were regulars to the class at the time and we shared pleasantries. Hari came out a few moments later and sat down with us as we discussed elements of the class. It was so nice just listening and hearing people share. In some ways, they were all weird like me; interested in the soul, the spirit, the unseen world, and all the things that I had been reading about. I had so many questions but felt a little shy to ask. As people left, I felt a little more comfortable to ask the hundreds of questions which had been brewing in my mind; careful not to let the tsunami of thoughts overwhelm the conversation. Hari shared his journey of how he became a Sikh as well as how and when the centre came to be. We spoke about the Sikh gurus and how to find your purpose and meaning in life. He was caring, thoughtful, and funny. I felt that I had always known him. I felt like a young child excitedly talking with his father, or great uncle, about the adventures of spirituality. I walked home that evening feeling full of light, and full of even more questions. The evening seemed so quiet – still and serene - and all I could think of was when I could return again.

 I continued to visit the studio for Hari's regular class and made an extra journey to the studio on a Sunday to join them for the Gurdwara program. Here I met some of the other members of the sangat - or community - and other teachers who taught at the studio. I met Hari's wife Guru Raj Kaur Khalsa, the lady whom I had seen on the front page, who had started the centre way back in the early 70s. Dharam Kaur Khalsa, one of the teacher trainers at the centre, and I remember her being mean and slightly grumpy; not even looking up to greet me when Hari was introducing me.

 Everybody was really nice to me, and interested in how I came to be here. They seemed inspired by my story, as well as worried about my awakening experience and how it had led me here. There were many members of a similar age staying after Gurdwara to help clean and pack away things. I got to know them – to share and hear their personal stories, their spiritual perspectives and their understanding of what all this spiritual stuff meant. It was like they totally got who I was and what I was going through. When I left the centre, I would always feel sad; like I was leaving my closest friends. It was as if it existed in an alternate universe - a different plane of existence. It felt like coming out of the wardrobe from Narnia back to the normal world every time I left and I longed for the time we would be together again.

 Over the months, I began attending classes more regularly and joined a weekend-long course on studying Japji -sacred prayer of the Sikhs which was developed by Guru Nanak. I felt intimidated and a bit stupid as I was Sikh and had never read Japji or even knew what it was, yet here were all these 'westerners' - white folk, to boot - that were following the Sikh way of life. All the answers that I was looking for were contained in these 39 verses and for the first time in my life I was chanting these sacred words. The format in which they relayed the teachings was perfect. All the verses came with English translations and were explained in English, so for the first time I could follow along. It was here that I met a few other Indian Sikh people who were also very warm towards me and quite intrigued to find another Punjabi Sikh in their midst. I was making friends, eating and sharing Indian cuisine like chapatis. I never thought that I would miss chapatis but having them reminded me of home and it made me feel a little less homesick. This was the complete opposite of my life back home, wherein socialising mostly meant going out clubbing, drinking, doing drugs and basically getting fucked up all weekend.

Here I was – in what seemed like a million miles from home - having the most magical and sublime time. The only way that I can describe it is that my soul was at peace and for the first time in a long time I was happy.

CROSSING THE THRESHOLD

As the winter months approached, the studio prepared for their annual teacher training program and I had heard about this from others who were either teachers, or who had been coming to the centre for longer than I had. I was considering to start the training but i had no interest in being a yoga teacher.

Hari mentioned it to me and suggested that it would provide many of the answers which I had been looking for.

That weekend, my ex-girlfriend had called me from back home and we had gotten into a huge fight. She had basically insinuated that I had run away from responsibilities and she told me that she blamed me for everything; going on to make mention that "all this spiritual stuff" – as she put it - was not me. I'll never forget her telling me that I was wasting my time and my life. I got off that call totally upset and, in some ways, I believed that she was right - what the hell was I doing?

That night I had a dream of being swallowed whole by a snake and then I burst out through its stomach. When I came out of the stomach it was me but I did not recognise myself. I awoke feeling frightened and confused. Then I heard that same voice that I had heard while I was still in England. It was a calm but stern voice; a knowing voice that was wise but not forceful - 'Become a teacher' was the message. After hearing the clarity in the guidance of this voice, I knew what I needed to do. I would train and become a Kundalini yoga teacher.

TESTS, ALLIES, AND (FR)ENEMIES

It was a bitterly cold Vancouver evening that chilly fateful Friday. The wind blew with a crisp iciness as I weathered the storm and made my way to the studio. The room was packed with the energy of anticipation and excitement. Myself and about 50 other bright-eyed, eager souls had all made the effort to attend the training and to begin this journey together. Our lead trainer, Guru Raj, welcomed us and explained a little about the coming months as well as the structure of the course. We sat in a huge circle and introduced ourselves, saying a little bit about how and why we came. We were given personal mentors and a 'buddy' that we would check in with for the duration of the course. There were also *other sevadars present; sitting around the room to hold space. Their roles were to act as anchors for the energy and they literally just sat with closed eyes, which was a good thing because there was one lady that I could not stop looking at. She was sitting quite close to me but I felt butterflies and a strange attraction to her. She was totally stoic and steady; sitting there in a graceful and powerful manner. I wanted her to open her eyes so that I could see her and see if there was a connection there, but she didn't move nor did she open her eyes. When the introduction was over, I looked everywhere to see where she was but she had gone. We were put into our groups which we would be in for the duration of the course, and there was much excitement. The air was filled with the chatter of people talking. People were buzzing, laughing, and sharing; excited for the journey which we were all about to embark on. My group mentor was a lady named Cindy whom I had met at Hari's class. She was super nice and friendly. She was a great support and helped me orientate myself despite the fact that she had only just finished her training the year before. She was kind of my first real friend in Canada - and the first friend I had met that had a car. I missed driving. I had been walking, cycling and using buses for the last year and this was a pleasant relief. My course buddy was Linda, from America. She was literally flying in for each of the training weekends and we got on really well. I was finally beginning to feel at home. I was no longer missing the UK or my old life. I had a new purpose and mission now - to complete this training.*

Saturday, September 10th of 2005 at 9am we were all together and we tuned in for the start of the course. This is where I met Bart who was some international DJ and uber cool. He had also decided to participate in the course at the very last minute. He had just returned from Africa and his sister was already a yoga teacher working at the centre. She had convinced him to join. We got on straight away and he told me that he was looking for a place to rent near the centre. I was living at least 45 minutes away by bus and thought it might be a good idea to move. I'd been in the busy and noisy downtown area since I arrived so being able to move somewhere closer to the centre would allow me to fully immerse myself in the training.

Truth be told; I was also running out of money. I had borrowed a thousand pounds from a friend to keep me going, but I had just now spent all that on the training course. My parents were super helpful; sending me money when they could, but there were times that I could not eat due to lack of funds. I would hold out until the next day and hope some money had been transferred. In my mind moving would definitely help me to cut costs.

We managed to find a great place very close to the centre and found that a lot of the regular teachers and other students also lived quite close to the centre. It was like a little community of yogis and there would be regular potlucks as well as mediation evenings as part of regular hang out events.

There were always lots of events at the centre during the week in addition to Sunday Gurdwara. These were some of the happiest and greatest days of my life; surrounded by like-minded friends who were all on a similar journey. We shared the same path; exploring, laughing, and hanging out in one of the most beautiful cities on earth.

As part of the course, we were also required to complete certain homework activities with our groups as well as individually. We were given a 40-day practice to help us establish new ways of being. We were to complete a certain number of classes and were required to come to the centre to do seva - or selfless service - which would include cleaning or doing maintenance work on the centre. I would normally attend my regular class with Hari at our usual time but that one particular week I had decided that I would fulfil my homework requirement and do a class after my seva. As a requirement we needed to complete 20 classes and I was eager to get them all completed so, I opted to join the evening class. I walked in and to my pleasant surprise was the woman from the opening night. I felt stunned and shocked as she welcomed me in. She had piercing blue eyes that twinkled, and it was as if her gaze saw right into the core of my being. She instructed me to find a place and make myself comfortable. It was the hardest yoga lesson ever - not because of the postures, but because I had to pretend my eyes were closed for the whole time. I had been trying to catch her gaze through the dimly lit room and in some vain attempt to impress her I made the most effort I had ever given in a yoga class, hoping to prove myself worthy.

After class, a small group sat and shared tea as I tried to play it cool. I was desperate to talk to her and find out who she was. As we sipped tea, we discussed meditation as well as the various practices and their effects. I listened eagerly; hoping to add something relevant to the conversation. She shared some of her experiences with spirituality and said that her most powerful experience of meditation was through a practice called vipassana meditation: a meditation practice that required one to be silent for an entire 10 days. She mentioned that it really took quite the amount of willpower to do and that if anyone was brave enough to try it, they should go! 'Great,' I thought, 'So in order to impress her I need to go on this 10-day retreat!' On the way home I couldn't stop thinking about her and I was already planning to attend her class the following week.

"Well now at least I know her name. Lidija"

APPROACH TO INNERMOST CAVE

I was finally loving my time in Canada and I was experiencing fulfilment. It was a happiness I had never known. I didn't ever want to go home. I wanted to stay here and be with my new family and friends. My only problem was that my passport visa had expired months ago and I was - for all intents and purposes - an illegal immigrant. My money had all but run out and I was now relying on handouts from my parents, back home, to keep going. My credit cards were maxed out and I needed to get something done about this quickly. My plan was that if I could travel to the USA, I could cross over for the day and then return the next day and that would set me up for another 6-month entry visa. If I could raise some money at home then I would have enough to finish my yoga training.

In our yoga training, we had 3 Korean students from across the border in Seattle, who had come to learn about this specific yoga practice due to a relationship and collaboration with their master, Sung, who was a world-renowned samurai and kendo warrior. He had a large health-line business in America and had been hoping to introduce it in Canada via the yogic community. An exchange trip had been planned to visit him and his other students in Seattle. Several cars were arranged and my friend, Mandeep, said that we could drive out there together. We had become very close as we were 2 of only 3 Sikh Punjabi men on the course.

There was a trip planned and I would go with them to do their training; staying behind to get my passport done and travelling back the following day. Seattle to Vancouver is only a 2-hour trip – one-way - after all. We had a powerful workshop using qigong and learning kendo as well as sword fighting techniques. We were pushed hard. The master had healed one of his students from cancer using his energy healing and dietary methods. I learnt how they – as his students - had to endure various challenges. One of them literally had to dig holes every day for 5 years until the master accepted him for training. These were hard core students so the pressure was on us to represent. The master allowed me to stay at this house that night and I remember standing in the doorway as my friends and Community left and drove away. I felt such pain. I felt alone in the world again; out of my comfort zone and hoping that I could get my passport stamped in order for me to get back to Vancouver ASAP.

The visa office was busy and I had a long wait until I was seen. I found a quiet room and completed my daily sadhana as well as the homework practice. A few others were coming in and out of the room. Normally, I would be very self-conscious about being the weird dude in the room, but I no longer cared. I was becoming more comfortable with my new identity as a yogi and besides - no one knew me. I was free to be myself. I had no identity nor personality to protect and uphold. I was also feeling slightly nervous because if they did not give me the visa, I didn't have much in the way of a backup plan. I was in the middle of nowhere with about 100 dollars in my account. It probably wasn't even enough for a hotel and perhaps just enough to get a bus back, but I had been learning about trusting the spirit.

God would take care of me.

The whole idea of this yogic training is to put faith and belief in the unseen world; knowing that it would guide us and protect us. I knew everything would turn out fine. After a long meeting with the immigration officers, they asked me what I was doing in Canada. I could not tell them that I was studying or that could've possibly gotten me into heaps of trouble for not having a student visa. So, I told them that I was holidaying and visiting friends. Their response went in the opposite direction. They told me that they thought that I was trying to extend my visa by re-entering Canada and said that they would not grant me a visa. I would be allowed to come back to Canada - and the USA - if I went home and spent at least 6 months there. Conditionally, I would have to be employed in the UK before they would consider my re-entry. I sat there; shocked, but half smiling as I was hoping that it was a joke and that they would stamp my passport and say:

"Not really. It's fine. You can go back."

But that reply never came.

I got up and stumbled out of the building with my suitcase and one travel bag. I had no idea what to do or where to go. The universe had let me down. I knew at that moment that this was all bullshit.

"Spirituality is stupid and now I'm stuck."

What would I do and where would I go now? I felt dizzy and lost; shocked as I walked aimlessly in downtown Seattle. People were walking past in their own worlds; rushing around to their jobs and appointments. I felt invisible again; as if the whole world was moving and I was an anomaly. The odd one out. I found a coffee shop and rushed in as if I were jumping out of the rapids and grabbing the only piece of stable, dry land that there was. I was in a full-blown panic. All of my belongings were in Canada. I could not even go back to retrieve them. Our next teacher training weekend was 3 weeks away, and if I could not get back to Canada, I would fail the training; making all of my time and the sacrifices that I had made meaningless. I would return home empty handed. I longed for my friends and my community. I needed to get back to my tribe. I thought about calling them but what could they do?

I felt totally abandoned.

I went to an internet cafe and thought I would try to find a place to stay for the night. I felt too embarrassed to call the master and ask them if I could come back. I had to keep moving forward. I felt embarrassed to tell anyone my naïve plan had backfired. I felt angry at all this stupid spiritual stuff and felt totally defeated. Following this silly inner calling had ruined my life. I wished that I had never left home. I wished that I had never started this stupid journey.

Whilst looking for a hotel I had a thought to check out locations for the meditation technique that Lidija had mentioned in Canada. I had nothing else to lose and at least I would have somewhere to stay for 10 days free of charge. I went to their website and checked their course schedule. There was a 10-day course starting in 2 days and there were a few places available. I thought that this would work for now. I applied and I was accepted. I called their office and spoke to a caring, soft spoken man, explaining my situation to him. He was so kind and compassionate; telling me not to worry. He gave me instructions about where to go and what bus to get; saying that he would collect me from the bus station when I arrived. I felt totally relieved - at least for now. I had somewhere safe to go and at the very worst, I would be in a quiet place to work out what I'm supposed to do next. I went to the bus station and booked my bus; managing to fulfil a lifelong dream of riding a Greyhound bus. I'd seen this particular bus company in movies and I had always imagined one day riding across America in one.

It was a 5-hour journey to Washington and the night drew in. The sun was setting as I stared out across the barren American landscape. I felt mostly numb as my mind tried to process what was happening; running through thoughts of my time in Canada and reflecting on this journey that I was on. It was a busy bus and I marvelled at all of the people aboard. The difference in lifestyle and language was amazing, but I was too closed down to connect with anyone. I was practically hiding under my baseball cap. I felt like a criminal on the run - with no valid passport or visa. The bus arrived at the final stop late into the night. There were only a few people left on the bus and as I turned to collect my bags, they had all dispersed into the night. As I looked around for a man I had never met, the bus began to pull away. I tried to say thank you and goodbye to the driver but nothing came out. I was here; alone in the dark, and the night felt so cold. If the weather had ever matched my mood perfectly, that was the night. I wished that the ground would just open up and swallow me whole. I just wished that I was back home - safe in my house; watching movies and having pizza. Ten minutes later, headlights pierced the pitch-black night like the eyes of hope coming closer; promising me rescue and salvation. The car pulled up and a small man wearing very thin glasses came out; asking if my name was Jag.

"Yes, yes! I'm Jag!" I quickly replied as if by taking my time to answer I would in some way lose my ride to safety.

We drove for about an hour, and we exchanged pleasantries, but we were mostly silent thereafter. We were out in wild-country - no lights, no signs, and no noise. I stared up at the night sky which was crystal clear and the stars shone vividly. We arrived after midnight. The poor guy must have been going out of his way to collect me, yet still he asked If I would like any fruit or a drink. I declined politely; hoping not to impose on him any further. He said that the course would not start for another day and that there was no need to wake up early; mentioning that he would come and get me at some point in the morning for breakfast. I smiled, thanked him, and then collapsed in a heap on this donated, wooden makeshift bed; wondering what happened to the good life of driving around in a Mercedes and going out to restaurants. I thought about how this was not fun or spiritual in any way. My mind raced:

"What a load of shit!"
Why did I listen to that stupid voice?
Now I'm totally stranded - a proper loser.
I just want to go home.
Maybe it's not meant to be.
I don't actually have the money for a flight home.

I feel asleep to the sound of grasshoppers and the familiar dripping sound of an old tap.

THE ORDEAL

Tim came back to this cabin around 9 AM with some fruit and tea. "Probably the same crap he was going to give me last night," I had thought to myself. I had been up a short time and had just finished my homework meditations. It seemed that I had slept in their office and the bed from the night before was actually some sort of massage table. The place looked a bit chaotic, with things laying all over the place. It seemed as though there was hay and grass on the floor; making it feel like a barn house. Tim asked if I would like to help him set up some of the course and - as I had nothing else to do except mope about and complain about my current situation - I agreed. I helped him set up things in the huge mediation hall, and got to see the rest of this expansive area. It was very well kept. Everything was clean, simple, and in its place; surrounded by green fields and woods. It was far away from roads and traffic. It was one of the most peaceful places I had ever visited. We kept busy well into *the afternoon when other people who were attending the course began to arrive. As the attendees flooded in, they announced that day one had begun. After an introductory talk we entered the meditation hall and noble silence began. The following 10 days were some of the most difficult experiences I have ever encountered. The day would begin at 4am marked by the deep chimes of the gong. We were given only one meal away that was finished by 11am (so all energy and focus could be used for meditation). We were given small breaks but encouraged to meditate even during this time. Whilst sitting my body would shake and vibrate as eons of pain and inner blocks began to release. I lost track of time and space and felt I was losing my mind with no escape. On day 4 whilst on my break i heard a voice. Not the inner voice but another old ,ancient gruff voice. I looked round and could not see anyone. The voice began to tell me about the many years it had been here and all the people that it had seen. I looked up at the huge tree that seemed to be glowing and the sound was coming from the tree. 'YEP' i thought I am losing my mind and began a full conversation about the changing seasons and how the tree is connected to all surrounding life and is known as a wild elder in this forest. We spoke for some time until the gong signally the end of break was chimed and I bid the tree farewell. I have summarised the 10 days below.*

10 DAYS OF NOBLE SILENCE: ENTERING THE VOID

Day 1 – Entering the Cave
Day 2 - No Escape
Day 3 - Painful Sensations
Day 4 - Talking to Trees
Day 5 - 12 hours of meditation everyday
Day 6 – Losing the Plot
Day 7- Electricity
Day 8 – Strong Determination
Day 9 - Annica, Annica
Day 10 - Celebration

Memories of being in space, isolation, past life flashbacks, like a monk, in prison
Last day noble silence lifted

THE REWARD: LEAVING THE CAVE

After 12 days in silence - being away from the world and all of the noise - we began our slow descent back into the normal world. I still was on cloud nine not only due to going through hell and coming out the other side but also for being able to return to Canada and finish my training. I felt like I had won the lottery and still there was a niggling doubt as to whether or not I would be allowed to cross the border. I tried to put the thought out of my mind and remember the voice of the Force telling me everything would work out fine.

The sun was shining.

The laughter and voices of all these happy meditators filled the grounds. People were sharing contact details, sharing stories, and saying farewell as people packed their belongings. We all went off in different directions - back to our lives. I was fortunate to meet a lovely couple who had offered a ride-share back to Vancouver. They were from The States but were on a driving holiday where they would be visiting a friend and a weird synchronicity occurred in that they were the only people going anywhere near Canada. At about 2 PM after - cleaning the centre - we set off in their car and we shared some amazing conversations during our car journey about our retreat experiences, but I had something worrying me which I had not been entirely honest with them about. I tried to smile and act natural; not having told them about my expired passport. I was scared that they might not give me a ride. I was very anxious as we approached the border crossing. I was tense, and my breathing turned shallow as I tried to feel my way through those sensations.

We passed the 3 passports over.

The lady who had received them, began checking them and looking into the car. My heart was beating fast and I did my level best not to look at her; knowing that if I looked at her too long – or looked away for too long – my guilt would become obvious. I tried to stay as calm as possible. The voice returned:

"Everything will go smoothly and easy."

As the thought crossed my mind, the border guard handed the passports back and told us to have a nice day.

What!?

I was shocked.

How had she not seen that my passport had expired? I felt such relief and such a huge gratitude to the higher voices. It felt like a miracle had just occurred as I shared the story with my new travel companions. My friends mentioned how cool I was during the police check and I told them about the voice; how it was telling me that I would be fine, but that my mind was going crazy.

"You've got one serious poker face, dude." One of them chuckled.

We stopped off at a nice cafe on our way back and we shared our plans for the future; pondering where we would go next. As much as I was enjoying our time, I could not wait to get back into familiar surroundings and connect with my yoga community again - and finish my training. I sat and reflected on my last 10 days - how my understanding of life and myself had completely changed. It was like I had been reborn; coming out of a cocoon. I was opening up and ready to see the world with new eyes. I had connected to my body for the first time. I had always felt like I was floating above my body - observing the world - and now I felt like I was inhabiting my body for the first time.

Armed with this new insight, the inner voice told me that my time there was nearly up and that it was time for me to go home; that I had to go back and work out my karma. I was so sad about this and also somewhat scared as the inner voice had been 100 % spot on with the border crossing, and me coming to Canada in the first place. I knew this was beyond just exerting my will. A higher power was at work here and I had to follow the guidance. I really just wanted to stay in Canada; to have a new life and a new beginning, but this was not my fate. I remembered the scene in Star Wars: Episode V – The Empire Strikes Back when Luke decided that he needed to leave his training halfway; with Yoda encouraging him to stay. Luke knew that he needed to go back to help his friends. Perhaps armed with my new tools and experience, I could return and help my family, friends, and community in the UK. People have no idea of these other inner worlds and experiences, maybe I could help them to wake up and behold the reality of the soul. After an almost 6-hour car ride, I returned home to downtown Vancouver. Once again, I was struck by the amazing synchronicities happening all around me, as the couple dropped me off just a few blocks away from my apartment. I took this as another sign that the universe was working for me in these synchronistic events. I took a slow walk home; soaking up the noises and vibe of the streets. I stopped off for some sushi; my first meal outside of the retreat. I watched the matrix unfold all around me. People going about their business; moving busily between the rushing traffic and I started to feel overwhelmed by all the sensory input. Everything felt noisy, and fast. I, on the other hand, was operating on a different timeline. I began to wish that I was back in the peaceful retreat; feeling safe and contained. I didn't realise how sensitive my system had become over the weeks as the busyness began to drain me.

I returned home to find the apartment empty; wondering where my roommate was. I sat on the balcony as the sun was setting; sipping tea as I processed the last 3 weeks. My body was tingling with sensations as the words of the teacher continued to echo within me; annica, annica, annica - the pali word for change. It speaks of impermanence. Everything changes; moment to moment. For me, the previous 3 weeks had changed my understanding of life - of meditation, of my own body, and my relationship with life. I felt emotional and found myself crying. I wasn't even sure as to why. I felt overwhelmed by this journey I had undertaken. I reflected on the good times, the dark times, and I reflected on the fact that some strange Force had got me back home.

Moreover, I reflected on how grateful I felt to have been given the gift of this realization. I went to bed sensing the rhythm of my breath and the sensations of my body.

THE ROAD BACK: SUMMER SOLSTICE

I was awoken very early the next morning by the sound of a creaky car door being opened and then what sounded like an explosion as it was being slammed shut. I woke up startled as I tried to get my bearings. I then heard the sounds of keys jingling. My hearing continued to become crisper and sharper like all my senses were tuning into these sound vibrations. I heard the key clinking as it entered the key column and the chinking of the lock mechanism as the keys turned. I was amazed that I was hearing to such a degree, like I had gained super hearing. It was like I was hearing every sound for the very first time. I felt my body tighten as the thunderous sound of a car being started filled the air before it pulled away. It felt intense to be experiencing sounds this way and I found myself feeling sensitivity to the lights and smells of the room. I got up and decided I would go to morning sadhana as it was already 4am anyway. My body had become accustomed to those early morning starts.

Walking back into the studio and seeing all the familiar faces - my teacher, friends, fellow students, and my roommate - was the most welcoming sight. They welcomed me back just with their eyes and smiles. It warmed my heart. The familiar feeling of being home - a feeling of belonging that I had never felt before - washed over me once again. After sadhana my friends were eager to find out where I had been and what had happened over the 3 weeks prior. Like a weary traveler returning from the great wilderness, I shared tails of my great adventure. My trials and tribulations, my fears, and my successful return were all on the agenda. I spoke of the help that I had been receiving from some form of mystical force; a force that I could not logically understand. We shared breakfast as I relayed the epic journey of the last 10 days.

As my roommate and I walked back to our apartment, I shared with him what I had not been able to share with the rest of our friends - that I would be leaving Canada after our training had finished. We both walked in silence for the remainder of our journey. Later that day, I went to the yoga studio and met Lidija who was coming into the yoga centre to teach. "Hey! You made it back. Where have you been? We were all worried about you," she said as she greeted me with a hug

I told her about the journey and my 10 days of silence. She was surprised that I had done this, as she knew how difficult it was and I had in some way earned her respect - like a knight being sent out on a mission to win the hand of the princess. We agreed to meet later to discuss the experience. Over the weeks we became good friends and I think I may have been falling in love. I asked if she would come to the final requirement of teacher training and to come to Mexico with me to do white tantric yoga.

She agreed and a plan was made.

Those last few weeks of summer in Vancouver were some of the happiest in my life. I felt as though I had finally found somewhere that I belonged. I had friends and I was amongst people that were on the same path of spiritual discovery that I was on. We all shared the same spiritual home - our yoga studio. There was a sense of safety and security that my soul had always longed for.

I was at the peak of my experience in Canada. Bart had also decided to come for the final leg of the journey. Lidija had planned my farewell party and everything was kept quiet. As it turned out – or as I found out thereafter – it was a surprise party. It was the most loved I think I have ever felt. We danced, we shared, we laughed, and we cried. Once again, I found myself leaving Canada in much the same way as I had left England; I had come full circle. Leaving a lot of my belongings behind, and giving them away, took me back to the moments before I had left England. Bart and I were leaving our shared apartment. We gave all of our furniture to charity as the journey was coming to a close. I was left with a few boxes of things; almost the same amount that I had when I first arrived all those moons ago. I said my final goodbyes and made one last visit to Yoga West and the Gurdwara; offering my prayers and blessings for all of the divine help I had received.

RESURRECTION: 3 DAYS

So, the final box was packed; with all of my things plus all of our luggage packed into the back of Bart's parents' station wagon. We were all set to go. My 3-year spiritual odyssey was coming to an end. I reflected on my time in Canada. All the memories, adventures, experiences, and the many people who became like a family to me flashed through my mind. We had planned to drive the whole 1551 miles from Vancouver to Espanola, New Mexico and so we began the final road trip adventure. The drive allowed me ample time to process all that had happened. We drove continuously for almost 4 days. It was a long drive; with Bart and I taking turns along the way. Lidija arranged the food and took care of all of our camping arrangements for the duration of our drive. As we drove, I began to lose track of time. The hours blurred; my sleep was filled with strange images and dreams of ancient sites and mystical beings. The whole trip felt like some sort of weird acid trip.

One evening, I dreamt of being in a wild forest. I was lost and the night was dark apart from the light from the huge silver moon that shone on high. In the darkness, I saw a pair of yellow eyes staring at me and slowly approaching. I stood frozen and deathly quiet as I tried to work out what I was seeing. Then, in the darkness, another set of eyes - and then another and another - as they circled around me. The sound of a deep growling followed by the loudest howl I had ever heard filled the still night air. I slowly began to see these wild wolves coming closer. They were all different shades; big, powerful animals. Their fur was glistening in the moonlight. They came closer and I realised that they were friendly; allowing me to stroke them as they looked deeply in my eyes. Their eyes were full of love and acknowledgement of me as one of the pack. We began running wildly through the night air; climbing trees, playing, and hunting.

I awoke with the taste of blood in my mouth.

Our journey allowed us to stop off at beautiful parks and lakes. I saw mountains and vistas that took my breath away under sunsets and moonlit skies. We experienced every type of weather as we drove through different states - wind, rain, and shine, even snow and a lightning storm that lit up the skies. I felt like I was in a wormhole; flashing through the farthest reaches of time and space. We were sleeping where we could; camping out when we could and sometimes driving for almost 19 hours a day. I noticed how the landscape continually changed and the people changed too. After 5 days we arrived at the Española border; bedraggled, tired, and exhausted. We made our final ascent to a high mountain top where the ashram was located.

We had arrived.

The summer solstice celebration in New Mexico was an annual event where Kundalini practitioners came together to celebrate the solstice with 3 days of tantric yoga. Legend says the land originally belonged to the Hopis Indians who had allowed the yoga group to buy and set up the retreat there.

So here we were in the middle of a desert. There was no hotel or traditional accommodation. We had to find a place in the desert and set up camp. There was a palatable excitement in the air as more and more people arrived for the festival. I had never experienced anything like this ever before. It felt like I had landed on an alien planet. We were out in the elements and away from all human civilization. It felt like true freedom, being at one with nature and the great outdoors. Being out in the wilderness, you realise how little you need; how the land, air, and sky are supporting us always. I thought about my life in the modern world with all the conveniences and it felt so fake; like an artificially created matrix. Here we shared the land with the insects, flies, birds, and the flesh-biting ants. By mid-morning the heat was almost unbearable and this was probably the only time I had truly enjoyed taking cold showers. There were over two thousand people attending, from countries all over the world. Every colour and nationally was represented; creating a sea of white that extended as far as the eye could see.

I was not in Kansas anymore.

It didn't even feel like I was on planet earth. It felt like we were joining up with all our extended family from all over the world. We all shared the same teachings, values, and lifestyle. We all worked together; everyone pitching in and taking a role in the camp operation. Many of my friends - from teacher trainers to teachers alike - had attended s. There was a great sense of community and celebration.

So began the 3 days of white tantric yoga. This was an ancient yogic practice to heal deeply held experiences from our subconscious. The practice of working together in pairs created a powerful zig zag energy that cut through long held phobias and wounds. It was a gruelling 3 days where we were required to hold specific yoga postures and mudras for up to an hour at a time. The process can bring up many issues. It enabled Lidija and I to work through our individual processes as well as to navigate our relationship knowing that I would soon be leaving.

This was a deeply healing inner journey. I experienced moments of bliss and moments of despair; with 10-hour days of constant meditation. On the very last day I experienced a phenomenon that is well known to regular attendees of the event. The group created so much electromagnetic energy that it caused a storm to form over the massive tantric tent - a 2-by-2-mile tent with no walls. It was mid-afternoon on a bright, cloud-free, sunny day, and as we practiced, a dark cloud formed over the top of the tent. Our eyes were closed for this particular kriya and I kept peeking out to see this weird phenomenon happen. The storm cloud became darker as we heard the first drops of rain begin to fall. That sound slowly became louder and louder. Within moments, gusts of rain began to cascade down over the tent; creating a loud rumbling as if huge drums were being beaten. A thumping sound became apparent as the rain crashed down all around us. All of the surrounding skies remained blue. After a short time, the rain stopped, and the clouds passed. The sun continued to shine. On the final night, there was a huge celebration of dance and music as we revelled in awe of the last 7 days. I felt overwhelmed with emotions; crying tears of joy. The experience had changed something within me.

I was no longer the person I was when I left UK shores all those years ago.

RETURN WITH THE ELIXIR

Almost as soon as it had started, the festival came to a close. We packed our things into the car and set off again on the open road. We had made it through to the other side with the bruises, scratches, and bites to prove it; nursing our aching bodies and drinking water to recover from heat stroke. We were sharing our experiences of what had occurred during our time at the festival. We were all in agreement that we had shared something unmistakably divine; a peak experience of consciousness. My flight was to leave from Las Vegas as it was too risky to go back through the Canadian border. There was a slightly sombre air as we drove through the scorching desert. Many hours were spent silence; reflecting on our time together. Leaving the calm deserts of Mexico and arriving in the craziness of Las Vegas was like moving between two polar opposite universes. The sounds, the lights, and the energies of this human amusement park was unmistakable and it was a jarring experience. Once again, I found myself feeling like I had just landed from another planet; being dumbfounded by how people lived and existed here. We shared one final meal together and there was not much talking. I had the same experience that I had had all those years ago. The pain in my heart for leaving my loved ones behind - the anguish of leaving my soul mates – was almost unbearable. I was only comforted in knowing that we would always be connected thanks to this journey. We cried and laughed as we said our goodbyes at the airport. I had come full circle as I sat on the plane and cried as I left behind all of those magical experiences.

The questions came again:

What have I done?

Did I make the right choices?

Were the choices even mine and have I truly been guided by spiritual forces?

I was, once again, travelling into the unknown with no fixed destination or idea as to what I would do. Maybe I would open up a yoga studio and start teaching yoga. Perhaps I would offer therapy to people wishing to know and discover their soul. I had a mission to help uplift humanity; to awaken the souls within them and to share the gifts I had received. I had this divine purpose to bring peace and healing to others; something that the world desperately needed.

I had a destiny to fulfil.

***

CHAPTER 7: THE ARCHETYPES

> *"Any legend, any creature, any symbol we ever stumble on, already exists in a vast cosmic reservoir where archetypes wait. Shapes looming outside our Platonic cave. We naturally believe ourselves clever and wise, so advanced, and those who came before us so naïve and simple...when all we truly do is echo the order of the universe, as it guides us."*
>
> - Guillermo del Toro - Movie Director

The world of myth and storytelling draws heavily from archetypal characters. The Star Wars movies are full of archetypes and archetypal themes. Archetypes can be said to be recurring patterns of human behaviour; symbolised by standard types of characters as seen in movies and stories. "Plato may very well have been the first philosopher to refer to archetypes. He called them Forms. For Plato, there were two realities: the world we live in; and the non-physical realm where the Forms exist. These Forms, for Plato, are pre-existing ideal templates or blueprints. They include characteristics like roundness, softness, hardness, greenness, blackness, and so on. Forms is another term for archetypes. In modern times, psychiatrist Carl Jung made us aware of archetypes. He saw archetypes as the fundamental units of the human mind." (24)

'Archein' in ancient Greek means old, while 'typos' means pattern. Archetype, is a combination of those words, meaning original pattern. This would mean all other patterns would be copied from this original – kind of like a mould to fit. Archetypes are all around us. They possess us, rule us, and guide us. They most certainly influence your behaviour, some to much higher degrees than others. It is believed that they influence over 90% of our behaviour! Your level of consciousness will be determined by how aware you are of the archetypes which are operating within you. Ultimately, you want to get to a place where you can choose which archetype to work off or depending on what the situation in front of you is demanding of you. According to Carl Jung, these archetypes form the keystone patterns of our collective unconscious and we again see this common thread of us all being connected to one another at subconscious level. Just as we can inherit instinctive behavioural patterns; so too can we inherit archetypes – at least this is what Jung proposed.

He defines the 12 core archetypes in his book The Archetypes and the Collective Unconscious. These archetypes are so inherently a part of us that we still tell stories about them to this very day, as noted by Campbell's monomyth. We see it all around us in popular books and film just like the Star Wars franchise. Almost all of us will be predominantly one archetype while having a blend of the others at work in the background. Once we understand our own archetypes, we will be able to gain insight into our behaviours.

Just as Larson referred to the trinity, Jung believed in a trinity of his very own – the trinity of the psyche. This trinity consisted of the ego or the conscious mind, the personal unconscious or the memories – both in awareness and suppressed, and the collective unconscious, or psychological inheritance; containing the knowledge of all experiences on earth.

ORIGINS OF THE ARCHETYPES

In his writings, Jung suggests archetypes arise in the collective unconscious. He explained that these models are innate, universal, and hereditary. Archetypes have always existed and will continue to evolve and develop with human experience. Archetypes help us understand the world we inhabit and the multiple energies of how we experience certain things. "All the most powerful ideas in history go back to archetypes," Jung explained in his book *The Structure & Dynamics of the Psyche*. "This is particularly true of religious ideas, but the central concepts of science, philosophy, and ethics are no exception to this rule... For it is the function of consciousness, not only to recognise and assimilate the external world through the gateway of the senses but to translate into visible reality the world within us," he suggested. (25)

Other philosophers proposed the notion of tabula-rasa which stipulated that the human mind was a completely blank slate at birth. Instead, he proposed that through our collective unconscious we had the wisdom of fundamental, unconscious, biological aspects of our ancestors. These 'primordial images,' tell us how to be as a human being before we even leave the womb. Which archetype dominates you will be entirely hinged upon your upbringing and unique experiences.

THE 12 ARCHETYPES

An outline of the 12 archetypes and their most common traits can be found in the Appendix. These 12 archetypes offer us guidance that can help us to understand our motivations and draw on our strengths while working on our weaknesses. Understanding which of the 12 archetypes dominates our personality, or which is currently most active, can help up to realise what is important to us.

The 12 archetypes are:
1. The Innocent,
2. Everyman,
3. Hero,
4. Outlaw,
5. Explorer,
6. Creator,
7. Ruler,
8. Magician,
9. Lover,
10. Caregiver,
11. Jester, and
12. Sage.

JEDI EXERCISE: ARCHETYPAL PSYCHOLOGY

Archetypal psychology is a powerful way of getting to know your psyche. It's also a means of understanding the motivations of others. The more you can identify the archetypes in others, the more you can see the patterns of behaviour within yourself. Conversely, the more you can witness these behavioural patterns in yourself, the more understanding you'll have for others. Read the list of archetypes in the Appendix and write down the ones you are most drawn to or speak to you on a deep level. Remember that we each have the Child, Victim, Saboteur, and Prostitute, so you will need to select only eight more to fill out your circle.

What myths, fairy tales, or spiritual stories that have meaning for me do I associate with this archetype?
Has this archetype appeared in my dreams?
Does thinking of this archetype make me feel empowered or disempowered?

These exercises are just the beginning of your exploration and self-examination, we encourage you to deepen your learning through further research on this topic so you may continue to study this rich and valuable topic. Make notes in your Jedi journal.
The world can be a hard place to exist sometimes. Some days you aren't feeling like you are up for the challenge in front of you. You are tired and sore; exhausted, beaten down, and ready to hide under the covers. Everyday life can feel like a battlefield. The many daily obstacles we meet and the variety of enemies that we have to defeat can wear us down. These people could show up as the nagging boss, our children who decide that today is the day to have a revolution, the heavy traffic, the queue for lunch, or perhaps the crappy weather. There are things all around us that can have you feeling that it might probably be best to take the day off. You might feel as though you are ready to admit defeat and back down, but that's just your fear talking. In truth, you are much more powerful than you think you are.

Some people just don't know when it's time to give up and for some, it's never a good time to start. Being pulled around by our various commitments and responsibilities can leave us feeling like we are not in control of our life anymore. Capitalism and materialism have distorted the natural balance and order of things. We can feel deep down that something is wrong with the world but we are encouraged not to look up and not to question anything. We are kept so distracted that we don't have the time or energy to look. Health issues such as diabetes, high blood pressure, cancer, allergies, heart disease, fibromyalgia, ADHD, autism, stress, immune dysfunction, obesity, anxiety, sleeplessness, depression, and mania, are all-natural responses to the artificial, abnormal conditions we exist in. Yet we generally "medicate" them away, through tv, media, consumerism, drugs, and alcohol abuse; much to the delight of big pharma and political strategists. It's all a part of the mission to keep you in line.

In the words of Indian sage and Jedi Knight Jiddu Krishnurmurti; "It is no measure of health to be well adjusted to a profoundly sick society." This matrix system wants you to conform in order to keep the financial and commercial world turning. The system is saturated in the frequency of fear which causes us to back down, retreat, and give up altogether. We are forced and moulded into distortion; losing a sense of who we truly are. In the words of Jedi Master the Buddha; "We see The First Noble Truth in Buddhism is usually translated as "life is suffering." So if this ancient wisdom teaching is true, how do we approach this arena we call life and be victorious in it?"

The way to claim victory and reclaim your sovereign self is by embracing your inner warrior energy. This is the path of a Kundalini Jedi Warrior!

THE WARRIOR ARCHETYPE

Warriors tend to live life like a battlefield. They can be arrogant and overconfident. They wish to push past their fears and inadequacies and fulfil the mission at any cost. Warriors have the courage to fight back. It is in their nature to challenge injustice and wrong doing. The inner warrior is guided by his inner values, or by royal decree, not by public pressure or opinion. There exists a warrior within all of us. We have an innate ability to activate the warrior archetype within us. When we are disconnected from our warrior archetype, we may let other people push us around, or we might lack direction, or even fail to achieve our goals because we cannot persist. At the same time if we use too much warrior energy, then every interaction becomes a contest —we want what we want and insist on getting it; whatever the cost to others or our relationships. A true warrior is not just considerate of his own personal battle, but is also in tune with the world and the greater needs of society as a whole. The true warrior is self-sacrificing; being free from pride, vanity, and personal ambition. The way of A Kundalini Jedi Warrior is to walk the middle path - a higher path.

It is a warrior in balance.

***

CHAPTER 8: A NEED FOR WARRIORS

> *"I fear nothing. For all is as the Force wills it."*
>
> *- Chirrut Imwe – Rogue One: A Star Wars Story*

A TRUE WARRIOR

Warriors are selfless, free of pride, ego, and ambition. They are intelligent, logical, and rational. They protect the fragile and needy like a good-hearted parent would. He offers the world all of his actions in a consistent and steadfast manner.

Yoga is about nurturing compassion and understanding of the sacredness of life. A true yogi is sensitive to the presence of God in all things and sees the good in all of us. His actions are gentle and tolerant, bringing healing and nourishment to those in their path.

A true warrior doesn't weigh themselves down with over-sentimentality but rather chooses to be pliable in the world; adapting to everything that they're presented with and surrendering to the present moment. They are swayed by neither a win nor a loss. They are passionate in their demeanour; acting with strength and courage as they navigate the roads less travelled. They are not too proud to ever compromise and they seek avenues to give and receive love to those around them. These yogic warriors know that we are all a part of the same life Force, or source, and thus loving each other means loving ourselves.

While being aware of the suffering in the world, this warrior conducts himself with a calmness of spirit as well as discipline and humility. He is disciplined in his work; making every effort to work hard and to serve those in need.

These warriors are not afraid to venture into the unknown; learning new things and trying new methods as they go. They are objective, practical, fair and goal-oriented; choosing not to discuss trivial matters and gossip.

WARRIOR EVOLUTION

As mentioned before, the warrior, like any archetype, is neither good nor bad. However, some forms of an archetype are no longer appropriate for the current times we live in. Due to the dawning of a new age, the quality of consciousness in people within all cultures is changing. The current time offers us the opportunity to participate in the archetype's evolution by how we choose to live it. In doing so, we can see that we do not need to be at war with ourselves, or with others. We are all on the same warrior team to some degree, playing different positions.

An important thing to learn very early on is nonviolent, or NVC, communication. It will help us to navigate conflict in a positive manner; striving for the best possible outcomes for all who are involved. It helps us to take care of our own needs, while compassionately meeting the needs of others.

As we continue to develop the qualities of the knight, the yogi, and the Jedi we create a new model and way of being; thus, becoming the Kundalini Jedi Warrior. We can become active participants in the creation of this warrior energy through the understanding and skilful use of archetypal energies. As we develop the qualities of compassion, and care - the nurturing qualities and sacred approach of the yogi - we can create a warrior for the modern age. We can create a warrior that is in balance with themselves; who overcomes challenges through love and understanding, not through force and violence.

*

WORTHY ARCHETYPES ALONGSIDE THE WARRIOR:

There are some notable, worthy archetypes that run alongside the warrior. These have been eloquently unravelled by Ariel Hudnall, self-proclaimed dream smith and writer.

THE SAGE

The qualities of the sage archetype can also be known as the scholar, expert, detective, thinker, teacher, mentor, savant, and philosopher. The Sage seeks to understand the world in analytical ways, processing reality with the logic and the wisdom of their often-long life. In Star Wars the sage is represented by a Jedi who has established themselves in the force and has some experience under their belt. Obi-Wan and Yoda embody the qualities of the wise sage. The Sage seeks nothing but the truth. Whether that truth is uncomfortable or heart-rendering, it will be accepted as the only meaningful path in life; the path of truth. Personal truth based on falsehood is one of the great fears of the Sage, and so they are always questioning what they know to be true. This eagerness to find contradiction sometimes leads the Sage to be misled or even manipulated by others who are aware of their weakness. The Sage can be addicted to learning; spending so much time pouring over books and information that they never actively engage in the threat facing their world. The Sage, being one of the pillars that the Hero can depend on, is not easily corruptible. Though the Sage can function in ignorance, when the wool over the eyes is removed, they often more easily accept that change than the other archetypes. But a shadow Sage is not impossible. A Sage surrounded by profound ignorance may become fed up with such an unenlightened world, and would be happily engaged in its political, religious, moral, and spiritual sabotage. A Sage can also become overly critical, impractical, or even unsympathetic to those not on their intellectual plane. Due to the nature of genius, a Sage may also become addicted to mind-numbing substances. (26)

The warriors who are fortunate enough to have access to the Sage archetype are those who will not take action until they can verify the truth. For them, there is no black and white when it comes to right and wrong. They believe that there are almost always systemic problems responsible for people who engage in wrongdoing. They often have a very broadened world view and will be concerned with the issues of the world such as climate change, pollution, and more. They always try to understand the underlying motivations behind why people do the things that they do. In essence, these people always try to see the bigger picture and understand an issue from both sides of the spectrum.

They are genuinely worried about the happiness of others, and the potential threats to these people's survival. They often advocate for others and are seen as true global citizens; trying their best to engage in capacity development. They are caregivers; striking the perfect balance between self-interests and altruism.

Develop the Strength of The Warrior,
The Compassion of a Healer,
and The Spiritual Wisdom of The Sage. (27)

The Warrior, the Healer and the Sage are the three facets of a human being who has become complete. While most people will disjoint their way of being and choose to focus specifically on one area – led by one archetypal form – the Kundalini Jedi Warrior will try to encompass all three. This is because many of us possess fragments of all of these archetypal constructs. Think about martial artists who possess the knowledge of the Warrior, the calm of the Sage, and the know-how of the Healer. Historically, the people who learn to master all three facets will have a more centered and balanced way of being.

Holding onto one of the three facets in the belief that it will make you whole simply is not true. It would be like taking one shade away from your lenses and still attempting to see the world in all its colourful glory.

THE MAGICIAN

Hudnall goes on to explore the Magician, also known as the visionary, catalyst, charismatic leader, medicine man, healer, and inventor, the Magician is the archetype that seeks transformation, and a deep connection to the cosmos, whatever their definition of that might be. The Magician is not involved in every day of regular people; they do not find 'mortal' concerns interesting or curious. Rather, they seek the threads beneath the surface that tie a world together. Unlike the Sage, however, knowledge isn't enough. The Magician wishes to harness magic for their purpose. Similarly, unlike the Creator, who uses the rules of the physical world, the Magician seems to draw his power from supernatural skill or resources.

The Magician is known as the catalyst for a reason. In the Hero's Journey, the Magician is the pin in the balloon of a hero's sheltered life. While the Magician, in fiction, is powerful, he is also often maimed by the same power, restricted (or wilfully determined) from assisting the transformation of the world, except from a distance. The Magician is the chess-player. One of the reasons that a Magician might not be willing to risk life and limb is because his power is born of ego-to in turn be corrupted or otherwise consumed by "evil" is one of his greatest fears. The Magician has an extreme duty to his self-preservation.

The Magician is one of the less flexible archetypes when it comes to fiction. The faults of the Magician are typically unvarying, as if those limitations did not exist, most epics would end in the second chapter. This means that the Magician is often perceived to be a coward, manipulative, dishonest, and even cultish. However, when a Magician aligns himself fully to the light, away from his Shadow, he can be a force of great healing and transformation for others. The Magician can often return after a fall from grace as a galvanizing force for the Hero, and make all the difference in the world's darkest hour. (28)

In the Star Wars franchise, for example, the evildoers are seen as cruel fascist, while the rebels are seen as pure of heart; energised by the Force to restore balance to the universe. Ultimately, as these rebels evolve within their roles, meaning archetypes don't fall away or die, they simply evolve within the consciousness of those who possess their qualities.

JEDI EXERCISE: EVOLUTION OF THE WARRIOR

Our relationship with the Warrior archetype changes over time, it evolves as we do:
1. Do you need less or more of the warrior archetype to deal with a current threat or challenge?
2. Where do you see the warrior in yourself and in what you think and do?
3. What forms of the warrior do you see in yourself and the people around you, and how is their influence affecting you?
4. How might you like your inner warrior to change and evolve in its attitudes and behaviours?

Record your insights in your Jedi journal.

*

LEGENDS

Every great civilization, creed, culture, and religion has its own great warrior tradition. Christians have a wrathful God and the Israelite warriors. The Mediterranean region had the Spartans and King Leonidas. The Persians had Xerxes and his immortals. The Romans had their gladiators and the Byzantine emperors had the Varangian Guard.

Irrespective of where these warriors came from, or what their beliefs were, the best of the lot were always those who trusted in their own intuition. They act in an anticipatory fashion. Some of the best of these warriors lived on the other side of the world and were the most feared warriors in history. The Japanese samurai was an expert in horse riding, archery, and the wielding of a sword made from the finest and sharpest steel yet to be seen anywhere else in the world. Samurai attached great importance to the circumstances of their own death. If a samurai died of his own accord, it was considered a valiant end. Rather than suffer defeat or humiliation at the hands of an enemy, samurai warriors often chose ritual suicide, known as seppuku, or hara-kiri in the west.

It is said that their courage came from living their lives as if they were already dead men walking. They lived according to the way of the warrior, also known as Bushido, which was founded in Confucianism. This code of ethics that they lived by demanded that they be loyal to their masters – similar to the Jedi and their Masters. They had to be completely disciplined and showcase a respect for themselves as well as others. However, this wasn't an art form that was strictly reserved for boys becoming men. Contrary to popular belief, many girls received this stringent martial arts training. They were cutthroat enough to wage war, and humble enough to return and till the soil when the war was over. Sound like a farm boy that we know and love?

Much like the Jedi, samurai warrior training began in childhood and combined physical training, spiritual discipline, and poetry. They followed Zen Buddhism, studying Kendo – or the Way of the Sword – as well as the moral, ethical code of the Samurai.

While these warriors went boldly into battle, never shying away from the light, there were more covert opposites to that spectrum in the form of Ninjas. The Ninja was a highly trained spy with a focus on assassination and sabotaging tactics. They were silent but deadly; mastering the art of the lethal throwing star.

Fast-forward a little further down the line and we are then led back west where the emergence of the Medieval Knight came to the fore. These men rode in cavalry and developed the art of persuasion; often never needing to even commence battle before convincing the enemy that they would surely lose.

SIKH WARRIORS

All of these warriors were incredibly revered in their time. They held such a high status in society and were regarded as heroes. Possibly the most peaceful but adept to war is the Sikh. Sikhism is a religion which although is centred around peace, was founded through strife, self-defence and defiance. They would often forge battles with adversaries who would have them heavily outnumbered, only to win victory with little collateral damage. They were incredibly brave and even more ruthless, especially amongst the ranks of the Sikh Khalsa Army.

The Nihang, also known as The Immortals, was an order of armed Sikh warriors who originated in the Indian subcontinent. It is believed that they originated either from the attire of Fateh Singh or from the Akali Dal – Immortal Army – of Guru Hargobind.

If one were to look back at the early history of Sikh military, they would come to see how it was dominated by the Nihang. They were brave and ruthless warriors who formed a part of the guerrilla squads of the Sikh Khalsa Army.

It wasn't until Guru Gobind Singh – the tenth and final Guru of the Sikhs – came to the fore that Sikh faith was transformed; creating the Khalsa community of faithful Sikhs in 1699. Today the Khalsa is totally composed of practicing Sikhs.

WARRIORS OF OLD

Contrary to the previous chapter, this one will look at some warriors who used their warrior energy for their own selfish pursuits; conquering nations, hell-bent on world-domination. They absorbed the troops of other nations, aiming to have the fiercest armies at their disposal. They moulded these fighters into the tactical units that would send shudders down an enemy's spine and stop them in their tracks before they even had a chance to fight back.

Human beings, at the end of the day, are incredibly combative beings, not because we love to fight – although some do – but because we fight for what we believe and seek to protect it at all costs. One such warrior was none other than Marcus Cassius Scaeva. He was known as the 'die-hard' of all warriors after being shot in the eye with an arrow during a battle between Julius Caesar and the Gnaeus Pompey army. History tells how he yanked the arrow from his eye socket, screamed out a battle cry and carried on fighting.

Another one-eyed warrior was Xiahou Dun. If you thought Scaeva was a renegade, then you will find that Dun was totally insane by comparison. During his time serving Warlord Cao, Dun got shot in the eye during a battle. It is recorded that he pulled the arrow from his socket; stopping only to assess the fact that his eyeball was hanging off the tip and eating it before continuing his fight.

Alcibiades on the other hand was known for being somewhat of a military genius. An Athenian warrior, Alcibiades was such a skilled fighter that his enemies would often submit to him completely; offering their daughters to him for marriage.

However, when it comes to Roman Gladiators, few were more prolific than Flamma. He turned down the right to walk free from the Colosseum on four separate occasions, staying to participate in the fights that he so enjoyed.

Sticking within the Mediterranean, we take particular note of Pyrrhus of Epirus. As King of the Greek Molossians, and one of the greatest Generals to ever live, he consistently pushed back the notorious Roman Legions.

Brought to fame by popular films like Troy and Sparta are the Spartan warriors. King Leonidas of Sparta is possibly one of the most legendary warriors for his ability to wild immeasurable damage to throws of opponents with just a few men. It was during the Battle of Thermopylae, at the legendary Hot Gates, that the Spartan 300 would take on 100,000 Persians. While the Persians would eventually kill the 300, they would lose a whopping 20,000 of their men to Leonidas' fearless army.

Alexander the Great, or the great conqueror was so selfish in his ways that he went on to conquer almost all of the known world during his lifetime. He had an insatiable thirst for world domination. He was an ingenious fighter.

From ingenious to quite possibly insane; next up is Galvarino. Galvarino was one who liked to stab his victims – a lot, and repeatedly. If there was a picture next to overkill in the dictionary, it would be a picture of Galvarino's face. When he was finally captured by the Spanish, they cut off his hands, but so deep was his love for knives that when he was eventually released, he continued fighting by strapping knives to his arms.

Across the globe was none other than Miyamota Musashi. He was the most skilled swordsman in Japan in his time. He began duelling at the tender age of 13 and would go on to win over 60 sword fights in his life. Some of his musings on combat and warfare are still around today.

If you've ever heard of the Battle of Shiroyama, then chances are that you have heard the name Saigo Takamori. Takamori led a 40,000 strong army of Samurai against a staggering 300,000 Imperial soldiers during that particular battle. Talk about going in guns – or swords – blazing.

Now, fewer names are more synonymous with death than our next sinister warrior: Attila the Hun. He claimed that his sword had been forged by Ares himself and even the most inexhaustible armies feared him; handing over gold and jewels in return for being left in peace.

Although the Huns were terrifying, when it came to war, the master of it all was Sun Tzu. He was an unmatched tactician, and would work on his enemies' minds before even stepping foot onto the battlefield. In one instance, Tzu was so incredibly outnumbered by his opponent that he decided that reverse psychology would be best. He simply opened the gates for his opponent who believed that it was surely a trap. Said opponent eventually retreated without there being any bloodshed whatsoever.

Perhaps not the intellectual that Tzu was known for being, Lu Bu was, however, the most feared warrior of his time. He was skilled in all forms of combat but his lack of loyalty and discipline saw him bouncing around China for quite some time. He would eventually defeat Warlord Cao, but would recede into the shadows as he usually would.

Finally comes a name that almost everyone will know: Ghengis Khan. He was known as the 'Holy Warrior' as many believed that a man as powerful as him was surely sent from the heavens. Not only did he control areas to the equivalent size of the entire continent of Africa, he also sired so many children that geneticists believe that every 1 in 200 men today is a descendant of Khan. (29)

These are all gladiators, mercenaries, army generals, leaders, and heroes that conquered lands and people. These great warriors used their skills and attributes to kill, maim, and overpower the enemy at any cost. They used their innate warrior capabilities either for a king, or the people, and perhaps even for the hand of a fair maiden. Warrior energy can be used for many purposes and ultimately depends on the intentions of the warrior themselves. Their purpose was to destroy the enemy. Being single minded, they were either heroes of their lands or enemies of others.

In the modern world of business and politics some of these same strategies are being used to gain competitive advantage; to overtake companies and assets. The world over, strategies are used to overthrow governments; all for the purpose of power, prestige, position, and dominance over those deemed less than them. Today we see warriors in combative competitive sports such as mixed martial arts – or MMA – which are literally the modern versions of the ancient gladiator arenas. Sports teams do battle every week; with each player being willing to give all of their talents and skills to beat the opposing team in a bid to claim victory over all.

The Jedi Warriors realises that his enemies and challenges are within himself and that by conquering those inner enemies and claiming victory over their feelings, they will arise as true masters. Mastering their minds to create higher and higher states of positive feelings and emotions only leads to a higher vibrational output that uplifts oneself and those around them.

WARS IN THE NAME OF GOD

Wars in the name of God are seldom just that. They are more to do with power and economic interests. When innocent people had to flee from ISIS militia in one of Iraq's latest Holy Wars, they lost everything. Just about everything of value was taken from them, even earring from little babies. They incite violence in the name of Sharia law; quoting Prophet Mohammed and insinuating that what they do is in the name of Allah. It is either convert, pay a bribe, or die; so, they all fled.

"Religious wars claim victims in other parts of the world as well. In the Central African Republic, Christians and Muslims are fighting to the death. In Asian Myanmar, Buddhist monks bash in the skulls of Muslims because otherwise "they'll cut our heads off," says monk Wira Thu from a Mandalay monastery. Meanwhile, in Nigeria the Islamic group Boko Haram is terrorizing non-Muslims and abducting schoolgirls in the name of Allah.

It is not the belief in Allah, Yahweh or God that unleashes religiously motivated violence. The religious systems merely provide the mask under which the banality of evil can hide. Killing and robbing are sanctioned by invoking God or Allah." (30)

If we look at the history books, this thread is common. The Crusades for example, only came into play in order to gain control of holy sites that were deemed sacred by opposing parties. This repainted the face of Christianity, showing a bloodthirsty side to the religion that seemed hell-bent on land accumulation in the Middle East.

*

THE BAD REPUTATION OF THE WARRIOR

So, we learned how to make guns, and we mechanised warfare which led to rampant trauma on national and global scales. No longer was the way of the warrior some form of sacred art-form but anyone – even those who were not mentally adept to being a warrior – would venture out onto the battlefield. It is because of this that the warrior as an archetype was rejected by so many people and why we have moved towards the idea that peace is the best way forward. However, sometimes aggression is called for and we should not forget that the way of the warrior wasn't started with the idea of brute force being at the forefront of the ideology.

In modern times, people are generally uncomfortable in the presence of warriors because we've been preconditioned with such awful imagery of the warrior throughout a most ugly warring history. Nonetheless, the warrior archetype is incredibly prevalent today. We are currently fighting this war against ourselves – split off into different faction wars, which can't be one by defeating some 'bad guy'.

But there are bad guys – believe you me they're out there. If we look towards capitalism and commercialism, we see how some sully the warrior archetype image by using it for personal gain. They create monopolies and deals which benefit only them and their counterparts. While the energy of the warrior is still so prevalent the true warrior nature has become lost and it is most likely due to the fact that we are not engaging our warrior spirit as warriors did so many moons ago. Instead, it becomes bogged down in a swamp of policies, with peacekeepers being used as pawns for capitalism.

While being 'nice' is great for all intents and purposes, the reason why society is encouraged to be docile is because if we were to rise up correctly within the warrior spirit once more, we would actively take our power back. We only view the negative aspects of this archetype and that's why it's so easy to be tricked into believing that it is bad. The problem isn't the energy, but the people who are not using it in synchronicity with other spiritual qualities that are more commonly possessed by the Sage and the Healer, for example.

Whereas before we sought out new hunting grounds for exactly that - hunting – now we seek them out for greed and personal gain. When we go back to our roots of what the warrior archetype is actually supposed to be, we are able to push ourselves towards worthy goals and causes in order to achieve the greatness that is befitting of this archetype. The only way, however, to do this is to live like the Samurai – like you are already dead, but with the same love and conviction that you would otherwise have. Once you feel like nothing external can conquer you, you will know the true way of the warrior.

THE GOOD FIGHT

The warrior needs a battle to fight. Fighting itself is not a bad thing. What is important is to know why we are engaged in this spiritual struggle today. Our war is being fought on the battlefield of our consciousness. As warriors, we fight our own inner and collective demons. The warrior has an incredible amount of courage and composure under the toughest of circumstances. He has been trained over a long period of time and is dedicated to the mission. Spiritual warriors appreciate life and teach this appreciation to the individuals around them. He understands that the Force flows through us all. By fighting and defeating his inner conflicts and negative thoughts, he reconciles with the warring nature of humans and defends the innocent. It is through self-control that the Warrior harnesses his power. He knows when and how to use aggression. His energies are under his control; he can release them and pull them back, deciding in advance what attitude to take in different scenarios instead of letting a situation dictate what he feels.

The warrior, unlike the Hero archetype, relishes pain. He believes that pain is necessary and even goes so far as to look forward to it on his journey. He will actively learn how to master this fearlessness of death and pain by learning how to open up beyond his body. He listens with his whole being; sensing the world around him.

To sense the force in all things.

To develop sensitivity.

To be in tune and in touch with developing our subtle nature.

As previously explored, history has shown us that the best warriors are those who trust their intuition. There is a particularly poignant story about Alexander the Great in

Steven Pressfield's book *The Warrior Ethos*. "Alexander the Great was an ancient Macedonian ruler and one of history's greatest warriors and military minds who, as King of Macedonia and Persia, established the largest empire the ancient world had ever seen. Alexander, while in India, encountered some gymnosophists (literally "naked wise men") yogis, sitting in meditation in the sun on the banks of the Indus. Alexander's party was trying to get through the busy street, but the yogis had their spot and they wouldn't move. One of Alexander's zealous young lieutenants took it upon himself to chase the holy men out of the king's path. When one of the wise men resisted, the officer started verbally abusing him. Just then, Alexander came up. The lieutenant pointed to Alexander and said to the yogi, "This man has conquered the world! What have you accomplished?" The yogi looked up calmly and replied, "I have conquered the need to conquer the world." At this, Alexander laughed with approval. He admired the naked wise men. "Could I be any man in the world other than myself," he said, "I would be this man here."

What Alexander was acknowledging was that the yogi was a warrior too. An inner warrior. Alexander looked at him and thought, "This man was a fighter when he was my age. He has taken the lessons he learned as a warrior duelling external enemies and is turning them to use now as he fights his own internal foes to achieve mastery over himself." (31)

JEDI EXERCISE: THE GOOD WARRIOR

Who is your favourite warrior race?
What qualities did you most admire in them?
Take a moment, and reflect on their story and legend.
Why does this particular hero/warrior speak to you?
If you could be any warrior throughout history, who would you be and why?
Collect images, quotes and stories of warriors that inspire you in your Jedi journal.

SPIRITUAL WARRIORS

A spiritual warrior will always seek the means to move forward in the evolution of their spirit. No matter whether the choices presented to them are difficult or easy, they will always prioritise that growth. Robert Bessler, owner of the *Abode of the Eternal Tao*, explored this notion of a spiritual warrior and had some profound theories on the matter. Below is an excerpt of that exploration:

Spiritual Warrior lives from a place of non-attachment and will change everything in their life if need be, in the pursuit of spiritual Expansion. I have found that once you seriously begin seeking the spiritual path, you will eventually be faced with the decision of graduating from a Spiritual Seeker to that of a Spiritual Warrior. It is only by passing through these stages that you can become a Spiritual Master. The Spiritual Seeker is one who is just starting or dabbling in spiritual or religious teachings. They read and attend seminars and workshops, practice many different systems and techniques and begin to make some real progress. Sooner or later though they will be faced with the decision to remain a Seeker without making any further discernible advancement, or to become a Spiritual

Warrior, understanding what it is to rely on their own Divine nature for what they need. The professional Spiritual Seeker continues through life experimenting in this and that, going from one New Age fad to the next, lost in the fog in fear of truly discovering their Divine nature and personal power. They continue to rely on others to make their decisions for them and are easily thrown at the first hint of distress or improvement. (32)

A spiritual warrior, on the opposite end of that spectrum, walks briskly into the unknown in the name of progress. Stopping along their progress would mean going backwards in terms of their spiritual evolution so they avoid this at all costs. Instead, they harness all of the systems that will serve their spiritual journey; drawing from several spiritual, or faith, systems to create one that is unique to them. They respect that there is truth in all beliefs, all practices, and all religions. They move away from drama and towards tranquillity; choosing to be accountable for everything that happens to and for them. They cultivate their skills in ways that allow others to feel safe. They offer help and healing to those who need it most.

They are always looking for a means to connect to the Force; remaining true to themselves along their journey, even in the face of adversity or death. The heart of the Kundalini Jedi Warrior must, therefore, be strong.

Martial arts are such an amazing platform for achieving this because it is an art-form that requires you to engage from a centred heart. One must be filled with the love and respect for both the art-form and their opponent. That being said, our heart centre is prone to closing off when we're under fear of death – or when there is a perceived threat. That is why it is so exceptionally important to engage in art-forms and meditations that encourage us to keep our hearts open; no matter what the danger is. This is the basis for an unshakeable heart. This is what allows us to evade danger without anger. Simply put, it removes the need to control and avenge ourselves or others because we are connected to our divine Force at all times.

In essence, your heart must come first in all that you do. It must be developed as a precursor to any other skill set, including those of combat. Fighting skills cannot come before a strong inner balance which can only be achieved through engaging in consistent spiritual practices.

More often than not, those around us will not be comfortable with our progress; not because they don't love us, but because it highlights faults within themselves that they do not wish to see or address. Be resilient and keep pushing on in spite of this; knowing that once you progress far enough along your path, you will have the tools to turn back and help them. They may also be afraid of losing you; or the version of you that they have grown to love. Be kind to these people, but persevere nonetheless.

As you go through this process of doing the practices in the book and connect to your Kundalini Jedi Warrior nature, your vibrational frequency will begin to rise. This will not go unnoticed by those in your life, and you should expect two very different types of feedback. Eventually, you can expect random statements from friends and family members that you have changed, and hopefully they state that it's for the better. They may praise you for the transformations they notice and may even encourage you to keep doing what you are doing, even though they don't understand exactly what you are going through.

The planetary, evolutionary shift that is happening as we prepare to transition into the Aquarian Age, has led to this calling for you to become the person that you ought to be. The rewards will be well worth the effort; I can promise you that much, but you must commit to the process completely and not look for excuses to walk away from the journey. As you rise higher in your vibrational energy towards the Force, those around may feel conflicted; even threatened. They may encounter feelings of insecurity; closing their hearts from you and others. This will lower their vibrational energy and it is imperative that you do not let these energies overcome you.

Your love will reflect their fears.

Your bliss will reflect their unhappiness.

Your divine truths may reflect their ignorance.

Be kind.

Persevere.

Encourage them to embrace their own growth; to use you as a mirror for that wish they hope to be and see in the world. It is then that their hearts will be allowed to open fully and to be filled with freedom and appreciation. Remember, this reckoning was how you began your own quest. However, you must remain fluid. Don't become arrogant in believing that you are ahead of someone on the spiritual path. Just when you think you know the path in front of you, it will change; forcing you to change along with it. Stay fluid. Keep learning. Keep growing.

This book will give you the tools to transform yourself into a Kundalini Jedi Warrior. It will show you how a warrior doesn't need to fight to prove a point, but rather fights for what is right without giving up. You will learn how to develop the compassion of a healer alongside your warrior qualities so that you can evade any negativity that comes your way. This compassion will be extended to those around you, allowing your vibrational energy to rise even further. Once you have developed the sensitivity to the subtle energies around you, by living through your heart centre, you will be able to develop an intuition that will guide you away from what is bad for you and towards what is good for you. Making decisions based upon how you feel instead of what you think is the true approach of the Kundalini Jedi Warrior.

It's very important that you become aware of the distractions which may cross your path. In this social media driven 'info age' that we find ourselves in it is so easy to fall prey to the trappings of distraction and mental fatigue. These distractions will diminish your productivity and lower your vibrational energy.

The trinity of the warrior personality is discipline, sensitivity, and responsibility. Try to avert your eyes from anything that will dampen that trinity. While all things possess a certain level of sensitivity, ours as humans is distinguished by our consciousness. Spiritual warriors are some of the few who develop that sensitivity more than others.

Within the trinity there is also responsibly, as we've just seen, "Responsibility is an attitude born of the most profound consciousness. In an attempt to explain the ineffable, we could say that consciousness exists on two levels: one that appears through the "small self" and which moves and reacts—nervously, bitterly, ignorantly—to the ups and downs of daily life; and the elevated consciousness or the interior being, whose reality, unlimited and immortal, unites with the Supreme Consciousness of the universe." (33)

While all warriors are destined to return to the supreme Force from whence, they came, their biggest challenge in the realm of consciousness is to strike a balance between his 'small-self' and his 'elevated consciousness'.

It is believed that at the inception of the universe a supreme consciousness broke up in to billions of pieces; all of which would eventually find their way into the bodies of those who inhabited the universe. We are all to return to this supreme consciousness of Force one day.

Throughout his time on earth, the warrior will experience the push-and-pull between his small-self and his higher-self. The warrior within him will try to expand his consciousness, while the common man within him will attempt to satisfy the wants of the small-self. Whichever one of these personas within you wins is the one that will dominate your thought processes and thus your actions. You will be challenged as a Kundalini Jedi Warrior and the challenges will most likely come from within. As such you must allow your physical health and mental equilibrium to depend upon the decisions of the "small" but healthy "I." The development of disinterested love and the pursuit of the highest ideals are inspired by a higher consciousness.

As Guillermo Marín Ruiz explains, the consciousness of man includes all of humanity's knowledge and wisdom. The problem is that people never stop to check in with their interior; they no longer pick up the inner call of consciousness or even recognise its existence. Nevertheless, consciousness is the ally that inevitably indicates what to do and what not to do. Since consciousness exists eternally and independently of the physical body, upon making contact with each individual body, it gives rise to the cosmic game of learning and transcendence. On the other hand, if a person directly or indirectly turns all of his efforts towards the satisfaction of the mental and physical ego, he will miss out on the thing that distinguishes him from an animal: consciousness. And so, both the "small self" and the potentially all-encompassing consciousness integrate themselves into the duality of a person, without which "project man" would not exist.

Discipline is the third element in the warrior's arsenal. This is not the sort of military discipline that blindly obeys others, but rather the discipline that comes from a committed, personal decision. This sort of discipline constitutes a personal achievement, because it is one thing to know what to do, and it is another thing to acquire the strength of will to actually carry it out. Discipline is an attitude. There are those who prefer that someone sets on them with a whip and takes responsibility for their decisions and, on the other hand, there are those who don't allow others to take responsibility for what they need to do. It is from this group of people that "warriors" arise.

Although discipline is an attitude and a personal decision, it needs to be cultivated for it to be strengthened and consolidated. Discipline responds to a premeditated intention, conscious and unceasing, that gradually gains a powerful inner strength that we call "will." The warrior develops an unyielding will to transform himself. As a result, he begins to notice subtle changes in his inner workings and in the world that surrounds him. Without this strength, human beings are no more than dust in the strong winds of the surrounding world. (34)

CHARACTERISTICS AND TRAITS

A war of fear will rage within you as you attempt to embark on your warrior journey. To win this war you will need to be entirely self-aware; acting with courage, and discipline to transform your emotional plain. To win the war against fear requires awareness, courage, discipline, and commitment to transform the emotional body. Let's explore these, and other qualities, that you will need to possess in order to win that spiritual war.

AWARENESS OF THE SPIRITUAL WARRIOR

The first and most vital tool of the spiritual warrior is awareness. It is easy to think we are aware, but pure awareness has no thinking involved. It has no thinking because it has no interpretation. Awareness is to perceive with clarity the truth of what is happening without interpretation or opinion. In a moment of awareness, the dialogue in the mind stops. We are "seeing" from a point or view separate from the reasoning part of our mind. This could be described as an epiphany. Practiced seer's live in this awareness at every moment.

Awareness is essential because it is the state of consciousness that allows us to discern between the facts and the Truth, and between the story and the lies in our mind. The realm of our mind is filled with false perceptions and false beliefs. While the mind can be very clever with stories and lies, it is the consciousness of awareness that is the discerning intelligence. We may use very intelligent reasoning to make a decision that is not good for ourselves. Only to look at it in hindsight and realise that we discounted indicators that told us otherwise. This can be done in something as simple as a stock investment. The mind is clever, but it is also full of assumptions and limited paradigms of perception. Conscious awareness allows us to see clearly instead of being blinded by these false belief paradigms.

Self-awareness is the clarity to know who and what you are, and not get caught up in self-important images of ourselves. These self-important images in our mind distort our sense of who we are. False images can lead us to low self-esteem and self-confidence, or they can take us into being self-centred. If you have an idea of who you are, then consider that you are not that idea in your mind. You are the one creating the idea, and observing it. Self-awareness that you are not any of those images in your mind is essential to becoming free of self-importance. (35)

COURAGE OF THE SPIRITUAL WARRIOR

The courage that makes for a good soldier also makes for a good Spiritual Warrior, but the intent becomes completely different. A soldier has courage to face a challenge that may bring physical harm. The Spiritual warrior has the courage to question and challenge his or her own beliefs. By challenging our own beliefs, we can dissolve the lies that cause our suffering. To challenge our own beliefs requires courage because it means the end of our illusion of safety. When other people challenge our own beliefs, we are usually quick to defend. We defend them even if they cause us to suffer. As a warrior we learn not to defend what we believe, and then to challenge those very beliefs ourselves. In this way we are able to sort out the truth from illusions. (36)

DISCIPLINE OF THE SPIRITUAL WARRIOR

A soldier has discipline to follow orders and continues on when faced with challenges. The Spiritual Warrior's discipline to continue on with their path when faced with challenges from their mind. It is easier to follow orders as a soldier, because we are threatened with consequences and rewarded to motivate us. This is in line with our years of conditioning. A warrior must have the discipline to deal with their own mind without someone else providing the motivation. A warrior must exercise their own will at the command of their heart, not an outside authority figure. This often means going against the fearful opinions in our mind that tempt us with illusions of punishment and rewards. We must also have the discipline to follow our own heart even when tempted by another person's opinion. This way of living requires disciplined practice. (37)

THE LOVE OF THE SPIRITUAL WARRIOR

A soldier has a commitment to love his/her country. The Spiritual warrior must have the commitment to love himself or herself. The warrior then extends that love to humanity. The commitment is required because in our journey we will certainly fumble and fall many times. It is in having a strong commitment that we get back up again. It is common to fall to judgment. It can be easy to love some people, particularly the people that like us or treat us well. However, it requires a tremendous commitment to love in the face of those that reject us. This commitment will cause us to challenge our beliefs about our judgments and not being compassionate. We must be committed to love beyond our own self-serving interests of what it will bring us. This is how we will become happy beyond our current paradigm of beliefs. In time we become committed to love for the sheer enjoyment of expressing love. This becomes our commitment. We nourish ourselves with the love we express. A warrior acts in this committed way, even when challenged.

In my point of view, Jesus Christ was the greatest Warrior. He had the courage, discipline, and openness to Love unconditionally even as he was being rejected and physically persecuted during his days. Even when his body was in physical pain, the only emotions he created and expressed were of love and compassion. He did not use a reason in his mind to hate or judge. This is extraordinary impeccability. If he could love in his challenges, then we can learn to love unconditionally in our challenges. (38)

MYTHS OF THE SPIRITUAL WARRIORS

BHAGAVAD GITA

Spiritual warriors are prevalent in more than just Christianity as we have come to learn. For example, the Bhagavad Gita, often referred to as just "the Gita", contains the teachings of Lord Krishna to the great warrior Arjuna. The pair were recognised as the ideal follower and devotee. The teachings, or conversations, take place in India during the Great War over the kingdom. This Great War is indeed historically accurate and we can take it as a metaphor for the spiritual war waging within us. Below we explore these teachings through the musings of Bina Mehta.

THE GREAT WAR

The war in the Bhagavad Gita takes place on the Dharmakshetre Kurukshetre field, which is physically located to the north of the modern city of New Delhi. Interpreted literally, Kurukshetre means "field of consciousness," a term which also refers to the metaphorical field where we are the actors at the centre of our own stage. We are constantly waging war within ourselves to make discriminating choices each moment of every day. To do or not to do, to be or not to be. Kurukshetre, the battlefield of the heart, is in every human being. The tension between human good and evil as humans is eternal. On the battlefield, Lord Krishna delivers his instructions to Arjuna to fulfil his dharma by fighting the battle and relinquishing all the fruits of action to God. (39)

DHARMA, THE SACRED DUTY

The word dharma seems rather simplistic but has a thousand meanings. Dharma, which means "sacred duty," is constantly repeated throughout the Gita and attests to its significance for the Indian civilisation. The term Dharma expresses the idea that sustains the Hindu concept of religion — one's sacred duty refers to the moral order that sustains the cosmos, individuals, and society.

The spiritual warrior faced with the inner conflict in the Bhagavad Gita is Arjuna, whose name means "one who makes sincere effort." Here, he represents the soul of everyman or atman. Krishna represents the centre of Divine Consciousness, the higher self of everyman or the charioteer of the soul.

The problem that Arjuna faces symbolises the moral struggle between the two halves of human nature, forces of light versus forces of darkness. IT is interesting to note the similarity to Anakin's journey in which the forces of dark won out and how Luke Skywalker was faced with a similar challenge and chose the light side. This narrative of light versus dark continues to be played out in the dynamic between Rey and Kylo Ren. This is the inner war, or the War Within, that every human must wage for self-mastery over his sensual and animal instincts. Emerging victorious in this war is attaining truth or moksha, which is freedom from attachments and worldly entanglements. (40)

ARJUNA'S DILEMMA

Arjuna is fearful, frustrated, and despondent as he looks across the Kurukshetre field to see all his cousins, friends, teachers and kinsmen. He has to wage war against them. Although he is a great warrior, Arjuna finds that his courage has failed him and is unwilling to fight against all of his loved ones. As a dharmic duty of a Kshatriya - the warrior caste - if he does not fight, he will achieve the reputation of a coward. If he does fight and is defeated in battle, he will be honoured for having performed his duty. Arjuna has to rise above this dilemma and perform his selfless service as a warrior without any expectation of results. He must rely on his resolve to act according to his dharma. That decision in itself will lead him to a state of deathlessness or liberation.

Krishna instructs Arjuna to embrace the spiritual path to end his suffering. When Arjuna renounces his fears and accepts his duty, his yoga begins. Hence, the dark night of the soul of this spiritual warrior is viewed as a preparatory ground for his yoga sadhana. The Upanishads call this "the razor edge path," as this path is not for the meek or frail at heart. Making a choice to rise above one's situation will require the alchemy of tapas, the trial by fire, being burnished and brandished in order for the fierce warrior to emerge as a shining jewel, radiating his true authentic Self. (41)

SHAMBHALA

This idea of battling a war within in order to face the external wars is present in Tibetan beliefs as well. The universal enemy, according to Tibetan Buddhism, is self-ignorance. A hero must be brave and ethical; compassionately helping others with their wisdom. This is known as the Bodhisattva ideal – or the Buddha-in-waiting.

Tibetan Buddhist teacher, Chogyam Trungpa, established the Shambhala Training Program as a way to teach peaceful warriorship that was based on sitting meditative practices. To these Buddhists, warriorship was not defined by seeking war with others, but by being brave within oneself. They believed that overt aggression was the source of all problems and not the solution. Many people today, as we've discussed, feel this way about aggression, but only because it has historically been misguided. We, as Kundalini Jedi Warriors, must see with the heart, that which is invisible to the naked eye, as Trungpa believed.

After the adoption of Mahayana Buddhism in Tibet, the concept of Shambhala was incorporated and became synonymous with a mythological kingdom of peace and beauty where people lived in harmony. It is said that people who lived here were wise, courageous and compassionate.

These ideas were first brought back to the West by a Portuguese Catholic missionary Estêvão Cacella, who had heard about Shambhala and sought it out. For centuries thereafter, explorers scoured the areas surrounding Tibet in search of the Kingdom to learn its secrets.

Helena Blavatsky is the one who brought these teachings to the west after she made such a journey to Tibet in the 19th century. We'll explore the great prophecy of Shamballa below.

PROPHESY OF SHAMBHALA

It says that this is a time when two great powers, one in the West and one in the East, are set on destruction and, though they have much in common, are focused only on the accumulation of weapons of unimaginable horror, intent on crushing each other. "Coming to us across twelve centuries, the Shambhala prophecy comes from ancient Tibetan Buddhism. The prophecy foretells a time when all life on Earth is in danger. Great barbarian powers have arisen. Although these powers spend much of their wealth in preparations to annihilate each other, they have much in common: weapons of unfathomable destructive power, and technologies that lay waste to our world. In this era, when the future of sentient life hangs by the frailest of threads, the kingdom of Shambhala emerges. It seems the survival of every sentient being is at threat. It is a time of apocalypse. It is at this time of great turmoil and fear that the kingdom of Shambhala arises. And from this kingdom comes warriors to overthrow the purveyors of hate and weapons. (42)

WHO ARE SHAMBHALA WARRIORS?

Shambhala warriors have no uniform, no insignia, they may not even recognise each other on the street. It is an individual path. But these people of spirit are called upon to go into the corridors of power and to dismantle the weapons of mass destruction. From within, the Shambhala warriors bring about great change and healing. The Shambhala warriors know that the forces of destruction do not come from outside ourselves but from within; that it is our own greed and fear and hate that creates the weapons that now threaten the world. (43)

TOLTEC WARRIOR

The Toltec culture thrived in what we now know as Mexico; ruling from their capital of Tollan - known today as Tula. They were known across the region for being incredibly fierce warriors. This is the story of the Toltecs

The Toltecs, led by Mixcóatl (meaning 'Cloud Serpent') sacked and burned Teotihuacan around 900 AD. Indeed, the Toltecs were famed as warriors, and it was under them that militarism was introduced into Mesoamerica. For instance, the Toltecs had various military orders, including that of the Jaguar and the Eagle, which were introduced to the Maya, their southern neighbours.

In a way, Toltec warfare may be said to have had a religious aspect to it. The Toltecs were worshippers of the God Quetzalcoatl, and they sought to spread his cult amongst the peoples they defeated in war. This effort was successful, considering the fact that Quetzalcoatl's cult spread as far south as the Yucatan peninsula, where he was worshipped by the Maya as Kukulkan. Moreover, in the pantheon of the Aztecs, who may be considered to be the successors of the Toltecs, Quetzalcoatl was one of the major Gods.
(44)

According to Toltec expert Allan Harman, there are three masteries on this Toltec path: Awareness, Transformation, and Intent. In the mastery of awareness, the human awakens to discover they are dreaming an old dream fed into their mind by others—parents, siblings, friends, teachers, religious leaders—and that it has little to do with who they really are and who they came here to be. They discover how those beliefs and agreements filter and distort every bit of incoming information from the outside world…then and only then can the human become a spiritual warrior and free himself or herself from the constraints of the past. We say "Warrior" because there is a battle to be fought. The warrior must fight the forces that expect quiet servitude to the agreed-upon rules of a small life. The warrior knows this struggle for freedom begins within, and then carries its power into the world. The warrior enters this battle not even knowing if he or she will win, but knowing there is no choice but to fight for the freedom the soul demands. This battle is fought with love and a gentle strength that grows stronger and more resilient as a gift from the very struggle itself. With awareness, the new warrior can "stalk" their limiting and confusing beliefs, and begin to determine which ones don't serve their adult life.

As the old dream is revealed and changed, the apprentice enters the mastery of transformation. A new dream is created from the release of old fear-based beliefs and a conscious choice of new ones based in love and acceptance.

As the Toltec warrior continues to transform their dream, a time comes when he or she realises they are experiencing real personal freedom, and a loving relationship with themselves and with all of creation. This is the mastery of intent, the mastery of love. The many fears from the past no longer rule the warrior's life and he or she is free to simply be happy and IN love for no reason. This, then, is the goal of the Toltec Path of Transformation.
(45)

The young men and women that were referred to as warriors undertook the battle to control their ego. Once they were able to do so and move away from material desires, their spirits could flourish. The spiritual warrior, after all, is someone who challenges the fears and false beliefs that have created suffering in their own lives. Their war does not take place on the battle ground but in their own hearts and minds. In order to win that battle, you must also go into it with the understanding that the supreme truth and unconditional love are on the other side of the internal battlefield.

The purpose of the battle was to fully rid the warrior of temptations towards materialistic tendencies. The body is merely a vessel through which you can reach spiritual transcendence. You will never be able to live wholly if you live for the satisfaction of material impulses. The more you gain, the more you'll want. Therefore, power and wealth are elements of the material world and do not serve you if they are your only driving force in life.

The Toltecs were incredibly humble. Humility is something that can only be derived from wisdom, and wisdom can only come through experiencing your warrior journey. When you live within your ego, you appear arrogant and overbearing; losing all sense of humility and the knowledge that pre-empts it. Lowliness is as much the aftereffect of an internal devotion to poise as it is the development of awareness and, consequently, of comprehension.

Shaolin Monks, much like Toltecs, were regarded as the most loyal soldiers. Shaolin is a martial art but it is also part of a complete spirituality that is grounded in Buddhism. Shaolin Monks are known to give up almost all material facets, and restrain themselves from typical pleasures that we enjoy. They are completely dedicated to their faith. It is one of the most respected forms of martial arts in the world. Let's explore the Shaolin ways as according to Learning Shaolin Kung Fu.

ORIGIN OF THE SHAOLIN

The origin of all martial arts leads back to the famous Shaolin Temple in Henan Province in China. 1500 years before the Indian monk Bodhidharma - also known as Ta Mo - came to the Shaolin temple and found the Shaolin monks in a catastrophic health condition. He taught Buddhism to an already existing group of monks, and also taught some form of martial arts based on Indian martial arts and/or dance. The reason he did this was variously given as the monks were out of shape, or needed to defend themselves, or China was too cold to sit in yoga meditation and so he invented a moving meditation. Bodhidharma developed the 18 boxing techniques of Shaolin and trained the monks to prepare their body condition willingly for the long meditations. The exercises should promote the health of the monks, the steely muscles and stimulate the internal organs, so they live longer. (46)

Shaolin Kungfu practiced by monks from Shaolin Monastery takes martial arts to a brand-new level. As Shaolin warriors believe the strength comes only from the mind, there are almost no limits to what can be done with their bodies during the training. They practice techniques centred around balance, strength, endurance, and self-defence. They can endure incredible amounts of pain while barely flinching. The design and arrangements of their movements are based on the medical knowledge of ancient China and conforms to the rule of movement of the human body.

WHAT DOES SHAOLIN MEAN?

The 'Shao' in "Shaolin" refers to "Mount Shaoshi", a mountain in the Songshan mountain range. The 'lin' in "Shaolin" means "forest". Literally, the name means "Monastery in the woods of Mount Shaoshi". Chinese folklore related to this practice include "All martial arts under heaven originated from Shaolin" and "Shaolin kung fu is the best under heaven," indicating the influence of Shaolin kung fu among martial arts.

The monks use Qi Gong and a special method of breathing with the lower abdomen to transform their bodies into armor. This allows them to withstand powerful blows, including those from dangerous—and sometimes sharp—objects. By cultivating their inner calmness, they are able to ward off mental, physical, and emotional stress. They also use QiGong to ward off injury.

Meditation helps with pain. Breathing and relaxation are known to combat discomfort. To take one's mind away from the source of pain, an individual may focus his or her mind on other parts of the body.

While Shaolin monks seem to achieve the impossible, they have simply developed their minds and bodies in ways that allow them to perform extraordinary feats of mental and physical strength by tapping into their internal energy and through physical conditioning. (47)

A Harvard study confirmed that Tibetan monks can actually raise their body temperatures with their minds. Known as g-tummo meditators, these individuals are able to dry wet sheets that are wrapped around their cold, naked bodies. It is worth noting that few possess this rare skill. Only a handful of monasteries in the Chinese provinces of Qinghai and Sichuan practice this type of meditation.

Dr. Benson, the Director Emeritus of the Benson-Henry Institute and Mind Body Medicine Professor of Medicine, Harvard Medical School, carried out his research in the 1980s. He determined that finger and toe temperatures increased due to vasodilation, which involves widening of the blood vessels to reduce blood pressure. (48)

WARRIOR QUALITIES

Warriors are forceful souls and do their best to balance their self-interest and altruism. They embody qualities of strength, courage, and determination. They are action-oriented beings, who are down-to-earth, single-minded, and very wilful. Warriors are willing to lay down their lives for king and country – for a cause, religion, or crusade. For justice. They strongly value both courage and loyalty. Warrior souls approach their work and life as a kind of personal battle or test. Remaining always alert and awake - ever vigilant - they have a keen situational awareness, developed through years of training and experience. They keep their senses sharp and they never let complacency lull them to sleep; instead, he is always watching, observing, studying, and planning.

They have a positive outlook and respect for the impermanence of life and so they are not afraid to die. Life's shortness brings clarity to the mind. You may have a lot of warrior energy by default; either learned or part of your basic makeup. It may even be an aspect of yourself that you feel you need to develop.

WARRIOR QUALITIES

- Courageous
- Fearless
- A knight in shining armor
- Loyal
- Generous
- Self-sacrificing
- Driven
- Mastery of self
- Focused on victory

Warriors are also closely linked with the knights of old but in a somewhat more refined way. The classical idea of a knight is someone who is a medieval gentleman-soldier, usually high-born, raised by a sovereign to privileged military status after training as a page and squire. A man belonging to an order or brotherhood. Think of the Knights of the Round Table in the tales of King Arthur, or the Knights of the Jedi Council in Star Wars. Knights are portrayed as being a defender, a champion, or an upholder of a worthy cause or principle - which at the time would usually be the king, the queen, and the kingdom.

The most well-known depiction of the knight archetype is the knight in shining armour; the devoted champion of a fair maiden. We see Luke inhabiting this quality as he searches for the princess and then attempts to rescue her. However, take note of how Princess Leia was a warrior in her own right; having to save Han and Luke via the trash compactor in their failed attempt to rescue her.

In the Star Wars movies, the Jedi are described or named as Jedi knights for a good reason. I previously mentioned how George Lucas used inspiration from Arthurian legends and the knights of the round table who are chivalrous and who embody many positive qualities that parallel the Jedi.

Luke seems to embody these qualities naturally, wanting to devote himself to the honourable mission of saving the princess; believing in the larger mission of the rebellion that goes beyond his own wants and needs. The medieval knights have common characteristics and ways of being which could be thought of as knightly virtues. Let's have a look at these 7 Knightly Virtues according to Mark Toci.

COURAGE: More than bravado or bluster, today's knight in shining armour must have the courage of the heart necessary to undertake tasks which are difficult, tedious or unglamorous, and to graciously accept the sacrifices involved. A trip to the dentist can become a courageous act or perhaps going to our mundane 9-5 job with a boss we don't like and even standing up for human rights violations we wish to stand up for.

JUSTICE: A knight in shining armour holds him- or herself to the highest standard of behaviour, and knows that lying or bending the rules weakens the fabric of society for everyone and would be a dishonourable thing for a knight to do, they have an inherent sense of integrity doing what's right when no one is looking.

MERCY: Words carry a powerful vibration and can be used to create or to destroy. Our attitudes can be painful weapons or a healing balm that literally creates the world we experience. At first glance it may seem like a weakness "to let somebody get away for their injustices" but for the knight the opposite is true. This act of compassion or forbearance shown especially to an offender could be seen as "a blessing that is an act of divine favour or compassion." which ultimately makes the knight stronger showing their true power.

GENEROSITY: Sharing what's valuable in life means not just giving away material goods, but also time, attention, wisdom, and energy — the things that create a strong, rich, and diverse community.

FAITH: In the code of chivalry, "faith" means trust and integrity, and a knight in shining armour is always faithful to his or her promises, no matter how big or small they may be. They continue to serve their missions with the belief they will always succeed.

NOBILITY: Although this word is sometimes confused with "entitlement" or "snobbishness," in the code of chivalry it conveys the importance of upholding one's convictions at all times, especially when no one else is watching.

HOPE: More than just a safety net in times of tragedy, hope is present every day in a modern knight's positive outlook and cheerful demeanour — the shining armour that shields him or her which also inspires people all around. When the community sees a knight people naturally become hopeful and uplifted feeling safe in their presence. (49) While each virtue is admirable in itself, when blended together these qualities portray the incredibly high value that chivalry has in the modern-day world. Kundalini Jedi Warriors should strive to keep these virtues. They should inspire those around them to do the same.

KNIGHTLY QUALITIES

- Hope
- Nobility
- Integrity
- Faith
- Mercy
- Justice

***

CHAPTER 9: YOGA

> *"True. yoga is not about the shape of your body, but the shape of your life. Yoga is not to be performed; yoga is to be lived. Yoga doesn't care about what you have been; yoga cares about the person you are becoming. Yoga is designed for a vast and profound purpose, and for it to be truly called yoga, its essence must be embodied."*
>
> — Aadil Palkhivala, Co-Founder of the Purna Yoga College

YOGIS

The conventional image of a skinny flexible person who spends their time levitating - or maybe they are just sleeping while sitting up - is what normally comes to mind when we think of a traditional yogi from far off distant lands. In this manual, however, we define a yogi as any person who practices yoga in the pursuit of aligning the mind, body, and spirit; with aims to be reflective in their attempts to understand the mystical side of life as well as how they embody qualities similar to the Jedi from Star Wars.

The Yogis are the Jedi of our galaxy. They are skilled, disciplined, focused, and are seekers of the truth and guardians of peace. Yogis are people that live a certain lifestyle and exude certain qualities. They practice in clear, step-by-step means and strive to refine and control the body through close examination of the heart and mind. To them, this is the only real way to become liberated and come to a self realisation. They will seek to evolve to their fullest spiritual potential. They constantly work towards shaping their own habits and behaviours in order to align themselves more wholly with the teachings and ethics of yoga.

Whether we like to admit it or not, we are all longing for a connection to the Force and to each other. They aim to solidify this connection through the embodiment of kindness, compassion and patience. As we know, the Jedi possess these qualities too, and we have the choice to create unity using our Kundalini Jedi Warrior skills. Yoga is, therefore, not an activity, but a way of life.

A yogi will practice meditation, moderate his diet and sleep patterns, and do daily yoga to keep alignment with the supreme force. They will be disciplined, self-aware, and constantly looking to achieve inner balance and harmony.

The lifestyle of a yogi can seem very boring to the everyday person. They spend their time not indulging the senses through intoxication but through the exploration of their mind-body connection; as opposed to hanging out down at the pub and having a few cigs with friends. Yogis tend to spend a lot of time in nature, or in solitude; staying away from negative people and chaotic environments. They are not interested in human dramas and do not watch the latest soap operas on TV. They live in a simple way; staying away from unhelpful situations to reduce stress, and anxiety, which in turn allows them the peace of mind that they need in order to connect deeply with the Force energy. They aim to be at one with the Force around them and fulfil their potential as human beings.

Jedi seek harmony with the Force and the principles that govern the universe. They are committed to perfecting themselves until they connect with their Jedi nature. The general idea is that, individually, we are like the waves of a great ocean. That means that we're all connected and we share the same essence. We're all made of a body, a mind, and a soul - an individual soul that is united and is part of a universal soul. Yogis believe that they can increase how much of a reflection of this absolute Force that they are; believing that it is within them and of which they are the means.

There are two types of yogis: renunciants or householders. Renunciants leave common life to retreat to their spiritual practice in a cave or near a mountain top. In Star Wars - a new hope , we find Obi-Wan all alone in the desert - not an uncommon place for a yogi to retreat to. This way they can strengthen their connection with the Force. The other approach - the householder's yogi - wishes to connect to the Force but retain their responsibilities to their family, work, bills, and social life. The path of the Jedi warrior may be filled with householder duties. This path can be more challenging and we can have a harder time establishing a regular practice, but we are also more likely to interact with other people and contribute to the common good.

HABITS OF THE YOGI

Yogis get up early to begin their "sadhana" or spiritual practice. They go to bed early and wake up early with great precision. They are very disciplined; quickly connecting with their breath and with the new mental state to make universal energy manifest through them. They make gentle unblocking movements; visualising their day, and using external and internal cleansing methods such as, drinking tea with lemon and moving their abdomen in circles to allow good movement and expulsion of toxins.

They utilise a combination of asanas - or yoga positions - breathing exercises, and meditation. The idea is to internalise and connect with the self. They must, therefore, transcend the body itself. They must charge themselves with energy, direct their senses inward, appease their thoughts, and meditate on the individual or absolute self.

They may drink vegetable juices or eat oats with nuts and rice milk, for example, but they don't forget that they should not live on food alone. Yogis nourish not only their physical bodies but also their energetic and spiritual bodies. Some of the methods they use are:

- Eating essentially fresh food, especially vegetables;
- Doing breathing exercises to get oxygen and eliminate carbon dioxide residues;
- Exercises to vitalise the body but not lower their energy; and,
- Going out to get some fresh air and to be in the sun for a while.

They eat in moderation to facilitate digestion and eat fibre to facilitate evacuation. Not wasting too much sexual energy is essential, as this brings great vitality. They nourish their spiritual body with meditation. Their goal is to maintain a meditative state all day.

Regarding work, Yogis understand that they have the right and duty to work in order to generate sufficient resources so that they and their families can live with dignity. They seek to fulfil a job according to their talent or nature, or one that is rooted in their social or family environment. They always seek a role with a vocation for service. They also seek to participate in projects that offer a social service; improving people's lives, and helping them to develop awareness. Yogis renounce the fruit of their actions. They do everything the best way they can, without worrying about the results since they know that results depend on many factors. They work with enthusiasm; maximising positive actions, and following the life principles of traditional teachings based on respect, nonviolence, truthfulness, and honesty.

When they return home, it's time to share and enjoy life with their family. They eat a light dinner and combine it with time for self-study; observing how their day has gone. They read a paragraph of the sacred texts and finish their day meditating to reconnect and offer the fruits of their actions. They freshen up and wash before going to sleep with high consciousness.

So, if the Force is truly existent then there are things, we can do to manifest it and qualities we can develop that will allow us to connect and flow with the energy of the Force. The yogi will practice and develop certain attributes to help achieve this. Let's explore them below.

ATTRIBUTES OF THE YOGI

1.**EVEN MINDEDNESS:** According to the ancient yogic scripture, until one attains the state of oneness and connection to the Force, most of our lives are based on action-orientated effort to get things done. Once a connection to the Force is felt and experienced, we develop an even- mindedness or oneness with life and the things that happen knowing that there is a greater force at work. So, we give up our desires, attachments, preferences, and expectations, and put our will and trust in the Force. The Kundalini Jedi Warrior remains unattached to anything and anyone and keeps a balanced mind in everything that they experience.

2. **SELF LOVE:** This is not a sort of "I love myself", self-help affirmation approach to self-love but a way of relating to yourself as if you are a unique expression of the universal Force. The yogi has perceived and accepted this ultimate truth so thus they have no inner conflicts. In the Star Wars saga both Anakin Skywalker and Kylo Ren experience a great conflict within themselves - the pull to the Dark-side of the force. The yogi/yogini overcomes this pull through their behaviour and self-restraint, which gives a true reflection of his inner purity and tranquillity. Since they do not engage in any self-destructive and inimical actions they can best be described as a friend to himself.

3. **SELF-CONQUEROR:** By conquering his mind and body, the yogi remains peaceful and tranquil; with his mind absorbed in the contemplation and service of the Force. Further, with complete control over his mind and body, and free from desires, attachments, attraction and aversion, he remains undisturbed and serene amidst the pairs of opposites such as heat and cold, pain and pleasure, honour and dishonour.

4. **CONTENTED SOUL:** Free from desires and attachments, the yogi is content with whatever he has and in whatever situation he finds himself. You could say that they live in a frequency of gratitude and do not struggle or strive to improve their condition or try to Force divine will. Treating gold and clay alike, the Yogi is endowed with knowledge and wisdom that everything is the will of God. They accept all and go with the flow; doing their duties and living their lives as a sacrifice.

5. **BALANCED AND RESTRAINED:** The ancient scriptures clearly state that, for a yogi, balance is a key development on the spiritual path towards liberation. Yoga is not for the one who eats or sleeps excessively, or for the one who does not sleep or eat at all. The yogi is working towards moderation; taking the middle-path by controlling what they eat, and getting the right amount of rest to function effectively. Their approach is one of coming into balance with the environment around them; living as nature intended and living in balance with the Force.

6. **ONE WITH THE FORCE:** Through the practice of yoga the yogi is able to overcome the desires and cravings of the mind by withdrawing and restraining his senses. He remains totally focused through meditation; mastering his chattering mind and leaving him undisturbed as well as completely absorbed in the Force. In that state of connection, he is happy in himself, and experiences infinite bliss and Oneness. This is in contrast to the ordinary people whose minds remain disturbed and preoccupied with worldly matters and materiality. They remember God only in times of distress or when everything else they have tried has failed.

YOGI QUALITIES

- Self-loving
- Compassionate
- Even minded
- Self-conqueror
- Intuitive
- Oneness
- Balanced
- Nurturing

*

JEDI LIFE

"For over a thousand generations, the Jedi Knights were the guardians of peace and justice in the Old Republic."
- Obi-Wan Kenobi, Star Wars: Episode IV - A New Hope

Jedi, like Yogis, make lifestyle choices that bring them towards a place of "sattva" - or purity - a state of equanimity and inner peace. They aim to clear the body of all toxins, thought forms, and habits that would stop or inhibit the flow of the Force energy.

THE CREED

I am a Jedi, an instrument of peace; Where there is hatred, I shall bring love; Where there is injury, pardon; Where there is doubt, faith; Where there is despair, hope; Where there is darkness, light; And where there is sadness, joy. I am a Jedi. I shall never seek so much to be consoled as to console; To be understood as to understand; To be loved as to love; For it is in giving that we receive; It is in pardoning that we are pardoned. And it is in dying that we are born to eternal life. The Force is with me always, for I am a Jedi.
- The Creed was adopted from the Prayer of St. Francis of Assisi, author unknown, 1915.

A large reason for the success of Star Wars has been the creation and introduction of the Jedi Knights. The classic narrative of good versus evil is played out through the battles and confrontation between the Jedi - who represent the light-side of the Force - and the Sith - who represent the dark side. All the movies tell the story and saga of the Skywalker family who was strong in their connection to the Force.

According to the history of Star Wars, the Jedi have existed for more than 25,000 years and at their peak, there were almost 10,000 strong Jedi in the universe. Through the films, we became familiar with the remaining Jedi as we shared their adventures fighting for the light against the dark.

Jedi Knights respect all life by defending and protecting those who cannot do it for themselves. A Jedi was a Force-sensitive individual, most often a member of the Jedi Order, who studied, served, and used the mystical energies of the Force; striving for peaceful and non-combative solutions to any altercations they encountered and fighting only in self-defence for those they protect.

The Jedi aim to remove blockages between them and the Force while simultaneously helping the individuals that they come into contact with. They are active peacekeepers and are charitable in nature. They denounce negative emotions such as fear and anger; believing that these cause us to lash out; impeding our rationality.

JEDI AND STOICISM

The Jedi are exceptionally stoic in their ways, much like Yogis. Adam Klinker, of Creighton University, perhaps said it best as he unravelled the parallels between historic stoics and the Jedi. The Jedi present themselves in a very stoic way. Stoic philosophy arose in ancient Greece around 300 B.C. and enjoyed a significant following in Rome. The Stoics taught a philosophy of living in agreement with nature while calmly fulfilling all of one's familial, social, and professional roles. To live in agreement with nature, they believed, required accepting the aspects of the world that you cannot change, doing the best you can with what you've got, and focus on improving what is in your power — namely, your own beliefs, judgments, and emotions. Some two dozen centuries onward — although placed in a time long ago and in a galaxy far, far away — Yoda and the Jedi seek to impart similar lessons on disciplining one's mind to harmonise with the logic and reason of the Force.

In Star Wars and Philosophy, an essay about Stoicism in the films, William Stephens compares the Jedi philosophy to Stoicism. "The Stoics teach that true power is self-mastery," says Stephens, "... its self-fulfilment, self-containment. It's not controlling other people. That's tyranny and that's what Yoda and the Jedi fight against when it comes to the Dark Side." (50)

Kevin Decker and Jason T Eberl tie in their own take on the matter in their paper on popular culture and philosophy. Stoicism holds that the key to a good, happy life is the cultivation of an excellent mental state, which the Stoics identified with virtue and being rational. The ideal life is one that is in harmony with Nature, of which we are all part and an attitude of calm indifference towards external events. To recap, the virtues the Jedi shares with the Stoic sages are patience, timeliness, deep commitment, seriousness (as opposed to frivolity), calmness (as opposed to anger or euphoria), peacefulness (as opposed to aggression), caution (as opposed to recklessness), benevolence (as opposed to hatred), joy (as opposed to sullenness), passivity (as opposed to agitation), and wisdom. Given all these virtues, Yoda certainly resembles what the ancient Stoics described. The Stoics also keep an eye out for signs of the future, another trait held in common with the Jedi. Yoda employs this tactic with some caution — "Difficult to see, always in motion, is the future," he tells Luke when the Jedi-in-training wishes to abandon his studies to help his friends. When young Anakin Skywalker reports his premonitions of his loved ones suffering and dying, Yoda cautions him that the fear of loss is the path to the Dark Side and that death is a natural part of life. These are important Stoic teachings. (51)

QUALITIES OF A JEDI

- Stoic
- Reflective
- Aligned to a Higher Power
- Aligned to Nature
- In service of others
- Negotiators
- Calm
- Protector
- Teacher
- Guide
- Skilled in the Force
- Accepting
- In the flow
- Wise

*

KUNDALINI JEDI WARRIOR

A Kundalini Jedi Warrior will train their mind to be calm, balanced and non-reactive. They will uplift others through word and deed. They will be hopeful and optimistic about the future and wish to establish a golden age of peace through service and love. They will have a deep connection to humanity and the plight of the planet. They will also possess a deep desire to help, heal, and save wherever they can; with their ultimate aim being to leave the earth in a better state than when they found it.

They will be unique in the way that they inhabit and use the Force. Being a Kundalini Jedi Warrior is not about being some perfect, ideal copy of Luke Skywalker - or some other hero, for that matter. In the movies, the Jedi inhabit the same principles but deliver them in very unique ways. Becoming a Kundalini Jedi Warrior will change you to bring out the fullness of your nature and the fullness of your potential; not to be different, but to be more of who you are. Life can be a serious business and we need some light and laughter to raise our frequency. Being a KJW means you can uplift people with your presence.

A Kundalini Jedi Warrior is someone who understands that they are a spiritual being having a human experience who is willing to dedicate his life to the service of the Force, to uplifting the frequency of the planet through battling their dark side, and to raising their inner frequencies.

What type of Jedi would you like to be? Take some time to reflect on the qualities below and record your observations in your Jedi journal.

QUALITIES OF A KUNDALINI JEDI WARRIOR

- Stoicism
- Reflective
- Higher power alignment
- Natural Alignment
- In their flow
- Negotiators
- Possesses Force skills
- In service of others
- Possesses oneness

- Protectors
- Teachers
- Guides
- Calm
- Accepting
- Balanced
- Compassionate
- Nurturing
- Intuitive

- Self-conqueror
- Even-minded
- Self-loving
- Hopeful
- Noble
- Person of Integrity
- Faithful
- Merciful
- Just

*

POWER OF THE UNIVERSE

"If you want to find the secrets of the universe, think in terms of energy, frequency and vibration."

— **Nikola Tesla, Inventor, Engineer, Futurist**

In the previous chapters, we explored the qualities of the warrior, the yogi, and what a Kundalini Jedi could be. Now we will begin to look at how the tools of yoga can help us develop and actualise our new archetype.

I used to think that yogis were just these skinny weird dudes who lived in remote caves high up in the Himalayan mountains or wandered around dense Indian forests with a loin cloth and no job. I believed that they could levitate, lived for 100s of years, and didn't need food because they had special powers, but I had no real aspirations to become one or ever meet one.

Although, to be quite fair, living in a cave away from the world sounded rather appealing. Now that I am a 'grown up ' - I use this term loosely - I've realised that these yogis were masters of the human condition. They had a scientific approach to finding out how to connect with the divine. They researched through personal experience; trying and testing different methods to understand the energy of their body and to uncover the mysteries of the universe. Through fasting, body postures, and various breathing techniques they attempted to merge with the powerful energy of the divine - to realise the truth of reality. These yogis were interested in self-actualisation so that they could achieve God realisation and reach a state of perfection, as well as an enlightened way of living.

Today, in the west, we now have access to these ancient practices, tools, and technology of yoga. They aid us in living healthier lifestyles and restoring balance back to the world. Through the consistent practice of yoga methodology, we can experience a huge individual transformation of our being and manifest a healthy change in the world.

Although yoga is a powerful self-help tool that we receive many personal benefits from, we must also be aware of the greater application of yoga. We are not here merely for ourselves but our practice of yoga also extends to our friends, families, communities, even to all citizens of the earth and the future generations. When we practice with this intention, we are healing the wounds of 7 generations past and preparing the path for the next 7 generations.

We have a lot of work to do, but before we do it, we must first learn how to tune our bodies in. You must know how to raise your vibrations before you begin with your first Kundalini yoga experience.

*

SOUND, VIBRATION & FREQUENCY

We live in a sea of sound. Everything around us is giving off a vibration - however subtle that may be. Vibes are the emotional signals that a person gives out to those around them with their body language and social interactions. An example of good vibes is a happy person smiling and having a positive effect on those around them.

When people say 'high vibe', they're usually referring to something positive. High vibe is another way to describe when something is operating at a high energetic frequency. The higher the frequencies are, the closer to unconditional love the person is. On the opposite end of that spectrum, the lower the frequencies are, the closer to fear the person is.

You will usually be able to feel whether something is vibrating at a high or low frequency from the way you begin to feel emotionally. The heavier it feels in your body, the more uncomfortable you will begin to feel. This usually signals you to move away from that person, place, or experience. The lighter it feels in your body, and the sense of well-being you begin to experience, will usually signal that you are closer to the vibration of love.

The experiments by Japanese scientist Masau Emoto provided real evidence of this vibrational phenomena. In his ground-breaking book, *'The Messages in the Water'*, Dr. Emoto demonstrates how different sound frequencies changed and altered the structure of water. He found that water exposed to loving, benevolent, and compassionate human intention resulted in aesthetically pleasing physical molecular formations in the water. While water exposed to fearful and discordant human intentions results in disconnected, disfigured, and "unpleasant" physical molecular formations. He did this through magnetic resonance; analysis technology which gradually freezes the water whilst a camera captures high speed photographs. You can find examples of this photographic evidence in the Appendix.

JEDI VIBRATIONAL EXERCISE

List 5 people that you personally know whom you feel a high positive vibe from. You will notice this vibe in the form of a feeling that you enjoy their company, or feel uplifted around them. These are also generally people that you regard as good people.

Now make a list of 5 people who you feel have a negative vibe from. You will notice that when you spend time with them you leave feeling, irritated, down, or sad. These can be people who always seem to have a dark cloud hanging over them regardless of what is happening around them. They could be argumentative people who are easily able to find fault with most things.

Collect your insights in your training manual. Reflect on times you have felt you had positive vibes and circumstances where you felt low vibes.

*

MANTRAS

The mantras which we use in Kundalini Yoga are traditionally a sacred Indian language known as Gurmukhi. Some of the mantras will be in English, but they will both contain peaceful vibrations, as well as those of prosperity and connection. Before we begin any of our yoga practices or meditations, we tune our frequency to a higher vibration. See if you can experience any change in yourself when you do this. Try it a few times and, if you still have resistance, continue on to the exercises. So, we have spoken about the power of the fear frequency and how our thoughts, sounds, and environments change our vibrations. Mantra and sound healing has been used for thousands of years to change our state of consciousness and even alter our state completely. These sounds bypass our natural defences and impact us deeply on a cellular level. The sounds we hear around us affect our health and vitality. The Universe is made up of vibration and, as such, sound is not only a most potent tool in maintaining and creating our sense of well-being, but it can also be used to heal the body, mind, and spirit.

TUNING IN MANTRA

Before we can begin with any Kundalini Yoga, we must use the Adi Mantra. Adi means 'first' or 'primal' and it is a powerful sound frequency which sets our mind and body up for deep inner practice. It clears the energetic space around us and within us. Ong Namo Guru Dev Namo is an Adi Mantra which means 'I bow to the Creative Wisdom, I bow to the Divine Teacher within, or I bow to the teacher within me and I bow to all the teachers that have existed before.' This tuning in mantra is used to connect to the divine flow as well as our innate internal knowledge. The Adi Mantra connects us to the Golden Chain, also known as the chain of teachers. The Golden Chain is the channel through which the energy, the wisdom, and the protection of the tradition flow to you.

By chanting this mantra and linking ourselves to the Golden Chain, the exercises and meditations that you practice are guided by your higher consciousness. They are guided by all of the teachers that have brought this opportunity to you. It makes you very receptive and sensitive to the message of your body, mind, and intuition.

We chant to connect to the essence of all sound or Naad. Even in perfect silence, there is always a sound within us – the beating of our own hearts; the rushing of our blood streams. When we actively regulate our own sounds through the use of such tuning in mantras, we can alter our health and overall wellbeing for the better. It is no secret that our thoughts can have a profound effect on our health, and we can, therefore, bio hack our way to good health using mantra, breathwork and rhythms.

SAT NAM

One such mantra, as described in this excerpt from 3HO, is *Sat Nam* or *Truth is my identity*. This mantra reinforces the divine consciousness in everyone and is one of the most used mantras in Kundalini Yoga. It is used as a greeting as well as the mantra for Kundalini Yoga exercises, inhaling Sat (truth), exhaling Nam (name, identity). Chanting the mantra, Sat Nam, awakens your soul and gives you your destiny. Sat means Truth—the reality of one's existence. Nam means name or identity. It instantly attunes us to our highest self. Sat Nam affirms that Truth is our Identity. Sat Nam is a bija mantra, a seed sound. Within the seed is all the knowledge of the fully grown tree. Bij mantras are sounds that rearrange the habit patterns of the subconscious mind. (52)

WAHEGURU

This mantra expresses the indescribable experience of going from darkness to light. It is a mantra of infinite ecstasy. It could be Translated as "Wow!" The divine inner teacher, or the dispeller of darkness is beyond description, or I am in ecstasy when I experience the Indescribable Wisdom. Its sound vibration has a positive effect on the mind and body whilst uplifting and connecting our spirit to something greater. It is the infinite teacher of the soul.

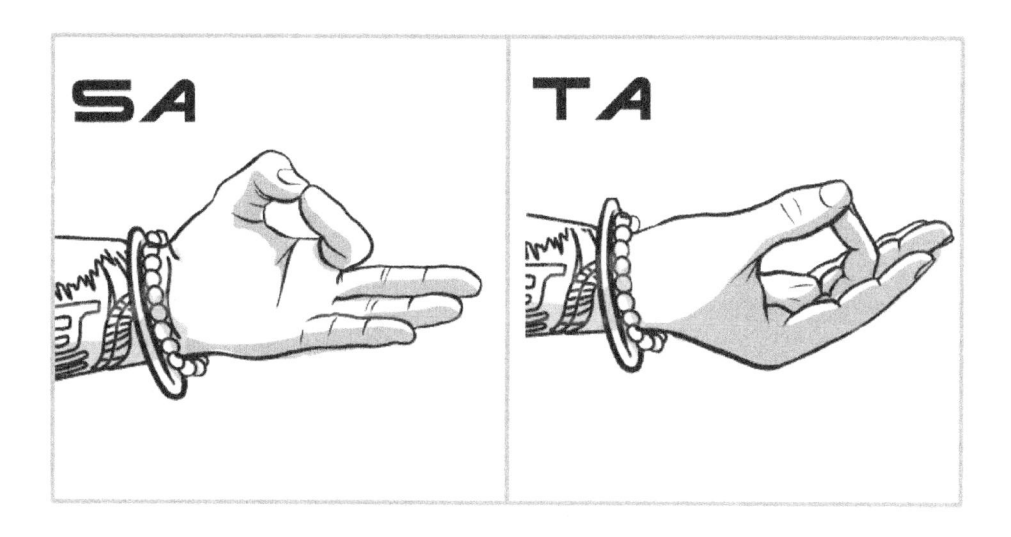

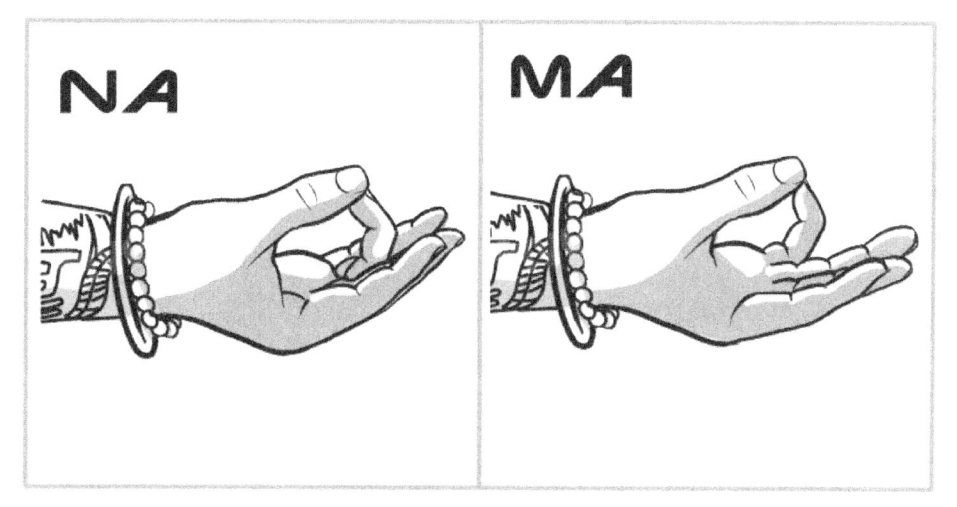

SA TA NA MA MEDITATION.

Sa ta na ma ties in the nuclear sounds of Sat Nam. It uses deeply primal sounds to connect us to the very thread of the evolution of existence itself. It is also commonly referred to as the Panch Shabad – or mantra with 5 sound currents. As we chant the 5th sound – "A" – in sa ta na ma, we imprint this evolutionary coding into our own psyche.

SAA: *Infinity, cosmos, beginning*
TAA: *Life, existence*
NAA: *Death, change, transformation*
MAA: *Rebirth*

Let's try this mantra as a meditation now. You will need to set aside approximately 15 minutes to complete this exercise. Go to your quiet sacred space - see instructions for this under Jedi Exercise: Create your Sacred Space - and sit crossed legged with a tall spine. Tune in with the Adi Mantra described above - ONG NAMO GURU DEV NAMO X 3.

JEDI EXERCISE: SA TA NA MA MEDITATION

This meditation brings a total mental balance to the individual psyche. Vibrating on each fingertip alternates the electrical polarities. The index and ring fingers are electrically negative, relative to the other fingers. This causes a balance in the electromagnetic projection of the aura. Practicing this meditation is both a science and an art. It is an art in the way it moulds consciousness and in the refinement of sensation and insight it produces. It is a science in the tested certainty of the results each technique produces. Each repetition of the entire mantra takes 3 to 4 seconds. This is the cycle of Creation. From the Infinite comes life and individual existence. From life comes death or change. From death comes the rebirth of consciousness to the joy of the Infinite through which compassion leads back to life.

Mudra:
This mantra can be done in many different mudras. Most common is to begin in Gyan Mudra. The elbows are straight while chanting, and the mudra changes as each fingertip touches in turn the tip of the thumb with firm pressure.

Mantra and Mudra:
Chant Saa, Taa, Naa, Maa. With each sound, alternate through four mudras:
On Saa, touch the first (Jupiter) finger; Gyan Mudra (knowledge)
On Taa, touch the second (Saturn) finger; Shuni Mudra (wisdom, intelligence, patience)
On Naa, touch the third (Sun) finger; Surya Mudra (vitality, energy of life)
On Maa, touch the fourth (Mercury) finger; Buddhi Mudra (ability to communicate)

While doing the meditation, you may experience pictures of the past come up like on a movie screen in your mind. Let them dance in front of your eyes and release them with the mantra. This is part of the cleansing of the subconscious mind.

Time:
2 minutes out loud
2 minutes in an audible whisper
3 minutes chant silently. Keep the hands, L in the head and tongue moving.
2 minutes whisper.
2 minutes out loud.

Then sit quietly and listen inside, hear the mantra vibrate within for 1 min.

To finish, inhale deeply, raise the arms up in the air and vigorously shake the arms and fingers. You can involve the whole body and spine. Exhale. Repeat. This is an important part of this meditation as it helps move and release the energy in the body. Relax for a few minutes sitting Or relax on your back.

- Kirtan Kriya (Sa Ta Na Ma Meditation) – The KRI Institute

JEDI EXERCISE: CREATE YOUR SACRED SPACE

Ideally you will have a separate room or space to do your practice. This will become your recharge cave. It's good to choose a quiet space in your house. Ideally you could have a whole room dedicated to your sacred space. The space should be clean, light, and airy. It should be a place where you can switch off your phone, come away from your distractions in life, and just *be*. It is a place that - over time due to your practice and meditations - will build energy and hold a certain vibe, so that when you enter the space, you can tune into yourself easily.

Create an altar and find a suitable cushion or chair to use for your practice. My altar has my lightsaber and imagery of my favourite Jedi masters as well as other spiritual teachers. You can add whatever feels sacred and peaceful for you. Be creative. Use flowers or smelling oils if that suits you. Some people like to have crystals. The main thing is that it feels welcoming and sacred for you - a place away from the world.

Setting up your meditation space can be hugely beneficial and it will aid your daily practice. This may be difficult if you live in the city, so experiment with earplugs and set a time either in the early morning or later in the evening when there are fewer distractions.

Make your space welcoming and inspiring yet simple.

*

MY FIRST YOGA EXPERIENCE

I remember going to my first yoga class and feeling weird and out of place. The class was being held in a cabin in the woods - already weird - and I was working in a stressful sales environment at the time. I felt that I needed a way to wind down and destress after a long day. I had mostly been coping with the stress by drinking and partying on the weekends up until that point, but this was beginning to take a toll on my health. I thought going to yoga would be cool; plus, everyone was saying it's good for you and I had nothing to lose.

Walking into this huge room packed with people of all ages - but mostly women - as we began the practice, I began to feel embarrassed that I was not able to do all of the moves correctly and that I kept falling over. Then my mind started whispering:

"What the hell are we doing here? You're such a wimp. Shouldn't we be out doing something more manly like boxing or weight training?"

The teacher instructed us to tune in to ourselves and I inwardly protested:

"I'm not a bloody radio!!"

I found myself getting more and more agitated as the class went on. I couldn't wait for the class to be over and thought that I would never be going back there again.

And so my journey with yoga ended as fast as it began.
Many years, and a huge spiritual awakening, later things have changed.

Today more and more celebrities and athletes are now using yoga to enhance their performances. Many top business executives use it as a tool for productivity and business success. As a stress and wellbeing tool, it has transferred across all areas of life; helping parents become calmer caregivers, providing students and academics some help with exam stress, and now it's also being used for the eradication of substance addictions as well as prison rehabilitation programmes. This just goes to show you the diversity and powerful effects of yoga. Here we will be using yoga to become Jedi Warriors

Yoga and meditation have become buzz words in the health and wellbeing industry but yoga isn't just about stretchy pants, fancy yoga mats, and finding out how flexible you can be. Although flexibility, stronger abs, and having a perfectly pert bottom can be some of the more material side effects of practice.

To a beginner, yoga can feel intimidating. Firstly, there are so many different types of yoga practice available. Then there's all these different sayings and languages as well as strange body postures that can make us feel out of our depth.

Yet, it is an ancient, time-tested practice that scientific masters of the body and mind spent thousands of years perfecting. Ultimately, the yogis were looking to achieve oneness with the universe; to become connected to the divine source so that they could realise 'Godhood' and their essential nature. They have left us a roadmap of teachings and guidance that can allow us to master aspects of mind, body, and spirit.

The physical body is the temple in which you can build credit or create debt. When you are young, you can often play mischief with the physical body without feeling the adverse effects. However, in old age, the body reminds you of your earlier actions. The body doesn't forgive debts; it records the results of your actions. Yoga is not as strange or mystical as you think and you will find that it has a most practical application. Whilst no magic is involved, it will require you to let go of what you know, work hard, and take your first steps into a wider world.

*

THE AIMS OF YOGA

"Yoga is the practice of tolerating the consequences of being yourself."

— **Bhagavad Gita**

Yoga has seen a huge increase in practice around the world. People are coming to yoga as a way to reduce the stress and commotion that they are feeling in life - and this is a great tool for such things - but true yoga goes much deeper.

As the world and pace of life speed up our bodies and energies desperately try to keep up we are experiencing higher levels of stress than any generation before. We are suffering from an information overload through social media and the internet; leading to a rise in mental health problems such as anxiety, attention disorders, sleep irregularities, and depression. As these ailments increase, frustrated and burnt-out people are turning to alternative healing methods to alleviate the pain; using a 5000-year-old technique to solve the problems of the 21st century.

People can see how the current way of living is unsustainable, and that the system no longer works. Losing trust in the establishment, some are taking the first steps towards empowerment. In a culture in which we rush from one day to the next, yoga creates a space within us which opens up the possibility of connecting to what we already have –
and to the perfection of who we already are.

Initially, people come to yoga for increased flexibility and fitness but throughout practice, things begin to change within themselves. Once this happens, the real journey of yoga begins. Our approach to life changes our perspective and we become more self-reflective. The awareness gained through mindful yoga practice teaches us kindness and self-compassion. Our practice gives us continued growth and self-awareness; most often changing to spirituality or self-actualisation. It brings us a sense of fulfilling our potential.

When you practice yoga on a regular basis you have a positive impact on your strength and endurance. It allows you to facilitate an air of friendliness, compassion and self-control while making you incredibly calm. These physical and psychological changes lead to an increased self-awareness and vitality.

The yoga poses that you will engage in will cleanse your body by increasing blood circulation; helping you to flush out toxins which have come about through irregular posture and poor habits. Breath control in combination with these poses can rectify a number of physical disorders.

Generally speaking, humans are rarely satisfied. We may have moments of contentment, but usually, we are looking for something more to fill us. Perhaps we are hoping for a different job, a new partner, more money, food, alcohol, or more yoga. Once we attain what we have long desired for, it opens the door for countless more desires. We want more of what we have attained already; maybe in a different colour or maybe the object of our desire didn't meet our expectations. Our mind is always changing - fluctuating; guided by the insatiable cravings of the senses. Yoga says that beyond this continually changing mind and intellect, there is an unchanging and formless Spirit that is unaffected by time, space, cause, name, or form. It is veiled by Maya - the great illusion of life which creates a veil over reality - in the individual - or jiva - according to his or her stage of evolution. Each moment, we have the choice to create unity or division with our thoughts, words, and actions. Every moment, therefore, is an opportunity to practice. Yoga is not something that we go to, it is something that we live.

Let's try some yoga. If this is your first time trying yoga, start slowly with the minimum time stated. Be mindful if you are carrying any injuries; reduce the pressure and slowly work to build that area. This is a powerful set of asanas - also known as postures - that will begin to prepare the body for the meditations later in the book.

KUNDALINI JEDI WARM-UP EXERCISES

Before we begin our Kundalini Yoga practice, we always tune in with the mantra that we introduced in the sound and mantra chapters.

ONG NAMO GURU DEV NAMO*: I bow to the infinite wisdom within me. I bow to the wisdom and teachers that have come before.*

The mantra balances and opens up the energetic channels. This helps us to bring our attention and awareness to the moment and helps to create a sacred space beyond the noise and distractions of our daily lives. The war-ups help to burn off any nervous and scattered energy so that we can be fully present in the moment. The idea is to get the heart rate going and get the blood flowing throughout the body. Kundalini Yoga is the yoga of awareness. Listen to your body; do what works for you.

Challenge yourself to extend just past whatever you think your limits are. For instance, if you think you can only do one minute of an exercise, then try for one minute and ten seconds.

Nota Bene:
Female Jedi; when you are on your moon cycle, it is suggested that you avoid strenuous yoga. In particular, do not do: Breath of Fire, Stretch Pose, Root Lock, Sat Kriya, or strenuous leg lifts. Instead, visualise yourself doing the postures.

This warm up practice can also become part of your daily routine. Doing this set first thing in the morning and even last thing at night will bring many health and psychological benefits. It's a good idea to have a space that you can set up and use regularly for practice. Turn off your phone and anything else that may cause distraction. Wear loose, comfortable clothing and a natural-fiber head covering such as a bandana, scarf, or cap.

Have a sheepskin or natural fibre blanket to sit on and a shawl or second blanket to cover yourself during relaxation and meditation. Through time, yogis find it to be the best insulator to keep grounded during meditation. If you are tight in the lower back, hips, or legs, have a pillow or cushion to elevate your lower body during meditation and seated postures.
-TUNE IN WITH ONG NAMO GURU DEV NAMO x 3

1. SHOULDER SHRUGS:

Inhale, bringing both shoulders up to the ears. Exhale, bringing the shoulders down. Keep the spine straight and do not stretch the neck. Continue at a gentle pace for one minute and then for another minute. Begin inhaling up and exhaling by dropping the shoulders down so that the breaths shake the body a little bit. To finish, inhale both shoulders up to the ears, suspend the breath for a few seconds, and relax.

2. SPINAL FLEX:

Sit on the heels in rock pose. Inhale and rock the pelvis forward; pulling the chin into the throat to open up the spine. Push the chest forward and uproot the sitting bones into the ground. Exhale round the lower back; rocking the pelvis back. The head does not move up and down, but the chest rises. Keep the hands to the thighs. Continue for 1-3mins or 108 times.

3. FROG POSE:

Squat down on your toes with your heels touching. Raise up the heels and keep them up during the whole exercise. Place your fingertips on the ground between your legs to help you balance the posture. Inhale as you raise the hips and stretch the legs up keeping the fingertips on the ground. Keep the knees locked. Exhale and come down to the starting position; face forward slightly and lift the chin. The knees will be outside of the arms. It is easiest to do this at a quick and rapid pace. Continue for 11, 26, or 56 reps depending on your level of fitness. Inhaling up and exhaling down counts as one rep.

4. FRONT PLANK:

Begin by lying on the stomach place the palms flat on the ground just underneath the shoulders and push yourself up by straightening and locking the elbows heels push the toes towards the ground the neck is in alignment with your spine there should be a straight line from the neck to the feet hold this posture whilst taking long inhales and deep exhales, continue to hold for 1-3 mins depending on your level of fitness.

5. NECK ROLLS:

Roll the neck slowly round in circles, left ear goes over left shoulder right ear over right shoulder inhaling as you go back and exhaling as you bring the chin to the chest continue one minute and then change direction for another minute, image all the tightness and tension around the neck and shoulders melt away, to end bring the head back to centre inhale deeply suspend the breath for a few seconds exhale and relax.

Time: 2 minutes. 1 minute in one direction. 1 minute in the other direction.
Once you have completed the warm up exercises take some time to sit still or lay on your back in deep relaxation. Focus on your breathing and notice the sensations in the body. Drink some water. These powerful movements, when practiced correctly, will tune the body to optimal performance and you will feel a heightened vibration in the body. These movements charge your positive vibrational frequency.

*

COSMIC ENERGY

"I know that what you call 'God' really exists, but not in the form you think; God is primal cosmic energy, the love in your body, your integrity, and your perception of the nature in you and outside of you."
- **Wilhelm Reich - Austrian Doctor of Medicine and Psychoanalyst**

So, if it's not just about stress reduction and tight abs what is the ultimate purpose of yoga? Yogis were very interested in working with the cosmic energy that exists outside and inside us. They wanted to connect to the absolute truth and experience their creator first hand; living in the bliss of that pure connection. They found a way to raise this cosmic energy within their bodies to achieve union with the universal cosmic field; thus, fulfilling their individual potential and purpose of their lives as yogis. Cosmic energy is said to be a trifecta of omnipresence, omni-potency, and omniscience. It is what created the universe and what makes everything in this universe so deeply connected. It is our very own version of the Force which flows through our bodies via the chakras (see Appendix for description) and through a field that is referred to as the aura.

It nourishes our bodies and supports proper cellular functioning. It breathes life into everything and goes by many names including chi, life force, prana, and higher consciousness. Prana is believed to be the Force that is responsible for life outside of earth, but it also acts as the main component of brain activity within our own bodies. We are, thus, inextricably linked to all energy throughout the universe. It is the source of Kundalini energy and the reason for our brains being alive. Coming up, we will explore the world of Kundalini and how this ancient practice may help us create the Jedi of the future.

***

CHAPTER 10: THE POWER OF KUNDALINI

"The Kundalini is the life force; it is the essential energy of existence. It is the hidden ingredient in life. It is what makes it all work."

- *Frederick Lenz*

KUNDALINI

The Sanskrit word, Kundal, means 'coil' and shakti means 'coiled power'. Kundalini Shakti is therefore commonly compared to a sleeping serpent which is coiled at the base of our spine. While this energy has many different names across the world, it is always referred to as an organic Force which is necessary for uniting yet another trinity: mind, body, and soul.

One also finds symbols of Kundalini in many different cultural legacies, such as Mercury's serpent which is an alchemical symbol for the process of psychic metamorphosis. The Gnostics understood the serpent to represent the spinal cord. In ancient Greek and later, Roman mythology, we find Asclepius, the God of healing. He is seen holding a staff which is entwined with a serpent - or sometimes two.

Why did the Greeks relate to this symbol to healing? The staff represents the central support of the human body or spinal cord, which is the physical location of the Sushumna, or the central cord of the 7 chakras that run along your spine. In Rome, Aesculapius came to represent mercury who usually held a healing staff called the Caduceus. The one or two coiled snakes or serpents entwined around the staff represent the Kundalini which rises along the central subtle channel in a spiral double-helical movement. (54) It is made up of the two great forces of repulsion and attraction. It is electrifying and sometimes referred to as 'universal electricity'. It has the power to eradicate some of our most deep-seated fears and tensions. It can help us ease into our best selves – the confident and connected versions of ourselves. It is a primal life force that we are all naturally born with.

Yogic science suggests that this energy is present in all beings and is the fire that ignites the creation of us as humans. The energy enters the top of the head and triggers the formation of the child in the womb. Once the charge has kick-started the formation of our organs, cells, and body it is said to then coil 3 1/2 times at the base of the spine to hold the energy field in stasis until we die when it uncoils and returns to its source.

The yogis knew about this powerful dormant energy and developed practices and methods to release this stored energy - to direct it from the base of the spine up to the top of the head; connecting the energy back to the source from whence it came and achieving a connection and oneness reminding them of the truth of reality. This, in essence, helps them to achieve cosmic consciousness and this peak experience changes the fundamentals of who the person believed they were. The experience reconfigures the personality and our understanding of self as a separate identity. We become enlightened to who we are and begin to live life from a different perspective.

*

WHAT IS THE FORCE - REALLY?
"What gives a Jedi his power. It's an energy field created by all living things. It surrounds us and penetrates us. It binds the galaxy together."
- Obi-Wan Kenobi, Star Wars Episode IV: A New Hope

One of my favourite things about the Star Wars movies was the magical quality of the Force - this mysterious energy that allowed Obi-Wan to do Jedi mind tricks; easily convincing evil stormtroopers that "these are not the droids you are looking for". The Force allowed Luke to communicate telepathically with Leia when he needed help. It gave him the power to magically jump up and escape the carbon freeze trap set up by Darth Vader in Star Wars: Episode V – The Empire Strikes Back. The Force is beyond death; with Luke still being guided by the Force ghost of Obi-Wan who had helped him to trust the Force to deliver the torpedoes in Star Wars: Episode IV – A New Hope. He ultimately destroyed the death star and claimed victory for the resistance. I would spend hours running around pretending that I was a Jedi; imagining that I could move things with my mind and influence my mum to let me pay out longer. Sometimes she did; proving to me that the Force worked. I pretended that I could jump to great heights just like Luke could, when in fact, I was only jumping up on the staircase in our living room.

This magical energy of the Force gave me hope that miracles could truly happen. You didn't have to be big or strong or even look a certain way to use the Force. With the force as our ally, we could be our own unlikely heroes. Yoda's use of the force made me believe that anything was possible. In the Star Wars: Episode V – The Empire Strikes Back, Luke crash lands his x-wing into a swamp as he searches for a fabled Jedi master that lives there. Once he finally finds him, he begins his training to become a Jedi. In one powerful lesson, Yoda shows Luke how our thoughts are related to the power of the force. Yoda challenges Luke to raise his x-wing out of the swamp. As Luke tries to levitate his X-wing from the Dagobah swamp, and fails to do so, and fails, he tells his Master, "You want the impossible." With that, Yoda, less than half of Luke's size, calmly raises the star fighter. "I can't believe it," says Luke. "That is why you fail," Yoda replies!

Yoda's teaching here shows how our beliefs can limit us and how appearances can be deceiving.

Luke had to open his mind to possibility

Watching this as a child was super inspiring. I would've done anything to have these sorts of magical powers; having access to a Force energy that would make me special and powerful. In a strange twist of fate, I became a yoga teacher who works with energies; developing inner guidance through my intuition. I have practiced to connect myself to the divine source of all creation. My psychotherapy training gave me a deep understanding of how powerful our thoughts and beliefs can be in shaping our life experience. When I started to train in TaeKwonDo, I remember thinking that I would never be able to do high kicks or remember a 34-move pattern, but with training and self-belief, I eventually became a black belt. I believe that this journey which I undertook was guided by the Force.

As we continue to experience great change on the planet, many people are beginning to question the quality of their lives. Increased stress from the pace of life, with our health and mental well-being being affected, has many of us feeling like we've lost our place in the world. Work-related stress and lifestyle changes have seen people begin to question what is really going on. If we can acknowledge that money and possessions do not buy happiness then what is the purpose of life?

There must be some deeper meaning to it all.

*

THE FORCE AND GOD

People have lost their trust in organised religion which may be due to bad earlier experiences with their church or a general loss of faith. Believing in an all-powerful God sitting up in the clouds, granting our wishes or punishing us for bad actions, seems laughable and outdated. It's not cool to believe in a God anymore. Some people just find it too difficult to believe that a "just God" would allow so much evil to happen in the world. These people misunderstand the spirit of the Force-consciousness.

Even if you are an atheist there would still be some semblance of agreement that we have energy that runs through us and that there is an energy, or life force existing in all things. This energy can be guided, directed, and channelled so that you may experience the fullness of your being. You are a conscious or unconscious creator with the energy that flows throw all things.

"For my ally is the Force, and a powerful ally it is. Life creates it, makes it grow. Its energy surrounds us and binds us. ... You must feel the Force around you; here, between you, me, the tree, the rock, everywhere, yes."
- Grand Master Yoda, Star Wars: Episode V - The Empire Strikes Back

It was traditionally the role of religion to bring people together and raise consciousness so that they could remember their infinite connection, but man's interference and power structures have decimated that. With all of the wars, and spiritual leaders being exposed, people have understandably turned their backs on religion. As more and more sexual misconduct in church has come to light, we have begun to doubt that these are houses of God and pure energy. So, the time has come for individual transformation through the Force. It's time to elevate yourself to your true identity.

The Force is the modern-day version of God, a generic term we can use to understand the unknowable energy and to explore the mysteries of creation. Without this connection to something beyond us, we are left feeling confused and lost in a random and chaotic universe when in truth there is a divine order. There is an intelligence, and a Force that runs through all things. The Force of the spirit is neither good nor bad; it is neutral. We manifest the Force through us in our own unique ways.

There are many names for this spiritual energy. In Catholicism it's called God, in Taoism it's the Chi, in Hinduism it's Brahma, in yoga we call it Cosmic Energy or Kundalini Energy. These different versions and meanings are all from the one reality. Tuning into the Force will allow us to embrace the truth of reality and who we are.

It will empower us to fulfil and complete our mission.

THE UNIVERSAL FORCE

"I used to wonder that myself. Thought it was a bunch of mumbo-jumbo-magical power holding together good, evil, the dark side, and the light. Crazy thing is, it's true. The Force, the Jedi, all of it. It's all true."
- **Han Solo, Star Wars: Episode VII - The Force Awakens**

The Force is a mysterious thing and it can be difficult to give it an accurate description. Words and descriptions such as otherworldly, energy, power, intelligence, higher wisdom, flow, electric, emanating, heavenly, spiritual, God, magical, flowing, and mystical begin to connect us with the energy.

According to a fan contribution, the concept of Force was one of George Lucas's first ideas regarding the story and the Jedi, the idea of an energy field that connected all living things in the galaxy. Lucas used the term the Force to "echo" its use by cinematographer Roman Kroitor in the film *'21-87'* (1963), in which Kroitor says, "Many people feel that in the contemplation of nature and communication with other living things, they become aware of some kind of force, or something, behind this apparent mask which we see in front of us, and they call it God".

Although Lucas had Kroitor's line in mind specifically, Lucas said the underlying sentiment is universal and that "similar phrases have been used extensively by many different people for the last 13,000 years". The natural flow of energy known as The Force is believed to have originated from the concept of qi/chi/ki, "the all-pervading vital energy of the universe". And the yogis call this energy prana or Kundalini. (55)

In Taoist beliefs on the other hand, they practice is qi – or chi. The word qi means "breath," 'air" or "gas, but figuratively, qi is life-force—that which animates the forms of the world. It is the vibratory nature of phenomena—the flow and tremoring that is happening continuously at molecular, atomic, and subatomic levels. This principle of a driving life force is, of course, common to many cultures and religious traditions. In Japan it is called "ki," and in India, "prana" or "shakti." Did you know Shaak Ti is a female jedi in the Star Wars movies; a colourful and exotic alien species, from the planet Shili. Shaak Ti is a member of the Jedi High Council and is a Jedi General during the Clone Wars and surely influenced by the Hindu yogic term, "shakti", which translates as divine feminine power. The ancient Egyptians referred to it as "ka" and the ancient Greeks as "pneuma." For Native Americans it is the "Great Spirit" and for Christians, the "Holy Spirit." In Africa, it's known as "ashe" and in Hawaii as "ha" or "mana." (56)

***Nota Bene:**
For the remainder of our Kundalini Jedi Warrior training journey, we will refer to the divine, God, higher power, and holy spirit as The Force.

PROTECTING YOUR ENERGY

The technology that we use today is so present in our lives that they constantly interfere with our energetic fields. Our natural flow of chi or qi is thrown out of balance due to the electromagnetic vibrations or frequencies that our computers, TVs, tablets, cell phones, smart watches, and other gadgets emit; not to mention the frequencies emitted by power lines, microwaves, and wi-fi signals. Thankfully there are certain materials that you can use to protect your energy; materials like copper, aluminium, and mylar. Wearing bracelets and other products that contain these properties will scatter the electrical photons as they pass through you; effectively deflecting or absorbing the radiation. As you begin to practice yoga as part of your Kundalini Jedi Warrior journey, you could do well to invest in some of these products so that you're protecting the precious energy that you're working so hard to balance.

Luke: Breathe. Just breathe. Reach out with your feelings. What do you see?
Rey: The island. Life. Death and decay, that feeds new life. Warmth. Cold. Peace. Violence.
Luke: And between it all?
Rey: Balance. Energy. A-Force.
Luke: And inside you?
Rey: Inside me, that same Force.
Luke: And this is the lesson.

- Luke Skywalker; Star Wars: The Last Jedi

SUNIA MEDITATION

Sunia is a Sanskrit/Gurumukhi word that translates to "the art of extreme deep listening." It involves moving beyond the words; listening to the tones, inflections, and inferences that are spoken. It involves hearing each subtlety of the sound. It's through these subtleties that you actually connect to the root understanding of what a person truly means. It gives you almost a vision of where they've come from to speak their words. It highlights what they're intending with these words, and how sincere they intend it to be. Even without the expression of exact words, one can extract the true meaning through Sunia listening.

JEDI EXERCISE: HEARING THE FORCE

This exercise will take 10 minutes. If you have more time, by all means, sit for longer and go deeper into feeling the Force. Sit in a comfortable position, get quiet, and close your eyes. Be very still, and listen. Listen to your breath, listen to the sounds inside and outside the room. Feel the weight of your body as you sit. Sit in a comfortable position with your back straight and eyes closed. Tune into your hearing and begin to notice the sounds in the room. Mentally take note of the sounds that you hear. Now, expand your listening to include your house or apartment and note all of the sounds. These could include a ticking clock, the sound of the fridge, and so on. Now extend your listening to include the sounds outside your window and continue expanding your hearing as you can.

Now, connect to any bodily sensations that you can feel. Notice your body posture and become aware of your feet and sitting bones. Take note of your hands. Notice the temperature of your body and become aware of the parts that feel heavy. Develop an awareness for any parts that are tingling, tickling, or twitching. Just take note of all of the sensations in the body.

Take some time to notice the smells in your environment and the taste in your mouth.

By practicing this exercise, we can increase our sensitivity and connection to ourselves as well as to the world around us.

In time, we will start to become aware of the subtle vibrations of the Force moving in all things.

POST-EXERCISE JOURNAL

- How many different sounds or noises were you able to become aware of?
- How often have you used sound to uplift your spirits when you are feeling sad or bad?
- Do you sing a song, play a CD, or call a friend and talk? Reflect on the types of music you normally listen to and how that music makes you feel?
- How often have you brought yourself and others down by words used in anger and frustration?
- Can the sounds we utter heal ourselves and others?
- How do you feel when you hear the opening few bands of the Star Wars theme?

Make some journal entries into your Jedi manual and reflect. Spend 10 mins in complete silence; capturing your insights about this experience in your training manual.

Write down 10 different sounds you heard.
List 5 smells that you smelt.

List 10 body sensations you had whilst sitting.

JEDI EXERCISE: HAND SENSITISATION

THIS EXERCISE WORKS WELL WITH A JEDI PARTNER

In the previous chapter on feeling the Force, we began training our listening function by becoming aware of the sounds and sensation in and around the body as a way to feel the energy of the Force. The following exercise will allow us to continue developing our sensitivity by focusing on movements and touch to feel the flow of the Force.

Find a partner. If you don't have anyone around, use both of your palms together instead of yours and someone else's. Face each other. One of you holds a palm face-up. The other places a palm just above that one so that the two palms are facing each other. The hand on top moves around in small circles that gradually become larger. Notice any sensations that take place.

It is easier to feel the Force from another person than by placing your own palms together. However, you can still achieve sensitisation on your own. Place your own two palms together. Make some small circles with one palm while the other palm stays still. Make the circles bigger. Practice doing this with your own palms every day, and you will become much more sensitive to the Force.

Here are some tips on how to enhance the efficiency of this sensitivity practice.

Before you begin the hand sensitisation exercises, place the thumb of one hand on the pressure point in the centre of the other palm. Massage the pressure point using a lot of pressure. Now, do the same with the other palm. This increases your sensitivity. You can also rub your hands together vigorously to generate a lot of heat.

The development of sensitivity also comes more easily when you do this practice mindfully. Take a few deep breaths before you begin. When you do the exercise, relax into it. Make your circles slow enough so that you can feel the subtle sensations. The more relaxed and mindful that you and your hands are, the greater the sensitivity. Your capacity for sensitivity will grow with each recurrent practice session.

Now, place your left palm in front of you; facing your right hand. Point the index finger of the right hand to the pressure point at the centre of the palm without touching it, about an inch or two away. Keep the left hand steady. Make small circles with the index finger of the right hand. Let the circles gradually become larger. Remember to relax the hands and keep them soft and supple. Take notice of what you feel. The sensation that you notice will increase over time.

Switch hands.

Try different distances between the finger and palm. Let your palms face each other about 12 inches apart. Imagine that they are holding a ball of white light. Squish that ball and make it smaller. Let the ball "rebound" back to its original size.

Record your experience in your Jedi journal.

Nota Bene:
The above exercises are for sensitivity. With sensitivity, you can learn how to use the Force and work with the Force more efficiently. This requires daily practice and diligence. Awakening is gradual. There are no shortcuts. With daily practice, you will be pleasantly surprised at how much more information you are processing as time goes on.

*

LUMINOUS BEINGS

"Luminous beings are we, not this crude matter."
 – **Grand Master Yoda, Star Wars: Episode V – The Empire Strikes Back**

The yogis believe that we are spiritual beings having a human experience. Have you ever wondered where you came from? Have you ever thought of how you came to be here? Have you ever contemplated the meaning of your existence?

Yogic thought tells us we are just energy transforming from one form to another with the human incarnation being the highest because we are able to have free will, and self-awareness. We are able to realise our true self.

The universe consists of everything. As far as we now can approximate, there are about one hundred thousand million stars in our Milky Way alone. The saying that there are more stars than there are grains of sand on all of the beaches and deserts on this planet combined is accurate.

If you see the earth revolving around the sun, the moon that is making its rounds, the stars near and far that are shining in the sky, the sun shining bright, and every other activity of the wind, earth, water, and fire you will slowly come to see that it is all possible because of the spirit of the universe.

In the Star Wars universe this same energy is called the Force.

It's the spirit that grows in everything and allows it to expand and when the time comes for the spirit to leave, the physical manifestation of it tends to contract. Even the things that carry the spirit do perish for this is the law of nature. The form goes through a process of growth, expansion, and contraction. Be it plants, animals, humans - or anything that exists in the physical form - it has to go through the process of G.O.D: generating, organising, and decay. It is the same in Star Wars, everything returns to the Force. All is energy and energy is never destroyed, it just transforms from one form to another.

This universal energy macrocosm is reflected in the microcosm of our own bodies. We can see the same process within. Every cell of our body grows, multiplies, and dies; only to be reborn and for the process to begin again. It is the way for the Force to continue to flow.

It's you.

It's all you.

You're a feature of the universe in the same way that your cells are features of your human body. You're not a person made of cells, as if there were something in you distinct from the entire biological structure that's more real to you. You are the aggregate functioning of all of the cells in your body. You don't live 'in' it, you are it.

Your origin is space dust and particles. You are made from the same material as the planets and stars; relying on the energy of the universe. You develop faith and remember that we all come from the one true source and all return there.

In Star Wars: Episode II – Attack of the Clones, a young Anakin Skywalker comes to Master Yoda for advice after having nightmares about losing his love, Padmé, to which Yoda replies; "Death is a natural part of life. Rejoice for those around you who transform into the Force. Mourn them do not. Miss them do not."

With this knowledge that we are energy, and that we will also one day transform into the Force, we can become fearless in our approach to life; understanding the impermanence of all things and living life without fear.

*

KNOWING THE FORCE

Yes, the Force can be known, and the way is to realise your spirit that works beneath your mind. The word spirit has been used by saints, seekers, sages, and yogis attempting to describe the very essence of life and existence.

The whole universe can be observed in one's mind, provided that you experience the whole mind. If you are habituated to perceive only outside life and have no clue what's going on inside your mind, the truth of life will always remain an elusive thing.

This body and mind are animated and alive due to the spirit and Force flowing through us. So with this realisation, we see that we must be in a relationship and consciousness connection of this energy. Knowing the unknowable is a worthwhile pursuit for a Jedi, to strengthen that condition and come to a true realisation of the self and who we really are.

To create wholeness within ourselves there must be a balance and understanding of the mind, body, and spirit. Mostly in the modern world, enhancing and connecting to our spiritual nature is something we do now and again. We go on a weekend retreat in the countryside or pick up a good self-help book which we thumb through on our way to work. In general, we are more focused on our social, human interactions and how we function in the outer world, with little attention to our inner world.

Being a Kundalini Jedi means practicing deep inner reflection, to make the connections between our inner experiences and how these manifest in our outer reality.

*

A WAY OF SEEING LIFE

Lucas's inspiration has always been present in the field and seeking the inner spirit involves changing our understanding of the greater universe. We need to remove ourselves from the orientation of there just being a physical world; moving towards the idea that something exists beyond us.

"The Force is really a way of seeing; it's a way of being with life," Lucas has said. "It really has nothing to do with weapons. The Force gives you the power to have extra-sensory perception and to be able to see things and hear things, read minds and levitate things. It is said that certain creatures are born with a higher awareness of the Force than humans. Their brains are different. The Force is a perception of the reality that exists around us. You have to come to learn it. It's not something you just get. It takes many, many years...Anyone who studied and worked hard could learn it. But you would have to do it on your own."

- **George Lucas**

Although you will be doing a lot of this work on your own, we are here to provide support and guidance to you throughout your journey in order to connect to the Force. So, we begin the exploration of what spirituality involves and how you can view life. Dr. Maya Spencer, of the Royal College of Psychiatrists, comments on what spirituality entails; stating that spirituality involves the recognition of a feeling or sense or belief that there is something greater than myself, something more to being human than sensory experience, and that the greater whole of which we are part is cosmic or divine. Spirituality means knowing that our lives have significance in a context beyond a mundane everyday existence at the level of biological needs that drive selfishness and aggression. It means knowing that we are a significant part of a purposeful unfolding of Life in our universe. Spirituality involves exploring certain universal themes – love, compassion, altruism, life after death, wisdom, and truth, with the knowledge that some people such as saints or enlightened individuals have achieved and manifested higher levels of development than the ordinary person.

Aspiring to manifest the attributes of such inspirational examples often becomes an important part of the journey through life for spiritually inclined people. (57)

Star Wars can be thought of as a spiritual movie if we are using the above definition of spiritual. The films tackle the intricacies of relationships, love, family, compassion, good, evil, the impermanence of life, and balance. It clearly shows the consequences of following a dark path as opposed to one of selflessness, and ultimately losing who you are whilst exploring the idea of being a hero as exhibited by the Skywalker family.

YOGI SIDDHIS AND JEDI POWERS

When we are young and small the world can feel like a big place. We are dependent on others for our survival and our caregivers provide us with rules and protection. When I was young - and even now - I dreamt of having Force powers; the power to overcome bullies, the power to get out of homework, and the power to push people back with a wave of the hand. However, those were just movies and make believe, so having Jedi powers was total fantasy, or was it?

If we look towards the franchise for inspiration, we can see that there were two main wielders of the Force – the Jedi and the Sith. They each had their own unique powers as delivered to them by the use of the Force. Some could sense impending attacks while others could lift and push physical objects with their minds and even influence the thoughts and rationale of others. The Jedi stood firmly in their belief that the Force could be used for many purposes such as wisdom, the manipulation of matter, protection, and persuasion.

In the Star Wars films, only certain individuals were Force-sensitive, but in reality, we are all connected to some unseen power. We can awaken latent abilities within us, similar to those used by the Jedi. It is because of this that Force-sensitives could feel a "disturbance in the Force" whenever there was a great loss of life, and in a similar way we are also connected by a unified oneness field that we all share. Even our thoughts are some form of collective unconsciousness of the planet. In essence, we are all one living organism.

*

YOGIC SUPERPOWERS

Patanjali's Yoga Sutras are some of the most classic yoga texts. They were written about two thousand years ago and tell us if we sit quietly, pay close attention to our minds, and practice diligently, then we will gain supernormal powers. These yogic superpowers that bear resemblance to those of the Jedi are known as siddhis. They are ordinary capacities that everyone possesses. When we remove distractions, we can access them. They are commonly grouped as such: extra-normal, paranormal, ultra-normal, and supernormal.

The extra-normal powers are those that represent a heightening of the normal capacities, The paranormal include such capacities as remote viewing, astral travel, telepathy, and the like. Ultra-normal powers would include such abilities as being able to sit in a fire without getting burned; being able to go without eating or drinking for extended periods, even for years on end; shape-shifting; true mind reading; accurate prophecy;

prodigious pranic healing power; and much more. We therefore view the categories of siddhis also as follows:
1. **EXCEPTIONAL** mind-body control;
2. **CLAIRVOYANCE**, and,
3. **PSYCHOKINESIS**.

PATANJALI'S YOGA SUTRAS

In Patañjali's Yoga Sutras IV.1 it is stated, Janma auṣadhi mantra tapaḥ samādhijāḥ siddhayaḥ, "Accomplishments may be attained through birth, the use of herbs, incantations, self-discipline or samadhi". Possible siddhis or siddhi-like abilities mentioned include:

- **Ahiṃsā**: a peaceful aura
- **Satya**: persuasion
- **Asteya**: wealth
- **Brahmacharya**: virility
- **Aparigraha**: insight;
- **Śauca**: sensory control/cleanliness
- **Saṃtoṣa**: happiness
- **Tapas**: bodily and sensory perfection
- **Svādhyāya**: communion with the Divine
- **Ī' varapraṇidhāna:** Samādhi

EIGHT CLASSICAL SIDDHIS

According to different sources, seven of the eight classical siddhis (Ashta Siddhi) or eight great perfections are:

- **Aṇimā**: the ability to become smaller than the smallest, reducing one's body to the size of an atom or even become invisible.
- **Mahimā**: the ability to become infinitely large, expanding one's body to an infinitely large size.
- **Laghimā**: the ability to become weightless or lighter than air.
- **Prāpti**: the ability to instantaneously travel or be anywhere at will.
- **Prakāmya**: the ability to achieve or realise whatever one desires.
- **Ī' itva**: the ability to control nature, individuals, organisms, etc. Supremacy over nature
- and ability to force influence upon anyone.
- **Va' itva**: the ability to control all material elements or natural forces. (58)

JEDI FORCE ABILITIES

Force protection is a power that can only be achieved by high-ranking Jedi Masters. It allows the user of this power to become invulnerable to a plethora of attacks. It is revered as the ultimate form of self-defence. This is similar to the protection bubble, which can also inflict damage on an opponent as well as protect the user.

Force defend, on the other hand, doesn't shield one entirely, but reduces the damage taken by Force powers. Force absorb allows the user to absorb the incoming negative energy from attacks and redirect it. It is a counter strike technique, of sorts.

These Force-sensitive beings who were capable of these amazing feats, were those who were highly attuned to the flow of the Force. With the correct training, they could develop the ability to manipulate the Force. Not all users of the Force can access all of these techniques because how you engage with the Force is completely unique to you. Some techniques are so incredibly difficult that only a handful of masters have been able to accomplish them. When you access the light side of the Force, you will be able to use the techniques in this book for protection, and for increasing your mental as well as physical capacities. They are used defensively, but can be accessed for the offensive if not to inflict physical harm.

SELF-MASTERY

The teaching method of the Jedi Order was focused on a preliminary basis of control – self-control that is – which was taught to Jedi initiates as the foundation for opening their minds to the Force. One had to learn how to control their own body, as this self-control was the precursor to all other teachings. It is a skill that would be constantly cultivated throughout a Jedi's life as a means to prolong life and avoid decay.

Patanjali explains that there needs to be mastery of this eight-fold path, and that after that the siddhis will be obtained. It is also at this point that you would be able to hold an unwavering focus in meditation without mental chatter affecting you over a prolonged period of time. As you begin your meditative practice you might find that you can only achieve this for a few seconds or maybe even minutes, but as you master the eight-fold path, you'll be able to have this level of mental control for hours on end.

We will learn some mind and meditation techniques in the coming chapters, but I think that you are beginning to see how the yogis have all been suggestive of the idea that we could develop real Jedi powers. These ancient traditions suggest that through the practice of yoga and meditation, we could influence another's mind just like with a Jedi mind trick. We could even have foresight into events that could happen; feeling disturbances in the Force. Both Yoda and Obi-Wan can be seen experiencing the distress of planets being destroyed and feeling the energy of the people being affected; uttering, "I feel a great disturbance in the Force." It was as if millions of voices suddenly cried out in terror, and were suddenly silenced ". (Star Wars-A New Hope)

"I fear something terrible has happened."
- **Obi-Wan Kenobi, Star Wars: Episode IV – A New Hope**

Through yoga, we will be developing our sensory system and increasing our awareness of our inner world which will heighten and develop our sensitivity to the subtleties of life. Only through practice and dedication will you begin to access your own Jedi siddhi powers.

Certain locations in the galaxy had strong connections to the Force, such as the cave that Luke Skywalker entered during his training on Dagobah. There were also entire planets that had strong connections to the Force. These places included the Wellspring of Life, Mortis, and Moraband. This strong connection to the Force is also present on our planet. There are many known areas in the world which hold some strange mystical energy; places that provide healing or that feel energetically charged, thus elevating the spiritual work that we'd associate the elementary siddhis with garden-variety psychic phenomena. They, today, include telepathy (mind- to- mind communication); clairvoyance (gaining information about distant or hidden objects beyond the reach of the ordinary senses); precognition (clairvoyance through time), and psychokinesis (direct influence of matter by the mind, also known as PK).

The idea of energy points is not just science fiction. Here on Earth We also have something known as ley lines. Just like we have veins that flow in and out of the heart, Mother Earth has Ley Lines, which are lines of energy that coil around the earth in a similar fashion as a strand of DNA. These Ley lines carry positive or negative energy creating a magnetic field very much like our own bodies. These lines that cross the earth in certain places, causing a vortex of energy, like Stonehenge in Glastonbury, Mount Shasta, the Bermuda Triangle, the Egyptian pyramids, and Peru's Machu Pichu. These places give us a glimpse of this power, but technically speaking, The Force energy wasn't created there. It was always there.

The Jedi and Sith orders can understand and, to varying extents, manipulate this Force. Some consider The Force to be a sentient being which controls all of the above. However, as its earlier name, "The Way" suggests, it can be thought of more as a ubiquitous flow/energy/feeling/aura.

The concept of The Force in Star Wars seems to resonant universally. Today people have lost their faith, trust, and connection to the church and organised religion. What was once a place to go to in order to connect with God, they are now places that people avoid for many reasons; included - but not limited to - some bad early experiences. As the world continues to wake up to their essential nature and sovereignty, people are not willing to give their power away to a structured organisation anymore. However, that deep and natural need for spiritual connections and meaning has led many to adapt to understanding a higher power as the Force.

It has no identity, no face, no man in the sky with a big beard fulfilling our wishes from the Argos' catalogue.

But why do we respond so powerfully to it?

We can usually all relate to The Force in some way because it reminds us of basic ideas, feelings, and the beliefs behind most of our most ancient and enduring religious mythologies. Even better for us is that it does so without settling on exactly one in particular.

*

MIDI-CHLORIANS AND PRANA

The prequel movies sought to further explain what the Force is supposed to be by introducing the concept of midi-chlorians - an attempt at bridging the science-religion gap, which is a leap not needed in an allegory. "I'm assuming that the midi-chlorians are a race that everybody knows about [in the world of Star Wars]," Lucas has said. "The way you interact and interface with this larger energy field [the Force] is through the midi-chlorians, which are sensitive to the energy. They are at the core of your life, which is the cell, the living cell. They are in a symbiotic relationship with the cell. And then, because they're all interconnected as one, they can communicate with the larger Force field. That's how you deal with the Force."

In the movies, the power of the Force could be used by individuals who were sensitive to it, a power that was tapped through the midi-chlorians.

Midi-chlorians were intelligent microscopic life forms that lived symbiotically inside the cells of all living things. When present in sufficient numbers, they could allow their host to detect the pervasive energy field known as the Force.

The Force is the inner source of energy that powers all living things and is manifested as an intracellular symbiotic life form called midi-chlorians. The name is a combination of Mitochondria - the endosymbionts that power your cells - and Chloroplasts - the endosymbionts that perform photosynthesis in plants.

Throughout the original trilogy, the Force is depicted as an unknown and mystical entity. Obi-Wan tells Luke of the power it holds. He further goes on to tell him of the "light side" and the "dark side," and encourages him to embrace good, not evil. Furthermore, the original trilogy introduced both sides of the spectrum; the Jedi Order and the Sith.

Like any energy of creation - prana, electricity, or atoms - this energy can be activated and misused by those who are not spiritually motivated or have not completed this process and are therefore not free of personal patterns. It is very helpful to understand the process and the intention of your life Force as it awakens you so that you may discover wisdom, love, and authentic direction in your own life. Simplicity, contentment, unconditional acceptance, and presence are hallmarks of an awakened life.

In the yogic term, this same energy is represented as prana.

Prana comes into the body from the food we eat, the air we breathe, and from absorbing the energies of the earth and heavens. Prana travels through thousands of tiny channels called nadis to every cell in the body. Normally, prana is restricted from flowing through the Sushumna by locks above each chakra.

Prana is the Sanskrit word for "life force"; in yoga, Oriental medicine, and martial arts, the term refers to a cosmic energy believed to come from the sun and connecting the elements of the universe.

*

KUNDALINI AWAKENING

"The kundalini energy enables us to do things that would not happen otherwise, to apply an occult pressure, to use energy to create effects perhaps thousands of miles away."

- Frederick Lenz, AKA Rama

The capacity to intensify and raise energy in the body has been explored for thousands of years. It is a natural human potential. Through various practices, for the most part the Kundalini is a result of mental/spiritual progression as in working on the chakras and the body through meditation, prayers, bodywork, breath work, or various yoga or sexual practices.

The power points are worked with, cleansed, and healed. For what good is the Kundalini if the energy is blocked and cannot move upward? Through practices and lifestyle, we clear the path for the energy to rise up the spine. You will find many tools and meditations to help you in this endeavour.

American comparative religions scholar Joseph Campbell, who George Lucas based the mythology of Star Wars on, describes the concept of Kundalini as "the figure of a coiled female serpent —a serpent Goddess not of "gross" but "subtle" substance—which is to be thought of as residing in a torpid, slumbering state in a subtle centre, the first of the seven, near the base of the spine: the aim of the yoga than being to rouse this serpent, lift her head, and bring her up a subtle nerve or channel of the spine to the so-called "thousand-petaled lotus" – or Sahasrara - at the crown of the head...She, rising from the lowest to the highest lotus centre will pass through and wake the five between, and with each waking, the psychology and personality of the practitioner will be altogether and fundamentally transformed. (59)

Kundalini awakening offers a profound opportunity for those called to follow a spiritual path. It gradually releases many patterns, conditions, and delusions of the separate self. In some people, the Kundalini force can awaken spontaneously for no apparent reason other than it is spiritually time to do so. Spontaneous Kundalini activation seems to increase in frequency as well. Perhaps this is due to an overall global transformation toward enlightenment. The awareness of the Kundalini is a spiritual step in transforming human consciousness, an emergence to our natural state of Being One with the cosmos. The mystical mind is forever changed by the Kundalini awakening. (60)

Yoga's purpose is redirecting the life force up the spine. To achieve this lofty goal, our outer life has to reinforce our meditative efforts, otherwise, contractive attitudes bring our life force downward and opposite to where we are trying to go spiritually.

As well as prana mastery, yogis are also trying to raise and work with their Kundalini energy. There are many reasons to take this arduous journey, but for whatever reason you take it, the heart and the courage of the warrior is required to walk this path.

WHAT ARE THE BENEFITS OF COSMIC K ENERGY?

1. Feeling more at peace and bliss;
2. Increase in IQ level;
3. Much better sense of sound, colour, and sight;
4. A feeling of purification;
5. Psychic abilities are enhanced;
6. More compassion and empathy;
7. Slowed down ageing and an increase in creativity;
8. Blissful vibration of energy perceived inside the ears as sound (OM);
9. You become more magnetic and can attract situations or people into your life with your thoughts;
10. Increased spiritual connection;
11. People tend to feel less stressed and relief of anxiety;
12. Generally, you feel much more focused;
13. More energy and increased vitality;
14. Relaxation;
15. Life seems clearer and the purpose is more apparent;
16. Better concentration and performance; and,
17. Alleviation of pain and physical ailments.

When the Kundalini is awakened, it is the ultimate tool for self-improvement, allowing long-term positive change. The nature of Kundalini is that it can't be held back when the floodgates are open, there is no way to stop it. That's why it's a great idea to find guidance through an enlightened teacher.

One thing we can be sure about is when the Kundalini is awakened, the life we know will never be the same again. One of the Kundalini awakening benefits often understood is when the energy moves up your spine, your unconscious thoughts can be brought forward as conscious thoughts. Nothing will be buried, whether you want to deal with it or not. It will be out there. This is one of the main reasons why Kundalini awakening shouldn't be carried out alone, without a teacher who can guide you through this extreme emotional process. (61)

HOW DO I GET MORE COSMIC ENERGY?

Cosmic energy never stops flowing no matter what. It also never gets depleted. Cosmic energy is really important for a person's spiritual and physical well-being. It is also considered to be the fuel for life. As we mentioned earlier, cosmic energy is available to us in abundant supply. It is up to us to tap into it if we're on a path of healing or spiritual development. There are different ways in which a person can get his cosmic energy activation. The easiest way to build a relationship with the cosmos is by limiting the level of negativity in one's life. You can do this by harmonising your breathing through techniques such as meditation and yoga. In the next subchapter we will take a deeper look at a specific type of yoga as a way of receiving cosmic energy.

*

KUNDALINI YOGA PRACTICE

"Kundalini Yoga is the crack cocaine of yoga. If Hatha is a mild weed high, Iyengar is a deep hash glow, and Ashtanga is amphetamine, Kundalini blows the fucking doors off."
— **Russell Brand, Comedian, Actor, Activist**

The rise and popularity of yoga has also led to new yoga styles being created. This only further makes the choice of which style to opt for even harder. There are in general 9 major schools of yoga which focus on different aspects; hatha yoga for the body, bhakti or devotion yoga, ashtanga, vinyasana, Bikram Yoga, Jivamukti Yoga, Power Yoga, Sivananda Yoga, and Yin Yoga.

In this manual we will be focusing on the practice of Kundalini yoga. Known as the mother of all yoga, Kundalini includes elements from all other systems. It delivers them in sets and kriyas that will elevate your consciousness.

As you may remember from the story chapter in the hero's journey chapter, I experienced a spiritual awakening in 2003 which led me to leave the life that I knew behind and go on a search for the meaning of life. I was guided by a higher power to go to North America where I would find happiness and the answers that I was so desperately looking for. During this time, I began to meditate for the first time in my life and, whilst I was meditating, a strange word would come up into my consciousness. This one simple but weird word which had been permeating my consciousness from even before I had left the UK was 'Kundalini'. At the time I had no idea what it meant and I guessed that it had to be some funny word that I had read in a book or heard in a song. It was much later on in my journey that I randomly came across the word again in a local community newspaper. The article spoke about strange spiritual practices that were carried out in the early hours of the morning; practices that developed spiritual powers.

I was intrigued.

The same inner voice that had been guiding me all along directed me to search out the place and solve the mystery of the Kundalini. What I found was my spiritual home for the next 3 years and the beginning of my journey as a Kundalini yoga teacher. Kundalini may be known by different names within different belief systems, but it is always the same unwavering and unifying Force. It is the organic catalyst necessary to unify our body, mind, and soul. It is the divine light that invites poetry into our lives. It is the secret to living this human life as divine beings.

Many cultural legacies such as Mercury's serpent, also possess the symbol of Kundalini. As the alchemical symbol for the process of psychic metamorphosis, the Gnostics understood that the serpent also represented the spinal cord. Even if we were to look at the Greek God of Healing – Asclepius – he holds a staff which is intertwined with a serpent, and it has become a symbol for modern-day medicine. The staff represents the spine, and the serpent represents our Kundalini energy. This symbolic energy is the core of your personal power.

The practice of Kundalini Yoga, aims at awakening this energy. The practice includes practice of asana, pranayama, bandha, mantra chanting and meditation. The practice is designed to raise complete awareness of body and mind; to prepare the body and mind to handle the flow of Kundalini energy as it travels to the highest chakra. The goal is to increase consciousness and build compassion and healing.

Kundalini yoga is a powerful and sometimes complex set of movements and postures that will help to unite you to yourself; to empower yourself; to create a vehicle strong enough to be able to contain the Force. It all arms you with power and wisdom to use the Force. It will include breath work, asana, mantra, and movement; all to develop and strengthen awareness.

During your training you have your eyes closed. This is to help you withdraw your senses from the outside world to take your consciousness inside, in order to discover the world within you. You shut the world off outside in order to discover the power within you and to know yourself deeply. You will experience moments of 'no mind' so that you may hear the whisper for your soul – those individualised messages and guidance from the Force. The goal of Kundalini Yoga and all spiritual technologies is to create a conscious connection with the Divine.

Yoga means union.

The union is between our physical reality and God-consciousness - the universal energies and our soul. The practice of Kundalini Yoga removes our blocks and resistances. It raises our energy to higher frequencies and opens our awareness to expanded realities. If we train
ourselves to focus our attention on our goal of union, we can facilitate our transformation. The goal of this lesson is to set out guidelines on how we can train ourselves to pay attention to and hold the experience of the infinite in our consciousness.

JEDI EXERCISE - SAT KRIYA

This exercise works directly on stimulating and channelizing the kundalini energy, so it must always be practiced with the mantra Sat Nam. Sat Kriya strengthens the entire sexual system and stimulates its natural flow of energy. This relaxes phobias about sexuality. It allows you to control the insistent sexual impulse by re-channelizing sexual energy to creative and healing activities in the body.

Instructions
Tune in with ONG NAMO GURU DEV NAMO x 3
Posture:
1. Sit on the heels in Rock Pose, knees together.
2. Stretch the arms over the head with elbows straight, until the arms hug the sides of the head.
3. Interlace all the fingers except the index fingers. Men cross the right thumb over the left. Women cross the left thumb over the right.
4. The spine stays still and straight. This is neither a spinal flex nor a pelvic thrust.
5. Remain firmly seated on the heels throughout the motions of the kriya.
Locks & Mantra:
1. Begin to chant Sat Naam with a constant rhythm of about 8 times per 10 seconds.
2. As you pull the navel in and up toward the spine, chant Sat from the Navel Point. Feel it as a pressure from the Third Chakra.
3. With the sound Naam, relax the belly.
4. As you continue in a steady rhythm, the root and diaphragm locks are automatically pulled. The steady waves of effort from the navel gradually enlist the movement of the greater abdomen. The breath regulates itself - no breath focus is necessary.
5. The focus of the sound Naam can be either at the Navel Point or at the Brow Point (the point where the eyebrows meet at the root of the nose; the area that corresponds to the Sixth Chakra).
6. The force is through the navel but the two locks come along sympathetically. This natural pull of the two locks creates a physiological balance. Blood pressure is maintained evenly.

Time:
Continue for 3 - 31 minutes.

To End:
1. Inhale and gently squeeze the muscles from the buttocks all the way up along the spine.
2. Hold it briefly as you concentrate on the area just above the top of the head.
3. Exhale completely.
4. Inhale, exhale totally and hold the breath out as you apply a firm mahabandh - or root lock by contracting the lower pelvis, lift the diaphragm, lock in the chin, and squeeze all the muscles from the buttocks up to the neck.
5. Hold the breath out for 5 to 20 seconds according to your comfort and capacity.
6. Inhale and relax and the back for 3-5 minutes.

THE TEN BODIES

As humans, we are very attached to our physical body. We identify with it. We consider it to be the expression of who we are, we think of ourselves in physical terms and rely greatly on physical anatomy to enhance our potential. We often label ourselves based on our morphology; thin, fat or chubby, and carry this definition almost like a label. When we feel unwell, we try to heal the physical symptoms our body manifests. That is quite a limiting way of considering our existence.

Like other Eastern traditions, yogic teachings point out that in addition to our physical anatomy, there are also more subtle, energetic structures to consider when it comes to understanding our existence, our strengths and imbalances. Those structures constitute our subtle anatomy and include our life force energy and the channels through which it circulates within us, as well as our chakra system or energy centres which relate to physical, emotional and energetic capacities.

In Kundalini yoga, Yogi Bhajan also taught another way of understanding the subtle anatomy, which he referred to as the Ten Bodies or Ten Light Bodies.

"If you understand that you are Ten Bodies, and you are aware of those Ten Bodies, and you keep them in balance, the whole Universe will be in balance with you."

- Yogi Bhajan

The Ten Bodies are powerful capacities of the psyche (the psyche refers to the totality of the human mind, conscious and unconscious). Each of the Ten Bodies has specific gifts that manifest when strong, and certain deficit tendencies that surface when weak. Yogi Bhajan explained that the root of all disease exists first in one of these spiritual or energy bodies before it manifests outwardly.

Therefore, by learning about the Ten Bodies, we can understand where some of our imbalances lie and work on strengthening the weak bodies to make ourselves healthier and happier.

To follow, I intend to give you an overview of what the Ten Bodies are and how they manifest when balanced or weak.

1ST BODY: THE SOUL BODY

The first of the ten light bodies is your soul, your connection to your inner infinity. It is the foundation which connects you to your purpose and destiny.

When your Soul Body is in balance, you feel connected to your inner wisdom. Your intuition is strong, you are creative and come from a place of humility and understanding. Your heart rules over your head so you can trust and relax into the flow of life. When your Soul Body is weak, you tend to come from your head instead of your heart. You over intellectualise and feel stuck, not able to access your creative flow.

Tip to strengthen the Soul Body: Practice heart opening exercises (yoga kriyas and/or meditations). Lead with your heart in general.

2ND BODY: THE NEGATIVE (PROTECTIVE) MIND

This is the part of your intellect which gives you discernment and allows you to set boundaries. It keeps you alive so although its name sounds negative, the Negative Mind is a good thing. The Negative Mind is often our stronger body and it is constantly working to assess our environment and situations for danger or negative potential. When your Negative Mind is in balance, it warns you of potential dangers, keeps you safe and alive. It gives you patience to listen to your inner guidance. When your Negative Mind is weak, you may be overprotective and do not take action because you fear the worst consequences. You may also be aware of the dangers but choose to ignore them. A weak Negative Mind can cause you to go into self-destructive relationships.

Tip to strengthen the Negative Mind: Practice discipline and integrity.

3RD BODY: THE POSITIVE (EXPANSIVE) MIND

This body serves to identify opportunities and see the positive essence of all situations. The Positive Mind gives you willpower and encouragement to take the necessary steps towards your destiny. When your Positive Mind is in balance, you have a good sense of humour and sense of hope. You see the good in all and judge situations with honesty and clarity. Your communication is strong and direct. You meet your challenges with reverence. When your Positive Mind is weak, you might be over positive and ignore dangers or simply not consider the risks.

Tip to strengthen the Positive Mind: Strengthen your navel point through core work. Work on increasing your self-esteem.

4TH BODY: THE NEUTRAL MIND

The Neutral Mind evaluates the inputs from the Negative and the Positive minds and delivers neutral guidance to us. Your Neutral Mind brings you in alignment with your destiny. When your Neutral Mind is in balance, it is meditative and gives you guidance from a place of intuition. It gives you the ability to recognise polarities (good versus. bad, right versus wrong etc.). When your Neutral Mind is weak, you have a hard time making decisions, obsessing

over weighing the pros and cons. You'll have the habit of being victimised by life because you don't know how to integrate your experiences and find meaning in them.
Tip to strengthen the Neutral Mind: Meditate.

5TH BODY: THE PHYSICAL BODY

This body is the temple where all the other light bodies meet. The Physical Body allows you to experience life, balance yourself and fulfil your desires. When your Physical Body is in balance, you have the strength to physically go for and sacrifice for your hopes and dreams. You can share your knowledge with others. When your Physical Body is weak, there can be narcissism and too much concern with perfection of the physical body. You may be angry, greedy, jealous, or competitive. Your inner and outer realities will be out of balance.
Tip to strengthen the Physical Body: Regular Exercise. Teach others, share what you have learned.

6TH BODY: THE ARCLINE

You can visualise your Arcline as a line of energy, extending over your head from ear to ear. Women have a second Arcline in front of the body which extends from nipple to nipple. Your Arcline gives you your projecting power and your radiance. It is also a protective shield. When your Arcline is in balance, you have the ability to focus, concentrate and meditate. Your projective power is strong, helping you manifest what you want in life. You are less prone to aggressions and negative thoughts. When your Arcline is weak you may be overprotective and easily influenced. You may be unfocused and unable to manifest your prayers. Tip to strengthen the Arcline: Awaken the third eye, the pituitary gland; seat of your intuition.

7TH BODY: THE AURA

The Aura is the electromagnetic field of energy that surrounds your Physical Body. Your Aura acts as a container for your life force energy, your prana, and is also a shield of protection. It extends up to 3 meters (9 feet) around the body. When your Aura is in balance, it creates a sense of presence and charisma. It elevates you. It can attract positivity and repel negativity. When your Aura is weak, you may be paranoid and lack self-trust, and negativity can penetrate into the psyche and into the physical body. Tip to strengthen the Aura: Meditate. Wear white natural fibre clothing. White, which holds all the colours of the spectrum, is believed to expand and magnify your Aura.

8TH BODY: THE PRANIC BODY

This body deals with the prana, the life force energy which comes with the breath. Through the breath, your Pranic Body continuously brings energy into your system. When your Pranic Body is in balance and your breathing is deep and relaxed, nothing can bother you. This body gives you the energy and self-motivation necessary to take action and achieve your goals. When your Pranic Body is weak you may have constant low-level anxiety and chronic fatigue. You may be fearful and defensive or try to get energy from food or stimulants. Tip to strengthen the Pranic Body: All breathing exercises (pranayama) are beneficial.

9TH BODY: THE SUBTLE BODY

This body carries your Soul when you die. It allows you to see through the veil, beyond the immediate realities of life. When your Subtle Body is in balance, you become subtle. You have great finesse and a powerful calmness. You learn quickly and master situations easily. When your Subtle Body is weak you may be naïve and easily fooled, unintentionally crude or rough in your speech or behaviour. You may be restless. Because you lack the peace that comes from flowing with the way things are. Tip to strengthen the Subtle Body: Develop mastery. One way to do so is to practice a Kundalini yoga kriya or meditation for 1,000 days.

10TH BODY: THE RADIANT BODY

This body gives you radiance and courage. It allows you to act despite the fear. When your Radiant Body is in balance, you are charismatic. You exert a magnetic presence and inspire respect. You give 110% to all that you do. You have authentic relationships with others and an overall well-balanced life. When your Radiant Body is weak, you tend to have a "my way or the highway" attitude. You may be afraid of conflict. You may shy away from other people's attention, or feel ineffective and unable to come through in situations. Tip to strengthen the Radiant Body: Have commitment. This could be commitment to your practice, to doing the right thing, to being true to you and so on.

When all Ten Bodies are in balance, we reach embodiment, the 11th Body, the state where we are one with the Universe's play. Kundalini Yoga works to balance and activate the Ten Bodies. Each Kundalini yoga kriya (or yoga set) is complete in itself. A regular practice is a comprehensive way to work on all Ten Bodies at once, if you are aware of a weakness or imbalance in one particular body, and you wish to focus on strengthening and balancing that body in particular, you can choose a meditation which works that particular body, or which uses a mantra associated with strengthening that aspect.

In the coming chapters we will be using meditations that work on the positive, negative, and neutral minds as well as the 7th body: our auric field.

***

CHAPTER 11: A CODE TO LIVE BY

> "I'll never turn to the dark side. You've failed, your highness. I am a Jedi, like my father before me."
>
> - Luke Skywalker, Star Wars: Episode VI - Return of the Jedi

LIVING THE WARRIOR'S CODE

A code has value as both an internal guideline and an external statement of our values and commitments. The best foundation for focusing on ourselves is to articulate, define, and live by a code. A code is an operating system. It describes the way you behave, engage, and show up. Being a warrior is not just about fighting for some great cause in a haphazard way; warriors follow codes that influence and shape their behaviour so that they may be the most effective warrior that they can be. Having a code is also about developing the right character as well as good moral and ethical principles that allow the warrior to battle honourably and with the right intentions

When Yoda first meets Luke, he does not immediately introduce himself. Instead, he tests him. He tries his patience — of which Luke has very little. He eats Luke's food, wants his lamp, and invites him over for dinner. It's a brilliant way of seeing not what kind of Force-wielder Luke is, but what kind of person. Once Yoda lays down the oddball facade and begins to train Luke in the ways of the Force, his lessons are challenging and full of wisdom, even for the audience. Among his many teachings, "Luminous beings are we, not this crude matter," remains particularly powerful. It's a reminder that all life is equal and connected, and only that understanding can lead to true selflessness. "Do. Or do not."

THE ORIGINAL YODA

Patanjali, as we have already seen in earlier chapters, was undoubtedly the greatest expounder of Yoga. He was one of the first people to teach its ways and has become somewhat of an enigma to modern historians because almost nothing else is known about him. It is only through legends that we think we have a clear picture of his spiritual nature. He is thought to be the founder of Swadhyaya, or the study of self as the primary basis point for yogic power. In the Indian tradition, the legend is that Patanjali was self-born and that he was a highly-evolved soul who incarnated of his own will in a human form to help humanity. Akin somewhat to the idea of a Force ghost and being able to project yourself over time and space like Luke did when he astral-projected for the final battle in the last Jedi.

Yoga philosophy and practice were first described by Patanjali in the classic text, Yoga Sutras, which is widely acknowledged as the authoritative text on yoga. Today, many people identify yoga only with asana, the physical practice of yoga, but asana is just one of the many tools used for healing the individual; only three of the 196 sutras mention asana (postures) and the remainder of the text discusses the other components of yoga including conscious breathing, meditation, lifestyle and diet changes, visualisation and the use of sound, meditation, mudra, bhakti devotion, karma yoga (selfless service), and ethical guidelines. In Yoga Sutras, Patanjali outlines an eightfold path to awareness and enlightenment called ashtanga, which literally means "eight limbs". (62) Head back to the previous chapter for recollection on the original Jedi and yogis.

*

THE 8 LIMBS OF YOGA

DIAGRAM OF THE 8 LIMBS OF YOGA

Patanjali says, you can't just practice asanas in yoga class, feel the stretch, and then go home and have a stiff drink, order a takeout meal, yell at your employees, and cheat on your taxes. That is not practicing real yoga. There is more to yoga than that — yoga can help you cultivate body, mind, and spiritual awareness. The heart of Patanjali's teachings is the eightfold path of yoga. It is also called the eight limbs of Patanjali, because they intertwine like the branches of a tree in the forest. These can sound like commandments, laws, or hard and fast rules but really they are a code for living. They provide a framework and structure to living your life. These are Patanjali's suggestions for living a better life through yoga. The eight limbs work together. The first five steps — Yama, niyama asana, pranayama, and pratyahara — are the preliminaries of yoga and build the foundation for spiritual life. They are concerned with the body and the brain.

The last three, which would not be possible without the previous steps, are concerned with reconditioning the mind. They help the yogi to attain enlightenment or the full realisation of oneness with Spirit. (63)

LIMB 1 - Yama Yama is social behaviour, how you treat others and the world around you. These are moral principles. Sometimes they are called the don'ts or the thou shalt nots. There are five yamas.

LIMB 2 - Niyama
Niyama is about inner discipline and responsibility, how we treat ourselves. We begin to build a healthy and loving relationship with ourselves which will then translate in how we relate to others and life.

LIMB 3 - Asana
"The posture of yoga is steady and easy," Patanjali says. . Although Westerners often consider the practice of asana or postures as an exercise regimen or a way to stay fit, Patanjali and other ancient yogis used asana to prepare the body for meditation. To sit for a lengthy time in contemplation required a supple and cooperative body. If you are free of physical distractions and can control the body, you can free the mind.

LIMB 4 - Pranayama
Prana is the life force or energy that exists everywhere and flows through each of us through the breath. Pranayama is the control of breath. The basic movements of pranayama are inhalation, retention of breath, and exhalation. "The yogi's life is not measured by the number of days but by the number of his breaths," says Iyengar. "Therefore, he follows the proper rhythmic patterns of slow, deep breathing." The practice of pranayama purifies and removes distractions from the mind making it easier to concentrate and meditate.

LIMB 5 - Pratyahara
Pratyahara is the withdrawal of the senses. Pratyahara occurs during meditation, breathing exercises, or the practice of yoga postures — any time when you are directing your attention inward. Concentration, in the yoga room, at your writing desk, or the boardroom, is a battle with distracting senses.

LIMB 6 - Dharana
Concentration or dharana involves teaching the mind to focus on one point or image. "Concentration is binding thought in one place," says Patanjali. The goal is to still the mind — gently pushing away superfluous thoughts — by fixing your mind on some object such as a candle flame, a flower, or a mantra.

LIMB 7 - Dhyana
Uninterrupted meditation without an object is called dhyana. Concentration (dharana) leads to the state of meditation. The goal of meditation is not unconsciousness or nothingness. It is heightened awareness and oneness with the universe.

LIMB 8 - Samadhi
The ultimate goal of the eightfold path to yoga is samadhi or absolute bliss. This is pure contemplation, super consciousness, in which you and the universe are one. Those who have achieved samadhi are enlightened. Paramahansa Yogananda called it the state of God-Union. (64)

THE YAMAS AND NIYAMAS

Here, we'll focus on the Yamas and Niyamas; the first two practices of Yoga according to Patanjali. Yogis follow a set of ethics and observances outlined in the Yamas and niyamas. They are the first two stops on the path; even before the physical postures called asana. They are ethical principles that are supposed to guide how we relate to other people and how we take care of ourselves.

The idea of a yoga practice is really not just to focus and be aware and mindful and calm for the time that we're on the mat, but to carry this state of being with us when we leave class, so it can have a much deeper impact than just making us look good. The Yamas and Niyamas are moral codes which dictate the right way to live. Honouring these ethics as we progress along 'the path' means that we're always being mindful of each action. This in itself means that we are cultivating a more present and aware state of being.

THE YAMAS

The word 'yama' is often translated as 'restraint', 'moral discipline' or 'moral vow', and Patanjali states that these vows are completely universal, no matter who you are or where you come from, your current situation or where you're heading.

The Yamas traditionally guide us towards practices concerned with the world around us, but often we can take them as a guide of how to act towards ourselves too. There are five Yamas in total listed in Patanjali's Sutras:
- **Ahimsa** (non-harming or non-violence in thought, word and deed)
- **Satya** (truthfulness)
- **Asteya** (non-stealing)
- **Brahmacharya** (celibacy or 'right use of energy')
- **Aparigraha** (non-greed or non-hoarding)

By considering these aspects in our daily practice on and off the yoga mat, all of our decisions and actions come from a more considered, aware, and 'higher' place, and this leads us towards being more authentic towards ourselves and others.

THE NIYAMAS

The word 'Niyama' often translates as 'positive duties' or 'observances', and are thought of as recommended habits for healthy living and 'spiritual existence'. They're traditionally thought of as practices concerned with ourselves, although of course we can think of them as affecting the outside world too. Patanjali lists a total of five Niyamas, but again there are other traditions and texts that list more:

- **Saucha** (cleanliness)
- **Santosha** (contentment)
- **Tapas** (discipline, austerity or 'burning enthusiasm)
- **Svadhyaya** (study of the self and of the texts)
- **Isvara Pranidhana** (surrender to a higher being, or contemplation of a higher power)

Iyengar describes both the Yamas and Niyamas as the 'golden keys to unlock the spiritual gates', as they transform each action into one that originates from a deeper and more 'connected' place within ourselves. Whether you consider yourself 'spiritual' or not though, and whether you practice yoga or not, these are all ways in which we can help ourselves and the world around us to be a better place. (65)

The yogi code allows the development of attitudes and aptitudes that give the yogi a framework to achieve their goal of divine union. Let's explore the Jedi code and how applying it allows the Jedi to be an effective conduit for the force.

THE CODE OF THE JEDI

There is no emotion, there is peace. There is no ignorance, there is knowledge. There is no chaos, there is harmony. There is no passion, there is serenity. There is no death, there is the Force.

A code has value as both an internal guideline and an external statement of our values and commitments. The best foundation for focusing on ourselves is to articulate, define, and live by a code. As mentioned, a code is an operating system. It describes the way you behave, engage, and show up.

Being a warrior is not just about fighting for some great cause. Warriors follow codes that influence and shape their behaviour so that they may be the most effective warrior that they can be. It is also about developing the right character as well as good moral and ethical principles that allow the warrior to battle honourably and with the right intentions. Let's review the Jedi code.

THERE IS NO EMOTION, THERE IS PEACE

The Jedi believe in denouncing emotions since they are the root cause of mortal suffering. They believe that fear, anger, attachment, desire, and pride cause sentient beings to lash out in conflict. Emotions impede rational thought, disallowing them from doing what is an objectively correct action. The Jedi are the opposite of the Sith - who focus on the dark side of the Force - the Sith use their passion, and other strong emotions to fuel their power. This is similar to the Buddhist teaching that craving and attachment lead us to more suffering. When our emotions are out of control, or unchecked, there will be a discordance within us. The emotions become like storms on the inner calm sea of our awareness, so Jedi are aiming to create peace within themselves. For a Jedi in the real-world, emotion is required. However, commotion is not. In this daily challenge, we are moving away from being reactive based on our emotions and developing a neutral and balanced approach to empowered living.

Emotions are a natural part of life. As the great movie saga has shown us, Jedi are not immune to feeling emotions. Jedi Masters, Obi-Wan Kenobi and Yoda both openly express their sorrow when they discover the death of younglings at the hand of the newly-appointed Sith Lord - Darth Vader. Certain emotions are even encouraged, contrary to popular belief. These are emotions such as love when applied from the Jedi perspective.

This tenet is not to say that emotion does not exist but that it be transcended, not used as the motivation for our actions but understood in the right context. Emotions must be understood first, and it is a young Jedi's duty to explore his feelings. Unless a Jedi can confront his thoughts and feelings, he will never achieve inner peace. Emotions, then, are not to be overcome or denied, but rather understood and dealt with. This tenet could be modified to read "Emotion cannot take away my peace." Jedi calm is different from normal calm in many ways. A person is calm only when the situation needs it. They have to try to be somewhat calm in the face of tragedy, excitement, or challenging life situations; which usually only lasts for a moment. The Jedi, on the other hand, rely on their calm to access inner stillness so that they can access knowledge that the Force has to offer them. They must strive to keep this calm at all times so that they may correctly act upon the will of the Force. This calm is taught early on to young aspiring padawan. It is further strengthened during the various trials and tests that the Jedi undergo. The peace brought on by true calm is the only way to fully access the power of the Force.

This does not mean that we are emotionless; it means that once we have developed enough inner Jedi calm to understand and master our emotions, we find peace. This statement is a reminder that our actions do not come from our emotions, but from the compassion that comes from our peaceful state of mind.

JEDI EXERCISE: PEACE REFLECTION
In your Jedi journal, record the following observations:
- What brings you Peace?
- How does your Peace affect those in and around your space?
- How do things work out for you when you are calm? Which emotions do you struggle with the most?

THERE IS NO IGNORANCE, THERE IS KNOWLEDGE

Jedi are training to be whole and well-rounded in all aspects of their being. This is a line that means many things to a Jedi. Firstly, the surface meaning is that a Jedi should strive for holistic intelligence in all things that they have to deal with. They cannot be ignorant of the places they go or the situations they find themselves in. There must be an understanding of what they are involved with. Does the current challenge require action, reflection or would it be best to avoid it?

A Jedi must study hard and apply themselves to all aspects of life, not just the Force and the Jedi Way. There is a commitment to exploring different aspects of life thus becoming competent in relationship dynamics, financial management, personal healthcare, and good dietary habits. They must learn about anything that one may find useful in some dispute. They must learn the laws of the land, and understand the basic psychology of individuals and groups. They must practice and refine communication skills, develop negotiation skills, effective conflict resolution techniques, as well as communicating clearly and effectively. They should become receptive through trust in the Force. Only then will knowledge be attained. The Force tells us what we need to know when the need arises. Required knowledge is obtained from guidance by the Force in unexpected ways like stumbling upon a book that gives us the answer we were searching for, or seeing the same object or image repeatedly. This can help bring knowledge as we "connect the dots" in your mind.

Trust in the Force, and it will teach you much.

Ignorance is the absence of knowledge.

By keeping a closed mind to things, we become ignorant to the things that the world has to offer us. If we keep an open mind to things, we gain knowledge. Keeping an open mind on things allows us to take in information, separate fact from fiction, and research what we don't know. A Jedi must be discriminating and try to understand how the world that they exist in operates.

Ignorance is a part of life but it must not be feared. For more knowledge to light their way, the Jedi Temple Archives contain possibly the single largest source of information in the galaxy. In yogic philosophy, this is known as the akashic records. It is a compendium of all human events, thoughts, words, emotions, and intent ever to have occurred in the past, present, or future. However, this tenet also reminds the Knight that knowledge can be taken from the most unusual places. The great Master Yoda demonstrated this to the young Luke Skywalker on Dagobah when he acted like a fool; being childish in front of younglings. This performance was meant to teach Luke and the younglings the simple fact: even the foolish can be wise. Indeed, while instructing younglings, Master Yoda was often heard to remark that "Truly wonderful the mind of a child is." This tenet is what gives the Jedi his open mind and ability to accept what other beings would tend to see as unacceptable. In other words, this tenet points out that a Jedi must often use not only his rational mind but also his intuitive mind in order to ascertain the truth of a situation. This tenet is embodied by Qui-Gon Jinn's statement to Anakin Skywalker to "feel, don't think."

THERE IS NO PASSION, THERE IS SERENITY

This line speaks of the physical attachment a person usually has to other people and things. It is good to have the drive to do certain things, but to let that drive run everything that you are, is allowing passion to overrun you. The first tenet of no emotion relates to this. Passion in its negative expression is a path to the dark side. If you cannot control yourself, how can you ever hope to control the Force and maintain your inner peace? This also forbids attachment and possession to other people. To have an emotional tie is to have something blinding you from the greater good. The Jedi cannot afford to let personal feelings invade their thoughts and actions. Their duty is to the Force, and to the Jedi Order. If you were to have to choose between saving a person you cared for from dying, or saving ten people you didn't know from dying, chances are, you would choose to save the one you love. To anyone who has ever been in love and felt the desire for another and said that they would save the ten, quit kidding yourself. Passion comes from the Late Latin word "passio" - to suffer. By giving in to our emotions - becoming passionate about something - we suffer. Emotions are irrational and unpredictable, but by letting them guide us, we become irrational and unpredictable. We then struggle for peace within and suffer for it. We then make others suffer from our irrational behaviour. Sexual passion is a powerful energy; fiery in nature with the power to overrun our logic and make us do things which we would not normally do. Jedi are encouraged to live celibate lives for this reason. Chastity is a virtue related to temperance, and it is defined as refraining from unreasonable sexual conduct or romantic relationships. Chastity allows the Jedi to uphold their moral standards while adhering to the guidelines of the Jedi culture.

Serenity can be described as "an utter sense of calm." which comes from within. Controlling our passions allows us to be at peace and thus achieve serenity. However, passion in this context refers more directly to situations of extreme stress in which a Jedi might be tempted to react strongly. That a Jedi must draw his weapon only in defence is an expression of this tenet. While emotions and intuition must be understood and utilised in a Jedi's daily life, he must never act rashly. Passionate use of power leads to the dark side. A Jedi must always act with a calm hand and an even temper.

THERE IS NO CHAOS, THERE IS HARMONY

The Jedi believe all aspects of life are unfolding perfectly, just as they should, in their own perfect time for the greatest good of all. Too many who have no experience of the Force, the strong connection that the Jedi have to the unseen world may feel cynical; seeing the world as a random unpredictable series of events. This line of thinking automatically causes agitation, fear and an inability to be calm in an unjust and unpredictable world.

'There is harmony' reflects the cosmology of the Jedi Order. Whereas uninitiated beings see the universe as a chaotic and disconnected place, a Jedi realises that all things are interconnected and, more importantly, interdependent. While an uninitiated being sees sorrow and tragedy in the workings of the universe, through the Force, a Jedi is able to interpret and understand even the most painful of life's events.

The Jedi, through their training, understand the vastness of the universe. They look at the bigger; perceiving the mysterious workings of the universal force. Their will is connected to the will of the Force and over time have experienced the unfolding of events, that at the time seemed dire, actually turned out to be the best thing for everyone involved.

Every event has a purpose. Minor inconveniences such as failure, disappointment, and disagreement are also inevitable and should be taken in stride. Jedi do not deny the fact that tragic and terrible things happen; they merely point out that tragedy is simply another part of life. By developing this inner harmony through understanding the nature of the Force, the Jedi bring peace and understanding to all who come in contact with them.

THERE IS NO DEATH, THERE IS THE FORCE

The Force seems to be all energy, all things, all change. It always has been, and always will be, all-encompassing unto itself. It is an eternal aspect that runs through the fabric of the universe. The Force is responsible for all elements of creation. It sustains the elements, destroys the elements, and transforms the elements. Death is a factor of change, and thus a factor of the Force.

Without death, there is no life.
Without decay, there is no transition.
Without ageing, there is no youth.

This does not mean being a Jedi will make you live forever in physical form but that your essence continues through the Force. Our soul and our energy, is part of the Force. As such, we are luminous beings encased in a shell of tissue - organs, skin and bones. When the body dies, we do not die, but rather the physical vehicle is exchanged for another physical life form. We transform. We become one with the Force. The way we live our life, the principles we lived, the courage we brought to it, and the integrity that we embodied could go on forever inspiring people; thus immortalising the life we lived. As the great Jedi Master Yoda once told Anakin Skywalker, "Death is a natural part of life. Rejoice for those around you who transform into the Force. Mourn them do not. Miss them do not." To the Jedi, death is a natural part of life. Nothing to be feared. The Force is life itself. From the Force, life comes, and to the Force, life returns. So, when we "die" we become one with the Force, therefore there is no death. It can take time to fully adopt a new code and a new way of approaching life but with persistence and time you will find that it will bring you untold benefits. Just try it for yourself and see. Memorise the Jedi code. The Jedi Code should inform the way that you interact with the world and how you think about yourself. The Jedi code is your mantra whenever you get frustrated or worked up. It will guide you and protect you against the power of the dark-side.

ANALYSING YOUR JEDI CODE EXERCISE

Go to your sacred space. Take some time to become still and quiet; reflecting on the idea of living by a code.
Do you live by a code?
What would your experience of life be like if you lived by a code?
Maybe you have a code that you do live by, but have never thought of it as a code for life-energy. Make notes in your training manual; capturing any insights and benefits

*

BE YOU

"Always be yourself. Express yourself. Have faith in yourself. Do not go out and look for a successful personality and duplicate him."

— **Bruce Lee, Martial Artist, Actor, Philosopher**

It is very helpful to have maps and codes for living to orientate and guide us through life's many challenges, as we walk towards finding our unique place and contribution to the world. This can only be found and expressed when we are being true to who we really are and expressing ourselves authentically. You may be new to this type of work or you may be a seasoned warrior who has completed many cycles of the hero's journey. You may have collected many years of experience as well as many tools and techniques. If so, that is great. I encourage you to use them. We are unique and individual aspects of the force with different temperaments, personalities, and skill levels; so, we must find the approach that works best for oneself.

Growing up, Bruce Lee was an inspiration to me. I believe that his words and actions will continue to have a positive impact on future generations to come. He forged a legacy and destiny for his own life. His movies are an inspiration for me and so is his martial arts. His philosophy for life will stay in my heart and soul forever. Nowadays we know limitation as taking what is useful for you - not everyone else - discarding the rest. Always believe in yourself and always be yourself; not what others expect you to be.

"Absorb what is useful, Discard what is not, add what is uniquely your own."

— **Bruce Lee, Martial Artist, Actor, Philosopher**

I feel that this is the best way to approach a spiritual path. What worked for Buddha may not work for you; just as what Lao Tsu teaches may not resonate with you. If you hold to the ideas without understanding them, you will create discord in your life. The same thing happens when ideas become stagnant and we don't let them go. Go at your own pace and with your own understanding. No single person, or line from a book, can give you complete understanding.

It has to come from within.

Bruce Lee did not look to imitate others; he was committed to going deeply within himself to find the truth about his own unique essence and how to express it honestly in the world. He was constantly working on understanding his true self through active observation, questioning, researching and journaling.

Bruce Lee was unique; one of a kind! We are each unique in our own way and there's no one exactly like us. Be yourself, be true to yourself.

"Who's the more foolish, the fool or the fool who follows him?"
— **Obi-Wan Kenobi, Star Wars: Episode IV – A New Hope**

Master Jedi Qui-Gon is ahead of his time - a true visionary. He is the Jedi who shows Yoda the error of his ways, and guides Yoda as well as Obi-Wan towards a better future for the galaxy. He is quietly radical and rebellious, but not out of ambition or narcissism. Qui-Gon's independent streak, though, stems from his belief that he is in service to something greater. Qui-Gon's unconventional and open-minded approach to the Force, as well as a willingness to learn about it through disciplines other than those usually taught by the Jedi, make him a force to be reckoned with.

Each Jedi follows the way of the Jedi path, but in their own unique expression. They are not robots, but have found their unique connection and expression of the Force. They are committed to protecting the galaxy. You can apply the Jedi approach to your own life in whichever form that may take : A jedi mum or dad , jedi teacher, jedi officer, jedi student, jedi weight-trainer, you can apply it to any aspect of your life and make it uniquely your own .

"Every individual has the potential to be original."
-**Yogi Bhajan, Yoga and Spiritual Teacher**

THE REBEL JEDI

The spiritual teacher, Osho, shares his teachings regarding how to find one's path in the world as well as the power of following and creating your own path in life. In his words; "The rebel has no path to follow; those who follow any path are not rebels. The very spirit of rebellion needs no guidance. It is a light unto itself." (66)

Express yourself and have faith in yourself. The people who cannot rebel, ask for guidance, and want to be followers. Their psychology is that to be a follower relieves them of all responsibility. The guide, the master, the leader, or the messiah becomes responsible for everything. All that is needed of the follower is just to have faith. Just to having blind faith is another form of spiritual slavery.

The rebel is in a state of tremendous love with freedom – total freedom, nothing less than that. Hence, he has no saviour, no God's messenger, no messiah, no guide; he simply moves according to his own nature. He does not follow anybody; he does not imitate anybody. Certainly, he has chosen the most dangerous way of life, full of responsibility, but of tremendous joy and freedom.

He falls many times, he commits mistakes, but he is never repentant of anything because he learns a deep secret of life: by committing mistakes you become wise. There is no other way of becoming wise. By going astray, you become more clearly acquainted with what is right and what is wrong; because whatever gives you misery, suffering, makes your life a darkness without end, without any dawn, means you have gone astray. Find out, and come again to the state of being where you are peaceful, silent, serene, and a fountain of blissfulness, and you are again on the right path. There is no other criterion than that. Being blissful is to be right. Being miserable is to be wrong.

The pilgrimage of a rebel is full of surprises. He has no map, no guide, so every moment he is coming to a new space, to a new experience – to his own experience, to his own truth, to his own bliss, to his own love. (67)

It is said that followers will never truly experience the beauty of things on a first-hand basis as they will always be subject to second hand experiences. You must venture into paths less travelled instead of using second-hand knowledge in order to appear to be wise. Knowledge shouldn't just be borrowed and imitated but forged and discovered. We are not mere parrots to memorise knowledge without making discoveries of our own.

People who do this are said to not be taking their own lives into their own hands; they are not being respectful of their own dignity.

The following is an excerpt from Osho's work, *The Rebel*:

They are not trying to figure out, "Who am I?" They are simply trying to imitate somebody else. They can become good actors, but they can never become themselves. And your acting – however beautiful, however correct – will always remain something superficial, just a layer of dust on you. Any situation can scratch it, and your reality will come out.

You cannot lose your uniqueness; that is your very being. And particularly the rebel... his very foundation, his very spirituality, his whole being is an assertion of his own uniqueness. It does not mean that he is asserting his ego, because he respects your uniqueness too.

The rebel is the real spiritual being. He does not belong to any herd, he does not belong to any system; he does not belong to any organisation, he does not belong to any philosophy. In simple, conclusive words, he does not borrow himself from others. He digs deep within himself and finds his own life juices, finds his own life sources.

And remember, your path is not going to be anybody else's path, because each individual is so unique that if he follows somebody else's path, he loses his own identity, he loses his own individuality, he misses the most beautiful experience in existence. That's the beauty of the rebel – that he does not need a guide. He is his own guide, he is his own path, he is his own philosophy, he is his own future. It is a declaration that "I am all that I need and existence is my home. I am not a stranger here." (68)

*

BREATHE, JUST BREATHE

"Lesson one. Sit here, legs crossed. "The Force is not a power you have. It's not about lifting rocks. It's the energy between all things, a tension, a balance that binds the universe together. Breathe. Just breathe. Reach out with your feelings. What do you see?"
- **Luke Skywalker, Star Wars: Episode VIII - The Last Jedi**

Watching the Star Wars movie for the first time and hearing the deep scary mechanical breathing had me sitting wide-eyed with fear. There's no denying that Darth Vader is one of the most famous fictional characters ever created. However, it's not just his black cape or helmet that has taken the world by storm. Darth Vader, although being the villain, is an icon and his voice and breathing are recognised the world over.

The first of Darth Vader's breath sounds is an inhale, or "air in"; the second is an exhale, or "air out". Star Wars sound creator Ben Burtt created Vader's distinctive heavy breathing sound by recording his own breathing in a Dacor scuba regulator. Vader's suit is basically an iron lung that breathes for him. Anakin's lungs suffered severe burns on Mustafar and he can no longer breathe on his own. Could Vader's lack of proper breathing be one of the reasons he has a strong connection with the dark-side of the force?

As a general rule society does not breathe correctly. Our stressed-out nervous systems and the current frequency of fear lurking at every corner means we tend to breath in a shallow quick breath which further stresses out our nervous system. Over time these stresses impact our health and our ability to be effective Jedi warriors.

Your respiratory system works hard, logging 20,000 breaths daily. Every system in the body relies on oxygen; from cognition to digestion. Effective breathing can not only provide you with a greater sense of mental clarity, but it can also help you sleep better, digest food more efficiently, improve your body's immune response, and reduce stress levels.

PRANAYAMA

Pranayama - the Sanskrit word for "life force" comprises all cosmic energy; permeating the Universe on all levels. In living beings, this universal energy is considered responsible for all bodily functions through five types of prana, collectively known as the five vāyus.

Sound familiar? An energy field that surrounds us and binds us together is how Obi-Wan Kenobi describes the Force in Star Wars: Episode IV – A New Hope. The Jedi draw their powers from the Force; an energy field that is created by all living things. The Jedi don't seek to control the Force, rather they sense it and allow it to flow through them. They harness it. The Force in Yoga can be likened to a combination of Prana – or life-force energy - and Brahma – the supreme consciousness. Yogis harness their own Prana, and purify it through asana and pranayama; merging Prana with Brahma through meditation to achieve oneness with the universal Force. We'll explore this in greater detail in the chapters to follow.

Many ancient wisdom traditions teach us that life is one — yoga being a prime example, as the word translates directly as "union." The experience of oneness has been spoken of by mystics and sages, and is now sought out by contemporary practitioners of yoga, meditation, and other forms of spiritual or contemplative practice. When this awakening occurs and we catch a glimpse of the underlying reality that we are all connected, an appreciation of the Force has a profound potential to change our consciousness and our actions.

VAYUS

The prana vayus are the five movements or functions of prana or life force. Vayu means wind and the five prana vayus are prana vayu, Apana vayu, samana vayu, udana vayu, and vyana vayu. Each of these vayus governs a different area of the body. When they are balanced, they promote health and vitality of the body and mind. This then allows us to realise our full potential.

NADIS

Nadis are energy channels through which "prana" energy, life, and consciousness – streams. Within the human body, there is a subtle and perfect network of 72 Nadis - one for each of the 72 main body areas - each nadi can vibrate in 1000 modes (according to the 1000 petals of the crown chakra), that makes 72.000 vibrations) that distribute this life force throughout the whole body. On the physical level, the Nadis correspond to the nervous system, but their influence extends beyond this to the astral and spiritual planes of our existence. If all the Nadis are functioning correctly then we are healthy and generally feel happy. But nearly every one of us has some physical or psychological problems, which means that some of the Nadis is not working properly and need to be balanced. Prana is conscious energy, which means that the Nadis also transmit consciousness. Utilising the Nadis one can see and hear things at a great distance and move in other levels of consciousness. There are numerous reports from people who were clinically dead and then came back to life again. They nearly all described how they traveled along a tunnel with light radiating at the end. This tunnel is the Nādī through which life escapes from the body. We can also have such "tunnel experiences" in dreams and on astral journeys. With these, we are not really outside the body but in an altered state of consciousness. The Nādīs make it possible for us to take mental journeys of discovery throughout the entire Universe. With their help, our consciousness can go to any place we would like without the body having to move at all.

Three Nādīs are of special importance are **Ida, Pingala, and Sushumna**.
- **Ida** arises on the left side of the body and represents the moon principle
- **Pingala** begins on the right side of the body and symbolises the sun principle.
- **Sushumna** runs through the central channel of the spinal cord and represents consciousness.

On the physical level pingala - solar sun energy – is masculine and has its counterpart in the sympathetic Nervous System. Ida in the parasympathetic-left nostril - lunar moon energy – is part of the feminine Nervous System. Sushumna in the Central Nervous System itself.

The moon symbolises the mind with its changeable feelings, whereas the sun represents the intellect. Just as our emotions and thoughts change constantly, the moon is also constantly changing its form. The intellect, however, is a stable and constant principle like the sun.

Only when harmony and balance prevail between the moon system and sun system are we healthy and capable of developing further mentally and spiritually. We can activate and harmonise the Nadis through the breath. When we breathe through the left nostril in Pranayama we activate the Ida Nadi. The Idā Nadi cools, quietens, and refreshes body and mind like the silvery light of the moon. Pingala Nadi, however, which is influenced by breathing through the right nostril, has a warming and activating influence, in the same way as sunshine warms the earth and stimulates the growth of vegetation.

Nerves are normally described as beginning in the brain and going down into the body. However, Ida and Pingala nadi are usually described as starting in the root chakra and going up the spine; ending in the nostrils. Ida and Pingala sit at approximately the level of the Pituitary Gland. Idā affects the right side of the brain whilst Pingala influences the left hemisphere. To maintain balance both Nadis run in a snake-like course from one side of the body to the other. At the points where they cross, they also meet with the central Nadi; Sushumna. The first crossing of the Nadi at the top of the spinal column forms the Throat Chakra – also known as the Vishuddhi Chakra - and the last crossing at the base of the spinal column forms the Root Centre – also known as the Muladhara Chakra. Here the Ida Nadi flows on the left side of the body and the Pingala Nadi on the right side, and it is precisely here that our dormant consciousness lies hidden.

At several places along the spinal column, the Nadis form a type of knot - each of which constitutes a key point in our spiritual development. When these knots are untied, the energy located within them is activated and the hidden powers – also known as Siddhis or Jedi force powers - are given to us as healing powers. We are then able to enact these powers in the seeing of past and future, the seeing of auras, and other supernatural abilities. (69)

BREATHING POWER

Of all our physical processes, this is the most fundamental one. It goes without a thought, but once we place a focus on it, it has the power to change our vitality. It can enhance our self-confidence, sharpening our ability to focus, as well as easing stress and anxiety. Ultimately, we can strengthen the quality of our voices, and relieve pain.

BREATH AWARENESS FOR BEGINNERS

Warriors need to regulate their breath as the situation requires, in order to be calm and focused when needed as well as to be energised and quick like fire when called for. We will begin with a very simple but powerful practice that will serve as the foundation for all the breathing exercises that we will practice.

Find a quiet place or retreat to the Jedi space that you created - anywhere you won't be disturbed. Sit down comfortably and begin to notice the inhale and exhale of breath through the nose. Just become aware of the flow of breath and notice how you are breathing.
- Is the breath fast or slow?
- Is the breath deep or shallow?

Become aware of the sensations at the entrance of the nostrils.

You may feel some tingling or tickling sensations. Perhaps you will feel the flow of breath going through each nostril.
- Can you feel the temperature of the air as it comes in and goes out?

BREATHING INTO THE BELLY- BASIC JEDI BREATH TECHNIQUE

Sit crossed-legged with your spine straight. Close your eyes and begin to breathe just through your nose, keeping your mouth closed. You may place a hand on your belly to help you connect with the movements until you are familiar with them. Start by filling the abdomen, then expanding the chest, and finally lifting the upper ribs and clavicle. The exhale is the reverse: first the upper deflates, then the middle, and finally the abdomen pulls in and up, as the Navel Point pulls in.

Practice this by separating the three parts of the breath. Sit straight on the floor, in a chair. Initially have the left hand on the belly, and notice the movement of the belly as you breathe. Place your right hand on your chest to feel the movement of the diaphragm.

LONG DEEP BREATHING - JEDI BREATH TRAINING TO RELAX AND REGULATE THE NERVOUS SYSTEM

In our demanding high-speed modern world, we push ourselves to our limits. The constant barrage of things to do causes our systems to always be on high alert; ready for our next job or task. This can cause our body and nervous system to perceive this as an outside attack on our system. In this state, our nervous systems switch to our primal reptilian brain; engaging the fight or flight response as a way to manage the perceived threat.

The constant stream of negative fear-based messages means we are always on the lookout for the perceived danger. This activation of our sympathetic nervous system places us on high alert and affects the pattern of our breath.

In this state of fear, we tend to breathe shallowly; high up in the throat and chest with a rapid pattern of breath starving the muscles and cells from optimal functioning. Taking long deep breaths on the other hand will engage the parasympathetic nervous system. Note how when people are in shock or upset, we suggest that they take a deep breath. The body's ability to self-regulate and calm itself down through the breath, in times of danger and stress, is incredible.

This is a great breath to practice and master.

Use it on the train bus to work, and practice it whenever you are stuck or frustrated in a queue. Most importantly, don't take our word for it. Experience it for yourself. Here's why you should try it:

- Long deep breathing relaxes and calms you due to its influence on the parasympathetic nervous system;
- Increases the flow of prana;
- Reduces and prevents the build-up of toxins in the lungs by encouraging the clearing of the small air sacs (alveoli);
- Stimulates the brain chemicals (endorphins) that help fight depression;
- Brings the brain to a new level of alertness;
- Pumps the spinal fluid to the brain, giving greater energy;
- Stimulates the pituitary gland to secrete, thus enhancing the intuition;
- Filling the lungs to capacity revitalizes and re-adjusts the magnetic field;
- Cleanses the blood;
- Regulates the body's pH balance which affects the ability to handle stressful situations;
- Energizes and increases vitality;
- Aids in releasing blockages in meridian energy flow;
- Activates and clears the nerve channels;
- Aids in speeding up emotional and physical healing;
- Aids in breaking subconscious habit patterns such as insecurities and fears;
- Aids in fighting addictions;
- Re-channels previous mental conditioning on pain so as to reduce or eliminate pain; and,
- Gives the capacity to manage negativity and emotions, supporting clarity, cool-headedness, and patience;
- Raises our vibrational frequency.

DEEP BREATHING EXERCISE

Long Deep Breathing uses the full capacity of the lungs by utilising the three chambers of the lungs: abdominal or lower, chest or middle, clavicular, or upper. Begin the inhale with an Abdominal Breath. Then add the Chest Breath and finish with a Clavicular Breath. All three are done in a smooth motion. Start the exhale by relaxing the clavicle, then slowly emptying the chest. Finally, pull in the abdomen to force out any remaining air. Breathe through the nose. Continue for 26 breaths or 3 – 31 minutes.

ABDOMINAL BREATH:

Let the breath relax to a normal pace and depth. Bring your attention to the Navel Point area. Take a slow deep breath by letting the belly relax and expand. As you exhale, gently pull the navel in and up toward the spine. Keep the chest relaxed. Focus on breathing entirely with the lower abdomen. The diaphragm muscle separates the chest and thoracic cavity from the abdominal cavity and intestines. The diaphragm is a sheet of muscle that is normally in a dome shape. As you relax the diaphragm and extend the belly, the dome flattens and extra space is created to expand the lungs above it. When you exhale, the dome is re-created and the air from the lower lungs is pushed up and out. This pushing allows a portion of the lower lungs to be used efficiently. Place one hand on the Navel Point and one on the center of the chest. On the inhale, you will notice your hand rises as the belly rises, On the exhale lower it steadily. With your hand, monitor the chest to stay still and relaxed. Very soon you will notice all the muscles involved in this motion.

CHEST BREATH:

Sit straight and keep the diaphragm still. Do not let the abdomen extend. Inhale slowly using the chest muscles. The chest expands by using the intercostal muscles between the ribs. Do this slowly and focus on the sensation of expansion. Exhale completely but do not use the abdomen. Compare the depth and volume of this breath with an isolated abdominal breath. If you place your hands on the top and bottom parts of the ribs you can feel how the bottom ribs move more than the top ones. They are the floating ribs and are not as fixed as the upper ones to the sternum. So much of the contribution of the ribs and intercostal muscles comes from an expansion out to the sides of the lower ribs. (70)

ALTERNATE NOSTRIL BREATHING – JEDI BREATH TRAINING TO BALANCE THE HEMISPHERES OF THE BRAIN

This simple yet most powerful technique is a pranayama that is easy to do, and it creates a deep sense of well-being and harmony on the physical, mental, and emotional levels. It is integrating and grounding, and balances the right and left hemispheres of the brain. Relax and enjoy a feeling of well-being. The energy of the nervous system is directly proportional to one's breathing. The Creator in His wisdom gave us two nostrils. Ancient yogic texts explain that the nostril on the right is our sun nostril and it controls our energy level; our left nostril is our lunar nostril and it controls our emotions.

Consequently, if we are tired, breathing long and deep through the right nostril will give us added energy. Breathing through the left nostril will bring us calmness even in the midst of emotions (anger, nervousness, joy, sadness). When we breathe long and deeply through alternate nostrils, the whole nervous system is soothed, calmed, and energised simultaneously. All that is required of a person is to do this alternate nostril breathing for 3–5 minutes and his or her whole nervous system will be revitalised.

This particular technique is very simple, yet very effective. It is extremely helpful when we feel off-center and we still must function in the everyday world. For instance, we may be scheduled for an important interview, or business endeavour and find ourselves extremely nervous or irritable. This technique can help us calm ourselves and be effective in our communication.

TUNE IN WITH ONG NAMO GURU DEV NAMO x 3

Posture:
Sit with a straight spine. You may be in an Easy Pose or on a chair, wherever you can keep your spine straight and be comfortable.

Mudra and Breath:
Using the thumb and index fingers of the right hand, make a "U" of the two fingers, using the thumb to close off the right nostril and the index finger to close off the left nostril. Close the left nostril, inhale deeply through the right nostril. At the end of the inhale, close the right nostril and exhale through the left nostril.

Now inhale through the left nostril fully and deeply, then close the left nostril and exhale through the right one. Again, inhale through the right nostril and continue alternate nostril breathing. The breath must be complete and full-on both the inhalation and exhalation cycles.

Time:
Continue for 3 – 5 minutes.

To End:
Inhale deeply, hold the breath a few seconds, lower the hand, and exhale and relax deeply for a few minutes. (71)

BREATH OF FIRE – JEDI BREATH TRAINING TO ACTIVATE AND INCREASE ENERGY IN THE BODY

So, if the previous breath was to help us calm and ground ourselves down from hyperarousal then this one will work in a somewhat opposite way. If you feel tired and need a boost of energy or if you've been working long and hard every day, with your mind beginning to feel foggy, this will help clear all of that away

Breath of Fire is one of the foundational breath techniques used in the practice of Kundalini Yoga. It accompanies many postures and has numerous beneficial effects. It is important to master this breath so that it is done accurately and becomes automatic.

- Breath of Fire is rapid, rhythmic, and continuous. It is equal to the inhale and the exhale, with no pause between them (approximately 2-3 cycles per second).
- It is always practiced through the nostrils with the mouth closed unless stated otherwise.

- Breath of Fire is powered from the navel point and solar plexus. To exhale, the air is expelled powerfully through the nose, by pressing the navel point and solar plexus back toward the spine. This feels automatic if you contract the diaphragm rapidly.
- To inhale, the upper abdominal muscles relax, the diaphragm extends down, and the breath seems to come in as part of relaxation rather than through effort.
- The chest stays relaxed and slightly lifted throughout the breathing cycle.

ONE MINUTE BREATH- JEDI BREATH TRAINING TO MASTER THE BREATH AND MASTER THE MIND

Bruce Lee had the one-inch punch, and yogis had the one-minute breath. This powerful exercise will allow you to master your breath and your mind. The mind and the breath are intimately connected. When our mind is racing, you will notice that your breath is fast and shallow. As you noticed during long deep breathing, the slower and lengthier the breath, the quicker you will activate the parasympathetic nervous system; enabling it to kick in and relax your body and nervous system.

The One Minute Breath is a great Kundalini Meditation for developing intuition, relieving anxiety and stress, and strengthening the glandular system. It's simple, yet can be very challenging and profound. Practicing this breath regularly will calm your fears and worries and open you up to experiencing your spiritual nature. It's also a great meditation to choose if you would like to increase your lung capacity.

GET STARTED
TUNE IN WITH ONE NAMO GURU DEV NAMO

Sit with a straight spine and the hands in Gyan Mudra (index finger and thumb tip touching).

Eye Focus:
Eyes are closed, pressed gently up, focusing at the brow point.

Breath:
Slowly and steadily inhale 20 seconds, hold the breath for 20 seconds, and then exhale for 20 seconds. This may take days, weeks, or months to perfect. Start with the slowest breath you can manage at this time, but keep each segment equal in length. You might begin with inhaling for 8 seconds, holding for 8 seconds, and exhaling for 8 seconds.

Time:
Continue for 11 minutes.

HOW IT WORKS

For many people, the one-minute breath will be difficult at first. It may cause suppressed emotions to come to the uncomfortable surface, such as anxiety or fear. Practice for whatever length of time you can manage at first. Develop the capacity to observe, but not react to - whatever emotions are experienced. Gradually the emotional charge will dissipate and your breathing will deepen; increasing vitality. People who do breathing exercises will have the capacity for very long breaths. They will have extra prana. They are achievers. A happy person will never have shallow breathing, whereas the volume of energy in people who have a short breath is not balanced. Happiness is proportionate to your rate of breathing and the length of the breath. as the volume of oxygen that you have, will be equally proportionate to how much strength you will have. When we slow our breathing down to 8 breaths per minute, we induce relaxation and relief from stress. The parasympathetic nervous system is activated and healing processes are initiated. When we can slow the breath down to one breath per minute we calm anxiety, fear, and worry; integrating both hemispheres of the brain, and opening up to experiencing our spiritual nature. Intuition develops. The whole-brain works – especially the frontal hemispheres.

Now that you know how to balance your physical self in the ways of the warrior, we will now begin exploring the will of the warrior.

***

CHAPTER 12: THE WILL OF THE WARRIOR

"Fate whispers to the warrior, 'You cannot withstand the storm.' The warrior whispers back, 'I am the storm.'"

- Unknown

We see Luke start out as a nervous, shy, and frustrated farm boy; too scared and well behaved to confront his uncle. For Luke, this meant that he would have to work another season on the farm instead of going to flight school. He was easily dejected and accepting of his fate while his friends went off in search of something greater. As Luke takes his first steps on the hero's journey, we see him also develop his willpower and strength. Over the course of the movies we see his warrior's will grow stronger until it becomes strong enough to overcome the influence and power of the emperor who is the epitome of the dark-side.

These times are demanding that we live fearlessly; standing for truth, and lit from within by the radiance of the soul. The life of a spiritual warrior is a life of courage, compassion, strength and discipline. These qualities enable us to conquer our inner doubts and insecurities with steady determination and grace. As spiritual warriors, we are called to stand up for the dignity and human rights of our neighbours, our communities, our nation, and our planet. Every warrior will need to develop their 3rd Chakra as the seat of the warrior strength.

HARA CENTRE

The hara is not just an anatomical location but as the Dan Tian or centre of the energy of our body we gain our core physical, mental, emotional and even spiritual health, for in many ways we are as healthy and as calm, centred and peaceful as the hara. Most nations with enduring physical cultures have recognised this longstanding and as a result cross-cultural truth. From yogic and Qi Gong exercises of breathing, to belly dancing, meditation, martial arts, aerobics and more, these practices have recognised the importance of infusing the centre of the energy of life, the abdomen and the organs, with the breath of life to regulate the energy and blood of the entire body.

THE DAN TIEN

Explained from the vedic/yogic perspective the Dan Tien is something similar to, or to some identical to, the Sacral Chakra. In Japan, it is exactly identical to what they call the Hara. It's the centre of our creative power. When training in martial arts I frequently remind myself of the following.

All physical power comes from the waist.

All non-physical power comes from the heart.

It can be helpful to perceive the Dan Tien as a pearl of energy, for both its preciousness as well as its density due to layers and layers of calcium (or for us, energy) being built up over a long period of time. When we contract the perineum before and during exhalation, we can imagine that the energy now being drawn up the spine from the inward breath is being compressed into another layer of this energetic pearl in the centre of our body, an inch or two below our navel. A more advanced version is to also compress the stomach muscles, pulling them towards the spine during exhalation, though this is more forceful and therefore needs to be done with care. (72)

THE CHAKRAS

The word chakra means spinning wheel. These are the centre points of energy, thoughts, and feelings, as well as the physical body. According to yogic teachers, chakras determine the way people experience reality through emotional reactions, desires or aversions, levels of confidence or fear, and even physical symptoms and effects. There are said to be 7 major chakras with some schools of yoga claiming there are actually 114 in the body. The human body is a complex energy form; in addition to the 114 chakras, it also has 72,000 "nadis," or energy channels, along which vital energy, or "prana," moves. Head to the Appendix for descriptions of the major chakras.

The solar plexus-navel point, located in the centre of the abdomen, is referred to as the "hara". It is where the organs that give us life reside. Also, where we find the navel, we find the Chinese acupuncture point CV 8 Shen Que, or "Spirit Gate", which refers to the place where we received life from our mother by way of the umbilical cord. As such, these areas are the focal point of energy in our body from which life is given, sustained, and taken away. Located about six inches above your belly button within your diaphragm, the solar plexus chakra is associated with the colour yellow and the element of fire. This chakra is responsible for regulating the energy associated with action, intention, identity, and vitality.

Have you ever experienced great confidence, autonomy, and inner drive in your life? This was likely when your solar plexus chakra was healthy, harmonious, and functioning at its optimal state. However, there are many habits, mindsets, and traumatic experiences in life that can cause your solar plexus chakra to become blocked, suppressed or stagnant. If you have experienced a strict upbringing, bullying, authoritarian parents or figures in your life, mental, emotional, abuse, you likely have an impaired solar plexus chakra.

The Third Chakra, or navel point is dominated by the fire element, the Agni Tattva. It is the centre of will power, command, and control. It is the reserve energy center. Without a strong Third Chakra, you may have many ideas and good intentions but they may not come to fruition. With a strong Third Chakra, even your slightest intentions begin to manifest.

It is said that the Kundalini energy is initiated from the Third Chakra. The reserve energy at the navel gathers strength, and then goes through two small reserve channels down to the base of the spine and awakens the slumbering Kundalini which lies coiled through the First Chakra. Then the Kundalini energy begins its constant journey of awakening and arousal along the spine.

The stimulation, strengthening, and distribution of energy at the Navel Chakra is a central part of the warrior path. When the navel energy flows properly, it coordinates the organs of the body. The eliminative functions are triggered, the energy to support your actions is gathered, and the will to project that energy to support your actions is maintained. A person who has mastered the Third Chakra knows how to initiate and complete an action. That is why the Third Chakra is associated with the archetype of the spiritual warrior: one who is able to know one's mission and formulate the energy to act and complete it; to live with commitment, discipline, and stamina; to obey one's highest consciousness and command one's mind and senses. (73)

The modern world offers us many challenges and obstacles. We may be juggling a career whilst fulfilling childcare and family obligations, or we may be starting out in a new career and business that requires long hours and dedication. You may be challenged with ill health and an inability to complete tasks and obligations. We may have a cause close at heart that we are passionate about and wish to create some real change in order to help those less fortunate than ourselves. It can be difficult to influence outer circumstances and we thus feel that we don't have the energy to fulfil our good intentions. However, with the practices below, we will start to build energy reserves and strengthen our resolve to overcome.

Listed below are signs and symptoms that let us know that our solar plexus chakra needs healing. Tune into yourself and pay attention to your thoughts, feelings, actions, and physical sensations within your body.

Here are some signs to look out for:
- You constantly feel fatigued and lazy;
- You have a problem with overeating and overindulgence;
- You tend to manipulate others to get what you want;
- You frequently feel powerless and weak;
- You tend to be a bully or overly dominating around others;
- You feel insecure and unassertive;
- You lack self-confidence in most areas of life;
- You tend to seek approval from other people (i.e. you're a people-pleaser);
- You have low self-esteem;
- You have an excessively inflated sense of self (i.e. a big ego);
- You have addictive tendencies;
- You suffer from frequent gas, constipation or stomach upset; and,

How many of these signs can you relate to in this list? Make a note of these symptoms or others in your Jedi journal.

By strengthening and cultivating our inner strength, we put ourselves in a position to be true agents of change and guardians of our realms. As spiritual warriors in the Aquarian Age, we cultivate the qualities of living and dying fearlessly. The fear of death blocks our ability to live life fully. The essence of a spiritual warrior is fearlessness, and the ability to act with integrity regardless of conditions.

NAVEL POINT

From here, we will be referring to the 3 chakras – also described as the hara Centre – as the navel point to avoid confusion. The Navel Centre is the first point through which we are nourished while in utero. We are nurtured and given the energy to grow through this centre. Once that physical tie to our mother has been severed, it continues to collect energy, but from the cosmos instead. As we walk, our arms and legs perform this function whereby we can accumulate energy at this centre.

Our 3rd chakra is said to be the reserve pool of energy in our bodies. The Kundalini energy is initiated from here as the energy in this energy gathers strength before moving on to the 1st chakra to awaken our Kundalini energy. As this energy awakens and arises up our spine, we can use a stretch pose to further stimulate the Navel Point. When the energy begins to flow properly, it will create harmony amongst all of your organs. It is then that the will to project this newfound energy onto your actions is given to you. People who are strong at this 3rd chakra are known as the doers of the world. They know that the quality of their lives depends on their own actions and they act in ways that can shape, and direct their life path. They possess a fiery confidence about them and a willingness to initiate everything in their lives.

With confidence in yourself you will no longer have to battle your own aggressive egotism. You will simply feel comfortable in your own skin. You'll have trust in your own abilities and come to understand the power of choice – choice over your mindset and how you approach those around you.

This in turn, will give you the energy to set some healthy boundaries. Boundaries will keep you safe from lapsing into self-minimising roles around other people. Instead of engaging in conflict around your boundaries, you'll stand your ground respectfully but confidently. This newfound energy will allow you to relinquish addictive patterns so that you can carry out your goals with enthusiasm. You will feel empowered.

Whenever you feel this energy slipping, get out and do something. Taking action on a vision is a shortcut to hot-wiring that energy centre back up again. When you act in this chakra, you will rarely be still; always looking for something to do without the need of stimulants to get you through any given task.

When you are filled with emotions – bad or good – but you feel that you do not have the right to express them, that energy will undoubtedly pool up in the Navel Centre. With a strong 3rd chakra, you will be able to use this energy to action your plans and ambitions; initiating your awareness and your Kundalini energy.

Those who are strong in their 3rd chakra are the entrepreneurs, the go-getters, and the risk takers. They are the first to volunteer and the first to raise their hands. They are the first to lend a helping hand in a tough situation.

As Jedi, we can see that there are a lot of problems in the world. Injustice and suffering are rife and as the guardians or protectors of the earth, we have a duty to serve and help. This can sometimes bring about an apathetic feeling if we are unable to help. In the following pages, you will find Kundalini yoga postures that will allow you to develop your 3rd chakra and to develop the willpower as well as the strength of a spiritual warrior. You can begin practicing these now. Start with 1 minute and work up to longer times. Head to the next page for the stretch pose.

STRETCH POSE

The stretch pose is a challenging posture that, when done correctly, resets the entire nervous system and strengthens the abdominal area. It has a tremendous effect on the entire body. Stretch poses work on the navel point, which as we now know is the location of the 3rd chakra. By working on the third chakra, it boosts resolve and self-esteem. Stretch pose in conjunction with Breath of Fire - as we were made aware of in the previous chapter - is calming, rejuvenating, and it purifies the blood. For beginners, this posture can be difficult so start slowly and build up the duration of time. Start with 30 seconds, building up to one minute and work your way up to 3 minutes. 3 minutes is the optimal set time for max effect. Tune in with ONG NAMO GURU DEV NAMO x 3.

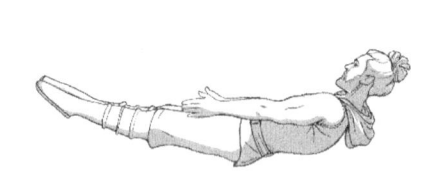

*Lie on your back. Legs stretched out arms by your side.
- Raise your head and heels 6 inches off the ground.
- Focus the eyes on the toes and stretch the toes so they point away from you.
- Place your arms either above your thighs with the palms facing down but not touching the legs or alongside your legs with the palms facing your body but not touching.
- Begin Breath of Fire.

Here are some tips and adjustments that will support your practice:
- Place your hands underneath your buttocks, this gives support to the low back and makes it easier to keep the legs up;
- You may want to start with alternating 10 seconds in Stretch Pose and 10 seconds resting.

Rest for 1-3 minutes when you finish. As you feel yourself getting stronger, increase the hold time and decrease the rest time. Allow your body to work into the posture; experimenting with these suggestions until you have built up the necessary strength of body and mind. Before too long, you will breeze your way through 3 minutes.

BENEFITS OF STRETCH POSE:
- Adjusts and strengthens the navel point, your power centre
- Tunes-up your nervous and digestive systems
- Strengthens the reproductive organs and glands builds abdominal strength improves posture gives you a sense of power and strength increasing self-esteem and wellbeing.

NAHBI KRIYA
This next set of exercises will help you build a warrior mindset, warrior body, and a strong will quickly and effectively. Nabhi refers to the Solar Plexus Chakra or Manipura Chakra, it is thought of as our power centre, located above the navel and slightly below the solar plexus; just below the belly button. The yogi says that the body has 2 heartbeats; one as the heart and the other being the nahbi/navel point. It's the place of willpower and action. Through our Solar Plexus Chakra, we harness personal empowerment, self-esteem, inspiration, and vitality. It will also help you get the abdominal area in shape – and there's nothing wrong with developing a warrior 6 pack.

JEDI EXERCISE: TUNE IN TO YOUR NAHBI
This is a challenging set so start with 2-3 mins for each exercise and then slowly increase onto the times stated. It's best not to eat anything for at least 2 hours before practice as the Kriya focuses on the midriff and belly.
Tune in with ONG NAMO GURU DEV NAMO x 3 .
Practice a few warm up exercises from the Jedi warm up set and When you are ready, come laying down on your back.

1. Alternating Leg Lifts: Lie flat on the back. Inhale and lift the right leg up to 90 degrees. Exhale and lower it. Repeat with the left leg. Continue alternate leg lifts with deep powerful breathing for 10 minutes. This exercise is for the lower digestive area. If you have any sort of back problem, it is advisable to put the palms on the floor underneath the lower back /bum to provide little support whilst you practice.

2. Leg Lifts: Without stopping, inhale and lift both legs up to 90 degrees. Exhale as you lower them. Stretch the arms straight up toward the sky, palms facing toward each other for balance and energy. Continue for 5 minutes. This exercise is for the upper digestion and solar plexus.

3. Knees to Chest: Bend the knees and clasp them to the chest with the arms, allowing the head to relax back. Rest in this position for 5 minutes. This eliminates gas and relaxes the heart.

4. This exercise flows from one position to the other without a break. Starting with the knees to the chest in position 3 above, inhale and open the arms straight out to the sides on the ground, and extend the legs straight to 60 degrees. Exhale and return to the original position. Continue for 15 minutes. This exercise changes the magnetic field and opens the navel centre.

5. Leg Lift: Lie on the back. Bring the left knee to the chest. Hold it there with both hands and rapidly raise the right leg up to 90 degrees and down. Inhale up, exhale down for 1 minute. Switch legs and repeat for 1 minute. Repeat the complete cycle for both legs one more time. This exercise sets the hips and lower spine.

6. Front Bends: Stand up straight. Raise the arms over the head so they hug the ears. Press the fingers back so the palms face the sky. Exhale as you bend forward to touch the ground with the palms, keeping the arms straight and hugging the ears. Inhale up very slowly with deep breathing. On the exhale, apply mulbandh.(root lock tightening the anus and sexual organs) Continue for 2 minutes, then increase the pace more rapidly for 1 more minute. This exercise is for the entire spinal fluid and the aura.

7. Totally relax or meditate for 10 to 15 minutes.

NABHII KRIYA TIPS: Remember to keep the breathing deep, and fully activate the navel centre. Keep the lower back pressed down and don't strain into your back, shoulders, or neck! When that burn in the core starts to happen, I find it helps to imagine the bright, unquenchable orange flame glowing brightly inside. Allow that burn to spread through the body; cleansing your body and mind of negativity and doubt. The increased strength and positive effects of the Kriya help us increase our vibrational frequency. Keeping strong with the force is not a one-day task but a difficult, daily task of strengthening our connection to the Force – it is not easy. It takes hard work, and most of it is pretty uncomfortable. However uncomfortable it may be, you need to do that work. No one else is going to do it for you, and that is the most important, empowering realisation that you can come to. You can and you will accomplish this. This is a fantastic set to practice for 40 days to really connect with your inner strength and power.

ARCHER POSE

In the great history of human evolution, there are many religious and mythological archers that have served their leaders in warfare. Great warrior archers like Apollo, Artemis, and Hercules were master archers. I love this posture as it allows me to channel my inner Robin Hood, or Legolas; if im having a Lord of the rings kinda day.

This is a powerful posture to develop overall body strength. It helps develop strength in the quadriceps and the intestines. The legs and knees are being strengthened. Outstanding physical stamina and strength are gained; while, remarkably, at the same time, there is an inner posture of feelings taking place that is equal in power to the pure physical connection of feet to the ground.

The posture develops Chivalry and fearlessness, inherent in this noble warrior stance.

Kundalini Jedi Warrior

Instructions:
Bring the right foot forward so that the feet are 2-3 feet apart.
The right toes face forward while the left foot comes to a 45-degree angle, with the heel back and the toes forward.
The left leg stays straight and strong as the right knee bends until the thigh is almost parallel to the ground. Do not let the knee go beyond the toes and tuck the tailbone.
Curl the fingers of both hands onto the palms, thumbs pulled back.
As if pulling back a bow and arrow, lift the right arm up, extended forward parallel to the ground, over the right knee. The left arm, bent at the elbow, pulls back until the fist is at the left shoulder. Pull Neck Lock. Chin in, chest out. Feel this stretch across the chest.

Eyes:
Eyes stare beyond the thumb to Infinity.

Time:
Practice for 3 minutes on each side.

Physical, mental and spiritual benefits of Archer, or Warrior, Pose:
- Makes you feel firm and grounded whilst it Strengthens the nervous system.
- Strengthens the knees, legs and intestines.
- Builds power in the navel and stimulates the alchemical fire that purifies and transforms us.
- Builds physical stamina and a reservoir of inner power.
- Opens the hips, giving you access to deep core strength.
- Gives steadiness & develops the ability to stay focused.
- Develops the qualities of a Warrior - courage, fearlessness and willpower.

- Builds self-esteem & self-assurance.
- Helps to promote a greater flow of energy and power throughout the physical and subtle bodies and thus promotes the expansion of consciousness.
- Works on all the chakras allowing them to open, heal and balance.
- If you need excessive sleep, it is said that this posture can help you cure this.
- Puts pressure on the thigh bone,
- It balances calcium, magnesium, potassium, and sodium in the body.

VIRASANA - HERO POSE

We don't normally imagine warriors slouching around on the sofa or sitting around aimlessly. Even when the warrior is relaxing, he is still keeping his posture and position as a warrior. We see Qui-Gon Jinn adopt this posture during his confrontation with Darth Maul in the climactic battle in 1999 Star Wars: Episode I – The Phantom Menace. During an intense lightsaber battle, the pair are separated by a forcefield; stopping their battle. As the Sith Lord continues to pace backwards and forwards, we see that the Jedi takes the warrior pose to close his eyes and gather himself in meditation, keeping his calm and posture even during battle.

Try this posture next time you're sitting down; swapping the sofa for the floor. This will build the warrior mindset whilst also benefiting your body physically.

STEPS OF HERO POSE VIRASANA

- First kneel down, at that point parallel your hip girth separately;
- Transfer a little in way over hip girth along with your higher than the level on the ground;
- Bend forward and twist the plump apart of calves external with the hands;

- Sit on the ground among the feet and breathe out. (During practice if you're feeling any distress or not able to sit properly on the ground, in that case, try to sit properly);
- Place your hands on top of thighs just near to knees, your palms should be facing down;
- Now relax your upper body and shoulders, your spine should be straight and tall;
- The crown of your head should point to the ceiling and looks straight ahead;
- During the process assume that you are hero or warrior, who sits tall and proud;
- Hold this pose for thirty seconds to one minute;
- During the process take normal breathing; and,
- After that, relieve your feet, ankles and knees. Shake your legs.

HEALTH BENEFITS OF HERO POSE VIRASANA
- Stretches the hips, thighs, knees, ankles and feet;
- Improves circulation and relieves tired legs;
- Strengthens foot arches, relieving flat feet;
- Improves digestion and relieves gas;
- Helps relieve the symptoms of menopause;
- Improves posture;
- Therapeutic for asthma and high blood pressure;
- It stretches thighs, knees, ankles and feet;
- Useful in meditation;
- Relieve legs tiredness;
- Virasana improves blood circulation in the legs;
- It improves digestion; and,
- Beneficial in gas problems.

ADDING A MANTRA
This pose can also be done in combination with a mantra adding; to the powerful effects of this kriya. We introduced you to the mantra 'Waheguru' in the sound and mantra chapter earlier. Here we have the same mantra, but in rhythmic repetition. Aquarian Sadhana's 'Wahe Guru, Wahe Guru, Wahe Guru, Wahe Jio' mantra generates a lot of heat in the body as well as a powerful magnetic field and expanded aura. It is the seat of the Warrior Saint.

MANTRA: WAHE GURU WAHE JIO
Complete Mantra pronunciation: Wha-hay guroo wha-hay guroo wha-hay guroo wha-hay jeeo · Language: Gurmukhi the word vāhegurūis traditionally explained as vāh "wondrous" + guru "teacher", together with said to carry the meaning, "The wondrous Lord/teacher who dispels the darkness of ignorance and bestows the light of truth, knowledge and enlightenment".

RECLAIM YOUR PERSONAL POWER

As warriors we must be aware of the thoughts and messages we tell ourselves. Many of our enemies are not lurking in the woods or on the battlefield but actually from our own repetitive self talk. Reclaim your personal power by repeating the following affirmations: "I can," "I will," "I have the power to decide," "I am strong and courageous," "I embrace my strength," "I love the person I am," "I stand up for myself," "I am responsible for my life," "I am worthy of love and kindness," "I am whole." (Say these statements out load now and notice how you feel after declaring them).These powerful statements, when repeated, start to influence our subconscious mind with the ultimate effect of raising our vibrational frequency.

The more you repeat these affirmations with sincerity, the more they will reprogram your unconscious mind, and therefore, open your solar plexus chakra. Try starting each morning with one of these affirmations. Stop seeing yourself as a "victim". It is best suited to eradicate deficient blockages.

As Aletheia Luna, for Loner Wolf, comments, one of the most damaging mindsets carried by those with blocked solar plexus chakras is the notion that they are "powerless" and defenceless victims of life. If you carry this mentality, it will manifest as the tendency to blame other people for your unhappiness. You might also find yourself constantly sacrificing your needs for others who don't always appreciate your efforts. This is also known as the Martyr Syndrome.

Secretly, there is a lot of energy put into playing the victim, and it is a facade that must be maintained - and reaffirmed - every day. If you see yourself as a person who is being victimised by someone else or something else, explore what it feels like to say "no." Playing the victim is so attractive because it allows us to bypass the weight of self-responsibility, so don't be surprised if you find yourself terrified of "stepping up" and reclaiming your power. It takes practice and courage.

So, what does a healthy and balanced solar plexus chakra look and feel like?

When you have a clear, strong and harmonious solar plexus chakra, you will firstly feel confident in yourself. You will no longer struggle with self-doubt or aggressive egotism, but instead, you'll feel comfortable in your own skin and you'll trust in your abilities. You'll come to understand that you have the power of choice, i.e., the power to choose your mindset, and therefore how you approach life and other people.

Not only will you feel more self-assured, but you will also have the energy and willpower needed to create healthy boundaries. You will no longer lapse into explosive or self-minimising roles around others, but instead, you'll stand your ground with respect for yourself and others. Your newfound energy will allow you to move out of lethargic and addictive patterns, and instead carry out your goals and dreams with enthusiasm. You will feel energised, focused, empowered, and in alignment with life.

Sounds great, doesn't it?

But remember, bringing about these changes doesn't just happen overnight. You will need to be sincere and patient in your dedication to cleanse the solar plexus, especially if it has been blocked for many years. Here are some of the best solar plexus chakra healing practices out there which will help you begin to heal this energetic centre:

If you wake up feeling energised and ready to take on the day, then you most likely have a high vibrational frequency. If you feel down in the dumps as soon as your feet hit the floor, then you're most likely suffering from a low vibrational frequency. Have a look at some ways to get out of the pits and back to soaring with high vibrations.

1. Break out of routine and take a risk

Lethargic and "safe" routines only tend to perpetuate our feelings of powerlessness. Break the dull inertia of your life and try something new. Step outside of your routine and go exploring, even if that means going to a different shopping center on your Saturday shopping trip. Even small breaks in routine will infuse you with energy and vitality. One small change can give you the motivation and renewed energy you need.

2. Cut ties with critical and negative people
If you can't cut ties permanently with belittling and critical people, try your best to keep a distance from them. During this time of your life, you'll benefit from supportive people who will encourage you to grow, not unsupportive people who will drag you through the mud.
(75)

3. Nature Walks
Get in some Vitamin D and some fresh air; truly allowing yourself to connect with nature by being present and turning off your phone. If you would truly like to see the benefits, walk barefoot. It has a healing effect known as 'grounding' which we will explore in later chapters.

4. Immerse yourself in Sound
Certain sounds can make us more receptive and relaxed. These include gongs and bowls or any type of deep meditative music. You can retreat to your Jedi Sacred Space or plug in some headphones to allow the deep vibrations to effect all the cells in your body with positive vibrations. You can find some relaxing music on our Youtube channel Kundalini Jedi warrior. Avoid sad and depressing love songs and limit your gangster rap playlist for more positive vibrations.

5. Be Kind
This is a great way to increase your vibrational frequency. Have you noticed that the Jedi interact with other people in a very kind and considerate manner? Giving to others makes us feel good. Performing a small act of kindness for just about anyone will elevate your mood. Sharing a smile or kind world can make a difference in someone's world.

6. Be Grateful
Practicing an attitude of gratitude can lift your spirits in no time at all. Create lists of things that you are grateful for. Do it as you wake up to prepare you for the day ahead or before

you go to sleep to wash away any thoughts of it having been a bad day. It will help you to end the day on a high note. I class gratefulness as a number one Jedi power for raising our vibrational energy.

7. Say No
Don't ignore your needs for the sake of someone else's! If you're really not up for something, say it. Just say no. This will help you create healthy boundaries and keep the force flowing strongly within you.

8. Think Positive
Sometimes things aren't as stressful as we make them out to be. Our thoughts have the power to convince us that they are. In a type of self-fulfilling prophecy, if you feel anxious, you will tend to draw yourself into anxiety-ridden situations. Don't suppress your negative emotions, but don't let them guide you either.

9. Find High-Vibe People
The people that we surround ourselves with can drag us down. Be sure to spend as much time with people who lift you up and raise your vibrational energy. In turn, give them that same nurturing support.
There are many safe, effective ways to raise your positive vibrations and your mood. Many of them are simple and straightforward: Move your body, find a bit of stillness, take some deep breaths, and spend time being kind to the people you love (preferably in nature).

Remember that the power is in your hands. It is up to you to decide who stays and goes in your life. If someone is frequently discrediting, underrating, or bad-mouthing you, take steps to remove them from your life. It is equally important to note that it is all too easy to be swayed to the dark side of your warrior nature if you are not careful with your intentions. We will explore this dark side in broader detail in the coming chapters.

***

CHAPTER 13: THE DARK SIDE OF THE WARRIOR

"*The dark side of the Force is a pathway to many abilities some consider to be unnatural.*"

- Emperor Palpatine, Star Wars: Episode III – Revenge of the Sith

The warrior archetype lives for the battlefield. He lives for conflict and overcoming his opponent. When not amid all-out warfare, this warrior is training to prepare and plan for the next confrontation. The warrior myth begins with the hero wanting to escape a confining environment; to go on a mission to defeat the enemy, and to save the day. The warrior is willing to risk their lives for a high ideal; to defend their kingdoms, and to protect the weak from harm. Luke begins his journey to save the princess and to help the rebel alliance; ultimately developing courage, strength, and new Jedi skills to complete his mission.

We are living in a warrior culture. It is not that we need more warrior energy, but we need to redefine the warrior energy so that it may serve the kingdom, not destroy it. It could be argued that our current warriors arc as much part of the problem as they are the solution. Our culture is one of competition and comparison. There is still the primary driver of "survival of the fittest". A 'Type A' personality is generally looked upon more favourably than a 'Type B' personality.

In her book *'Awakening the heroes within'* Carol Pearson says that any system based on competition - including all competitive sports, politics, judiciary systems, capitalist economics, and rivalry in education - is based on warrior modality. In the introduction, we saw how the war on things drugs, terrorism, poverty, and the wars between individuals and nations could not be the way forward. It is for this reason that the idea of warrior energy has gained a bad rap. However, the problem is not the warrior energy but our use of it. The warrior archetypes need an upgrade. Whenever we stand up to unfair authority - when we protect someone from harm and when we risk our livelihoods or even our lives for higher principles - we are activating the positive expression of the warrior.

But what happens when the warrior's energy leans towards the Darkside?

All energies have polarity, and all archetypes include the shadow qualities of the archetype. Some people take every situation as a contest. Others take it personally and rush to defend themselves, when someone disagrees with them. They sometimes even attack the other person. Pearson describes how this occurs in society's education system with educators who hold to competition as the only way to promote learning. The medical profession is a warzone; with doctors who wage war on disease, even if it makes their patients experience their body as a battlefield. Business leaders push their workforce to breaking point; whilst affecting their health and family life to suffer - as long as they can close the deal, they think they've won. This drive to succeed then becomes the driving force of intention. The human and social costs of gaining profit outweigh any human factors or respect for life. This single-minded warrior approach of being above others without respecting human feelings and higher values can end up doing more harm than good.

We see this more and more in the world today with people acting without regard to ideals or broader social objectives. The focus is solely on themselves. The quest to be number one - to have more power, status, or money - distorts the warrior's energy, and ends with them becoming more like mercenaries. They become people who are willing to lie, cheat, and steal in order to achieve their objective - thus becoming more of a villain than a hero.

The warrior energy, in its negative polarity, is the tyrant, mercenary, assassin, gun for hire barbarian, or mindless killer. Here, the warrior loses integrity willing to play dirty and break the rules if that is what it takes to win the battle and get their due reward. If we do not have enough access to the Warrior archetype, we may let other people push us around. We may lack direction, or fail to achieve our goals because we do not persist. Too much warrior and every interaction becomes a contest — we want what we want and insist on getting it whatever the cost to others or our relationships. Too little and we have no sense of direction. As the saying goes, a man who stands for nothing, falls for anything.

In the Star Wars movies, we see these polarities in their positive and negative expression of how the use of force energy is portrayed; the Jedi's complimentary use of the Force and the Sith's damaging exploitation of the Force.

WARRIOR IN ITS NEGATIVE EXPRESSION

"He who conquers himself is the mightiest warrior."

— **Confucius, Chinese Philosopher**

All this positive energy can turn hostile, rebellious, and arrogant. Overconfidence, coupled with aggression, can turn to rage; making the warrior move from having a goal serving to a goal of serving himself.

Many great things have been accomplished by warrior energy and a great many things destroyed by that same energy. Remember that each archetype has a light and a shadow side. For Jedi warriors, it is crucial to recognise which archetypes are active within us and work towards bringing them into balance. The warrior mentality can be all-consuming and obsessive. An unbalanced warrior chooses conflict over diplomacy every time. In the Shadow, the warrior archetype creates conflict where there is none. Too much warrior energy leads to rage and destruction, and in the same polarity not enough warrior energy leaves us weak and an easy victim for the tribulations of life.

An undisciplined warrior who has not mastered themselves seems to swing from composure to rage quite easily. Part of the healing challenge of this archetype is learning to manage emotions and find a healthy outlet for them. If we are undisciplined and engaged in drugs and alcohol - unable to stop our self-destructive habits - then our inner warrior is out of balance and will not function adequately or effectively. The suppressed and undisciplined warrior becomes the heartless barbarian. The violence is directed both outward and inward.

The aggression does not need to be physical. It is just as likely to be in words that perpetuate shame and a barrage of negativity from our inner critic.

This awareness is essential to the Jedi warrior if he is to continue to fight for the light side of the Force. If he loses that awareness, he will be tempted, seduced, and manipulated by the Darkside.

The Emperor: [to Luke] Good! Use your aggressive feelings, boy. Let the hate flow through you!

- The Emperor, Star Wars: Episode VI - Return of the Jedi

We see this play out in the prequel movies as we follow the rise and fall of Anakin. He goes from being a promising young Jedi who was prophesied to bring balance to the Force, to becoming Darth Vader - an instrument of the galactic Empire; ruling the universe with a tight iron grip. We see the emperor goading Luke into allowing his anger to consume him; for him to take his weapon and strike down his father.

Anakin, through manipulation, was turned towards the Darkside, due to his anxiety and fear of losing those he loved. This fear fuelled the development of his shadow qualities. The shadow warrior is numb to pain - both his own, and that of others. He slays and injures without remorse. The sanctity of life is lost on him.

In Star Wars: Episode II – Attack of the Clones - the 2nd film in the prequel trilogy - Anakin begins to have nightmares regarding his mother's wellbeing. Upset from the nightmares, and angry at himself for having them - Jedi don't have nightmares, after all - he goes back to Tatooine to find her. Upon finding her, just before she passes away, he becomes enraged; losing his composure. When his grief and pain overwhelm him at the loss of his mother he is completely overtaken by his emotions. He takes his anger out on the sand people that kidnapped her. Later he confesses his crimes to Padme.

"I killed them all. They're dead, every single one of them. And not just the men, but the women and the children, too. They're like animals, and I slaughtered them like animals. I HATE THEM!"

- Anakin Skywalker, Star Wars: Episode II – Attack of the Clones

He then becomes angry at his mentor for holding him back and declares that he will become the greatest Jedi ever. Padme tries to soothe the frustrated Anakin by reminding him that he is only human to which he replies "I'm not human I'm a Jedi."

Pearson, in her book, states that a 'warrior's greatest fear is being human - merely mortal.' It is as if he loses touch with his humanity; leading to the warrior in its ultimate negative expression when killing and murdering the sand people.

The sense of invincibility of the warrior can lead to an inflated ego as seen with Anakin's belief. He is a better Jedi and not being appreciated – according to his belief. When he is not granted the title of Jedi master, he becomes petulant and disrespectful. He overextends himself, believing that he has no limits. This leads him to breaking the rules and ignoring the chain of command; potentially putting himself and others in unnecessary danger. This is why the warrior needs to reflect on their actions and motivations, are they still fighting for the greater good or have they become overcome with vengeance, hatred, and anger. In Anakin's case, he falls in love with Padme and, ignoring Jedi protocol, actively pursues her. He is angry with himself that he cannot change reality, and the way that things are; believing that he should be able to. Anakin goes so far as to say that he will even stop people from dying and that he will be the greatest Jedi ever. His pain turns on him as he then begins to believe that his teacher and mentor is holding him back from progressing:

"It's all Obi-Wan's fault. He's jealous."

Unable to accept his feelings, he gets to project outwardly; making the other the enemy. In his mind it is far too human to get angry.

THE DARK WARRIOR ARCHETYPE

The Warrior archetype can detach themselves from emotions and human relationships when the need arises. This is a most valuable asset and most needed in the heat of battle. This sense of detachment provides the warrior with a much-needed focus on essential tasks and the ability to complete the mission. This valuable skill becomes a hindrance when it goes from serving the higher good to becoming a way of being; avoiding the elements of living a modern human life. The simplicity of this mindset can become so ingrained in a person that it becomes a normal way of functioning.

This way of functioning is a common dilemma for war veterans and people exposed to harsh environments which may have required them to develop that mindset whilst in the warzone. However, they find the transition back to everyday civilian life very difficult. Adjusting to life back at home, and finding their place amongst their families, begins to feel like an impossible task. With the subtle relationship dynamics and emotional needs of their current world, they have to set aside this survival skill from the previous environment. A commanding officer in the Army may try to rigidly run his family in the same way that he led his troops. The negative warrior creates unattainably high standards for himself and those around him; becoming abusive in an attempt to achieve his mission objectives.

This type of thinking is not reserved only for combat soldiers or workaholics. Still, it can also be true of lawyers, ministers, doctors, politicians, and other men who may be married to their job. Shifting from mission-mode to domestic-mode can be difficult for them. They're the men who take pride in working all night at the office and coming home at 7 AM; only to leave for the office again an hour later. They'll choose work at the expense of health and even family. They take the warrior's comfort with pain to an extreme and grind it out to get to the top. However, they're doing it because they really don't know what they want out of life. Continuously working distracts them from this fact. Once they do reach the top, they often feel empty, lost, and bitter. The warrior can become cruel, even to the most vulnerable; having a strong disdain for the weak, or for the very people he promised to protect.

In Star Wars: Episode II – Attack of the Clones we see Anakin being sent by the emperor to hunt down and destroy all Jedi. Anakin comes to the Jedi temple, finding the younglings or young padawan, also known as Jedi children in early training.

He slaughters them all.

Anakin knew that he had to slaughter innocent children - personally - to cause him so much pain, anger, and hatred - of himself - that there would be no way back. This heinous crime would fuel his dark-side energy; cutting off his connection to the positive warrior energy in the belief that this approach could save his own family. That's why we see him crying on Mustafar. It is why he hated himself from that point on, and why, eventually, he turned on the Empire. He almost immediately began to feel remorse for the things he'd done, but by the same token, he thought that the atrocities he'd already committed had set him on the path that he was taking. In its more extreme form, the suffering of others gives pleasure and observing that suffering feels good.

In domestic life, a father influenced by the hostile warrior becomes enraged. When a child comes home with a less than perfect grade, he puts her down and berates her mercilessly. A man with positive Warrior energy would have kindly shown disappointment, but then offered to help his daughter study for the next exam so that she could ace it.

HERO TO WARRIOR-BOY TO MAN

Fighting itself is not a bad thing, and the battlefield can be a place of honour and respect. When the hero archetype is underdeveloped, it can leave us open to the negative energies of the archetype. As a hero, we can become overly confident; having not yet met and respected our limitations, and leaving us arrogant as well as insensitive to the needs of others. We are, in essence, privy to a self-obsessed view of our powers and importance. The hero's approach, when left unchecked, ultimately leads him to self-destruct.

Likewise, the negative polarity of the hero would be the coward who lacks energy and motivation; pushing themselves into confrontation and thus never achieving anything of significance. Ultimately, this approach leads to self-hate and low self-esteem as the hero becomes frustrated and angry at their lack of success.

In the book *King, Warrior, Magician, Lover: Rediscovering the Archetypes of the Mature Masculine* Robert Moore and Douglas Gillette describe how the hero is the boyhood archetype which matures into the Warrior archetype. Part of this maturation process centres on a shift in one's loyalties. "The Hero's main motivation is to be the hero and to receive all the acclaim that goes with that and sometimes the hand of the princess and is really to himself–to impressing himself with himself and to impressing others."

The warrior's loyalties, on the other hand, "are to something beyond and other than himself and his own concerns." The warrior's loyalty centres on "a cause, a God, a people, a task, a nation– larger than individuals." The warrior has a "central commitment" around which he organises his life. His life's purpose is rooted in ideals and principles, which naturally strips away superfluities and pettiness and brings his life significant meaning. [76]

The Jedi offer themselves to the service and protection of the universe. They keep the Force in balance within themselves and never fight or battle for their own personal motives. We see this in Luke's journey from being a whiny teenager who just wants to go out with his friends and be a pilot, to slowly - through training and experience – learning to respect his limitations. He eventually matures into a warrior. He not only saves the galaxy, but redeems his father through compassion by not succumbing to the Darkside. He does not destroy the enemy for the sake of merely destroying them, but in his forgiveness, he comes into his power. If he had given in to the emperor's manipulation, he would have fallen into temptation. That, in itself, is the same way that it seduced his father. If he were thinking only of himself, as his father once did, he would've been turned to the dark, but Luke cared about his friends. He cared about the struggle that the rebels fought for. He cared about being a Jedi.

These things distinguish him from the boy; taking him to the heights of the hero. He matured into a warrior.

WARRIOR EVOLUTION THROUGH ARCHETYPAL PARTNERSHIP

"There's more to being a warrior than killing. A true warrior — the best warrior — isn't cruel or mean. He doesn't claw an enemy who can't fight back. Where's the honour in that?"

— **Erin Hunter, Forests of Secrets**

The point here is that the warrior, like any archetype, is not inherently good or bad. The current time offers us the opportunity to participate in the archetype's evolution by how we choose to live it. By engaging qualities from the other archetypal energies, we can balance and enhance the Warrior archetype so that it operates in its ultimate positive expression. The fact is, Warrior energy becomes destructive when it is not used in harmony with the other archetypes – even more so when it is not directed by compassion, empathy, contemplation, and discipline. In engaging the archetype in a positive manner, we can see that we do not need to be at war with others in our country. We are all on the Warrior team to some degree; playing different positions. We just need to talk with one another about what we see as the most pressing threats; assessing where we need to use force, where we need to provide support, where we need to use our words, and when the magic of love is required to win the day for everyone.

THE SAGE ARCHETYPE

The Sage is also known as the scholar, expert, detective, thinker, teacher, mentor, savant, and philosopher. The Sage seeks to understand the world in analytical ways; processing reality with logic and the wisdom of their often-long life. In Star Wars, the Sage is represented by Jedi master Obi-Wan as well as Yoda. They embody the qualities of the wise Sage who have established themselves in the Force and who have some experience under their belt. The Sage seeks nothing but the truth. Whether that truth is uncomfortable or heart-rendering, it will be accepted; as the only meaningful path in life is one that pursues the truth. He considers things carefully; taking all aspects and facts into consideration before jumping into action.

THE CAREGIVER

The person with this archetype is incredibly focused on taking care of others. Caregivers have a desire to help others. They are also known as the helper, parent, or saint. The Caregiver gives the warrior the ability to become a high-level warrior. The archetype now evolves from the single-minded approach of destroying the enemy at all costs to seeing the enemy as human and a part of humanity. A warrior is fighting for this could be providing water or medical care after the battle has finished or allowing survivors to return to their base camps. This level of empathy and understanding distinguishes the warrior from brute force and ultimately displays the warrior in their full, healthy expression.

THE MAGICIAN

As previously discussed, this archetype is also known as the visionary, catalyst, charismatic leader, medicine man, healer, and inventor, the Magician is the archetype that seeks transformation, and a deep connection to the cosmos, whatever their definition of that might be. The Magician is not involved in every day of regular people; they do not find 'mortal' concerns interesting or curious. Instead, they seek the threads beneath the surface that tie a world together.

When a Magician aligns himself entirely to the light, away from his Shadow, he can be a force of great healing and transformation for others. The Magician can often return after a fall from grace as a galvanising force for the hero, and make all the difference in the world's darkest hour. (76)

Kundalini Jedi warriors are focused on changing their inner world to affect the outer world. Jedi warriors are not competing with others, and they are not competing with themselves as this would cause unnecessary internal conflict. When we are approaching ourselves from the perspective that we are spiritual beings having a human experience, we let our spiritual identity guide us.

Pearson suggests working with our inner orphan and the energy of the innocent archetypes to develop a level of self-care and self-love towards ourselves. Pearson means the negative warrior needs to develop their inner orphan to increase their empathy while balancing their innocence. This way they can be relieved of their cynicism and fulfil their potential as true positive warriors.

The power of this archetype is the ability to release selfish ends and conquer evil forces. The enlightened warrior knows that the real enemy is the enemy within. The power to face and triumph over one's inner demons is the gift of the warrior. So too is a deep appreciation for the sanctity of all life. We must also be aware of the negative aspects of the Shadow. (77)

*

WORKING WITH ARCHETYPES

- To demonstrate what I mean by "moving an archetype along the spectrum," let's use the warrior as an example. If I am always angry, and my boss keeps yelling at me, my kids hate me, my dog keeps biting me, I am developing ulcers, I still fight with my partner, and whenever I am in the kitchen, I cut myself, ALL of that is negative Warrior energy playing out in our lives. It is within me - anger, ulcers, careless with sharp objects - and outside of me. Through the law of attraction, I exist entirely in this hostile warrior. On the other end of the spectrum, if we find ourselves focused on a target, there is a different experience. When we can separate what is essential from what is superfluous, fit, full of energy, practicing Tai Chi, fighting for a good cause and having great sex. All this belongs to the positive warrior. Most of us are not at either end of this spectrum. However, if you find yourself too close to the negative side, know that you have choices in how to move your inner warrior along the continuum towards the other side. You can do this with any archetype. This is how you heal. (78)

The Warrior archetype evolves as we do, so:

- Do you need less or more warrior to deal with a current threat or challenge?
- Where do you see the warrior in yourself and in what you think and do?
- What forms of the warrior do you see in yourself and the people around you, and how is their influence affecting you?
- How might you like your inner warrior to change and evolve in its attitudes and behaviours?

Make some notes from your insights in your Jedi journal.

HOW TO ACCESS THE WARRIOR ARCHETYPE

The recent COVID pandemic has impacted the world over as we continue to try to survive these troubling times . A general sense of helplessness to this unseen threat has seeped into our consciousness . However, if there's anything the world needs today, it's men and women in touch with the Warrior archetype ready to thrive again. It's the warrior energy that encourages us to do great things and to fight for worthy causes.

There are many ways to tap into and access this positive Warrior energy. Below you will find a list of things you can experiment with to bring more warrior energy into your life.

- Watch movies about great warriors. They don't necessarily have to be war movies.
- Read biographies about great warriors.
- Take up boxing or other martial arts.
- Do something that scares you.
- Work on becoming more decisive.
- Meditate, especially on death.

- Quit shoaling on yourself. The warrior is able to detach himself from the opinions of others to carry out his mission.
- Find your core values.
- Have a plan and purpose for your life.
- Boost your adaptability by strengthening your resilience.
- Study and practice the skills necessary for completing your goals. Whether that's marksmanship, computer programming, or being charismatic, become a master of your trade.
- Find the principles that you're loyal to.
- Establish some non-negotiable, unalterable terms and live by them.
- Strengthen your discipline by establishing habits and daily routines.
- Adopt a minimalist philosophy.
- Declutter your life.
- Simplify your diet.
- Get out of debt.

Once you've cleared yourself of negative warrior energy, you can begin actively working towards heightening your state of being. First up on that post clearing journey is facing your own fears.

***

CHAPTER 14: FEAR: PATH TO THE LIGHT SIDE

> "*Fear is a path to the dark side.*"
>
> *- Grand Master Yoda, Star Wars: Episode I - The Phantom Menace*

FACING OUR FEARS

Anakin feared loss: first, it was the loss of his mother, and then it was the loss of his lover Padme. It was this fear that drove him to the dark side, as he sought out a way to ensure that these losses never came to pass. This drive to overcome his fear ultimately led him to become Darth Vader; ironically becoming the most feared person in the galaxy. As Yoda had warned him earlier, his fear had led him to anger, his anger to hatred, and that hatred ultimately led to his suffering. His fear had so consumed him that he became a different person entirely.

Then along comes his son, Luke Skywalker, who insists to Yoda in Star Wars: Episode V – The Empire Strikes Back, "I'm not afraid!"

"You will be," Yoda responds "you will be!"

Luke confronts his fear in the cave on Dagobah, as he comes face to face with that which he fears the most - that which he may become; seeing his own face after striking Vader with his lightsaber in a dream sequence while on Dagobah during his Jedi training. By the final film in the trilogy Star Wars: Episode VI – Return of the Jedi, we see Luke's final confrontation with the Darkside. He stands above his defeated father with the emperor watching on and throws his lightsaber away, insisting, "I am a Jedi, like my father before me." He had faced and confronted his biggest fear. He has faced the possibility of becoming like his father, but instead of embracing the dark-side as his father did, Luke stakes his claim as a Jedi – just like his father once did. At this moment, Luke has faced his fear and, with compassion, he redeems his father.

Now a Jedi master, Luke begins training a new generation of Jedi agreeing to teach his sister's son Ben Solo, but upon seeing the Darkside in his nephew, he attempts to kill him. His fear of failure was complete, and Kylo Ren was born. In his view, he did fail Ben Solo, and this led him to self-imposed exile. But Rey forces him to confront this fear once more - as he is afraid of failing her too. He winds up confronting this fear, walking out to face the First Order; thus, buying the Resistance time to escape.

That self-sacrifice is the destiny of all Jedi and that's been a message of the Skywalker saga throughout. Fear is the path to the dark side, but it's not the absence of fear that makes a Jedi. It's confronting those fears and emerging better because of it, which makes a Jedi.

"*Confronting fear is the destiny of a Jedi.*"

- Luke Skywalker, Star Wars: The Rise Of Skywalker

Everyone gets scared, it's part of being human, and it is a normal reaction to danger or threat, but in today's world, fear has become the dominant frequency. We live in unprecedented times with massive changes and uncertain futures; leading to more stress-related illnesses and a nervous system struggling to cope.

We live in a fear-driven society. Our brains are hard-wired to respond to fear. From the dawn of time, fear has helped us to survive—to keep us alert; to anticipate trouble and keep us from getting eaten by predators. Fear is a powerful force that motivates us into action. Anything positive—our values, our passions, inspirations, and desires—lack the same brain punch as fear, and we find useless products, devices, and insurance plans as a futile attempt to quell this fear. Marketing companies and product developers know this too well and prey on our sensitivities with false promises; raking up high profits in the process.

But while our evolutionary ancestors had good reasons to be afraid, their anxieties came in fits and starts; once back in the cave, once the tiger lumbered away, so did their fear. However, in our modern age, we are forever vigilant. The primal brain is activated, and we find ourselves trapped in a game of survival. The reptilian part of our brain rules the day and although the reptilian brain served us throughout the ages and is the reason that we got this far, it's time to shift our perspective. In contrast, we have no reprieve: We are constantly bombarded by messages telling us that the world is never safe, and that danger is around the corner. As we are already genetically wired for anxiety, this barrage only provides more fodder for the problem. It's no wonder that anxiety is the primary problem affecting adults and children today. Humans crave safety, security, and peace. This is in some ways our natural state; we love being cosy and warm and safe. This is where we most lose our power and self-agency. In a world of savvy marketers and branding companies offering us this safety and peace that we crave, we are easy prey. We give our power away to governments and organizations who promise us a world without worry. They promise us that we will be taken care of if we trust them and follow their rules. We become like victims; giving away our power for the illusion of escaping fears.

We must not run away from our fears but face them for they hold valuable information. This is the counter-intuitive way of approaching fear. Ironically, fear wants the same thing for us; to move away from danger and get us to a place of safety and comfort. As a Kundalini Jedi Warrior, we turn towards the fear to listen deeply to the wisdom and message that it wishes to provide. As creatures of habit, we cling to what is known to us and do our best to avoid the unknown aspects of life. We are attached to the stories that we have about ourselves and our lives. With an attitude of 'better the devil, you know' we stay in bad relationships, unfulfilling jobs, and careers that we despise. We continue to engage in destructive habits with full awareness that they are bad for us because of the fear of change. The potential pain involved in that change seems too much to bear. We generally know the changes that we need to make but are frozen in our old comfort zones. Most of us will go to any lengths to avoid pain at any cost. Our fear of getting hurt may be related to the immediate discomfort or it could be due to the way that we have been injured in the past, which we may have forgotten consciously. Still, our body and subconscious remember and remind us.

So, we put up with it all and suffer along the way as we lose years of our lives; stuck in the same situations, and becoming bitter as well as resentful as our lives pass us by. The unknown presents itself as a threat - a place we should never venture - and ironically it is this unknown that holds the treasure we seek.

This is not so much about facing your fear and doing it anyway, but you feel your fear to see the message that it has for you. In this way, we are not ignoring our fear and relegating it to the deepest parts of our unconsciousness - where it will no doubt pop up at the wrong time and place - but working with it.

The nature of fear is that it causes us to shrink, hide, and contract. Our body language changes as we withdraw and cower. It is as if we are turning and squirming inwards in an attempt to avoid and shield ourselves away from the fear. The energy of fear is quick, cold, and sharp; activating our defence mechanisms to protect ourselves. We become small. This bodily contraction leaves us feeling tight, rigid, and constricted. Our cognitive functions are significantly impaired, and our thoughts become distorted. Our nervous system readies itself for fight or flight as we attempt running away to distract ourselves from further attack. This need to escape is generally a reaction with the intent to not feel.

On the other side of our fears are all of our dreams and goals. The polarity of fear is desire, and desire has the opposite qualities. It is open, expansive, and indicative of growth; promoting a feeling of joy and happiness.

This also manifests biologically. The hard wiring of thousands of years of evolution means that the reptilian, lizard part of our brain stem is primed for an instinctual response; to **react** to perceived threats and dangers. The Kundalini Jedi way is to develop our capacity to calmly **respond** to fear and not let it overwhelm or overpower us.

When we respond to life through our intuition - through the development of our sensory system - we become sensitive to how we process emotions so we may understand their valuable prompts and guidance. Generally, as a society, we manage our emotions as something to be ignored so we can live a stress-free life, or we numb out the fear with the use of substances or frivolous activity. A Jedi wants to develop a relationship to their inner whispers and guidance; to foresee not to ignore, and to create a deep self-trust, so that they are not manipulated by outside sources.

Once again, the Jedi warrior is approaching things counterintuitively and ironically. Really feeling and listening to the fear will result in less stress in the body and more vitality and energy for life. As we face our fears, we see that it has become a great change agent and that it is leading us to our most extraordinary life. Fear helps us to fulfil our destiny.

Society is currently geared towards being competitive; urging you to fight for likes and approval, where only the strongest survive and the most beautiful are valued. Our culture of social media ads and fitting in has us now always comparing ourselves to others; leaving us to ask "are we ever enough?"

YOU ARE ENOUGH!

We find temporary relief with distractions; constantly checking our phones, going shopping, watching TV, and even working to provide a momentary break from the inner noise. This gives us, at best, a fake peace that makes us feel more at war than at peace.

EYE OF THE STORM

Fear and excitement have a very similar energy signature. We enjoy the thrill of sensational news stories, drama, horror movies, and things like going to Disneyland for the fast rides. We are addicted to the adrenaline rush and have become addicted to this overstimulation. The same is true for our work life; where people hide and self-medicate with long hours of work. Here they are well rewarded and respected by their peers as well as society for being productive members of the community, whereas, in reality, they are pushing themselves to the point of burnout and exhaustion. The nervous system takes all these messages and images as a sign that it is under attack and must be ready to fight, flee, or freeze. Living in overwhelm will eventually cause you to stop; not out of wisdom that you are overdoing it but due to becoming ill. Sometimes we push so hard that we damage the system altogether. Most people's approach is to double down and go harder, faster, and stronger. This is the current approach people tend to follow - the beaten and worn path.

"You will know. When you are calm, at peace, passive."
- **Grand Master Yoda, Star Wars: Episode V – The Empire Strikes Back**

However, there is another way to approach this life. Jedi warriors adopt a counterintuitive approach. We need to be calm, passive, and slow down. We may need to eliminate specific responsibilities that we have over-committed to; reviewing our energy commitments and the impact that they have on our quality of life. As Jedi, we learn how to simplify areas of life and how to allocate ourselves free time. Maybe one of the most courageous things that we can do, to create some balance in our lives, is to get back in touch with ourselves and to become quiet enough to listen to the whispers of our inner wisdom. When we begin to crave serenity instead of chaos and drama, we are moving in the right direction. It can be hard to recognise these subtle attacks as they happen every day because we tend to normalise our reactions due to the stress. Maybe we have a challenging boss at work, and we try our best to ignore them in order to just get our job done; whilst not realising how much pressure we are under.

Our loud neighbours.
The constant barking of our neighbour's dog.
Being stuck in a queue and running late for an appointment.
Traffic.

When the body receives a shock, it has experienced a trauma and if we are highly strung out, a shock could be something as simple as a door slamming to trigger us into a flight, fight, fright response.

Our nervous system goes into high gear to protect itself against threat. Over time, this will weaken the nervous system; causing adrenal exhaustion and overactive glands. At the end of it all, we will be left unable to deal and respond accurately to life's challenges. Recovery of our nervous system requires a more relaxed approach. We can train our body and mind to respond in this way, we can do this when the storm is raging, but we begin to practice it when no fear is present; building reserves and giving us the ability to handle any situation.

The following meditation will help give you the confidence to handle stressful situations and develop the fearlessness to make courageous decisions. This will help to minimise the stress in your life. In the midst of chaos and fear you will be able to stay healthy and steady. You will be sitting in the eye of the storm; calm and collected.

MEDITATION: FEAR IN THE NOW

TUNE IN WITH ONG NAMO GURU DEV NAMO X 3

This meditation trains us to be calm in the now and feel that we can handle whatever the moment brings. The meditation will create a small feeling of fear and perhaps little panic as you suspend the breath; this stimulates your flight-fight response as the body moves into survival mode. The hand posture and repetition of the mantra creates a counterbalance to the small inner emergency and puts you consciously in control of your fear. When practiced regularly, it will train the nervous system to stay calm in the face of all danger and stress.

Take some time to sit in a cross-legged position and focus on your breathing and body sensations. Close your eyes. Relax your arms along the sides of your torso and press the elbows to the sides. Simultaneously lift your forearms up until they are parallel to the ground and your hands are in front of your body with the palms facing up. Separate the hands about 3 feet from each other so that the forearms form an angle of about 120°. Bring the fingers of each hand together so that all five fingertips touch and point up the arm. The position should feel very relaxed. Remove any tension from the shoulders and neck. Mentally focus at the top of the nose where the eyebrows meet. Regulate the breath precisely; deeply inhale and then completely exhale. Suspend the breath out for 16 regular beats and then quickly inhale and exhale again. Hold the exhale out and continue this cycle. As you hold the breath out, concentrate at the brow point with the mental mantra:

sa-ta-na-ma, sa- ta-na-ma, sa-ta-na-ma, sa-ta-na-ma
(Mentally vibrate the sounds, do not make them vocally.)

The sound regulates the time of the breath, so it is the same on each cycle. Continue the meditation for 11 minutes and finish with a few deep breaths and by stretching the arms straight up and shaking out the fingers and hands. You can relax in sitting posture or on your back for a few minutes. Use your Jedi journal to record your experience and any insights you may have gained.

THE GHOSTS OF FEAR

The real purpose of fear is that it wants peace for you and that may also include working with worries from the past, memories, and experiences that we continue to hold in the body. Until our memories are processed - as opposed to unconsciously being played out - so that our present feelings are distinct from the past, we will remain hyper-vigilant to unperceived threats. As such, we find ourselves remaining ever alert due to old dangers, feelings of being unsafe and we are then unable to handle our daily lives. This, added with the stress put on our nervous systems, can cause exhaustion and an inaccurate perception of reality. We need both aspects to be serving each other as can be achieved when we process the past.

As these memories continue to fester in the subconsciousness, we feel haunted in our present dealings and life. The subconsciousness is very powerful and vast; holding all of our memories and experiences - like a reference library ready to do the necessary background checks and provide supporting evidence. However, its major flaw is that it doesn't discern if the data is old or new. It doesn't interpret things based on the new reality but merely believes whatever is stored in the library as truth.

So, we need to assimilate the past and the associated memories with the current reality of our lives. When we are growing up, we experience lots of small hurts and upsets that can be construed as traumas. It could be something like having our heart broken for the first time; experiencing the loss of something or someone that we love - like a family member - or losing something we value highly. When we're at this very young age, we are not able to process some of these complex emotions, and we end up suppressing them; forgetting them and trying to run away from them. This builds up a memory bank of events which hold anxiety for us of that earlier version of ourselves. That younger you who wasn't able to defend or protect themselves. The subconscious doesn't know that you are smarter now that you have grown up and become an adult.

So, this is where we require the conscious self to intervene for us. It's about bringing the memories up from the subconsciousness; bringing those from the back of the brain in the primal stem and bringing them forward to the frontal lobe. As we integrate memories - bringing them from the back to the front - we can also gather the valuable lessons from the past experiences and put those in our storehouse of knowledge. All of these unresolved issues or feelings that we have can cause our system to overload, and when we experience an overload, our clarity of mind is reduced. The nervous system is overwhelmed with outdated data, or information, causing blockages. Think of it as a desk with job files being added continuously to make your to-do list. The files keep piling up and up until you can no longer see the desk or know which job is most pressing. It becomes like a vast crowd of people; all trying to get their voice heard, but it just ends up like a mass of indistinguishable noise. Alternatively, you can think of it as your computer's email inbox. Each day, more and more emails arrive; trying to get your attention. You can't respond to them because of the sheer number of them. Only once you can go through all the old, outdated, email messages and clear out our inbox will you be able to tell which emails are the most important so that you can respond appropriately.

MEDITATION: REMOVE GHOSTS OF FEAR

This meditation creates time and space to helps you bring up your protective thoughts and feelings that you usually ignore . These repetitive fears messages from the past once faced will allow you to relieve this old pressure. Listen to your fears ,worries ,concerns and dump these past memories that aren't serving you anymore. Clear any intense feelings that you have been avoiding and offload the toxic build-up of unheard messages. You will be able to tackle fears from the past when all of these old unread messages have been cleared out. Only then will you be able to distinguish the essential current messages from the old unread ones. Prepare yourself for this conscious confrontation. This meditation also works on the 4th body which is the negative mind.

TUNE IN WITH ONG NAMO GURU DEV NAMO

Take some time to sit in a cross-legged position and focus on your breathing as well as your bodily sensations. Tune in with your tuning in mantra and close your eyes. Make a cup with your hands; both palms facing up and the right hand resting atop the left. The fingers should cross over each other. Put this open cup at the level of the heart centre. Keep your elbows relaxed at your sides; keeping your eyes slightly open and looking towards your hands. Inhale deeply in a long, steady way through the nose and exhale in a focused stream through rounded lips. Feel the breath go over the hands and let any thought is negative or persistently distracting come into your mind as you breathe. Breathe the thought and feeling in and exhale it out with the breath.

    Continue for 11 minutes.

    After 11 minutes, exhale completely and suspend the breath out as you pull the navel point in. Concentrate on each vertebra of the spine until you can feel your spine like a stiff rod all the way to the base. Inhale powerfully and exhale completely.

    Repeat this final breath 3 to 5 times and then relax completely.

JEDI EXERCISE: JOURNAL YOUR MEDITATION OBSERVATIONS

- Refer to your Jedi training manual and begin to make notes about What happened to you during this meditation.
- What did you learn?
- What did you feel?

You may need to do this practice for a few days, or even up to 40 days, depending on how much stuff came up for you. You may feel relieved immediately afterwards. When you feel noticeably better, most of the time, it means that you are coming into real-time awareness. Now that you have emptied the contents of the past, you can now be fully present and address the concerns of the future more effectively.

*

FEAR OF THE FUTURE

If we are not preoccupied with our fears of the past, then we will be worried about the concerns of the future. There is a positive aspect that comes from fear because it makes you ask the big questions of life, like 'who am I?', 'where am I going?', and 'what does the future hold for me?' Always thinking and worrying about the future can create much anxiety within us and thus stresses out our nervous system with unfounded concerns. As the future is unknown, there is no way for us to satisfy our curiosity, and the mind becomes busy ruminating about possible outcomes. Not only do we make ourselves sick with worry, we also lose our connection to the present moment.

MEDITATION: FEAR OF THE FUTURE

Take your Jedi journal and - after slowly reading the following passage - make notes about your understanding of death and capture your thoughts, moods, and feelings.

Deathless nature of spirit:

So, imagine for a moment that there are 1 billion galaxies which have all sprung from nothing. It all started billions of years ago, and earth has been around for 4.5 billion years. 9 million different species live here on this planet. Nearly 8 billion people inhabit this earth. Now, see all of the people passing through this earth hotel; coming and going - old and new. We understand that we are part of this big play.

You are not living life; life is living through you.
You don't win life; instead, you belong to life - you are life.

Your atoms and energy - your cells - are made up of stardust; made from the same qualities as everything around you. Once you accept that you are part of all of it, there is nothing to protect or fear. Safety exists because energy cannot be destroyed; it can only transform and change form. It is our attachment to form that generates the fear. Once we release this attachment to this form, then we have true freedom to just be. We get to this feeling of fearlessness by recovering our self-trust. By trusting yourself, and trusting all that there is beyond this life and your human limitations, you allow yourself to let go and flow. When we experience fear, it signals that we have forgotten the bigger picture.

We are Deathless in our nature because this is the nature of spirit. We commit to the spiritual practice of remembering the Force with every breath. We simultaneously remember our inherent nature as spiritual beings connected to the Force. Once we arrive at the realisation that there is nothing to fear, we will become fearless spiritual warriors. When you can achieve the state of being dead while alive, you will know fearlessness. Your trust in the Force makes you brave. This is the destiny of the Kundalini Jedi warrior. At any moment, we can choose to believe the universe to be a hostile, cruel, and unjust universe, or a friendly universe that wants you to relax and enjoy the experience. A lot will depend on our early experiences and will depend on your history of trauma as well as the protective field that you created to protect yourself. The destiny of a Jedi is to face these upsets with our new realisation and begin to live life in a new way. This openness will create a loving environment where you feel safe; trusting the Force to be there for you.

*

DEATH

"Soon will I rest, yes, forever sleep. Earned it I have. Twilight is upon me, soon night must fall."

- Grand master Yoda, Star Wars: Episode VI - Return of the Jedi

On review, there are a lot of deaths in the Star Wars films. From the death star destroying planets and killing millions - perhaps even billions - of people as well as the satisfying end to some to the franchise's greatest villains such as Darth Maul, death is abundant in the franchise. The death and destruction of Emperor Snoke and the counterweight in the form of the death of some of our most beloved heroes highlights the polarities of our world. One most notable death for me was Luke Skywalker passing away; signalling another sacrifice on the part of a great Jedi Master and ushering in the most dramatic death in the saga. Though controversial - and inevitable - there is no arguing the power of Luke Skywalker's heroic effort to save the Resistance.

We see Mace Windu meet his end at the hands of Emperor Palpatine. Obi-Wan sacrifices himself, bringing us another one of the most dramatic moments in all of the Star Wars franchise. As the group of heroes tries to escape the Death Star, Obi-Wan duels Darth Vader to a standstill. He knows he can't win, and he knows he can't get away. He sacrifices his life to give Luke and the others the chance that they need to get away with the Death Star plans. It's a noble act and one of the most moving moments of the original film.

We see Anakin's death as a redemption. Anakin Skywalker wasn't a Jedi at the moment of his death, but his sacrifice led him back to the light; literally and figuratively. The redemption of Darth Vader remains one of the most climactic, cinematic moments in the entire Skywalker Saga. Defeated by his son, he watches on as the emperor tries to kill him.

According to Wookipedia, the ultimate resource for Star Wars Fandom on the net; mass death created disturbances in the Force, which was felt galaxy-wide by Force-sensitive individuals. When the planet Alderaan was destroyed by the Death Star, Obi-Wan Kenobi was visibly distressed and revealed to Luke Skywalker that something terrible had just happened, as if millions of voices cried out in terror and were then silenced. Nineteen years earlier, Jedi Master Yoda dropped his staff and became distressed as he sensed the death of many Jedi at the execution of Order 66. (79)

Although Yoda didn't die in battle, his death was still dramatic. He finally passed of old age on Dagobah, right as the Galactic Civil War came to a head. While he could not fight, he had passed down to Luke Skywalker all the tools he needed to become a Jedi.

The passing of Luke Skywalker in Star Wars: The Last Jedi upset fans all around the world. In real life we remember our favourite characters as they pass away. In the last few years, we have lost a number of key actors who played roles in the franchise. Losing Carrie Fisher was heartbreaking and recently - whilst I was writing a draft for this book - actors David Prowse (Darth Vader) and Jeremy Bulloch (Boba Fett) also left their earthly bodies and became one with the Force.

IT IS OUR GREATEST FEAR
"When gone am I, the last of the Jedi will you be."
- **Grand Master Yoda on his deathbed, Star Wars: Episode VI - Return of the Jedi**

The mother of all fears is the fear of death. It's the place that we are all going to, and there's nothing we can do about it. Throughout the ages, legends speak of those that have searched for the elixir of life; giving them everlasting life to avoid the inevitable. Upon considering death, we are faced with more significant questions:

"What is my purpose and meaning for life?" and
"What would constitute as having lived a good life?"

The thought of death can bring about an existential crisis. Whether referred to as an existential crisis, or existential anxiety, the main concerns are the same: that life is inherently pointless; that our existence has no meaning because there are limits or boundaries on it, and that we all must die someday.

This is said to bring life into focus for us. Some people even experience what is known as the death drive in accordance with Freudian psychoanalytic theory. This is when people march towards death by acting out in aggression, repetition, compulsion, and self-destructiveness. This repetition compulsion to self-destructive habits and attitudes acts as a defence against the reality of death.

Buddhism makes us aware that things are constantly changing. Nothing is permanent. Impermanence known as anicca or Pāli - or anitya in Sanskrit - is one of the essential doctrines of Buddhism. It stipulates that all things in existence are evanescent. If we are able to grasp this concept experientially through meditation, we can move to a place of serenity and peace. From embracing the fear of death by understanding the nature of impermanence, the passing of all things and the nature of constant change, our approach to life changes. In Star Wars: Episode II – Attack of the Clones Anakin approaches Master Yoda regarding his fear of losing the ones he loves. It is one that has been recurrent throughout this manual because it is so incredibly important to grasp it:

Anakin Skywalker: *I won't let these visions come true*
Master Yoda: *Death is a natural part of life. Rejoice for those around you who transform into the Force. Mourn them do not. Miss them not .Attachment leads to jealously. The shadow of greed, that is."*

- Star Wars: Episode III – Revenge of the Sith

But Anakin's fear and attachment to Padme, the one he loves, overpowers his emotions. Darth Plagueis was a Dark Lord of the Sith whose knowledge of the midi-chlorians was said to be so powerful and wise that he had the ability to keep those he cared about from dying. Anakin Skywalker, desperately seeking a way to prevent what he had seen come to pass in his vision of the death of Padmé Amidala, was entranced when Darth Sidious told him a tale of this and that it was possible to save the one that he loved. He was still grieving for the mother he could not save and did not want this fate to be the same for his love.; Skywalker's inability to let go of Amidala led to his fall to the dark side of the Force and ultimately become one of the greatest villains of all time.

"You are not ready. You want to learn the way to win but never to accept the way to lose, to accept defeat. To learn to die is to be liberated from it so when tomorrow comes, you must free your ambitious mind and learn the art of dying."

- Bruce Lee, Martial Artist, Actor, Philosopher

It may seem counterintuitive, but the more you try to win, and the more you're attached to the outcome, the more you need to let go of control. It doesn't mean that you shouldn't try your very best, but when you are doing that, you should - at the same time - internally let go of your need to be in control.

This understanding is essential if the warrior within you is to be fearless and effective. The warrior allows things to be as they are so that we can enjoy them. We realise that change is the only constant in the universe and we can relax. If we can accept that we are indeed spiritual beings having a human experience and we also realise that our essence is timeless, then death is not to be feared. We are just energy transforming. The energy never dies. The truth is that we are deathless by nature.

Remember, there is no death, there is only the Force.

***

CHAPTER 15: THE POWER OF ANGER

" *Fear leads to anger. Anger leads to hate. Hate leads to suffering."*

- Grand Master Yoda, Star Wars: Episode I - The Phantom Menace

ANGER

"Remember, a Jedi's strength flows from the Force. But beware: Anger, Fear, Aggression – The Dark Side, Are They. Once you start down the dark path, forever will it dominate your destiny, consume you it will."

— *Grand Master Yoda, Star Wars: Episode V - The Empire Strikes Back*

We all feel angry at times – it's part of being human. Anger is a normal, healthy emotion, which we might experience if we feel:
- Attacked;
- Deceived;
- Frustrated;
- Invalidated; and,
- Unfairly Treated.

With anger, we experience a range of sensations and feelings. Anger feels different for everyone. Anger can manifest as:
- A churning feeling in your stomach;
- Tightness in your chest;
- An increased and rapid heartbeat;
- Legs go weak;
- Tense muscles;
- Feeling hot;
- Having an urge to go to the toilet;
- Sweating, especially your palms;
- A pounding head;
- Shaking or trembling; and,
- Dizziness.

This can all feel very uncomfortable. Then there are the added elements of losing your cool in public and having your anger witnessed which can bring up feelings of shame or guilt. It also affects us mentally; leaving us feeling tense, nervous, or unable to relax. These are some of the other emotions that may run through you:
- Feeling guilty;

- Feeling resentful towards other people or situations;
- Feeling easily irritated; and,
- Feeling humiliated.

Recognising these signs gives you the chance to think about how you want to react to a situation before doing anything. This can be difficult in the heat of the moment, but a better understanding of anger can allow us to harness its powerful energy. Not everyone expresses anger in the same way. For example, some unhelpful ways you may have learned to express anger include:

- **Outward aggression and violence:** such as shouting, swearing, slamming doors, hitting or throwing things and being physically violent or verbally abusive and threatening towards others.
- **Inward aggression**: such as telling yourself that you hate yourself, denying yourself your basic needs like food, or things that might make you happy, cutting yourself off from the world and self-harming.
- **Non-violent or passive aggression**: such as ignoring people or refusing to speak to them, refusing to do tasks, or deliberately doing things poorly, late or at the last possible minute, and being sarcastic or sulky while not saying anything explicitly aggressive or angry.

Anger only becomes a problem when it gets out of control and harms you or people around you. In the Star Wars universe, we see The Sith - a secretive order of Force-users and sworn enemies of the Jedi - use anger and hatred to fuel their control over the Force. The Sith are aware of the power of this very energy and use it to overpower and destroy the Jedi as they attempt to control the galaxy.

Master Yoda has warned others of the dangers of anger and how for a Jedi they can lead us away from the light and into the dark. However, could anger be used constructively and not a path to the dark side? We usually think of anger as one of those ugly "bad" emotions. Anger is more than a big, mean monster. In society, we are encouraged to control our anger and outbursts are seen as negative. It isn't necessarily a 'bad' emotion; in fact, it can sometimes be useful. For example, feeling angry about something can:

- Help us identify problems or things that are hurting us;
- Motivate us to create change, achieve our goals and move on; and,
- Help us stay safe and defend ourselves in dangerous situations by giving us a burst of energy as part of our fight or flight system.

ANGER ISN'T GOOD OR BAD

The power of anger stems from the same power that digests our food and energises our cells in our body. You could say that without anger you would not be alive. Anger is neither good nor bad; it is a form of power, and how it manifests can be either destructive or constructive. This means that anger can either lower or raise our vibrational frequency. It all depends on how you work with it.

Anger comes from the Agni Tattva – also known as the fire element within the body - that gives us the strength of commitment, discipline, will-power, and the ability to carry out our intentions. Learning to use the power of anger constructively can help us achieve our goals, fulfil our dreams, and motivate our lives. The Agni Tattva is associated with the 3rd chakra solar plexus and is the same energy that the warrior uses for willpower and strength. It is the fire of aggressiveness that, once focused, can help us to achieve our life missions.

Padme: To be angry is to be human.
Anakin: I'm a Jedi. I can be better than this.
- **Star Wars: Episode II - Attack of the Clones**

POWER THROUGH ANGER

Anger is the great motivator; it's both the energy to protect yourself and the confidence to get what you need. It's the power that builds relationships, businesses, and empires, as well as the Force that destroys them. Anger is your source of intense, hot, energy in the pit of your stomach that allows you to handle any challenge that life throws at you. It will help you find your power and teach you how to use it for the greatest good.

"To answer power with power, the Jedi way this is not. In this war, a danger there is, of losing who we are."
– **Grand Master Yoda, Star Wars: The Clone Wars**

The teachings of Yogi Bhajan, the master of kundalini yoga, explains that anger is intoxicating because of the power it brings. Anger and Power are very closely related. As with any form of power, the outcome depends on how it is used. The goal of our work with Anger is to be skilful in applying its power. The image of a disciplined samurai warrior fighting only to defend and restore peace and honour can serve as an inspiration to harness the wild beast within and put it to good use. Used well, Anger brings just the right amount of energy to handle any situation. Think of it as your inner Jedi Master; taking care of you, and sending you the energy necessary for you to get what you need to live well. So, don't be afraid of your own power; when you claim it, you'll be safe. When your use of Anger is refined, balanced, and wise, you will instinctively use the right level of energy to get the job done.

Anger has received a bad reputation from all the damage that occurs in the process of releasing it, but your Anger is not the problem; no more than your stove is to blame for burning your dinner. Anger and power energy can both be thought of as forms of fire. They heat things up, make them move, and leave everything they touch changed; it just depends on how you use them:

Cook your food or burn it, warm your house or burn it down.

Create love or betray love. The choice is yours. When you learn to use Anger to protect yourself, you will become more comfortable. When you use it to serve others, you will be happy. Learn to enjoy the greater play of power and allow it to work through and around you.

ANGER AS AN ALLY

You have, at times, experienced Anger in the form you enjoy and need most: smooth, effective action to handle what needs to be done. You don't think of it as Anger, but as Strength. Intentional action and achievement are like nice controlled flames. When you hit an obstacle, the heat rises to match the situation. You take your efforts to a higher gear; you push harder or go longer until it's done. If that doesn't get you what you want, however, you start to feel irritated and frustrated. But you can channel that into clearer thinking or more decisive action. (80)

"There are a lot of sad things in life, but the saddest of all is when you do not recognise your anger, and you do not deal with it."

-Yogi Bhajan, Master of Kundalini yoga

JEDI EXERCISE: GAIN AWARENESS OF YOUR ANGER

Go to your Jedi Sacred Space and sit in a cross-legged pose. Get into a meditative state as you recall the event/person whom your anger has been targeted towards. Trace and track your emotions and bodily sensations.

This self-reflective practice is to help you gain some awareness of your anger and triggers.

When was the last time you became angry?
Think of 5 things that make you angry.
Which people in your life cause you to become angry?
Select only 5 situations that make your blood boil?
Think of 5 negative aspects or consequences of anger.
Think of 5 positive aspects or effects of anger.
Record your insights in your Jedi journal.

JOURNEY WITH ANGER

Anger can be your personal fuel and your teacher on your journey. It helps you to get what you need and to protect you by telling you that you do not like something that is happening to you. It can help you – by directing itself towards that person or thing – to uncover the source of what could harm you. You must learn to channel your anger so that you can unravel this side of your true power. You can then continually use it for self-protection. Once you are within your power and strength, you can use it to help others.

"It takes strength to resist the dark side. Only the weak embrace it."
— Obi-Wan Kenobi, Star Wars: The Clone Wars

MEDITATION TO TRANSCEND INDIVIDUAL CONSCIOUSNESS AND ANGER

Posture:

Sit in easy pose with the spine straight.

Mudra:
Make fists of both hands. Put both fists with the back of palms towards you, 6 to 8 inches in front of the brow point. Extend and press the thumb tips together until they become white. There is no need to press very hard, just firmly. It is important for the last joint of the thumb to relax and bend as much as possible.

Eyes:
After you see the tip of the thumbs turn white, close the eyes and see the white tips through closed eyes. Once you are in position, relax the body.

Breath and Mantra:
Inhale deeply. Let the breath out powerfully as you chant WAHE GURU. Chant this sound at the highest pitch possible. WAHE is about 1 second and GURU is until your breath is fully exhaled. Always take a complete breath and repeat the mantra rhythmically.

Time:
Continue for 5 – 11 repetitions, about 2 minutes.

This is not a practice to be done in a group. Practice individually or with a partner to end an argument. It is essential to keep the eyelids closed. If they are open, you will get faint and dizzy in a few repetitions of the chant. If your eyes are closed, you are protected, and the effects on consciousness will happen in 8, 9, 10, 11, or so repetitions. The mental frame from which you see yourself and the world will be shifted within and without by this exercise. (81)

*

MIND, BODY, SPIRIT

"Your mind, emotions and body are instruments and the way you align and tune them determines how well you play life."

— **Yogi Bhajan, Master of Kundalini yoga**

Living your life as a warrior takes great commitment, endurance, and courage. It is not a path for the faint hearted. In order to be a powerful Jedi Warrior, you will need to master your mind, body, and spirit. The Universe can demand a lot from us at times; testing our limits and capabilities. Changing and raising your vibrational energy takes a certain amount of work and effort.

In order to excel consistently, mastery within your body, mind, and spirit is essential. We have much to gain by harnessing the powerful potential of the mind body spirit connection for accessing intuition, healing ourselves, and becoming a refined warrior. Living a life full of vitality requires a connection between mind, body, and soul. Like a link in a chain, when one is broken the others become weak and vulnerable. Your body, brain, and spirit are constantly evolving. The more you use them the stronger they get. The less you use them the weaker they get.

In the next chapter of our training, we will explore each aspect of this mind-body-spirit trifecta and offer ways to develop your capacities as a warrior.

***

CHAPTER 16: THE JEDI MIND TRICK

" *Be mindful of your thoughts."*

- Obi-Wan Kenobi, Star Wars: Episode II - Attack of the Clones

THE MIND

The mind possesses the greatest power in the universe. Everything starts with the mind. Mastery over the mind is the work of a Jedi. It is incredible how the power of our mind can influence our whole life. It is said that we are what we think about and how we do it. The ancient yogis say that whatever we desire, we can achieve using Mind Power. Taming the mind, however, takes effort — you have to put in a certain amount of time and training to achieve this. This is why it should be the most important priority in your life.

Star Wars has numerous scenes throughout the saga that indicate - with timelines - the wisdom achieved, as well as the benefits of training and focusing the mind. Everyone from Yoda to Qui-Gon Jinn has encouraged their padawan learners to be mindful and master the present moment. Training the mind to stay focused and understanding the consequences of letting your thoughts, emotions, and feelings control you, underlies everything in the Star Wars universe. Throughout Star Wars we see the Jedi practicing mindfulness and concentration. As they do, they come to better understand themselves, the galaxy, their own personal suffering, and the dark-side within.

THOUGHTS

Zen Buddhists used the metaphor of a monkey mind to refer to the tendency for the mind to jump from thought to thought, constantly in motion, without conscious control. Several years ago, the National Science Foundation published a paper which estimated that our brains produce as many as 12,000-60,000 thoughts per day and approximately 18 million thoughts a year. From the moment of our birth until the moment that we depart, our mind never stops working. Even when we sleep, our mind is working; processing and synthesising the information taken in during the day and using it to shape our experience of the world.

This poses the question:
What are my thoughts?
Ask yourself, "How many of those thoughts are positive, supportive, and inspiring?"
It is estimated that a large percentage of these thoughts are negative and mostly repetitive thoughts patterns from the day before. These baseless worries are a major source of stress and tension. They are also a cause of exhaustion not only for the mind but also for the physical body. The mind can be a tool of transformation or destruction; depending on how you choose to use it.

MIND OVER MATTER

The Force can have a powerful effect on the weak-minded, a phenomenon Jedi sometimes take advantage of in pursuing their missions. An experienced Jedi can use the Force to implant a suggestion in the minds of those they encounter, encouraging them to comply with the Jedi's wishes.

The path of the Jedi requires us to become mindful of the thoughts as we work towards mastery over the mind. Luke, the Jedi apprentice, is plagued by frustration, impatience, and anger. Luke's mind is unfocused and full of fear. Luke's teachers, Obi-Wan and Yoda, teach Luke how to sense the Force within, as well as how to recognise and regulate his emotions; ultimately showing him how to discipline his mind.

You need to remember that you have a mind, but that you are not your mind. You have the power to separate yourself from your thoughts. We need to learn how to observe our thoughts but not get attached to them, because when you consciously control your thoughts, you consciously create the future that you desire.

How do we achieve this?

First off, one must understand the mind and how it works.

The mind is a set of cognitive faculties including consciousness, perception, thinking, judgement, language and memory. It is usually defined as the faculty of an entity's thoughts and consciousness. It holds the power of imagination, recognition, and appreciation, and is responsible for processing feelings and emotions, resulting in attitudes and actions

It is very important to be able to distinguish disturbed states of mind from peaceful states. States of mind that disturb our inner peace, such as anger, jealousy, and desirous attachment, are called 'delusions'; and these are the principal causes of all our suffering.

It is fascinating how various organizations – from corporations to churches—attempt to influence and control our interpretations, perceptions and beliefs in order to control the sheeple herds. Of course, not everyone is being underhanded; our families, friends, teachers and others are simply sharing the best knowledge they have with what their perceptions and beliefs have to offer. [82] We may think that our suffering is caused by other people, by poor material conditions, or by society, but in reality, it all comes from our deluded states of mind.

"The Force can have a strong influence on the weak-minded."
- Obi-Wan Kenobi, Star Wars: Episode IV - A New Hope

We must strive to eradicate our delusions and replace them with inner peace. This is the path of the Kundalini Jedi. Liberation from suffering can never be found outside of the mind because peace can only be found by purifying the mind.

We often hear the mind being described as powerful, limitless, complex and transcendent. We hear such phrases as "mind over matter," "be mindful," "we're only limited by our mind," and "the mind is a terrible thing to waste." Indeed, the mind is an incredibly powerful tool...if used properly. Your mind can be your greatest ally or your greatest foe. There is no in- between or grey area. Either our mind is used to our advantage or it's used to our detriment. This is because a mind that's not being used fully is a mind that is not achieving its purpose. We short-change ourselves and the world is not giving all of us. Our mind is extraordinary as it is complex. This complexity often results in our mind's racing and jumping from one idea to the next – seemingly without rhyme or reason. (83)

Buddha once described the human mind as being filled with "drunken monkeys," fledgling from flinging themselves from tree branches, jumping around, and chattering nonstop. It's always one thing to the next, and to the next, and the next after that. It was this discovery that allowed Buddha to offer a way out of our suffering and the ability to live with a peaceful, productive mind.

"Your focus determines your reality."
– Qui-Gon Jinn, Star Wars: Episode I - The Phantom Menace

Typical mind chatter sounds could include but are not limited to:
- Your mind-reading off a list of to-do items;
- Your mind listing its fears, both real and imaginary;
- Your mind recalling hurtful things that have happened in the past;
- Your mind judging the present; and,
- Your mind is creating catastrophic "what-if" scenarios of the future.

The monkey mind makes it nigh-on-impossible to calm ourselves and slow down. It dampens our mood; giving way to negative emotions. It messes with our ability to concentrate and it interferes with our interactions with others. It can be stressful but there are ways to get the monkey mind to calm down.

Obi-Wan Kenobi: "But Master Yoda said I should be mindful of the future."
Qui-Gon Jinn: "Not at the expense of the moment."
– Star Wars: Episode I – The Phantom Menace

Buddha realised that as powerful as the mind is, it required taming through discipline. Mastering the mind is one of the aims of Yoga. The aim is to control the mind, rather than allow it to control us. We want to make the mind sharper, clearer, more useful. We want to reach a state of calmness, neutrality and non-reaction.

NO MIND

I would like to present a brief look at the concept of 'mushin' – also known as no-mind - which has been addressed briefly earlier in this book. Being within a 'No-mind' state is different to being in a beginner's 'heart-mind' state. No-mind is usually understood as bringing the mind to a point where the thoughts become still. It is a moment when the mind is not thinking; not allowing the uncontrolled random thoughts generated by the ego to run rampant. When there is stillness of the mind - when it is void of thought - the ego is quiet and the heart can begin to be heard. It is during the suspension of thought that the consciousness of the heart-mind is free to assume the leading role. This is a good basic understanding, but it has layers of deeper meaning and greater skill. It is at this basic level that one begins to experience moments of inner peace and tranquility. This can be a highly profound event in itself, as so many people are burdened with the constant chatter running wild in their mind.

Another level of no-mind involves the understanding that once you are still in the mind, it is then possible to hear the Divine voice of your Higher Self, or of the Universal Source, or the Universal Force.

Once the continuous, uncontrolled thought patterns are slowed down and brought to a still point, the loud voice of the ego becomes barely audible and the voice of the Divine can be heard. This level is all about communication with your Higher Self.

It's the greatest power in the universe, and it all starts with the mind, mastery over the mind is the work of a Jedi.

"You weak-minded fool! He's using an old Jedi mind trick!"
—**Jabba the Hutt, Star Wars: Episode VI Return of the Jedi**

In Kundalini Yoga we speak about there being 3 minds – from the 10 bodies we discussed earlier. In yogic philosophy we claim that those 3 functional minds are the positive, the negative, and the neutral. The positive mind sees the potential, the negative mind sees the pitfalls, and the neutral mind assesses the input from both; responding from a neutral place.

The human being is made up of Ten Bodies. You can find their meanings in the Appendix. The second, third, and fourth bodies are mental bodies called the three functional minds: The Negative Mind, the Positive Mind, and the Neutral Mind. Let's explore them below as according to the teachings of Yogi Bhajan as recorded by the 3HO Foundation:

THE SECOND BODY: NEGATIVE (PROTECTIVE) MIND

Can I determine if there is danger in a situation? What do I need to consider?

The Negative Mind helps you to give form to the creativity of your Soul Body with the gifts of containment, form, and discernment. It instils in you a longing to belong which, in its highest expression, drives you to connect very deeply with your own God self. It gives you patience to be obedient to your own inner guidance.

If your negative mind is underdeveloped, your longing to belong can cause you to get into inappropriate self-destructive relationships because you are over-influenced by others; you aren't contained enough in your own centre.

The key words for the Negative Mind, or the Second Body, are "longing to belong.' Every two wants to be one. You've got this urge to merge. You've got this longing to belong that's definitely a part of human existence and consciousness. You want to be part of a group; you want to expand your identity. This is very much a part of human existence, that longing to belong, where every two wants to be one.

I want to make sure you know that this is something you need to have - this protective mind - because it does protect you. It doesn't have a negative connotation; it is a good thing. Setting boundaries is a good thing. Our society tends to be more positive-minded, so that makes our attorney happy here. There's a great need for attorneys because we aren't trained in protective mindedness and they are. You have to pay somebody a hundred bucks an hour to protect you.

The question for the Negative Mind is: "Can I calculate the danger in a situation?" or better yet: "In my urge to merge, in my need for completion, can I calculate the danger in a given situation?" I like to use the analogy of crossing the street, because it's something that you learn early on. You know how to stop, look, and listen. You want to go from point A to point B. If you get stuck - if you're stagnating in protective-mind - what happens is that you come to the corner, and even though you want to get across, you never move. You're overprotective. You're not willing to take a risk because no matter how you calculate it, you know you're going to get hit by a car on your way across. You'll never take a risk. That's over-protective.

What also happens when you're stuck in this mind is that you can calculate the dangers and ignore them. You want to get across the street so badly that even though you know it's dangerous, you miscalculate and do it anyway. You rush in between the moving cars. Sometimes you get hit. Sometimes you will calculate wrong. Sometimes you know it and you do it anyway, and you get into big trouble. A lot of people get caught this way - in their longing to belong - especially with relationships. You need to calculate the danger in relationships. It's the protective mind that helps you do that.(The meditation on dealing with fears in the earlier chapter deals with the negative mind)

THIRD BODY: POSITIVE (EXPANSIVE) MIND

Am I open to all possibilities that life has to offer? Do I let these into my life?
The Positive Mind sees the positive essence of all situations and beings. It is expansive and allows resources in. It gives you a strong will and allows you to use your power easily and humbly. It makes you naturally playful and optimistic and gives you a good sense of humour. It makes your communication strong and direct.

If the Positive Mind is weak, it is like receiving a daily injection of poison. You can be overwhelmed by the input of your Negative Mind which can be depressing and paralysing. You may be angry and intolerant or hesitate to use your own power, your own heat, because you are afraid of the responsibility it brings or afraid that you might abuse it.

The Key Question: "Will I allow myself to be hopeful? Will I allow myself to have the good things and experience the good things in life?"

With the Positive Mind, we're dealing with the risk/reward ratio. The key words are "Devil or Divine." The idea of "Devil," by my way of thinking, means that people who are over-projective can take you to hell faster than anybody else. What I mean is that if you're not calculating the risk of the situation, you get in trouble fast.

Our society is this way all the way: "Hype it up, build it up, sell it to the max and then take your lumps. It doesn't matter, I got my money." The false hopes projected range from those promoted by televangelists to the idea that if you drink a beer you'll have the absolute time of your life and feel completely fulfilled. That's the illusion, and that's a positive mind projecting.

The fact that you might have a hangover, you might be an alcoholic, that being sloppy drunk isn't necessarily attractive—all those things aren't considered in beer commercials. Everything is sold through projection. So that's the idea of de-will or "Devil." When there's no downside presented, put yourself on alert. Trouble is around the corner. After all, Newton said, "Every action has a reaction equal and opposite."

"Divine" means the ability to project your will into the Divine will. You have heard the expression, "Thy Will be done, on Earth as it is in Heaven." In other words, go with the flow; be at the right place at the right time; things are happening for you as they should when they should (or as they will in Thy Will). "Devil" is de-will, where you're unable to project your will into the Divine will.

Through your ego, you're trying to project your will when the time is not right, or when it is happening and the time is absolutely right for it to be happening, you're resisting and hanging back.

When your Positive Mind, your Third Body, is strong, you have a good sense of humour and you're able to be very hopeful and project that hope. You're like a candle in the darkness. If the Third Body is weak, there's a tendency to either "rush in where angels fear to tread" and not consider the risks, or to be over-positive to everyone's detriment including your own.

You can eliminate your negativity (i.e. your unwillingness to forge ahead) through meditating and through exercises which work on a certain part of your mind to release negativity. Most of all, you can actively and consciously develop your sense of humour. You can look at yourself with honesty and clarity.

Key to Balance: Strengthen the navel point. Increase your self-esteem. Use positive affirmations.

FOURTH BODY: NEUTRAL (MEDITATIVE) MIND

Do I allow myself to perceive and act upon inner wisdom? The Neutral or Meditative Mind is the ultimate "win-win" mentality. From here you look at the whole play of life with compassion. The Neutral Mind evaluates the input of your Negative and Positive Minds (and the rest of the Ten Bodies as well) and gives you guidance within nine seconds. It is a very intuitive vantage point and allows you to access your Soul. If your Neutral Mind is weak, you may have a hard time making decisions. You'll have the habit of feeling victimised by life because you don't know how to integrate your experiences and find meaning in them. You may have a hard time seeing beyond the polarities of life on Earth and tuning into the great cosmic scheme of things.

The Key Question: "Will I allow myself to be meditative and intuitively balanced in my thinking?"

The Neutral Mind (Fourth Body) is a meditative mind. It's a balance between protective mind and projective mind. When this body is working well, you have automatic balance between the two.

You strengthen the Fourth Body through meditation. Generally, you think that weighing and balancing things logically is the way to go. That's a conscious process. There's nothing wrong with being logical, but if the meditative mind is strong, this weighing and balancing is an automatic process. You can still consider things; it doesn't mean that you don't go through conscious weighing and balancing. When you're in a meditative mind, you make your decisions from the balance between protective and projective mind.

The key words of the Fourth Body are: "Cup of prayer." These are the words that my teacher gave. When you see a cup that's half full of something, you may think that it's half full or half empty. It has to do with your bias toward either protective or projective mind. Meditative mind is neither of those; it's a full cup.

Meditative mind makes you a good listener. If you get around somebody with a meditative mind, they'll pull you into their state right away. Their mental/emotional condition spreads out. That's the idea of a cup of prayer. Share this cup, have a drink out of this cup and you'll be fine.

When a meditative mind is working, you tend to balance out anyone around you or in your environment who tends to be overprotective or over-projective. A person with a meditative mind is quite valuable. They're intuitive, they have good timing, they know what to do and when to do it, and they make good listeners as well.

Meditative mind allows you to give and take criticism with equanimity. When you criticise somebody while you're coming from the meditative mind space, it can be quite good. But if you're being over-projective of your own self, or if you're being over-protective, then it won't work well as a result. You may feel bad at the time and later. Taking criticism with the meditative mind allows you to not dwell on it or feel bad about it at the time or later.

Meditative mind helps you to successfully work out recurring patterns in your life. The patterns that eventually will demote you are the ones in which you go radically off in one direction or the other, either over-projective or over-protective. You can work with those patterns through meditation, through developing a strength in this meditative mind.

Key to Balance: Meditate

Yogis believe you have a thousand-petalled lotus that's partly etheric and partly philosophical at the top centre of your head. For every petal, a complete thought is produced every second. So that's a thousand thoughts per second, which is serious computing power.

Some of these thoughts are conscious; most of them remain subconscious. All of these thoughts get channelled into different parts of the brain through neural-pathways. (84)

*

MEDITATION

Meditation is great for disciplining the mind as it makes the mind vigilant. By practicing meditation, we make our minds alert. The job of the mind is to translate external and internal sources of information; linking them together. Meditative yoga is done to calm the roving tendency of the mind. A distracted mind is not fit to practice yoga, after all.

A calm mind is achieved through the careful training with meditative yoga at the helm. You need to be as comfortable as possible to achieve this. You need to be free from illness, and pain to truly quiet your mind.

From the yogis' point of view, meditation is the result of your glandular system working. You're asking your glands to work a certain way and your brain to work a certain way in order to achieve meditative states. That's what yoga does. It works on the glandular system and the brain as well as the nervous system. So, if you can do yoga exercises, it makes meditation much easier. It's always good to do a little bit of yoga before you meditate because it gets you halfway there. The functioning of your body can either take you out of the meditative state or put you into the meditative state.

The second key to meditation is breath. I have found that to be profoundly important with myself, and I've found it very true with beginners as well. Breath will draw you into a meditative state faster than anything else. Breath and mantra - the combination of the two - changes your blood chemistry so much and so quickly that you will be drawn into a meditative state. You can't resist it. The breath is also a very good vehicle for retraining yourself because it's with you all the time. It is your most available and accessible tool. It's something that you can leave out of conscious control or put into conscious control. Control of the breath - or verbalised mantra - is probably the fastest and easiest way of changing your conscious state.

Main postulates of mindfulness, such as training the mind to stay focused and the consequences of letting your thoughts, emotions, and feelings control you, underlies everything in the Star Wars universe. Throughout Star Wars we see the Jedi practicing mindfulness and concentration, and as they do, they come to better understand themselves, the galaxy, their own personal suffering, and the dark-side within.

Anakin Skywalker: "Where do you go when you meditate?"
Obi-Wan Kenobi: "To a state of mind and body, where I reacquaint myself with simplicity."

- Star Wars: Rogue Planet

Meditation was a mental technique practiced by Force-sensitives and non-Force-sensitives alike, by which one attempted to get beyond the reflexive, "thinking" mind into a deeper state of relaxation or awareness. Many Force users such as the Jedi Order used meditation for enhancing emotional control over self and for better connection to the Force. Jedi often built meditation chambers in which outside disturbances could be muted and shut out to provide a more conducive atmosphere for deep meditation. While meditation could be attained without any outside means, some individuals chose to meditate with the assistance of a rare, naturally occurring meditation crystal.

Meditation within the Jedi Order was considered paramount to mastering oneself and the Third Pillar of the Jedi Path: Self-Discipline. Without self-mastery, Jedi scholars would argue that achieving mastery over the Force would be impossible. To the Jedi, meditation allows a practitioner to achieve inner peace, harmony, and serenity; three of the core principles of the Jedi Code. Due to the importance of meditation, the Jedi Council would instruct. Initiates and Padawans were then encouraged by their instructors to meditate whenever they had a spare moment, seeking deeper meditation during private time.
(85)

"Happiness can be achieved through training the mind."
— **Dalai Lama, Spiritual Leader of Tibet**

We commonly use meditation for relaxation nowadays as it can help us circumnavigate the stresses of daily life. During meditation you're able to silence the rambling thoughts in your mind; leading to enhanced physical and emotional well-being.

MEDITATION AND EMOTIONAL WELL-BEING
When you meditate, you may clear away the information overload that builds up every day and contributes to your stress.

The emotional benefits of meditation can include:
- Gaining a new perspective on stressful situations;
- Building skills to manage your stress;
- Increasing self-awareness;
- Focusing on the present;
- Reducing negative emotions;
- Increasing imagination and creativity; and,
- Increasing patience and tolerance.

Let us begin with some basic meditation techniques that will allow you to focus and train your mind so that you are its master and not a slave to your thoughts. Regular practice of these techniques will begin to allow you to focus; developing deep concentration and the ability to still the mind.

Serious training is required!

In actual fact, we are not just training our mind, we are recalibrating our whole being.

CREATING YOUR MEDITATION SPACE

Setting up your meditation space can be hugely beneficial and it will aid your daily practice. Find a place in your home - or anywhere that is quiet, clean, and away from any distractions or interruptions. This may be difficult if you live in the city, so experiment with earplugs and set a time either in the early morning or later in the evening when there are fewer distractions. Make your space welcoming and inspiring yet simple.

TRAINING PRINCIPLES

Some beginning tips. Like with any new skill, it may take some time to experience results. We are all different and will progress differently. The main thing is to be disciplined and to stick to your practice. Start with a few minutes instead of trying to do one hour at a time. If you are an experienced meditator you can meditate for as long as you would like.

It is like training a puppy. The puppy will want to get up, walk around, run around, and play, for this is the nature of the puppy as it relates to the nature of your mind. Your mind will wander; you will have thoughts and distractions. The practice requires gentle persistence. Every time the puppy walks away, gently guide it back to the practice. You may find yourself spending the whole session just getting the puppy to come back and be still. Be patient and try again. Over time, with continued training, you will notice you can hold your focus and concentration for longer periods of time.

At times you may become frustrated or angry or even deflated. Discipline and training must be directed with an attitude of kindness. Wilful force is counterproductive. A Jedi flows with the Force.

Nota Bene:
Early morning meditation during Armit Vela, which translates as the "ambrosial hours" (the two and a half hours just before sunrise), when the sun is at a sixty-degree angle to the Earth, the energy you put into your practice gets maximum results. The early hours are when the energetic charge is at its lowest to help you reach deeper levels of meditation.

CONCENTRATION MEDITATION

Concentration meditation involves focusing on a single point. The focusing will - over time - stop your mind from jumping around so much. In the beginning, you may become aware of how much noise and dialogue goes on in your mind, so it may feel like your mind is less focused than when you began to practice. Concentration meditation involves focusing on a single point. This could entail for example:
- Following the breath;
- Repeating a single word or mantra;
- Staring at a candle flame;
- Listening to a repetitive gong, chime, or bell; and,
- Counting beads on a mala.

With concentration meditation you simply refocus your awareness on the chosen object of attention each time you notice your mind wandering. Rather than pursuing random thoughts, you simply let them go. Through this process, your ability to concentrate improves.

BREATH AWARENESS MEDITATION

1. Sit comfortably.
2. Close your eyes.
3. Make no effort to control the breath; simply breathe naturally.
4. Focus your attention on the breath and on how the body moves with each inhalation and exhalation.
5. Notice the movement of your body as you breathe. Observe your chest, shoulders, rib cage, and belly. Simply focus your attention on your breath without controlling its pace or intensity.
6. If your mind wanders, return your focus back to your breath.

Maintain this meditation practice for two to three minutes to start, and then try it for longer periods. Use the 40-day chart in the Appendix to track your progress. Since focusing the mind is challenging, a beginner might meditate for only a few minutes and then work up to longer durations.

MINDFULNESS MEDITATION

This process allows us to acknowledge each mental note as it filters through our minds without trying to switch them off, control them, or judge them. It can work as a great first step into meditation for those who struggle to quiet their minds. You will begin to notice patterns in your thinking; being able to pre-empt them and flow with them as opposed to against them. You will eventually develop an internal balance of sorts as it encourages you to be fully present. Literally anything you do can become mindful meditation if you're giving it your all and focusing on it; even something as simple as washing the dishes. Many disciplines of meditation will call for some form of stillness – giving your all to the present task.

WALKING MEDITATION

Walking meditation is more than a simple stroll in the park. It is usually done much slower than normal walks and involves either coordination with the breathing, or specific focusing practices. It looks more like meditation than like walking.

The ability of focusing, developed in walking meditation, is easily carried into our daily life and also into seated practice, when there are actually less sensory stimuli. It's a powerful tool at your disposal. Unlike seated meditation, when walking your eyes are open, the body is standing and moving, and there is a bit more interaction with the outside world. Because the body is moving, it is easier to be mindful of the body's sensations and anchored in the present moment; for this reason, many people find walking meditation easier than seated meditation.

Here are some things to keep in mind, regardless of the "type" of walking meditation you choose:

- **PLACE**. Find a secluded place where you won't be distracted or disturbed. Ideally, the walking path should be slightly enclosed, so there is less distraction from the scenery, and the mind can more easily go inwards. Stay away from high-traffic and heavily populated walking areas. It's also important that you feel safe in your surroundings.
- **LENGTH**. Ideally, practice for at least 15 minutes. Since there is no discomfort of seated practice or of not moving, you can naturally do it for longer periods than seated meditation.
- **PACE**. Slow is better. Pace should be steady and even. If your mind is agitated, or your ability to focus is weak, walk very slowly, until you can stay in the present moment with each step.
- **ANCHORING**. Before you start your walking session, spend a minute or two just standing there, breathing deeply and anchoring your attention in your body.
- Stand with your feet hip-width apart and balance your weight evenly on both feet. Take the time to feel the stability of the ground.
- Take a few deep breaths.
- Close your eyes and do a scan of your whole body, starting at your feet. Make note of any sensations, thoughts or feelings and take the time to explore the sensations fully.
- Bring your awareness to your body, noticing how your body feels as you are standing, and becoming aware of all the sensations going on.
- **TECHNIQUE**. Choose one of the six techniques explained in this post. If you don't know which to try, read my recommendation at the end of this article.
- **RE-FOCUSING**. Just as in seated meditation, whenever your mind starts to engage with thoughts (or any type of mental content), bring your attention back to your walking and your breathing.
- **ATTITUDE**. We are not going anywhere. There is nothing to achieve, except mastering our attention and presence. Simply be with the process. (86)

CANDLE MEDITATION

Nota Bene:
Please take safety precautions when working with flammable objects; making sure you have created a safe space for this practice

The following is an excellent version of candle meditation.

Sit on a chair, the floor, or a cushion, so the candle flame is at eye level and about 60 centimetres away. How you sit is up to you, just be sure that you choose a comfortable position. Make sure that you're sitting up straight and can remain completely still while meditating.

Stare at the candle and allow it to be the main focus of your mind. Hold your eyes steady even if you feel distracted or bored. Your eyes may begin to water, but hold steady and the sensation will pass. If you blink or get distracted, just return your attention to the flame.

As you gaze at the candle, breathe deeply. Focus on the sensation of the light flowing into you with each inhalation. As time passes, the room around you will fade until your only awareness is the flame.

When your meditation is done, lay down and close your eyes for five minutes. This will allow your mind and body to come back to full awareness before you continue your day. (87)

*

A POSITIVE MIND

These are unprecedented difficult times filled with financial struggles, health challenges, personal isolation, social disconnection, and fear. We are mostly in survival mode. The struggles personally and professionally have made our lives challenging, making it easy to fall into the trap of developing a negative mindset.

Having a positive mindset can help you avoid stress. Even out of the most challenging and devastating situations, we can find a silver lining. A positive mindset is an attitude someone has who "expects" good and desired results. The power of positivity is immense, and it can help you convert that energy into reality.

With a positive mindset, you can avoid many physical and mental diseases as well. If you don't give weight to negative thoughts, you won't cause your body discomfort from stress, anxiety, worry, and frustration. A stress-free mind leads to a more robust immune system,

Half of life's battles can be won if you practice being confident in your abilities. A positive mindset cultivates confidence in your personality, allowing you to perform at your best because of a boosted self-esteem. You can make the right decisions at the right time with confidence. Another step towards crafting a "positive you" is to start any project or task with the goal of learning from it. Training to become a real-life Kundalini Jedi warrior could be your next project. Keep in mind, whether you complete your goal, and accomplish all the yoga kriyas and meditations, the journey will definitely add knowledge and experience to your life. If you start a task or objective with the intention to learn from it, you will never be disappointed. That is how you develop wisdom. (88)

The positive mind is one of three mental bodies, the others being the negative mind and the neutral mind. Its qualities are positivity, equality, and trust. The positive mind sees the good in everything. Its job is to calculate what is going right. It keeps the light shining strong no matter how dark things get. When your positive mind is healthy, you have a good sense of humour and a strong sense of hope. You are full of bliss and joy, and you are ready to succeed and take on life. The positive mind corresponds to the navel centre, to the seat of will, so a strong positive mind leads you to be action-oriented and organised. Your body is fit, and your mind is sharp. When your positive mind is sharpest, you can see that all good comes from the Creator and that all beings have access to this good, which makes everyone equal.

When the positive mind is weak, it finds data from the subconscious and magnifies it. It will find your hidden traumas, blow them out of proportion, and reinforce negativity. A weak 3rd body can lead to a blocked navel centre, making you sluggish, overweight, depressed, and unorganised. In extreme cases, you can become paralysed with negativity and feel like giving up entirely. A 3rd body that is too strong can lead people to become thin and dogmatic. (89)

JEDI EXERCISE: DEVELOP A POSITIVE ATTITUDE

This practice opens the heart centre and the feelings of the positive self. Here we are working with the third body, the expansive mind. The mudra is a gesture of happiness.

It has a great history and is said to have been practiced by many great and wise spiritual leaders including Buddha and Christ. The hand mudra became a symbol for blessing and prosperity. It works specifically on the 3rd Body. You'll recognise this as being from the 10 Bodies that we explored earlier. It works to uplift us and strengthen our positive mind.

TUNE IN WITH ONG NAMO GURU DEV NAMO X 3

Posture:

Sit with an erect spine.

Curl the ring finger and little finger into each palm. Bend the thumbs over top of them to lock them into place. Keep the first two fingers straight. Bring the arms so the elbows are by the sides, and the hands are by the shoulders with the two fingers of each hand pointing straight up. Bring the forearms and hands forward to an angle of 30 degrees from the vertical. Press the shoulders and elbows back firmly but comfortably. The palms face forward.

Eyes and Mental Focus:

Close the eyelids.

Roll the eyes up gently and concentrate at the brow point, the Third Eye area at the top of the nose where the eyebrows would meet.

Breath:

Create a steady, slow, deep, and complete breath.

Mantra:
Mentally pulse rhythmically from the brow point out to Infinity the sounds: Saa taa naa maa Saa is Infinity. Taa is Life. Naa is Death. Maa is Rebirth/transformation. This describes the cycle of life. This kriya brings a total mental balance to the psyche. The entire mantra means, "I meditate on Truth, Truth that I am."

Time:
Try it for 40 days. During that time eat lightly and speak only truth directly from your heart. Practice for 11 to 62 minutes. (90)

THE JEDI ATTITUDE

"A Jedi must have the deepest commitment, the most serious mind. This one a long time have I watched. All his life has he looked away...to the future, to the horizon. Never his mind on where he was."
— **Grand Master Yoda, Star Wars: Episode V - The Empire Strikes Back**

What are you really willing to give and do to become a Jedi? Are you willing to overhaul your way of thinking and your way of relating to the world? Are you willing to challenge your long held and, probably mostly, outdated attitudes? Our attitude will determine how we react to the outside world. When we approach situations with a positive attitude, we will have positive outcomes. When we approach situations with a negative attitude, we will have negative outcomes. We must be responsible for our lives and maintain a healthy attitude towards the things around us. Mastering your vibrational frequency will take time, practice, and repetition – a lot of repetition.

To be successful as a Jedi warrior, we will need to adapt our approach to life. We will need to train our mindset and have the discipline to keep our mindset healthy. Our attitude can serve as a superpower in these times. These reminders will serve us in the battle. Much of our success and fulfilment comes down to how we see things. It comes down to the meaning that we choose to give the events and circumstances which we find ourselves in. It comes down to what we believe this one, precious, life is all about. I'm not talking about being *Pollyanna*, wearing rose-coloured glasses, or ignoring real-world challenges. I'm also not talking about being fake or suppressing your not-so-positive emotions. What I'm suggesting is to use more of your intelligence; to become aware of how much power you have in this area and take responsibility for the impact that your attitude has on the quality of your life – and the lives of others. The actions you take, the energy you exude and, therefore, the results you create, are vastly different when you have a positive attitude rather than a negative one. While that might seem obvious, most people *react* to the world around them and allow their attitude to be dictated by their ever-changing circumstances. Look, even if you have good intentions, and you do the right things, and work really hard, if you don't also have this energetic skill mastered - this ability to maintain and express a genuine positive attitude - you're not going to be as successful or fulfilled as you deserve to be.

NEVER COMPLAIN

"Complaining is one of the ego's favourite strategies for strengthening itself."
- **Eckhart Tolle, Author and Spiritual Teacher**

Complaining keeps us locked in negativity and generally has a low vibrational frequency. We feel this when we hang out with someone who complains all the time. When we are around people like that, we end up coming away feeling tired, drained, or worse, we begin complaining about everything ourselves! So even complaining to yourself can alter your mood and lower your vibe. This is the source from which self-disgust, self-hatred, and self-sabotage springs and the ego loves it - this self-imposed separation. If we are able to maintain a practice of not complaining, we will begin to feel the results almost immediately. When we complain, we are creating negative images and associations in our mind, which will lower our mood. We might start blaming others for our problems, thus continuing the cycle of negative thinking. This thinking will affect our vibrational frequency and will likely attract more negative messages or experiences.

JEDI EXERCISE: STOP COMPLAINING.

Try it for a week and see what happens. See how your life opens up for you. If you need more motivation, start a complaining fund. Every time you catch yourself complaining, drop a **POUND** (or a **FIVER** or a **TWENTY** - whatever keeps you in line) into a jar.

BE GRATEFUL FOR THE FORCE

Whatever you focus your mind on expands. When you focus on lack, you operate from a position of loss and discontent; thus, experiencing more lack. You focus on what's missing from your life. When you focus on abundance, you have more of everything. Taking time to count your completions and successes creates a more profound sense of fulfilment. Gratitude is a superpower in its own right. It is one of the quickest and most effective methods to changing and increasing your vibrational frequency.

In the yoga chapter, we mention how people, in general, are usually dissatisfied and are always looking for the next thing to do, buy, or go to, and this seems to be the nature of us as human beings. Unfortunately, it is also a dead-end road because no matter how much we acquire, we always find ourselves wanting more. We yearn for a better car, a better job, or even a more fulfilling relationship. We live in a "me-me" society, and we want our desires and wishes to be met immediately in the name of instant gratification. How many of you have caught yourself beginning to complain about the most minor inconveniences when our lives are already rich and full. We might notice this fullness if we took the time to reflect. After completing an important job, do you move on to the next item on your agenda without taking time to savour the successful completion of the task you just finished? Do you dwell on your to-do list instead of savouring how much you've accomplished? It's hard to be down and out while also feeling grateful. Your life, no matter how bad you think it is, is a gift. This single realisation will raise your vibrational frequency considerably.

JEDI GRATITUDE TASK

Right now, spend 5 minutes and begin writing down all the things for which you are grateful. Here's an easy one to get you started: you could be grateful for the Star Wars' movies and how much you enjoy them. It doesn't matter if you can only think of one. Begin with being grateful for the air that you breathe, the sky, and the clouds. Once you start with one thing, you begin to feel other things to be thankful for. Now, keep going. Keep writing. Maybe your favourite show is on later. Just be grateful. Please write it down. This is your one small step back toward your path to higher vibrations. Some examples to get you started:

- A roof over my head and a warm home;
- Plenty of drinkable water;
- I don't have to go hungry;
- I can enjoy the small and free pleasures in life;
- Access to the internet;
- My friends and family;
- My health; and,
- The kindness of people I have never met before.
- After each statement say or write thank you, thank you, thank you!!

MONEY BACK GUARANTEE:

I challenge you to start a 40-day gratitude journal; writing 10 things that you are grateful for every day. If you are not feeling happier or more positive after the 40 days, send me proof of your journal for a full refund on the book you have purchased.
(Terms and Conditions Apply)

ACCEPTANCE

Acceptance is one of the most powerful states of mind that you can be in because once you've accepted the reality of something, you are then at your most empowered to do something about it.

Acceptance is allowing your thoughts and feelings to be as they are. It doesn't matter if they are painful or pleasant — stop fighting reality. Let your thoughts and emotions come and go naturally without forcing or silencing them. Acceptance doesn't mean giving up. On the contrary; it's acknowledging your feelings and life events. When you accept all your experiences — both pleasant and painful — you are expanding your mind. The opposite of acceptance is avoidance.

Accept yourself. There are many people in this world who have not learned to accept themselves. As a result, they lack confidence and they go through life at the mercy of others. A small insult, or unkind comment from someone else, can wound their self-esteem. When we accept ourselves, we are confident in who we are. That is because we aren't trying to fix ourselves. Yes, of course, we always should be trying to grow in wisdom and maturity, but when we accept ourselves, we like who we fundamentally are. Unfortunately, we live in a world in which we often aren't accepted. You may not be accepted for the colour of your skin, or your gender, or your sexuality. Some folks may not like your personality. But when you've accepted yourself, the opinions of others don't matter.

When you accept yourself, you are liberated from the opinions of others. They don't matter and that allows you to go into the world confidently; with a shield that protects you from the occasional unkind remark. Consider developing the life-changing skill of acceptance. It indeed will lead to greater happiness and peace in your life. The Serenity Prayer says, we accept the things we can't change, and we pray for the courage to change what we can.

"Use the Force, Luke. Let go!"
- **Obi-Wan Kenobi, Star Wars: Episode IV - A New Hope**

*

RESISTANCE

For many people, resistance can feel like an internal struggle between two parts of ourselves — one that overtly wants to change and one that covertly fights it. Every time you come up with a plan or goal that is important to your life, you will encounter some form of resistance. Things that take time and effort can be demanding mentally and physically. Your journey to becoming a Jedi will have many ups and downs. You will have good days when you feel you are making progress; feeling the Force flowing freely and experiencing life in a joyful, positive way. Other times you will feel like you are succumbing to the Darkside of the force. You can overcome this by focusing on the reason that you want to reach your goal of becoming a Jedi. Focus on the positive change you wish to bring into the world. Focus on your connection to the Force and how it inspires you and empowers you. To remember your mission as a Jedi knight ask yourself:

What am I always fighting against?
What am I afraid of?
What issues keep coming back in my life?

When you ask these questions and discover the answer, you'll uncover the most significant source of energy loss in your life. The next step is to learn how to preserve your energy and stop the resistance. Ask yourself:

What must I understand, love, or let go of that will free up my energy?

Often, we tend to invest vast amounts of energy towards fighting, avoiding, or suppressing something.

*

PERSISTENCE

There is a saying: "A river cuts through a rock not because of its power, but because of its persistence." Things will get in your way, and it will be easier sometimes to give up and do what is most comfortable instead of following your path as a Jedi. Persistence is an essential trait to develop in life because it is intimately interlinked with one's own personal development and self- improvement. You will only get better in life by failing at things; learning from those experiences and moving on. Many times, along the road to success, we get knocked down, and it often feels like we are going backwards or even losing. Well, often we have to lose - albeit temporarily - in order to win. I can assure you that there's no one on this planet that sailed painlessly and smoothly all the way to success. The critical thing about temporary defeat is learning the lesson from it. Each failure tells you something. That something is usually what not to do. From then onwards, we become wiser - and healthier - for the next attempt and we know what not to repeat. Each temporary defeat is like one of life's many battles, but as long as you don't quit, and learn from your losses – as long as you keep on persevering - you will eventually win. Bear in mind that Edison who invented the electric light bulb failed about 10,000 times before he succeeded. Although the Allies won both World Wars, there were many brutal defeats along the way. Even a world champion boxer has to take a whole load of punches along the way - but he doesn't quit. The most significant difference between winners and losers is their *response* to temporary defeat. Losers get disheartened and quit, but winners - although they also get discouraged at times - learn from the defeat. They become stronger and wiser. After a loss they pick themselves back up and persist.

*

KEYBOARD WARRIORS

The world is changing and evolving fast. The speed of information and content available on the internet and social media continues to rise and it is the highest it's ever been. The average person spends approximately 30 minutes a day on social media, and others have become addicted to the hits of dopamine reward-hormone that it produces. Whether it's Facebook, Twitter, Snapchat, Instagram, Tumblr, Pinterest, or any of the numerous other social networks out there, we waste so much of our time on social media and what for?

Oftentimes we are motivated by the ability to obtain "likes," "shares," "followers" and "friends"; constructing a feeble cyber alter-ego that craves for acceptance and the esteem of others. For this reason, social media can be a sickly environment; full of dark-side energy. Star Wars fans are some of the most passionate fans in the world and at times their emotions can run over. Star Wars' discussion groups can also turn hostile. Star Wars: The Last Jedi had fans furious with the film that was delivered and so enraged were the fans that they began a petition for the film to be scrapped. Characters such as Rose, Jar Jar Binks and even George Lucas himself have been berated and ridiculed for their efforts. This is not the way of the Jedi. To engage in negative talk and environments weakens our connection to the Force.

When we expose ourselves to social media each day it has a detrimental effect on our health, including an increase of depression and low self-esteem. Many studies have proven this. Connect with your friends, family, and other Jedi – sure! – but stop using social networks to build a false and unstable sense of self-worth unconsciously.

When a person posts a picture and gets positive social feedback, it stimulates the brain to release dopamine, which again rewards that behaviour and perpetuates the social media habit. Not only has social media been proven to cause unhappiness, but it can also lead to the development of mental health issues such as anxiety or depression when used too much or without caution. The constant barrage of perfectly filtered photos that appear on Instagram is bound to knock many people's self-esteem. We now have shorter attention spans and are generally more distracted; making it hard to stay focused on our Jedi path. Our battle in the modern world looks less like destroying sky fighters and lightsaber battles and more like the development of a healthy mindset. It looks like having the discipline to fight the impulses of our society. These tech distractions affect our relationships, productivity, and ability to learn — all of which require a certain level of concentration. Being constantly inundated with information also impacts our creativity and ability to be contemplative. As Jedi, we should conduct ourselves on social media in the same way that we do in the world - with integrity; not becoming involved in unfavourable chat rooms.

Stop spending so much time on social networks. The screen and unanimity of identification make the internet, and chat rooms, a haven for people to project and interact in unsavoury ways. Everyone has an opinion and wants to express it. People become brave on-line, and individual exchanges can become toxic; with some even leading to violence. We are better served by not wasting our time and energy exchanging or interacting in such discussions for they will drain our energy and lower our vibrations. Try to spend a minimum amount of time a day - or even stop using it for a whole week - to experience the effect for yourself. Put simply, better concentration makes life easier and less stressful. You will be more productive. To make this change means reflecting on what we are doing to sabotage personal attention, and then implementing steps towards behavioural change that will improve our chances of concentrating better. This means deliberately reducing distractions and being more self-disciplined about our use of social media, which is increasingly urgent for the sake of our cognitive and mental health.

Equally important is a strong body. A strong mind cannot remain strong alone. It needs the support of its vessel to clock at full speed. Just as an engine cannot go anywhere without a chassis, so too can a mind not get very far without a strong body.

***

CHAPTER 17: THE BODY TEMPLE

"I've seen this raw strength only once before, in Ben Solo. It didn't scare me enough then. It does now."

- Luke Skywalker, Star Wars: Episode VIII - The Last Jedi

THE BODY

Having a strong healthy body is essential if the Jedi warrior wishes to be effective in their use of the Force. The body acts as the sacred container for the Force energy. A healthy body equals a healthy mind; allowing optimal performance in life and a positive outcome in meeting the challenges of daily living. The pace of life and the increased pressures of modern living means that we have to develop a good relationship with our bodies if we are to fulfil our destinies as Jedi.

The physical body is the first aspect we must master in order to understand ourselves as humans. The body is not just skin and bones, but a complicated, intricate, and subtle energy system. It has glands, various circulatory systems, a brain, and a complex nervous system. All of these various functions and systems work seamlessly to make up our physical system. A weak body does no good except to dishearten your spirit. Lower stamina, nerve instability, and weak immunity exhaust your body. As a result, every physical task you do gets stressful and tiring. Yoga provides a natural and practical body workout to combat body weakness. The body receives, processes, and accomplishes the various orders of the day.

All of these functioning systems need cleaning, regular tuning, and care management of the system. Everyday living and the process of time and ageing create general wear and tear and various misalignments requiring corrections. If we are to function at our maximum potential, we must make those corrections. Our self-care and the preventive measures that we take will ensure that our bodies have longevity and can endure the requirements of fulfilling our soul's destiny. The balance and management of our bodily system will greatly influence our experiences and capacity to live in the world. Exercise and movement are well known for their health benefits and also for their positive effects on our mental health. It is a sure-fire way to regulate your mood.

The job of the Jedi is to develop the inner and outer elements of the body. Through yoga, we strengthen our nervous system and optimise the flow of energy in the body. The outer practice of conditioning the body allows us to feel more energy, feel more confident, and to develop a sensitivity to our bodies so that we may feel the Force flow through us.

How we feel in our body will have a big impact on the quality and experience of life as well as on our ability to fulfil our mission. Training and practice are key components of a Jedi lifestyle. Eternal students in the art of self-mastery, Jedi are willing to put the time and effort into physical trials in order to become strong with the Force.

Throughout the Star Wars saga, we see hopeful Jedi padawans being trained through tasks, or missions, while being guided by a Jedi Master. Yoda puts Luke through many physical challenges on Dagobah from handstands to swinging through trees with Yoda on his back; all while whispering the ways of the Force:

"Yes; feel the force flow through you."

In this way, Luke could grow beyond his limits and become stronger with the Force. We see Rey running the assault course in Star Wars: Episode IX – The Rise of Skywalker as she jumps, climbs, and attempts to become stronger in her connection to the Force. Developing a connection and sensitivity is of utmost importance to a Jedi for they need to feel the Force flowing within and without them. Your body's strength comes from its ability to exert a Force on an external object. The more weight you lift, the more strength you have. The intensity with which you apply the Force also counts. Apart from exertion, countering and resisting an external force also requires body strength. Adequate body strength is good for overall health, and it makes an easier life in general.

YOGA FOR BODY STRENGTH

It is unlikely that you'll think of yoga when you want to build body strength. Lifting weights at the gym or doing some form of circuit training is more widely accepted as forms of body strengthening while yoga is more commonly associated with flexibility and stretching. What you might not have considered is that yoga incorporates your body weight to strengthen you by movement instead of with the use of external objects like dumbbells. This culmination of body science and yoga movements to strengthen your body is magical. Strength training through yoga has an added advantage of improving muscle flexibility, which helps you avoid injuries. The complex movements bring balance and movement that are vital for strengthening your body. With yoga conditioning, not only are we strengthening our physical selves through the postures but the addition of breathing exercises and specific sequences allow us to strengthen our nervous system; giving us the added benefits of a regular detox of our system. Regular detox leads to a cleaner, healthier body whilst allowing our inner energy system to flow freely; giving us more vitality so that we can vibrate at a higher frequency.

There are several reasons why yoga is a more balanced way to do strength training. A regular yoga practice can reduce your risk of injury as well as condition your body to perform better at things you have to do every day like walk, sit, twist, or bend. It will work towards correcting our posture while we drive, as well as providing strength while lifting and turning.

Traditional gym workouts with gym equipment typically involve just going back and forth on a one-dimensional movement. For example, the forward-back motion of a bicep curl. Weight training exercises typically isolate and flex one muscle or muscle group at a time.

As a form of fitness, yoga moves your body in the ways it was designed to move in order to help ensure that it keeps functioning properly. In yoga you use both large and small muscles and move in many directions; holding various postures and associated movements for extended periods of time. This leads to overall body conditioning. The engagement of larger and smaller muscle groups helps tone muscles all over your body; keeping them in balance with each other.

Nota bene:
We are not saying you can't go to the gym or do any other sort of physical training, but as Jedi Warriors, we need strengthening of both our inner and outer selves so that our bodies begin to become strong enough to hold the flow and charge of the Force. Our yoga practice helps to increases muscle endurance because you typically hold any given pose for a period of time and
repeat it several times during a yoga workout. As a Jedi you will want to challenge yourself with your physical training, pushing yourself to your limit and then beyond it to become stronger over time. Care should be taken if you have had a previous injury. Listen to the wisdom of your body; not overdoing a posture if it causes pain that would result in an injury.

JEDI EXERCISE: SUN SALUTATIONS - YOGA SET FOR STRENGTHENING

Before we start our set it is advisable to perform some warm-up exercises to prevent injuries and prepare the body slowly. We always **tune in** before a set to prepare our mind and body for the practice. It changes the frequency of the body and aids beneficial practice. Tune in using ONG NAMO GURU DEV NAMO x 3: I bow to the teacher within me, and the teachers and wisdom that have gone before.

Complete the Jedi warm up set from Chapter 7. Sun salutations excellent setup increases cardio activity and circulation. It stretches and bends the spine; massaging the inner organs of the digestive system. It exercises the lungs and oxygenates the blood. It strengthens and works all parts of the body. You can start by practicing three rounds and then gradually increase to about 5-10 rounds.

1. Stand with your feet together; toes and heels touching. Keep your weight evenly distributed on both feet and feel yourself firmly planted on the ground. Find your balance point with your arms by your side; fingers together and straight. (POSITION 1 & 11)

2. Inhale; stretching up and bringing your arms up over your head. Arms touching; elongate the spine, lifting the chest up and relaxing your shoulders down. Be sure not to compress the vertebra of the neck and lower back. Look up at the thumbs. Inhale (POSITION 2 & 10).

Kundalini Jedi Warrior

3. Exhale and bend your torso forward. As you bend forward, keep your spine straight; elongating it as if reaching forward with the top of the head. Relax the head as close to the knees as possible. Ideally your chin will be brought to the shins or the knees. Keep the knees locked and straight. Place your hands on the floor at either side of your feet or reaching down as far as you can with your fingertips. Your eye focus is at the tip of the nose. Exhale (POSITION 3 & 9).

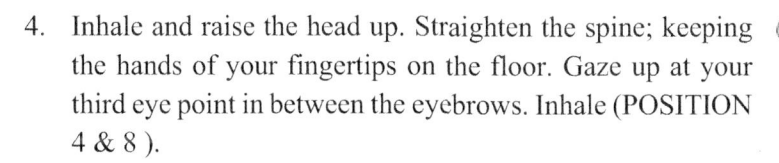

4. Inhale and raise the head up. Straighten the spine; keeping the hands of your fingertips on the floor. Gaze up at your third eye point in between the eyebrows. Inhale (POSITION 4 & 8).

5. Yogi Push-up. Exhale and bend the knees; stepping or jumping back so that the legs are straight out behind you. Balancing on the bottom with bent elbows hugging the rib cage. Keep your palms flat on the floor under the shoulders with the fingers spread wide. Your body is in a straight line from forehead to ankles. Keep yourself equally balanced between hands and feet. Do not push forward with the toes. Hold the pose briefly for a few seconds and from here transition into posture six. Exhale in this position.

6. Cobra pose. From this position inhale and straighten the elbows; arching the back. Stretch through the upper back so that there is no pressure on the lower back point. The forehead should face up at the sky and you should gaze at the tip of your nose. Fingers should be spread wide and apart. Try to keep your pelvis as close to the floor as you can. From here you can transition into posture seven.

7. Triangle pose. Tuck the toes into the floor. Exhale and lift the hips so that the body is balanced in an inverted V shape with your feet and palms flat on the floor. Keep your

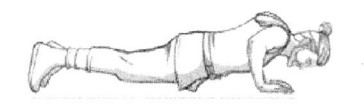

elbows and knees straight with your fingers spread wide. Gaze towards the navel point and hold this position for five breaths.

8. Inhale and jump or step back into position four.

9. Exhale and bend forward into position three.

10. Stretching up in healing and coming all the way up into position in order to transition back into standing up. Exhale and return to the original starting position with the arms by the side and fingers pointed straight.

AFTER FINISHING YOU MAY EITHER DEEPLY RELAX ON THE BACK FOR 5-8MINS OR SIT IN MEDITATION.

As well as our physical body we also have an energetic body. This is a great set that works the whole body and will leave you feeling energised after practice. As well as strengthening and conditioning our muscles and tissues, we also want this to develop a sensitivity within the body. In this next kriya we will build a lot of upper strength and really work the shoulders. In addition to body conditioning, we will also strengthen our aura. You may have heard of the aura before. This is like an energetic force field that surrounds our body. When this is weak, it can cause a weakness in our energy and we are easily affected by external forces.

In the Mind over Matter chapter, we introduced the concept of the 10 bodies and we explored the positive minds as well as how they relate to the sum total of all the bodies. Here we will touch on the 10th body, known as the radiant body. In the teachings of Kundalini Yoga, the human being has 10 bodies, not 1. The 10th body is the Radiant Body. This refers to a field of energy that extends 9 feet around us. Energy comes into the body through the crown chakra, goes up and down the spine; picking up speed, and then extends and builds up the Radiant Body. Some refer to the Radiant Body as a band that sits on top of the aura, almost like a golden tip or energy field.

A powerful 10th body makes one courageous and radiant. You project royalty and grace, both in how you act and how you present yourself. You carry yourself very well and have a special light about you. You are bold and have finesse. Good things come to you without much effort. Your presence is magnetic and attention comes to you naturally. A weak 10th body makes you timid. You become someone who lives in fear of conflict or recognition. You may have fluctuating energy and have difficulty with commitment.

STRENGTHENING THE AURA

The aura is the electromagnetic field that surrounds your body; it acts as a container for your life force, bringing confidence, security, mercy, and love. A strong aura attracts positivity and repels negativity, like a shield. Illness cannot penetrate to your physical body. It gives a

Kundalini Jedi Warrior

strong sense of security and an uplifting presence. A weak aura can make you feel paranoid or a lack of self-trust. Negativity can penetrate into the psyche and physical body.

In the yogic tradition, it is taught that this is a great kriya for keeping disease away and developing your aura. The time can be built up to 7 1/2 minutes for each side in Exercise 1, and 15 minutes each for Exercises 2 and 3. That will create a tremendous sweat. It can get rid of almost any digestive problem, give strength to the arms, and extend the power of protection and projection in the personality.

TUNE IN WITH ONG NAMO GURU DEV NAMO X 3
PRACTICE A FEW EXERCISES FROM THE JEDI WARM UP SET.

1. Stand up and bend forward so the palms are on the ground and the body forms a triangle. Raise the right leg up with the knee straight. Exhale and bend the arms and bring the head toward the ground. Inhale and raise up to the original triangle pose. Continue this triangle push-up for 1 minute. Switch legs and continue for 1 minute.

2. Sit in easy cross-legged pose. Extend the left hand forward as if grasping a pole so that the palm faces to the right. Put the right palm facing down crossed under the left wrist. Raise the right hand up over the back of the left hand so both palms face right and the fingers lock. Inhale and raise the arms to 60°. Exhale and bring the arms down to shoulder level; keeping the elbows straight. Breathe deeply for 2 to 3 minutes then inhale. Stretch your arms up and relax.

3. Put both arms parallel to the ground with palms facing each other about 6 inches apart. As you inhale, extend your arms backwards towards each other; keeping them as high as possible. Exhale and bring your arms forward to the original position.

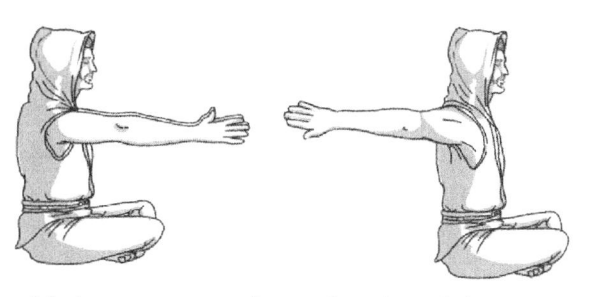

Continue for three minutes with deep rhythmic breaths. Move the arms powerfully in a backward motion; repeating the cycle for 3 minutes. Once finished you can begin another round of the same exercises. On completion sit in a meditative pose, with your eyes closed see if you can feel your magnetic field and feel how far your aura projects. Record your experience in your Jedi journal.

*

MARTIAL ARTS

Another fantastic form of body conditioning is martial arts. In Star Wars the Jedi are trained in the martial art of sword fighting similar to the samurai tradition and to the techniques of kendo. The Jedi use their martial arts skills to defend and protect; never to attack.

A young, but earnest, martial arts student once asked his new teacher: *"I am devoted to studying your martial system. How long will it take me to master it?"*
The teacher replied casually: *"Ten years."*
The student wanted to learn faster: *"But what if I really, really work hard at it? How long will it take then?"*
The teacher thought for a moment: *"20 years,"* he finally replied

The more you want to accelerate the process, the more time it will take. The student was asking the wrong question. He was so anxious that he only cared about the outcome: how long it would take him to accomplish it. Martial arts are a commitment and a chance to develop many qualities, including perseverance. The process of learning and training begins to impact other areas of our life. The martial art you choose or practice is just the outer covering. It's you that makes it come alive with your personality and your unique style. There are over 8 billion people on this planet, but only one of you. Don't follow the crowd, mimic others, or try to be someone else for this is a futile waste of energy. It is a waste of your authentic expression in the world.

I remember being on holiday in Ireland and watching the Wimbledon final on TV. It is an epic game with 2 masters of the sport thrashing it out to see who will be victorious. After 4 hours and 48mins Rafael Nadal claimed his first Wimbledon title; setting up the foundation for one of tennis' greatest rivalries. I was so inspired by what I had just witnessed that it prompted me to take on a personal physical challenge before my body got too old.

When I was younger, I had attended a few judo classes and also practiced karate – inspired, of course, by The Karate Kid - and enjoyed the classes immensely. However, as much as I had enjoyed attending, I did not complete any gradings. It was not until that moment – watching these masters of tennis battling it out - that the memory of these early classes came back. Then, aged 33, I made the decision that I would engage in Tae Kwon Do and obtain a lifelong dream to achieve my black belt certification. It was only by training later in life that I had evolved the level of commitment and discipline that I needed to complete my martial arts journey. And so in the summer of 2020 - almost 11 years to the day that I decided to embark on my martial arts journey - I passed my grading and became a 1st degree, assistant-instructor, black belt in Tae Kwon Do . I took my time; being sure not to exacerbate old injuries, but it just goes to show you that it is never too late to begin your journey.

The spirit of Tae Kwon Do is best epitomised by the 'do' part of Tae Kwon Do. It encompasses the advancement of body and mind. There is particular focus on the meditative aspects of the forms, as well as the way that people develop their concentration and physical strength.

I was also inspired by the tenets of Tae Kwon Do and how my training over time developed each of the tenets Tae Kwon Do teaches the foundation of good sportsmanship by teaching the five core tenets.

- **Courtesy**: Respect for others.
- **Integrity**: Acting ethically and morally.
- **Perseverance**: A can-do spirit in the face of adversity.
- **Self-Control**: Keeping your emotions in check.
- **Indomitable Spirit**: An unshakeable spirit.

Some of the top reasons why learning a martial art, whether it's karate, Tae Kwon Do, judo, or jiu-jitsu, is more than just a method of self-defence, according to Elite Daily, are highlighted below. There are many psychological, spiritual, and physical benefits of getting involved in martial arts.

Here are the top five reasons you should consider learning a form of martial arts.

It teaches honour and respect. It truly doesn't matter which martial art you study as pretty much any style is a great way to learn how to defend yourself. Martial arts not only teach you the techniques to defend yourself but also the way to think about defending yourself, which allows you to anticipate and avoid potential dangers.

Traditional martial arts, such as karate or judo, will teach you the importance of putting your ego aside and respecting your instructor, as well as others in higher positions, such as your parents or elders. Learning martial arts reinforces etiquette, respecting rules, and following a code of honour. You'll learn to show some humility, for someday, you'll be in a position of power and know what it's like to be in your underling's shoes.

It teaches you to use non-violent conflict resolution. Learning martial arts teaches you to mentally and physically refrain from violence and only use it for self-defence when it's the last resort. Martial artists will try to refrain from conflict and use non-violent conflict resolution skills, emphasising the importance of avoiding a physical altercation. In the real world, it's equivalent to having the mental discipline to refrain from getting into fights with stupid people. (91)

The mind, spirit and physical body are strengthened through the practice of martial arts. It requires diligence as well as a flexibility and speed that are unlike those of the layman

man. It will keep you physically fit, but it will also teach you that your body is capable of some accomplishing some amazing feats

I learnt many things from my martial arts journey and persistence was one of the most important elements that I learnt to master. The studio where I trained was almost 1.5 hours away from where I lived. A friend had introduced me to my teacher, Master De Silva, and I respected the relationship, time, and commitment he gave me and the other students. Changing clubs was a difficult decision for me for that particular reason, so twice a week, I would drive through rush hour traffic for 1.5 hours, fulfil my training for 2 hours and then drive back another 1.5 hours. When I look back on this now, it surprises me that I didn't give up. That is how we develop an indomitable spirit; by staying committed and not stopping until we complete our mission. During my years of training, I learnt many skills and attributes that helped me in other areas of my life.

Apart from the obvious benefits of getting fit, and learning a new skill, kicking and screaming was a good avenue for stress relief. A warrior cannot be effective and calm if they are stressed. They simply will not be focused enough.

More than sport, fighting, or self-defence, the martial arts are first and foremost about life. In an earlier chapter we explored living your own life as a rebel and creating your own path. We are only able to do this when we find out what that life essence is and begin expressing that essence.

> *"To be a martial artist means to be an artist of life."*
> **- Bruce Lee, Martial Artist, Actor, Philosopher**

Finding your unique expression of who you are; allowing whichever practice you choose to shape you and remove those aspects that get in the way of truly being yourself, is what it comes down to. Even the Jedi masters had their own unique take on the teachings and have their own unique personalities. Qui-Gon was always a little rebellious, for example. Living life is a creative endeavour. You are creating art with everything you do and everything you are.

You can learn a great many things about your own personality and so much more by engaging in a form of martial arts. One of those things is how to control your breath under pressure. From our previous chapters, we've already come to see how important breathwork truly is. Our breath, according to many martial arts practitioners, is guttural. It comes from deep within us; almost as if it were our soul-fire. It does not originate in our chests, but that is where it becomes a catalyst for the fuel that our entire physical being needs. Unbeknownst to many, we all engage in ineffective breathing techniques due to the amounts of stress that we are under – individually and collectively. Effective breathing can, therefore, take years of practice. Martial arts, meditation, and yoga are the holy trinity of spaces to learn breathwork.

I think you are really starting to see this common thread of threes if you hadn't already.

USING THE FORCE TO FLOW WITH OUR MOVEMENTS

Everything around us is moving at warp speed. This fast-paced lifestyle is the reason why we can't seem to get a firm handle over our physical selves, our health, or our overall wellbeing. However, if you really want to be a master of any given thing – including your physical movements – you have to slow it down. By slowing down, you can truly take the time to master something, and thus garner success in a chosen craft. You must crawl before you can walk, and walk before you can run. Martial arts of any kind offer great ways to teach yourself how to slow down.

AWARENESS IS EVERYTHING

The martial arts have the power to teach you heightened awareness. This ability can be the difference between life and death in intense situations. This isn't just harnessed from the fights but also from stillness. As any yogi will tell you, learning to be still can be more uncomfortable than any form of physical stretching.

CONFLICT BEGINS AND ENDS FROM WITHIN

All fights are fought on the battlefield within – even fights where you are going to go up against an opponent. The only time you can win is when you face yourself – internally.

THE JOURNEY IS WHAT MATTERS

As long as you are growing, it doesn't matter what the outcome is. You shouldn't be focused on the amount of time you can be still, the number on a scale or any solid outcome. Rather focus on your growth. We never stop growing internally; garnering wisdom with each passing day that we are alive. Up next, we explore the principles of discipline, flow states, movement and fighting through adversity according to excerpts from *5 Underrated Reasons You Should Pick Up A Martial Art* by Coach Eric Stevens.

DISCIPLINE AND SELF-MASTERY

"For a man to conquer himself is the first and noblest of all victories."

- Plato, Athenian Philosopher

We need discipline in order to live our lives efficiently. Discipline is based on the notion that short term sacrifices will lead to long term gain. It allows us to create habits and make routines, which ultimately lead to who we are on a daily basis.

Those who are disciplined are mentally tough. A disciple – the root of the word 'discipline' – is a student who is willing to learn. Martial arts are one of the fastest paths to self-discipline. All of our greatest opponents lie within us. The battle is won or lost before we step foot in any arena. Martial arts have helped many in areas of my life that are totally unrelated to 'hand-to-hand' combat.

Any art-form can be noted as the application of creative skill. When we engage in the martial arts, we discover truths about ourselves through the application of our skills. It allows you to discover your authentic self. The work of the martial arts is to juxtapose the internal and the external. Yoga, meditation, and martial arts all allow us to fuse our bodies to our minds.

These art-forms allow us to find mental stillness through bodily movement. It forces you to be present; teaching you how to breathe, how to move precisely and how to develop the right mindset.

As Jedi, we are learning to align ourselves so that we may become one and flow with the energy of the Force. Many martial arts, from judo to Brazilian Jiu Jitsu, are learned in this manner. Just like the Force Absorb, you can realign offending energy and redirect it to your advantage. "Martial arts teach you both successful offence as well as successful defence, when to attack and when to retreat. These concepts are just as applicable in the ring as they are in the boardroom. The martial arts will help you find a way to flow with the current, and through it." (92)

*

STRENGTHENING THE NERVOUS SYSTEM

Our nervous system controls all of our basic functions. It encompasses the nerves in our body which run up our spinal cords and into our brains. They carry important messages that allow our brains to enact instructions to our bodies. The following practices that we will explore will help you develop your nervous system so that it is steady and unshakeable.

HYDROTHERAPY - THE POWER OF COLD SHOWERS

As Jedi we need to be sharp, alert, and awake. We need our body to be open and functioning well. One of the best methods to promote healthy circulation and build a strong nervous system comes from taking cold showers. You may have heard of the Hoff method - submerging yourself in ice. The yogis of old could regulate their body temperature allowing them to stay in the cold high mountains of the Himalayas.

The process is called hydrotherapy or ishnaan. There's a lot more to it than just getting outwardly clean. When the cold water hits your body, all the blood rushes to the organs. The blood moves in order to protect the organs and keep them warm. This is an automatic self-defence mechanism.

As the blood moves inward, it flushes the capillary system. In this way, the capillary system of the body gets a powerful work-out. cold showers open the capillaries and clear toxins at the deepest level of the body. open your capillaries, increase your circulation, wake up and strengthen your entire nervous system.

Cold showers stimulate the body in a way that can vastly improve circulation and flush the organs clean. This, in turn, keeps your skin radiant and the blood chemistry young and healthy. It also stimulates healthy secretions from the glandular system and strengthens the nervous system.

This will be a challenging process for the mind, it will think why the hell are we doing that and this will be the first challenge, to ignore the mind hear, focus on your breath, it is a battle of your will versus the perceived experience of pain - as far as I know no one has ever died of having a cold shower.

- Follow these steps for the first victory of each day:
- Massage your body with a small amount of oil. Almond oil is highly recommended. It contains lots of minerals. You won't be greasy after the shower. When wet, the oil gets absorbed by the skin.
- Wear cotton shorts or boxers that cover your thighs. Make sure they are loose, in order to create an air pocket around the thighs. Avoid skin-tight, polyester athletic shorts. The shorts protect the femur bone which controls the calcium-magnesium balance in the body.
- Get the cold water flowing. Move-in and out of the water several times, constantly massaging your body until the water no longer feels cold (really!)
- Feel free to do a victory shout (shouting or screaming is not required but you may find it helpful, a mantra, like I am one with the force and the force is with me 'or 'I have the power' something empowering to block out the mental chatter)
- Start with the extremities – feet and hands, arms and legs.
- Go slowly if you have high blood pressure or problems with the sciatic nerve.
- Make sure to massage the chest and breasts to increase circulation to that area and clean out toxins.
- Dry off briskly with a rough towel to make the body shine.

Nota Bene
Female Jedi Warriors: Don't take cold showers while menstruating.

A cold shower can also be a little intimidating. It can help to make sure the bathroom is warm (use a space heater or run hot water to get it steamy). This is for very young padawans - If you really can't take a full cold shower, at least wash your hands, elbows, face, ears, and feet with cold water. Above all, be kind to yourself. How about taking a hot shower first, then ending with cold water? He replied, "That is like eating a lot of junk food and then having a healthy meal." If you really love hot showers, wonderful. Take them at night or another time for bathing your skin and hair. The morning shower is for your circulation and stimulation of your nervous and glandular system.

Do not take a cold shower if you have a fever or some other health condition, you can get advice from your doctor if you have heart problems. (93)

As warriors we are ready to respond and act on any situations that arise with swift energy, but also place importance on getting rest and knowing how to put our bodies in ease. This is a very important aspect of being a Jedi. Getting the right amount of sleep and the right quality of sleep.

SLEEP

Jedi need a good sleep. You need to be able to wake up feeling well-rested and refreshed. You must be able to cycle through the four stages of sleep with ease. These include:

1. **Falling asleep:** We will toss and turn in order to burn the last of our energy and get comfortable.
2. **Light dream:** Also known as the reverie stage.
3. **Dream state:** This burns the most of your energy during the night.
4. **Deep, dreamless sleep:** Your heart rate slows as does your breathing.

You must ensure that your breathing in the waking world is just as steady as it is in deep sleep. If it isn't, your nervous system will be wrecked by moving between these two states. Your sleep time will, of course, be dependent on your individual needs.

PREPARING YOUR SLEEPING SPACE

- The darker and cooler your room, the better.
- Get a firm mattress to support your spine and relax your central nervous system.
- Orient your bed east-west to cut across the earth's north-south magnetic field.
- Consider very low volume, low frequency positive affirmations or white noise to play in the background while you sleep.

Make sure that you engage in good sleep hygiene just before bed – about an hour or so.

- Make sure you refrain from heavy exercise an hour before bed. Light walking is fine.
- Avoid loud music.
- Avoid caffeine after 3PM.
- Make sure your oral hygiene is up to standard.
- Drink a glass of water, but not so much that it will make you wake up to use the bathroom.
- Have a lukewarm shower – too cold and it will wake you up, too hot and it will tamper with your internal temperature.
- Do a few Kundalini Yoga exercises like the Jedi warm-up set in Chapter 7.
- Read something inspirational, meditate, or say your prayers.

If you practice these as you lay in bed, you will have a chance to go quickly through the preliminary stages of sleep and almost immediately reach the deep dreamless sleep state.

- Take all your worries, concerns, ideas, and problems, and ask the Force for guidance, to be shown a way for inspiration. You'll be amazed at how many are gone, solved, or improved by the time you wake up.
- Set your mental timer to wake you up in the morning. Yes, your subconscious mind has a great sense of time and will respond to your directive.
- Lie on your stomach, turn your head so your right cheek is on the pillow. This automatically opens your left nostril to bring in the cooling, soothing, calming energy.
- Do long, deep breathing through both nostrils. (See the Yoga Chapter)
- Block your right nostril with your hand and continue long, deep breathing through the left nostril.
- Once you feel drowsy, turn over onto your back, side, or your preferred sleeping position.
- Continue long, deep breathing until asleep. (94)

THE JEDI DIET

To achieve peace, we must be at peace in our body. To be at peace in our body, we must develop an intimate relationship with our body. An intimate relationship is based on two-way communication. How do we develop this relationship with our body? First, we must care for and love our body. Second, we must listen to and pay attention to what our body is communicating to us. We can begin by noticing what type of relationship we currently have with our body. How do we feed it? With nourishing food and drink? Do we chew our food so that it can easily digest the nourishment?

Another very important aspect for the warrior is his diet - the quality of the food that he uses to nourish his body. Foods that will energise him and those which have a high vibration should be on the very top of the grocery list. Certain foods are also beneficial in strengthening and maintaining our nervous system. Jedi Warriors need to be eating food that is high in life Force energy.

THE FORCE IN FOOD

When a food has just been picked, it's alive with life Force and nutrients! Life force is vital energy or Qi/Prana. Head back to the Chapter on the Force to explore this again. After harvesting, the life Force gradually declines. At the very last stage of decline, microbes take over. It disintegrates, dies, and gets recycled back into the earth. When food is processed at high heat, it loses its life Force. High temperature cooking such as baking, frying, and irradiation cause a loss in nutrients. When raw foods are dried or dehydrated, they can be stored for long periods without losing life Force or nutrients. If you live mostly on organic, fresh veggies, fruits, seeds and nuts, you're getting the best that nature has to offer. However, if you're eating packaged foods which are designed to last for months, the life Force is much lower. Be aware of the fact that many so-called "health foods", even those labelled "organic" or "GMO-free", may be so ridiculously low in nutrition and life Force that it's a waste of your time and money. If they've been processed at high temperatures or extruded, the finest and most expensive organic nutrients may be lost. If they contain lots of sugars, then there's much less benefit.

We can't expect to eat junk food and consume artificial foods and preservatives and expect to feel vital and powerful.

BUYING ETHICAL FOOD

As Jedi warriors we are protectors of all sentient beings. Being mindful where and how we buy our produce goes a long way to increasing our vibration; as does being aware of the impact of our buying habit. Positive buying is favouring ethical products - be they fair trade, organic, or cruelty free. This option is arguably the most important since it directly supports progressive companies. Negative purchasing means avoiding products you disapprove of such as battery eggs, cars with high carbon emissions, or anything that you feel impacts our environment negatively. Ethical eating, or food ethics, refers to the moral consequences of food choices; both those made by humans and animals. Common concerns are damage to the environment, exploitative labor practices, food shortages for others, inhumane treatment of animals reared for produce, and the unintended effects of food policy.

YOGIC DIET: LIFE FORCE FOODS

A Yogic diet includes fresh simple foods that are free from meat, and eggs. You can get all the proteins, vitamins, and minerals you need without them. You should work towards living on:

- Nuts;
- Vegetables;
- Grains;
- Fruits;
- Dairy products; and,
- Legumes.

When your diet consists of nutritious, fresh foods that are easy to digest then you will have much greater health than you've ever had.

GUIDELINES FOR PREPARING FOOD

- Prepare the food you - and others - eat with love and care. An important ingredient of the yogic diet is the vibration that is put into the food. When you chant and have a positive projection as you are preparing food, you enhance the nourishment and healing power of the food.
- Eat-in a relaxing, pleasant environment. This helps with the digestion and assimilation of the food.
- Serve food gracefully. The act of serving others instils a consciousness and sacredness to the eating experience.

- Take a minute before you eat to be grateful. Blessing food adds prana or life force. Prayers don't always have to be eloquent and inspired.

Please refer to the Appendix for further information on the specific energy of certain food groups.

'Thanks a lot, God. I bless the Force for providing this food."
Remember the Giver.

GUIDELINES FOR GOOD DIGESTION AND ELIMINATION

Yogis have known for thousands of years that one of the easiest keys to health is slow conscious eating. It takes practice. You have to retrain yourself. Eating is something you have done for your entire life without thinking about how it is done. Changing this habit will take some serious reprogramming. It starts by counting your chews.

- If you can't digest it, don't eat it.
- Eat only what you can eliminate within 18-24 hours.
- Stop eating before you feel full.
- Rest after meals: nap after lunch, walk after dinner.
- Don't eat after sunset.
- Chew more than you think you need to. The stomach has no teeth.
- Have regular eating times, and eat only when you are hungry. A great way to get relief from overeating is sitting in Rock Pose (on the heels). Sit in Rock Pose (Vajar Asan) for a few minutes after dinner. It is said that one can digest rocks in this posture. (95)

DARK SIDE INTOXICANTS

"I have absolutely no pleasure in the stimulants in which I sometimes so madly indulge. It has not been in the pursuit of pleasure that I have periled life and reputation and reason. It has been the desperate attempt to escape from torturing memories, from a sense of insupportable loneliness and a dread of some strange impending doom."

— Edgar Allan Poe, Letters as Kept by the Edgar Allan Poe Society

This section has been added to encourage you to start thinking about your body and the things that you put into it. The following items are known to be bad for our body.

MEAT: I used to love eating a good hamburger made on the grill and sometimes would eat meat for quick convenience. Then, through the yogic teachings, I realised how our body digests the meat. Basically, after consuming meat it sits in our stomachs for 24-48 hours -decomposing. Basically, it sits and rots away and whilst it rots away like with any type of meat it will begin to release toxins. These toxins will find their way into the bloodstream and system through the cells and skin tissue. Then there is an obvious inclination to engage in good eating practices which do not harm life. As Kundalini Jedi Warriors, we uphold and protect all life forms, we bless the sacredness of life; understanding that the Force runs through all things and to this we hold a sacred bond to protect and uphold. We all have our vices. For some, it's a treat at the end of the week, while for others the pressures and stress of modern-day life mean they crave something more. Some need their caffeine while even cups of tea can be thought of as an intoxicant to get them up and going for work. These seemingly harmless warm beverages can be stimulants to see them through important tasks, while others may find relief at the end of a liquor bottle. When was the last time you saw an intoxicated Jedi?

ADDICTION: In today's society, everyone at some stage has faced signs of anxiety, stress, and depression. Whether it be work-related, home-related, or due to financial worries, it's something that impacts everyone. Alcohol, drug and other process addictions are on the rise as we continue to distract and avoid the reality of our world. Substances are also known to lower the levels of serotonin in the brain; causing changes to an individual's mood. Excessive drinking causes increased levels of anxiety, stress, and depression - a most certain path to the dark side.

Alcohol and drugs can disrupt the daily functioning of the human brain. Alcohol, for example, is a depressant which will cause disruptions to the balance of the brain; affecting thoughts, feelings, and actions. Alcohol and drugs cause the brain to release chemical changes that create stimulation by weakening the part of the brain associated with inhibition. This leads to risky increases in confidence. However, alcohol and drugs affect the brain in other ways. It may create mood changes leading to aggression, anger, anxiousness, and depression. These symptoms will reduce your vibrational frequency and lead us further into apathy and despair

Addictions can manifest in many different forms from workilism ,coffee and even to yoga. Using awareness to understand our behavioural patterns and the reasons for our addictions are the first steps to recovering our true power and becoming the jedi of tomorrow.

Nota Bene:
Refer once again to the chapter on yimas/nimyas and the ethical and moral foundations. If you are struggling with substance abuse and have used it for a while - or have come to a point in your life where you would like to make these changes - then we suggest getting a therapist or joining a 12-step programme to help you on your road of recovery.

BODY POSTURE AND CONFIDENCE

We live in a forward-facing world – sitting behind computers, driving in cars, preparing dinner, carrying children – all of which wreak havoc on our posture. Over time the spine becomes curved; our shoulders rounded forward and we are moving about the world with compromised spinal alignment - or bad posture. Poor posture has been linked with lower energy levels, and depression, as well as body aches and pains. Good posture, on the other hand, can make us look taller, appear thinner, and feel more confident.

What is the link between yoga and improved posture?

1. **Awareness**: Good posture is all about being aware of your body. A regular yoga
2. practice brings increased awareness to your thoughts, feelings and body.
3. **Strength**: Maintaining good posture throughout the day – straight spine, square shoulders, chin up, chest out, core engaged – requires a strong spine and engaged core. Regularly practicing yoga poses like baby cobra, locust and boat strengthen core muscles and will improve your posture over time.
4. **Flexibility**: Tight chest and hip flexor muscles pull the body forward, forcing the spine into flexion. Yoga poses that focus on spinal and hip extension, like upward facing dog and low lunge, open the front body and counter slouching.

Just like our bad habits, that were developed over time, our good habits take time to build back up as well. Practicing yoga a few times a week is an easy and healthy way to improve your posture. People who stand tall look more confident and feel energised. They project a positive energy and this inner feeling translates to living in a higher vibrational frequency. When we see someone with their head down and shoulders slumped it can seem like they are walking around with a heavy cloud over their heads. We automatically assume this person must be down. It communicates that their vibration is low and we tend to avoid them in order to stay away from this energy; hoping that we don't become influenced by it. When it comes to body language, faking it until you make it can have a profound effect on your self-confidence. Below are 10 tips to use your body language as a means to boost your self-confidence as according to Arlin Cuncic for Very Well Mind.

1. **Make eye contact**. Appear confident by maintaining eye contact in social interactions. Good eye contact shows others that you are interested and comfortable. Look the other person in the eye about 60% of the time. If direct eye contact feels too intimidating, start by looking at a spot close to the person's eyes.
2. **Lean forward**. When you are in a conversation, leaning forward indicates interest and attention. While it can be tempting to maintain distance if you are socially anxious, doing so conveys the message that you are disinterested or aloof.
3. **Stand up straight**. Don't slouch! Those with social anxiety tend to try and take up as little space as possible, which can mean sitting slumped over in a protective pose. Straighten your back, pull your shoulders away from your ears, and uncross your arms and legs.
4. **Keep your chin up**. Do you look at the ground when you are walking? Is your head always down? Instead, walk with your head up and your eyes looking forward. It might feel unnatural at first, but eventually, you will become used to this more confident pose.

5. **Don't fidget**. Fidgeting is an obvious sign of anxiety and nervousness. Appear more confident by keeping fidgeting to a minimum. Nervous movements draw attention away from what you are saying and make it hard for others to focus on your message.
6. **Avoid your pockets**. Though it can be tempting to shove your hands in your pockets, particularly if you are worried about them shaking, doing so makes you look more anxious and less confident. Keep your hands out of your pockets to look more self-assured.
7. **Slow your movements**. Fast movements make you appear more anxious. Everything from hand gestures to your walking stride can make a difference; slow down and notice how you feel more confident.
8. **Take larger steps**. As you slow down, try to take longer strides when you walk. Confident people take larger steps and walk with authority. Doing so will make you feel less anxious.
9. **Watch your hands**. Be careful about touching your face or your neck; both are indications that you feel anxious, nervous, or afraid. Confident people don't make these types of movements.
10. **Give a firm handshake**. How is your handshake? A weak or limp handshake is an obvious sign of a lack of confidence, so work on making sure that you offer a firm hand when meeting others. After practice, it will come naturally. (96)

*

AN ATTITUDINAL SHIFT

SMILE

Smiling is a powerful way to move our energy and put us in a higher vibrational frequency. Studies show that people think they already know someone if that person smiles at them, even if it's an absolute stranger. The theory: Scientists believe the need to bond is rooted in our evolutionary past. Survival was more likely when people combined forces, so humans acquired the smile as a way to signal friendliness and to induce an agreeable sense of shared history, whether there was one or not.

Today, when someone smiles, a glum mood is lifted, an apology is accepted, a person's shaky self-confidence gets a boost, a deal is struck, a physical attraction is communicated. But change the cast of a smile and the consequences shift. A rival grins in order to get under your skin; a bully smirks to unsettle his mark. Understanding the nuances helps ensure that you send—and receive—the right mouth message. Here, some intriguing insights about this familiar gesture. (97)

LAUGHING

We don't usually associate laughter with warriors engaged in battle but laughter is essential in the outlook of a Jedi. Every single Star Wars movie has always utilised humour in some fashion. Indeed, the saga is full of hilarious scenes, from the original 1977 film, Star Wars: Episode IV - A New Hope, all the way to Star Wars: Episode IX – The Rise of

Skywalker. The internet is overflowing with Star Wars memes and funny jokes based on the space opera from a galaxy far, far away.

Laughter can boost your immune system and improve your resistance to disease. It releases endorphins and other feel-good chemicals in the brain which have been known to act as natural pain-relievers. We will meet pain when we are challenged and taking a lighter approach can have many health benefits. It may even help us be successful in our endeavours.

"People suffer only because they take seriously what the Gods made for fun."
- **Alan Watts, Writer and Speaker**

This would be reaching the understanding and experience of being one with the Force and the Force being within me. When we can laugh at ourselves, and find humour in life, we have power. Even the darkest periods of life can be infused with humour. Humour is a great source of strength and reminds us that life is always in a state of transition. Nothing ever truly remains the same! When we find humour, we find freedom. The more serious you are, the more disconnected you are from your source of power.

All of these aspects together will begin to form a strong foundation for the work that comes. Engaging in these simple and yet also difficult practices will begin to make us strong and focused; increasing our vibrational frequency.

THE GREAT COSMIC JOKE

The cosmic joke is rumoured to be the greatest joke ever told, it is a long joke, it takes the entire length of your existence to tell but I am reliably informed that the punchline is amazing. Some say the secret of life is to live believing that life is truly part of a joke, that life is what happens whilst we are being told the set up to the joke and to live a good life is to live in anticipation of the laughter that follows being let in on the punchline.

That is the nature of the cosmic joke, it is not a cruel joke, it is the joke that everybody gets to share when we are released from this experience and return to being part of a single consciousness. When that happens we remember that we are a single part of oneness, we are everyone, every experience, every thought, we are part of the totality of all experience, and that every unique life is experienced and shared by everyone. If you are able to understand that, then your behaviour, your actions, your impact on others, every way you think or act towards others must by definition affect you in the same way in the end, after all what you do is who you are, and ends up being part of who we all are. (98)

In improving someone else's experience, we improve our own. It may require selfless action at times, but even those selfless actions are carried out for yourself. You are here to have your own experiences. When you decide how you would like to be present, your actions will flow accordingly.

You must acknowledge that even if your experiences create inadvertent negative impacts for others, that it may have a positive effect somewhere down the line. There is no way of knowing which of our actions will lead to certain chain reactions downstream, and we must simply accept our experiences and be present within them – good or bad. Just act in accordance with who you are.

In helping others, we find that we help ourselves. In protecting the weak from the strong, we too become stronger. Everything you do is a shared benefit to us all including yourself.

It could be that you learn the strength to act in a duty of care to those who are weaker - that they are an opportunity to show who you are and you gladly give those who are stronger the opportunity to be the best version of who they are. It could be that you come to believe in a world of peace, free movement, action, that we are honest and open. That we have a world of shared abundance, where uninteresting work is done by the robots, and instead we add real value to each other and maybe if everyone thought that it could be true, it would be. A world of imagination inspired by experience and made true by our joint belief that we already have such a world.

So maybe the cosmic joke is about how we actually chose this life, and that you chose your life with all its advantages, unique experiences and problems, and that you even chose it especially because of those unique challenges that we all have, and you did so with the full knowledge that you were going to face them.

"I laugh when I think how I once sought paradise as a realm outside of the world of birth. It is right in the world of birth and death that the miraculous truth is revealed. But this is not the laughter of someone who suddenly acquires a great fortune; neither is it the laughter of one who has won a victory. It is, rather, the laughter of one who; after having painfully searched for something for a long time, finds it one morning in the pocket of his coat."

— **Thich Nhat Hanh, Forefather of Mindfulness Meditation**

*

JEDI MINDFULNESS AND CONNECTING WITH THE BODY

The current times are challenging. Fear seems to fuel the media and influence the people. Many are feeling the pain and suffering of the planet. Watching the reality of what our species does to the Earth - and each other - can be horrifying; even traumatic. For some, it is too much, they can't be here, and suicide rates amongst teens and young adults are at record highs. The body can be the vehicle for states of bliss or a prison of pain and suffering. We are being scared out of our skins and bodies. We cannot fully embody our being and ourselves so we wish to escape the body however we can. We do our best to escape our present reality through distraction; preoccupying ourselves with thoughts of the good old times, the past, or an imaginary perfect future. Ironically, these thoughts only serve to make us upset with our histories or anxious about our future wishes. The many distractions and attempts to get our attention focused through the noise, visual interferences, and our phones which send constant notifications and updates, can leave our head spinning. Our minds become overactive as we are flooded with thoughts. We attempt to numb ourselves to the harsh realities and uncertain futures; settling for the fake illusions that our addictions, or lifestyles can provide. We need to find moments of time to disengage. We need to find somewhere quiet where we can just be and enjoy the moment as it is.

"But... There is no past and there is no future. The more you allow yourself to be free from thinking, the more you will be in the moment, the more you will experience life to the fullest. Clear your mind of all questions."
- **Grand Master Yoda, Star Wars: Episode V - The Empire Strikes Back**

A need to disconnect from reality is known as dissociation. It occurs when there's a breakdown in how you handle information. You begin to feel disconnected from your thoughts, feelings – both physical and emotional - and memories. It can affect your sense of identity and your perception of time. Some of the symptoms of dissociation include the following.

- **Depersonalisation** - Feeling disconnected from your own body.
- **Derealisation** - Feeling disconnected from the world around you.
- **Loss of feelings**.
- **Loss of control** of your bodily movements.

We have many things to distract us and take us away from being in the body, we will focus on 2 key areas: a) to connect with our body, sensations and felt sense and b) to strengthen our physical bodies and promote healthy functioning of our system.

The main thing to keep in mind is that the body, being the physical element, vibrates at the slowest frequency. The mind vibrates at a much faster frequency than the body. Therefore, the mind has to slow down to communicate with the body effectively. One of the best ways to slow the mind down is to slow down the breath. The mind follows the breath. The breath creates a link between the body and the mind. The body also responds to the breath because it can be felt in the body. My first yoga teacher introduced it to me at a time when my muscles were tight and my life was full of tension. I was out of touch with my body and my natural rhythms. He promised that it would complement the cleansing process initiated by yoga.

The other way is through the practice of mindfulness. Mindfulness is becoming aware. This awareness then lets us connect deeply with those around us and, most importantly, keeps us in the present moment. Living in the present moment means letting go of the past and not waiting for the future. It means living your life consciously; aware that each moment you breathe is a gift. The ability to be in the present moment is a major component of mental wellness.

GROUNDING

According to Melbourne Psychology Experts, grounding exercises are used to help bring us back into the present moment. These techniques can be used in many different situations, like when we're feeling "spacey", anxious or overwhelmed. They can be used when we are distracted by unhelpful or distressing thoughts, memories or impulses. Or if we're experiencing difficult or strong emotions like anger, shame or sadness. The main aim of grounding exercises is to bring awareness to the safety of the here and now, and to encourage our body and mind to connect and work together.

There are many ways of grounding ourselves. What works varies from person to person. What works for you now, may also be different to what works for you next week. Just like many of the other techniques we chat about on this blog, it helps to approach grounding like an experiment. Try something, then try something else and just see what you notice.

Below we've come up with a list of things that you can do to use your mind, senses and movement to come into the present moment. Some of the things on this list might help you to feel grounded and others won't feel like that at all. Give yourself some time to work your way through some of the ideas, and perhaps keep some notes in your Jedi journal so you can create your own modified list.

TUNING INTO THE BREATH

Focusing on our breath is one of the simplest ways we can bring ourselves back into the present moment. There are a whole bunch of techniques designed to hone in on your breathing. A simple technique is to start by simply taking a slow, deep inhale for 5 counts, and then a slow, deep exhale for 5 counts. Or exhale deeply three times and notice how your body feels when you're done.

Any of the Pranyama Exercises that we introduced in earlier chapters can be used here. The following breathing exercises will help you reconnect with yourself and help you feel more grounded.

- Abdominal breathing
- Slow breathing
- Mindfulness of breath

The beauty of the breath is it's always available to us. Whenever we need to ground ourselves back into the present moment, our breath is always within reach as an anchor.

RE-ORIENTING YOURSELF IN THE PRESENT

Try grounding yourself in the current time and place by answering these questions:
1. Where am I right now?
2. What is the day today?
3. What is the date?
4. What is the month?
5. What is the year?
6. How old am I?
7. What season is it?

Next, notice an object in your immediate surroundings. Notice it in detail – the shape, colour, texture and function of the object. Slowly move your focus to another object and do the same. And then another. What do you notice about your mind as you do this? How about your body? If you're feeling pretty calm as you read this, these might seem like strange questions to ask yourself, but when we're feeling flooded by emotions this can be a really effective way to bring yourself back into the here-and-now.

USING YOUR SENSES TO GET GROUNDED

- Tune into each of your senses and name one thing each that you can currently see, smell, taste, touch and hear.
- Take your shoes and socks off and find a patch of grass. Walk around and become aware of the sensation of the Earth contacting your feet.
- Take a shower and be mindful of the water running over your body. Or if that's not possible, run cool or warm water over your hands, or splash your face.
- Stop and listen to the sounds around you. Become aware of the sounds you can hear close by. Tune into the subtle sounds as well as the more obvious ones. Then gradually expand your attention outwards, so you are focusing on sounds in the distance. Again, try to focus in on the less obvious sounds, as well as the more dominant noises you can hear.
- Smell your favourite perfume, scent or essential oil.
- Practice some mindful eating. Take one thing like a piece of fruit or chocolate and slowly and mindfully be aware of the taste and textures as you chew and swallow it.
- Give yourself a mini massage. You can start on your feet and move upwards to help bring yourself back into your body.

IMAGINING YOURSELF SOMEWHERE SAFE

1. Imagine yourself in a safe, soothing, calm and comfortable place. This space can be either a real or an imagined place you associate with being totally relaxed.
2. Imagine this place in as much detail as you can
3. What does it look like? What is around you?
4. What does it smell like?
5. What are the sounds around you?
6. What is the temperature? Is there a breeze on your skin? Are you sitting, standing or walking?
7. Notice how it feels to be completely calm and peaceful here. How does your body and mind change when you imagine being in this place?
8. You might want to name or make a mental note of this place so you can come back to it at any time.

GROUNDING THROUGH MOVEMENT

- Take a slow stroll around the block or in a park. Tuning into the feeling of your body moving. The feeling of your legs moving as you stride, the sensation of your feet hitting the ground, your arms moving past your body. What else can you feel in your body as you walk?
- Head to the gym, go for a swim or book in for a yoga class
- Jump up and down. Notice the sound and what it feels like when your feet make contact with the ground.
- Turn some music on and move your body. If it feels right, have a dance! If you're needing something slower or less intense, just move along to the music in whatever feels comfy.

The training and methods for strengthening us as Jedi Kundalini Jedi Warriors is vast and varied. We want to have lots of ways to snap out of the matrix fear game and wake up to our mission. (99)

JEDI EXERCISE: SUFI GRINDS

Kundalini Circles, or Seated Torso Circles, are also commonly known as Sufi Grinds and traditionally practiced in Kundalini Yoga. It is a simple seated torso movement. As the name suggests this practice is done rotating the upper body, or torso, in both clockwise and anticlockwise directions; coordinating with the breath. Sufi Grind Pose focuses on your thoracic, or mid-spine, and brings balance to your root chakra. It also helps in digestion, works the core muscles, massages the inner organs and connects the body deeply to earth. Focus on grinding the sitting bones into the floor as you move.

Instructions:
Sit in an easy pose; crossing your legs. Hold the knees. Begin rotating the spine in a big circle for 1 minute and a half. Keep the head upright. Inhale as you circle forward across the knees and exhale as you rotate back. Close your eyes. Consciously grind the sitting bones into the ground as you move.

After 1 minute and a half change the direction to go the opposite way.

BODY LANGUAGE

The body is definitely impacted by our thoughts, but verbal communication is not the body's language. The body's language is attention and feelings. The body responds best when we pay attention to what we are feeling and to our physical sensations. When we do so, we are communicating directly with the body in a way that it understands. The body can respond back with sensations and feelings. In sum, we communicate with the body non-verbally.

This is an art that we must develop. We can train ourselves to bring our attention to and stay with the sensations in our body. The guidelines are actually quite simple. If we are thinking and have thoughts, we are in our minds. If we are feeling sensations and have no words, we are in our body. The body responds to touch, movement and rhythm. The body needs to be touched. The body needs to move. And the body needs to function at its own unique rhythm.

The practice of Yoga gives us a powerful opportunity to develop a loving relationship with our bodies. While we do the exercises, we pay close attention and build awareness to the effect that each exercise is having on the body. Our goal is to activate various parts of the body. We are creating alignment and stimulating the body to enter a phase of optimal functioning. We are not punishing, or beating the body up during our practice, but we are challenging ourselves outside of our comfort zone, there may be some pain involved (pain is just weakness leaving your body). We want to stretch and strengthen, not strain or hurt.

Our bodies know the difference. If we simply pay attention, we will sense the difference and be alerted to how far to go and when to stop.it seems obvious that when we feel pain we should stop but during practice try not to stop, slow down, do half the move, pull back but don't stop, we are retraining our minds to respond and not give up, apathy and giving in are states of the dark side. There is a fine, but clear, line between keeping up during a challenging exercise and injuring yourself. The more we pay attention to our bodies, the easier it is to identify that line.

Between exercises, we pay attention to the effects by feeling the energy and the sensations in our bodies. We often overlook this aspect of our training. Yet it is during relaxation when we are consciously "doing nothing" that we can actually listen to our body. This is the optimal time to stay present and let our bodies communicate with us. They have much to share if we would just stop long enough to pay attention, be patient enough to learn their language and be humble enough to give value to the messages.

Our ultimate goal is to enjoy being in our body. It doesn't happen overnight. It is a gradual process. Our first experiences are often uncomfortable. Discomfort is the main reason we stay in our minds and avoid a relationship with our body. Emotions are stored in the body. We get in touch with unresolved emotional traumas when we are present to the feelings in our body. The good news is that the emotions speak to us. As we listen to what our body and emotions are trying to tell us, we learn a lot about ourselves and resolve a lot of previously undefined malaise. Being present to the sensations in our body is how we consciously deal with the energy of our emotions and our desire-nature as human beings. Over time, the emotional energy becomes a means of communicating in the moment and a method to receive the messages from our soul.

Our body is like our child or a pet. It needs to be loved. We love it by paying attention to it and listening to it. It feels abandoned and abused when we are in our minds. It feels loved when we feel it and touch it. Many people have the powerful experience that they no longer feel abandoned and lonely when they start being lovingly present in their body. They realise that they had abandoned themselves and now know how to end the anguish of separation.

The body is an instrument of our soul. We fine-tune it with Kundalini Yoga. We start with the body. The tendency, of course, is to leave our body. I invite you to train yourself to stay present in your body no matter what. This is a challenge.

But the rewards for your efforts are great. You will learn to love yourself. You will be able to heal yourself. You will be able to manifest. You will develop a powerful presence and charisma. You will know what to do because you will be able to listen to your soul. You will love being alive at every moment. Your body will become your best friend. Here are a few guidelines to use to practice being in your body. Add to the list as your experiences enrich your awareness.

1. Feel your breath in your body.
2. Slow your breath down until your body relaxes.
3. Practice communicating non-verbally with your body. Be aware of what the body responds to.
4. Listen to the sensations in your body as ways that it is communicating with you.
5. When a sensation feels good, keep your awareness there and enjoy it.
6. When a sensation feels uncomfortable, keep your awareness there and allow it to express itself.
7. Allow without judgment or interpretation all sensations in your body.
8. Treat your body as your best friend. (100)

The body is the tool that allows the Force to flow through us if we are taking good care of it and overindulging in food and intoxicants; doing our level best to avoid unnecessary stress. It will continue to run smoothly and effectively long into old age if we can adhere to those simple principles. As with any form of machinery, it needs regular servicing and good care if it is to serve us well; taking into account our ages and stage of life. Cars can be traded in after a year, but we have one body for life, so respect and gratitude should be given to it, as well as an understanding about the functions of our human body. Yogic psychology will serve us well on our journey towards becoming a Jedi.

According to Ed Halliwel, during a body scan meditation, you'll notice how each body part feels, from your toes up through your legs, chest, arms, and head. The body scan is one of the most effective ways to begin a mindfulness meditation practice. The purpose is to tune in to your body—to reconnect to your physical self—and notice any sensations you're feeling without judgement.

It is designed to help you develop a mindful awareness of your bodily sensations, and to relieve tension wherever it is found. Research suggests that this mindfulness practice can help reduce stress, improve well-being, and decrease aches and pains.

Although in some ways it can seem quite simple, mindfulness is a multifaceted skill. The body scan is a great starting practice because it fundamentally trains so many aspects of working skilfully with experience. Here are seven aspects of mindfulness that are practiced in the body scan.

- **ATTENTION.** By consciously choosing to place the mind on an object, we are training our capacity to pay attention. Attention is also trained by moving the mind from one object to another, and by coming back to an object when we notice the mind has wandered. Training attention in a body scan is a bit like doing resistance work in the gym—it takes some effort, but it cultivates strength and flexibility. Remember, each time you practice a body scan, you are

strengthening the muscles of mindfulness.

- **AWARENESS.** When they first practice the body scan, most people notice that their mind seems to roam all over the place. We intend to pay attention consistently, but that's not quite what happens. This is not a problem—part of the practice is to bring awareness to whatever is happening in the mind, even if it's not exactly what we'd like it to be. Knowing our patterns is the first step to working with them skilfully. With awareness, we are open to the landscape of the mind, able to see the terrain of our being.
- **EMBODIMENT.** Repeatedly bringing attention to our bodies balances the tendency to "live in our heads." The body senses rather than thinks, so, by allowing body sensations to be felt, we can drop into a fuller sensory palette. Living from our bodies, we tune into a mode of perceiving that's more centred, grounded and directly in touch with the world around us, rather than always getting caught up in concepts.
- **LETTING BE.** Many of us are used to driving ourselves hard. We think of training as a way to try to force change, push, pull, cajole and badger ourselves into becoming something different. Mindfulness training encourages a different approach. Each time we come back to attention in the body scan, it's suggested we do so gently. When we notice the mind is wandering, we do so with acceptance—this is just the way the mind is, for now. While we may not always like what we find, we can practice allowing it as our starting point, rather than trying to resist it or try to force change, which just creates struggle and stress. (101)

JEDI EXERCISE: BODY SCAN

While often practiced lying down, it's important to recognise that the body scan is not a relaxation exercise—the point is not to feel calm (and particularly not to try to feel calm). The prime intention of a body scan is to incline the mind into sensory experience—to experience how it is to "be a body."

What we discover when we do this—mind wandering, tension, anxiety, boredom, peace, stillness, contentment, numbness, discomfort, irritation—is less important than our willingness to work with these arising phenomena gently and patiently, coming back to friendly attention each time we notice that the mind has drifted into thinking, or is buying into attachment or aversion. It can be especially helpful to practice the body scan with an attitude of "abandoning all hope of fruition." Just like a scientist, see if you can carry out the experiment of the practice, and explore whatever results occur.

Begin by making yourself comfortable. Sit in a chair and allow your back to be straight, but not stiff, with your feet on the ground. You could also do this practice standing or if you prefer, you can lie down and have your head supported. Your hands could be resting gently in your lap or at your side. Allow your eyes to close, or to remain open with a soft gaze.

Take several long, slow, deep breaths. Breathing in fully and exhaling slowly. Breathe in through your nose and out through your nose or mouth. Feel your stomach expand on an inhale and relax and let go as you exhale.

Begin to let go of noises around you. Begin to shift your attention from outside to inside yourself. If you are distracted by sounds in the room, simply notice this and bring your focus back to your breathing.

Now slowly bring your attention down to your feet. Begin observing sensations in your feet. You might want to wiggle your toes a little, feeling your toes against your socks or shoes. Just notice, without judgment. You might imagine sending your breath down to your feet, as if the breath is traveling through the nose to the lungs and through the abdomen all the way down to your feet. And then back up again out through your nose and lungs. Perhaps you don't feel anything at all. That is fine, too. Just allow yourself to feel the sensation of not feeling anything.

When you are ready, allow your feet to dissolve in your mind's eye and move your attention up to your ankles, calves, knees and thighs. Observe the sensations you are experiencing throughout your legs. Breathe into and breathe out of the legs. If your mind begins to wander during this exercise, gently notice this without judgment and bring your mind back to noticing the sensations in your legs. If you notice any discomfort, pain or stiffness, don't judge this. Just simply notice it. Observe how all sensations rise and fall, shift and change moment to moment. Notice how no sensation is permanent. Just observe and allow the sensations to be in the moment, just as they are. Breathe into and out from the legs.

Then on the next out-breath, allow the legs to dissolve in your mind. And move to the sensations in your lower back and pelvis. Softening and releasing as you breathe in and out. Slowly move your attention up to your mid back and upper back. Become curious about the sensations here. You may become aware of sensations in the muscle, temperature or points of contact with furniture or the bed. With each outbreath, you may let go of the tension you are carrying. And then very gently shift your focus to your stomach and all the internal organs here. Perhaps you notice the feeling of clothing, the process of digestion or the belly rising or falling with each breath. If you notice opinions arising about these areas, gently let these go and return to noticing sensations. As you continue to breathe, bring your awareness to the chest and heart region and just notice your heartbeat. Observe how the chest rises during the inhale and how the chest falls during the exhale. Let go of any judgments that may arise. On the next outbreath, shift the focus to your hands and fingertips. See if you can channel your breathing into and out of this area as if you are breathing into and out from your hands. If your mind wanders, gently bring it back to the sensations in your hands.

And then, on the next outbreath, shift the focus and bring your awareness up into your arms. Observe the sensations or lack of sensations that may be occurring there. You might notice some difference between the left arm and the right arm – no need to judge this. As you exhale, you may experience the arm soften and release tensions. Continue to breathe and shift focus to the neck, shoulder and throat region. This is an area where we often have tension. Be with the sensations here. It could be tightness, rigidity or holding. You may notice the shoulders moving along with the breath. Let go of any thoughts or stories you are telling about this area. As you breathe, you may feel tension rolling off your shoulders.

On the next outbreath, shift your focus and direct your attention to the scalp, head and face. Observe all of the sensations occurring there. Notice the movement of the air as you breathe into or out of the nostrils or mouth. As you exhale, you might notice the softening of any tension you may be holding.

And now, let your attention expand out to include the entire body as a whole. Bring into your awareness the top of your head down to the bottom of your toes. Feel the gentle rhythm of the breath as it moves through the body.

As you come to the end of this practice, take a full, deep breath, taking in all the energy of this practice. Exhale fully. And when you are ready, open your eyes and return your attention to the present moment. As you become fully alert and awake, consider setting the intention that this practice of building awareness will benefit everyone you come in contact with today. (102) This script was developed by Shilagh Mirgain, PhD.

JEDI EXERCISE: GATHERING THE FORCE

An essential element for learning how to use the Force is gathering the Force. The following exercise is best performed in a natural setting. Otherwise, just imagine the Earth under the surface that you are standing on. If you're indoors, try to connect with the trees, rocks, and other natural forms that are outside.

Stand with your feet a shoulder width apart. Look straight ahead while mindful of the Earth beneath your feet and the sky above you. Don't focus your eyes on anything particular. Try to feel inside the body with the eyes while being mindful of the Earth, the sky, and the whole field of consciousness.

Take a few deep breaths and get to know yourself for a minute. Place hands in prayer-position in front of your heart like Mother Mary. Now, pivot your hands so that the tips of the fingers point downward. Bring your hands close to the ground with fingers still pointing at the ground. Your legs are still in the same position. The upper body is bent over.

Inhale through the nose and slowly spread the hands apart, gathering up the Force from the Earth. Exhale through the nose and slowly bring the palms back together, gathering the Force from the Earth. Repeat this part.

You are relaxing more and more into each breath. You are also softening the hands more and more each time; becoming more sensitive. Imagine your arms are so long that you are gathering the Earth's magma. After a while, when you bring your hands back together for the *Nth* time, you have two hands full of magma.

Come back to a standing position and bring that magma to your heart – dominant hand touching your heart and the other palm resting on the back of that hand. Relax and absorb it into your heart for three breaths - always through the nose. With a lot of pressure, massage the heart region and the back behind the heart. Make sure that you feel the buzz from the massage. Massage all the way down into your body. Bring all that energy down. When you get to the feet, continue to massage the stagnant energy down into the Earth. This is part visualisation.

Come back up into your original prayer position. Take three deep breaths - always through the nose. Now pivot the hands so that the fingertips point forward. Extend your arms and point those fingertips to something in nature such as a tree or mountain. If there is none, just imagine that there is one. Pull your palms apart on a slow inhale. Slowly spread them apart; gathering the Force from the elements. Exhale and bring them back together, gathering the Force from the elements. Remember, you're softening into the breath while softening your hands.

"Scoop" the essence of the natural object and bring it to your heart, dominant hand touching the heart and the other palm on the back of that hand. Relax and absorb for three breaths. Soften into each breath. Massage the energy down just like before. This is powered by the imagination, but it triggers a very real energetic process. The Force responds to imagination. Imagination is a tool which acts as a radio tuning dial, while you're learning how to use the Force. Your fine-tuning abilities will increase with practice.

A real-life Jedi practices the conscious use of the imagination as a radio dial to tap into realms that are not easy to see with the naked eye.

Come to the prayer position again for three breaths. Hands go up, past the nose and over the head with palms still together. Pull them apart and gather from the sky. Bring the dominant palm to the crown of the head and the non-dominant palm to the back of the dominant hand. Relax and absorb into the head. Massage downward into the Earth. Prayer position for three breaths. Lift the hands above the head again in the same way. Turn the palms outward so that the backs of the hands are together.

Pull the hands apart and gather from infinite galaxies. When the arms are pointing out to either side, face-down, parallel to the Earth, you are collecting from all of nature. Bend down as the hands approach the Earth. Collect from the Earth again and scoop its magma into your hands. Now, you have the essence of the stars, nature, and Earth in your hands. Bring the hands back to your heart with the dominant palm touching your heart. You are standing up straight now. Relax and absorb. Massage downward.

Prayer position for three breaths. Become softer with each breath. Merge with the breath.

VISUALISATION

The exercise you just performed is part of visualisation. Visualisation is an approximation of very real processes that are actually occurring within you. The more you "tune in" to these processes through visualisation, the more sensitive you become to these processes. Again, imagination is essential for learning how to use the Force. Strengthen your imagination as well as your concentration and you will become more adept at controlling the Force.

As you become more sensitive to the Force, you have more control over it and it will flow more strongly. Remember again, that softening is your strength. A roaring waterfall is stronger than a brittle stick. Soften your movements and soften into your breath. Perform all these exercises mindfully because the Force, in itself, is consciousness.

The Force flows like a river. The more you soften, the less resistance there is to the Force as it flows within you. Condition your circuitry properly and the Force will flow more strongly within you. Be gentle, however. Learning how to use the Force is like the river carving the Grand Canyon. Don't overwhelm your circuitry. The Force cannot be Forced. You can perform grounding exercises to prevent overload.

"Kid, I've flown from one side of this galaxy to the other. I've seen a lot of strange stuff, but I've never seen anything to make me believe there's one all-powerful Force controlling everything. There's no mystical energy field that controls my destiny."
- Han Solo, Star Wars: Episode IV – A New Hope

The whole point behind the Force is that you have to believe in it in order to make it work. The force is always flowing, but we need to allow ourselves to connect to it. Luke's and Rey's whole journey, for example, is about connecting and believing in the Force. The Jedi teachers try to open the mind of the student and show them ways to understand the energy of the Force and a journey towards it in faith.

When was the last time you considered how the world came to be?

We might believe in God, or in some type of energy or power, that resides over everything but inevitably we are encouraged to think that we are the cause of all things. This is because even if there is a power such as the Force, we don't fully believe it is there in abundance - just waiting for us to ask for its help and assistance.

We can become attached to the outcome; losing ourselves in constant thoughts and strategies when in actual fact, merely letting go and trusting the will of the universe would serve us well.

Our mind and ego will cause separation and not want us to believe in the power outside ourselves. It takes skill and practice to let go and let the Force flow through us. Real progress is made in leaps of faith - some small and some large. Think back to the times when you got a lucky break or when the circumstances just all seemed to fit. The shift to trusting and depending on the Force is a slow and gradual one.

"I am a Jedi. I'm one with the force, and the force will guide me."
—Padawan Ganodi - The Clone Wars

The challenges of trying to make spiritual progress while living in a fallen world – that is also full of sin - can be daunting, but if you simplify your approach to spiritual progress by focusing mainly on the virtues of faith, hope, and love, you will have a far easier time accomplishing what you've set out to do.

***

CHAPTER 18: LOVE VIBRATIONS

" *You could say Jedi are encouraged to love."*

- Anakin Skywalker, Star Wars: Episode II - Attack of the Clones

JEDI AND THE POWER OF LOVE

Star Wars is known for some pretty epic battle scenes and nemesis duos, but it is also known for its magnetic love-pairs. While almost all of these romantic affairs ended in tragedy, there were some romances that had our hearts aching.

ANAKIN AND PADME

When Anakin was a slave on Tatooine, it was Padme that brought him hope. After multiple attempts on her life, he was assigned to protect her; knowing full well that he hadn't stopped thinking about her since his imprisonment. They bonded over an interest in politics and she embraced all of his flaws. Their love was forbidden, so they married in secret and soon after Padme fell pregnant with twins. His visions of her dying in childbirth stirred a fear in him that led to the Darkside. In a twist of self-fulfilling prophecy, it would be him that killed her; choking her in childbirth.

Padmé Amidala: Are you allowed to love? I thought that was forbidden for a Jedi.
Anakin Skywalker: Attachment is forbidden. Possession is forbidden. Compassion, which I would define as unconditional love... is central to a Jedi's life. So you might say that we are encouraged to love.

- Star Wars, Episode II: Attack of the Clones

HAN AND LEIA

The sexual tension between these two was palpable. A couple who didn't really get off on the right foot at first, Han and Leia would remain bewitched by another for many years. When their son, Ben Solo, would fall to the Darkside it would drive a wedge between them.

Accompanied by Luke and Lando, Leia would once again save Han; releasing him from the carbonite and professing her love for him.

These represent two subtle, and beautiful, romantic moments between the franchise's most iconic couple. A gesture that is both subtle and grand, Han attempts - in The Force Awakens - to turn his son, Ben Solo, back to the light. While Han is his father, which likely plays the biggest part in this gesture, Han does this, and risks his life. Undoubtedly this is seen as another gesture towards Leia, who had asked him to bring their son back.

A painful aspect of the film was knowing that Han and Leia did not last. When they see each other, and embrace, it is clear that they are still madly in love with each other. Han attempts to retrieve their son because he loves Leia and wants to see her happy once again; they, after all, long to be together once more. Although they could not be, it does not take away from the gesture itself.

HAN AND QI'RA

Han and Qi'ra bonded over their difficult beginnings. They dreamt of a better life; of escaping their misery and traveling the galaxy together. Their love story was a tragic one. Han would spend years trying to get back to her after she was captured, but she would choose to rise through the ranks of Crimson Dawn, instead of escaping with him.

REY AND KYLO REN/BEN SOLO

They are two sides of the same coin; equals in Force ability yet never being able to destroy the other; in spite of the fact that they worked for opposite teams, so to speak. They maintained this compassion for one another until the very end where Ben kills Supreme Leader Snoke to save her. Ultimately, he would turn back to the light; racing to Exegol to help Rey in her final showdown with Emperor Palpatine. As she is struck down and her life Force begins to leave her, Ben sacrifices himself to save her; giving up his own life Force to sustain her. (103)

Love can be the most unifying element of the universe or one that ends in despair. It is known as the elixir of life and joy as well as the remedy for what pains us. It transcends space and time; healing us from within and removing us from our own inner limitations to a place of our truest potential. It is our collective purpose to learn to live within the vibrational field of love; but not necessarily romantic love, but love for our fellow man and woman.

"That's How We're Gonna Win. Not Fighting What We Hate, Saving What We Love."
- Rose, Star Wars: The Last Jedi

Living this way allows us to embrace our God-qualities of compassion, forgiveness, tolerance, respect, generosity, and all others that enhance our life and the life of others. It removes us from the thoughts, feelings, and actions that victimise us. It means that we have to keep our egos in check in order to live this way. It can be quite challenging as our inner brokenness is often deeply rooted in past pains. However, we must navigate this valley in order to become heart centred. Once you are able to do that it will feel as though you are living on cloud nine in this natural high.

Deepak Chopra examines one of the oldest teachings of all time known as the Vedanta. It stipulates that "The ignorant man - engrossed in duality - desires material things; the intelligent man – or seeker on the path - desires enlightenment; but the wise man – or the knower of Oneness - just loves and receives everything."

Could it be possible to live in love and receive everything?

As previously discussed, the Yajur Veda, one of the oldest Hindu religious texts tells us what the Force of love is: "It is Omnipotent, Omniscient and Omnipresent. It is all-powerful, all-pervasive. It pervades, permeates, and penetrates all things and all hearts." This sounds very similar to the description of the Force: "It's an energy field created by all living things. It surrounds us and penetrates us; it binds the galaxy together." Obi-Wan Kenobi introduced Luke Skywalker, and most of us, to the Force for the first time in Star Wars: Episode IV – A New Hope. Live your life from love; recognise that you are the Universe. Be the Oneness, and everything will be yours.

Throughout history, warriors have been willing to die to protect tradition the things they love, be it the princess, the kingdom, nation or God. This warrior continues today with men and women working very hard to provide for their families. The warrior has evolved into many new forms that do not involve killing another, and right now, many are fighting in the name of love as they care for others and defend the earth. They embrace a love of truth; standing up against injustice in the name of love. Strictly speaking, Jedi are not to have attachments, and yet we see love being expressed throughout the film saga.

Luke's redemption of his father, Darth Vader, could be argued to have come from a place of love. He still believed that there was good in him, and the power of love brought Anakin back. This is also evident in the last part of the Star Wars saga and the redemption of Kylo Ren back to Ben Solo through the love and compassion of Rey.

When you operate from the ego, you operate from a shadow of your true self just as Ben Solo did. True love doesn't refer to something fleeting like emotions, it refers to that deep connecting aspect of the indomitable human spirit. When you are loved – and loved well – you feel safe; safe to explore, safe to express yourself, safe to be naked in spirit. Love is a safe space where you can be yourself as you truly are.

*

THE NEED FOR UNCONDITIONAL LOVE

In the need for love, the most important underlying need is the one for unconditional love. Let's explore this in accordance with the writings of Michael Brown in his ground breaking book 'The Presence Process'.

On some level, we are all angry because we were not loved unconditionally as we were as children. For many of us, even as children, we were all conditionally loved. This isn't an accusation. It is the predicament of being born into a world of constantly changing conditions. Since childhood, we have unconsciously spent our whole life attempting to live up to the conditions that we thought would earn us unconditional love. This has manifested as the endless physical, mental, and emotional "doings" or dramas we have performed in an attempt to gain attention and acceptance.

Unfortunately, unconditional love isn't an experience we can force others to channel in our direction through drama. All attention we attract through drama is by its nature conditional. The truth is that we fail at every turn to get the attention we seek. We have failed because unconditional love is not money; it is not something we can earn. Love isn't something we have to achieve through merit. We don't have to qualify to be loved. Love is our birthright. Love just is. Love is who and what we are.

During our childhood, the example of love set for us through our parents' interaction with us and with each other becomes our primary definition of love. This is the outcome of emotional imprinting. Consequently, as adults, whenever we seek to manifest an experience of love for ourselves, we unconsciously manufacture a physical, mental, or emotional scenario that will recreate the emotional resonance we experienced during our initial childhood interactions. This resonance doesn't have to be comfortable or in any way pleasant. It only has to be similar.

For example, if we received abuse when we asked for love, then abuse would then become part of our childhood definition of love. Consequently, as adults, whenever we feel a need for love, we automatically manifest an experience that includes the emotional resonance of abuse. We do this unconsciously, automatically. Why? Because this is the only way, we know how to get what we think love is. But the love we end up getting always hurts. It always hurts because of its conditions.

On a conscious level, we might then say, "Why does this keep happening to me?" The simple reason we keep manifesting the same hurtful experiences is because we don't know any better. This is the predicament we are all in, the open wound in the heart of humanity. This is why many of us automatically assume love hurts. Yet "hurting" is a condition, love is not. (104)

Because you exist, you are creating. All existence is creation in motion for that is what existence is. Existence cannot become stagnant. Creative existence will change, transform or expand, but it will never become non-existent. So you are a being of totality that is creative existence, and that is love. Love is all that you are as a creation in motion. That is who you are. When you are expressing yourself in the totality of your essence - in the fullness of your Jedi nature - you are coming from a state of consciousness that allows you to expand, believe, and become aware of more than you can consciously experience. You then live and create from the point of power that has a greater force and effect. This is the power of who you are. Think of everything as energy in motion, for that is all that existence truly is. View yourself as part of that energy in motion - the power that propels you. In that regard, the Power of Love is the non-tangible energy that permeates everything and propels you through life.

*

HEARTBROKEN

We all carry wounds from the past - things that happened, events, and losses. These are events that make us feel down. The pain of a breakup is one such event. These heartbreaks can build up over time; starting with a small upset when we were younger. As we get older, these heartbreaks mount up until we find that we have become cold, bitter, or cold-hearted. You could have had a traumatic experience or early childhood programming where you either consciously or unconsciously decided that tender feelings are weak and dangerous.

These pains, over time, cause the heart to become rigid and cold. We become suspicious and promise that we will never allow love to hurt us again. Anakin's heartbreak at losing his mum to the sand-people was a wound that eventually led him to becoming Darth Vader - the most feared man in the universe. And did Padme die from a broken heart when the man she loved began his decent down the dark path?

Our current climate of fear also causes us to shut down. The nature of fear is that it makes us contract, both physically and emotionally. We become protective; making us rigid and closed. We do this to make sure that our fear does not come true. When you compare this to the qualities of love, which include openness, joy, and allowing care for our fellow beings, we come to see the stark differences between the two means of functioning within love.

Below you will find meditations to help you open up to the power of love.

MEDITATION: HEAL A BROKEN HEART

Posture:
Sit in Easy Pose with a straight spine and a light Neck Lock
Tune in with ONG NAMO GURU DEV NAMO X3

Mudra:
Palms together, lightly touching. The tip of the Saturn (middle) finger is at the level of the Third Eye Point. The forearms are horizontal to the ground, elbows high. Look within. (No mantra or breath specified.)

Time:
Continue for 11, 31, or 62 minutes.

To End:
Inhale, exhale, relax the breath, and with clasped hands stretch the arms up for 2 minutes.
(105)

FORGIVENESS

Forgiveness transforms anger and hurt into healing and peace. Forgiveness can help you overcome feelings of depression, anxiety, and rage, as well as personal and relational conflicts. It is about making the conscious decision to let go of a grudge. Why would anyone want to forgive someone who has wronged her in the past? It is not about letting someone off the hook for wrongdoing, or forgetting about the past, or forgetting about the pain. It certainly does not mean that you stick around for future maltreatment from a boss, a partner, parent, or friend. It is about setting yourself free so that you can move forward in your own life. Forgiveness means giving up the suffering of the past and being willing to forge ahead with far greater potential for inner freedom. How do we give up a grudge and forgive someone who has hurt, disappointed, or betrayed us? Your grievance story is the one you tell over and over to yourself, and possibly to others, about the way you were maltreated and the way you became the victimised. Luskin teaches us to cast our story in such a way that we become a survivor of difficult times, or -- better yet -- the hero of our story.

"You can search throughout the entire Universe for someone who is more deserving of your love and affection than you are yourself, and that person is not to be found anywhere. You yourself, as much as anybody in the entire Universe deserve your love and affection."
– **Buddha**

COMPASSION

As we travel through life, we will encounter pain. It might be through the loss of a loved one, the end of a relationship, or recovery from a severe illness. Sometimes, it's the small stuff that brings up feelings of shame, inadequacy, or worthlessness. When this happens, the tendency is to get lost in judgment; we beat ourselves or others up in an attempt to stop the pain. This only intensifies our suffering. Caught in this reactive response, we forget that there's a real need to treat ourselves with kindness, love, and compassion. When we turn to face our suffering from a place of compassion, it helps us heal and reconnect with life.

Self-compassion involves acting the same way towards yourself that you would act towards a loved one during a time of difficulty, failure, or even when you merely notice something that you don't like about yourself. Perhaps most importantly, having compassion for yourself means that you honour and accept your *humanness*. Things will not always go the way you want them to. Compassion means offering patience, kindness, and non-judgmental understanding to others as well as oneself.

Stop punishing yourself for your mistakes. Accept that you are not perfect and be gentle with yourself when you are confronted with your shortcomings. You are valued by your friends and colleagues because of who you are, not because you are faultless.

Become aware of times when you derive a sense of self-worth from performance or perfection. Understand that you do not need to be a certain way to be worthy of love.

"If you don't love yourself, you cannot love others. You will not be able to love others. If you have no compassion for yourself, then you are not able of developing compassion for others."

- The Dalai Lama

*

THE JEDI PATH TO SELF-LOVE

" My love for you is a puzzle... for which I have no answers. I can't control it... and now I don't care. I truly, deeply love you."

— Padme, Star Wars, Episode II: Attack of the Clones

Throughout our early lives, we are taught to read, write, manipulate, calculate, build, destroy, theorise, study, and analyse life. We are taught how to say "please" and "thank you," as well as what is acceptable and unacceptable to others and society at large. However, most of us fail to be educated in one essential dimension of life: Self-love. Many people don't know how to say no because they are raised in cultures where no doesn't mean no, at least not to our elders. It can often lead us towards a dark path.

So how do we avoid this path towards the dark?

As Kundalini Jedi Warriors, we make Self-love the cornerstone of our approach to life. Self-love is the practice of understanding, embracing, and showing compassion for yourself. Self-love involves nurturing your entire being – that means taking care of yourself on physical, emotional, mental, and spiritual levels. We begin the courageous act of loving ourselves before we go out to save others. When engaging in self-love, we also work on forgiving ourselves; accepting our flaws, and embracing our inner demons, or our dark-side. This seemingly simple act of self-love has a great vibrational frequency in that by saving ourselves, we save the world.

HEART CHAKRA

Our heart chakra is undeniably important and Kristin, the Travel Muse enlightens us in the most beautiful way. The heart chakra, or anahata chakra in Sanskrit, is located at the centre of the spine at heart level. Anahata roughly translates to, "unhurt." Accordingly, the heart chakra acts as the individual's centre of compassion, empathy, love, and forgiveness. This chakra governs one's senses of trust, fearlessness, peace, generosity, gratitude, and connectedness, as well as change and transformation, healthy boundaries, depth in relationships with others, emotional control, and love for oneself.

The heart chakra is special because it is the fourth of the seven chakras, making it the exact halfway point of the system and the unifier of the physical and spiritual chakras. By connecting the lower three chakras — the root, sacral, and solar plexus — with the upper three chakras — the throat, third eye, and crown — the heart chakra acts as the bridge between the earth and spirit.

The heart chakra exists on the planet, too! The heart chakra of the earth is believed to be dually located at two towns in southwestern England about 30 miles apart from each other, Glastonbury and Shaftesbury. Another 25 miles beyond lies Stonehenge, which adds another layer of mystique to this earth chakra. All kinds of legends centre around this location, like the tale that Glastonbury Tor has a connection to King Arthur and the ancient mythological land of Avalon.

Glastonbury and Shaftesbury are the most commonly discussed locations for the heart chakra; however, another location which is sometimes considered is Maui's Haleakalā volcano. Apparently, the energy at the top of this dormant volcano gives off the same frequency as the beating of the human heart.

WHEN BLOCKED OR OUT OF BALANCE

When the heart chakra is out of alignment, a number of issues can arise. One might feel hard-hearted, broken-hearted, unhappy, lonely, insecure, easily hurt, or unable to receive love. One might choose to lead with the head and not the heart, to grow distant from others and put walls up, to shut down emotionally, or to hold onto resentment or bitterness.

Sometimes, in the busyness and stress of everyday life, the heart gets overlooked. We tend to pay attention to our physical needs and the thousands of thoughts bouncing around our brains, yet when it comes to self-love, generosity, and connectedness, we are quick to put the emotional work on the back burner.

However, by working to balance our heart chakras and keep them in alignment throughout the day-to-day, we only set ourselves up to be the best, most compassionate, and most joyful versions of us that we can be. If we can remain in touch with our hearts to do all things with love, the world and the people around us will be that much better for it. (106)

JEDI LOVING

It sounds like a paradox, but you cannot be altruistic, caring, or compassionate unless you're selfish. Unless you're capable of truly loving yourself first - even the darkest side of your being - you can never love somebody else.

Self-seeking is preached in most societies as sinful behaviour. We're encouraged to be self-sacrificial and martyrs for "the greater good." History is plagued with stories of the hero's willingness to sacrifice his or her own life for the survival of the group, but the truth is that the purpose of our social conditioning is to preserve and develop society as a whole. This in itself prevents most individuals from reaching their full potential. This is why taking care of yourself first is met with so much resistance from others: it's against our collective brain-washing.

But here's the thing; in order to be a positive presence in this world, and in order to care for others in an authentic and loving way, we must first focus on ourselves. We must first dedicate a large amount of time to our own healing, happiness, and self-fulfilment. We must be self-seeking. If you can't love yourself at a deep level, how will you ever be capable of true altruism or of truly loving anybody else?

WHAT SELF-LOVE ISN'T

You can't give away that which you don't actually have.

Self-love isn't egotistical. A person who engages in self-love understands that by loving others, they also love themselves, and by hurting others they also hurt themselves. Self-love is the furthest thing from narcissism, or vanity. Egotism is centred around the ego, while self-love is centred around the learning of one's self and the helping of others. Kundalini Jedi Warriors love themselves because they want to become the best that they can be. A Kundalini Jedi Warrior wants to explore themselves, practice inner work, do some soul-searching, work on their flaws, heal their traumas, and find inner peace.

On a side note, is there any such thing as altruism, really? The act of helping other people does benefit us: it makes us feel good. Therefore, altruism can also be thought of as a "selfish" act. If you truly love yourself, you want to take care of yourself. It's only self-hating egotistical people that harm themselves or others.

MEDITATION FOR A CALM HEART

This soothing breath practice (pranayama) relieves anxiety and promotes calmness and mental clarity.

Tune in with ONG NAMO GURU DEV NAMO X3

Posture:

Sit in an Easy Pose, with a light jalandhar bandh (Neck lock see glossary of terms in the appendix)). Place the left hand on the centre of the chest at the Heart Centre. The palm is flat against the chest, and the fingers are parallel to the ground, pointing to the right.

Mudra:
"Gyan Mudra" with the right hand (touch the tip of the index finger with the tip of the thumb). Raise the right hand up to the right side as if giving a pledge. The palm faces forward, the three fingers not in Gyan Mudra point up. The elbow is relaxed near the side with the forearm perpendicular to the ground.

Eyes:
Either close the eyes or look straight ahead with the eyes 1/10th open.

Breath:
Inhale slowly and deeply through both nostrils. Then suspend the breath in and raise the chest. Retain it as long as possible. Then exhale smoothly, gradually, and completely. When the breath is totally out, lock the breath out for as long as possible. Concentrate on the flow of the breath. Regulate each bit of the breath consciously.

To End:
Inhale and exhale strongly 3 times. Relax. This posture induces the feeling of calmness. It creates a still point for the prana at the Heart Centre. Emotionally, this meditation adds clear perception to your relationships with yourself and others. If you are upset at work or in a personal relationship, sit in this meditation for 3 to 15 minutes before deciding how to act. Then act with your full heart. Physically, this meditation strengthens the lungs and heart. This meditation is perfect for beginners. It opens awareness of the breath, and it conditions the lungs. When you hold the breath in or out for "as long as possible," you should not gasp or be under strain when you let the breath move again. If you have more time, try it for three periods of 3 minutes each, with one-minute rest between them, for a total of 11 minutes. For an advanced practice of concentration and rejuvenation, build the meditation up to 31 minutes. (107)

To heal the emotional wounds of the heart, we need to bring calm to the nerves that hold the wound. We know that a break in a relationship (to others or to our Self) has almost identical reactions in the nervous system and brain as a physical injury or loss of limb. The mudra used creates balance; it generates a subtle pressure which adjusts the heart meridian along the little finger and outer forearm, activating the "action nerve" junction with the autonomic system to reset itself by keeping the forearms parallel to the ground and involving the armpit reflexes; and finally, it uses the pranic influence of the middle finger and its Saturn and air qualities to quell residual emotional storms.

The next practice involves a 3-part meditation which forms a kriya to create self-love. Adi Shakti literally translates to 'the primal', first power. Feminine in its aspect, it divines the future - both known and unknown - and is the embodiment of creativity, balance, and completion. As a symbol, its impact transcends the rational mind.

The next kriya for creating self love has 3 parts , please follow the instructions carefully.

KRIYA FOR CREATING SELF-LOVE
Part 1

This exercise is called Reverse Adi Shakti Kriya.

Here you are mentally and hypnotically blessing yourself. This self-blessing is to affect and correct the magnetic field. It is said that doing this exercise will hurt if you have a lot of anger. Self-help is very difficult for those who are angry. After doing this exercise for 5 minutes, your muscles may start hurting if your diet needs cleaning up. The taste in your mouth will change if you are breathing correctly.

Posture: Sit in Easy Pose with a straight spine and hold your right palm six to nine inches above the top centre of your head. The right palm faces down, blessing you. This self-blessing corrects the aura. The left elbow is bent with the upper arm near the rib cage. The forearm and hand point upward. The left palm faces forward and blesses the world.

Eyes:
The eyes are closed and focus at the lunar centre in the middle of the chin.

Breath:
Breathe long, slow, and deep with a feeling of self-affection. Try to bring the breath to one breath per minute: Inhale for 20 seconds, hold for 20 seconds, exhale for 20 seconds.

Time:
Continue for 11 minutes. Then inhale deeply and move slowly and directly into position for Exercise 2.

Part 2

This exercise will benefit everything between the neck and navel. It will give strength to the heart and will open up the heart centre.

Posture:
Extend your arms straight out in front, parallel to the ground, palms facing down. Stretch out to your maximum.

Eyes:
The eyes are closed and focused at the lunar centre in the centre of the chin.

Breath:
The breath is long, slow, and deep.

Time:
Continue for 3 minutes. Then inhale deeply and move slowly and directly into position for Exercise 3.

Part 3

Posture:
Stretch your arms straight up with the palms facing forward. There is no bend in the elbows.
Eyes:
The eyes are closed and focused at the lunar centre.

Breath:
The breath continues to be long, slow, and deep.

Time:
Continue for 3 minutes.

To End:
Inhale, hold your breath for 10 seconds while you stretch your arms upward (try to stretch so much that your buttocks are lifted) and tighten all the muscles of your body. Exhale. Repeat this sequence two more times. (108)

"Can you spare seventeen minutes for yourself in twenty-four hours? This meditation will totally change you from the inside out. It will give you self-consciousness, self-experience, self-love and then you can love everybody. Become total."
                                                                            -Yogi Bhajan, Master of Kundalini yoga

PRACTICE AUTHENTIC SELF-LOVE

Practicing self-love and care for oneself is one of the most powerful ways to raise our vibrational frequency. We develop the capacity for challenging our negative inner critic and can begin to relate to ourselves in a more powerful way. Below you will find further suggestions for developing the right conditions so that you may fall in love with yourself.

1. TREAT YOURSELF LIKE YOU WOULD YOUR BEST FRIEND

Often, we are our own mortal enemies. To heal ourselves, it is important for us to consciously change our relationships with ourselves. We must treat ourselves with compassion and consideration just as we would with a best friend.

2. WELCOME SOLITUDE INTO YOUR LIFE

When we don't make space in our lives to be alone, it is easy for us to burn out, become disorientated and even ill. Each day, make time for yourself to rewind, relax, and reflect - alone. Solitude gives you insight as well as perspective, and it reinstates harmony in your life.

3. IDENTIFY TOXIC PEOPLE IN YOUR LIFE

Toxic people make us feel wretched and they significantly lower the quality of our daily lives. Toxic people are often judgmental, manipulative, clingy, backstabbing, ruthless, aggressive, controlling, deceptive, self-pitying, and self-destructive. Learning to cut away those who hinder your self-growth is a difficult, but absolutely necessary step on your journey of healing.

4. SEEK SUPPORTIVE COMPANIONS

Supportive people encourage us, uplift us, and inspire us. These people have often obtained a certain level of self-love, and because of their ability to respect themselves, they are easily able to respect and love others. Often it is not necessary to seek these people out as we naturally gravitate towards them on our paths! However, it always helps to instigate friendships and connections with supportive people as they can really help us out during dreary periods of our journeys.

5. SUPPORT THE WELL-BEING OF NATURE

All of life on earth, and within the Universe, is so interconnected, that the harm we do to others always comes back to harm us in one form or another. By supporting the well-being of nature – whether by becoming a vegan or vegetarian, or by choosing sustainable food and products, or even by replacing our cosmetics with organic "non-animal tested" alternatives – we are promoting the well-being of the earth and thus the well-being of us as individuals.

It is easy to fall into the trap of comparing yourself to those who have advanced more than you on their spiritual path. Don't do it. Part of practicing authentic self-love is being patient and forgiving with yourself. You don't have to push yourself or belittle yourself just because you haven't reached what you define as the epitome of self-love. Embrace your imperfections and know that you are worthy of all the love in the universe. You must be vigilant so as not to fall into a pattern of fear and self-loathing. You are still human, no matter how spiritual you think you are and this means that there will be setbacks on your journey. Don't condemn your vulnerabilities. With a clean heart, and a deepened understanding of self-love, one can begin to move with faith in the Force. Remember, this is not a blind faith, but an acknowledgment that what is meant for us will come to us, and that everything that we need is already abundantly provided to us through the Force.

***

CHAPTER 19: FAITH IN THE FORCE

"I Find Your Lack of Faith Disturbing."

"

- Darth Vader, Star Wars, Episode IV: A New Hope

How can we know for certain that the Force actually exists? At the end of the day, wasn't the Force just some unknown magic energy that George Lucas created for a "fantasy" sci-fi movie? There may not be a way to prove that the Force exists, but the power of the Force and an experience of it flowing through can be felt. Someone once said that, "The definition of faith is believing what you cannot see. The reward of faith is seeing what you believe." A large part of the power of the Force is believing in it and having faith that it exists. Here's how you can make your relationship to the Force real: by developing greater faith, hope, and love in your life. Listen and respond to the Force's guidance regularly. When you don't stay in touch with the Force, your life tends - by default - to be moving in a rigid, or controlled, way; relying on your mind and little ego. However, when you regularly connect with the Force, it empowers you; increasing the feelings of faith, hope, and love in your life. It reminds you of your place in the universe. Your faith says I believe there exists a power greater than myself that I do not understand, yet I am willing to trust and lean on this higher power.

Luke: *All right, I'll give it a try.*
Yoda: *No. Try not. Do... or do not. There is no try. [Using the Force, Yoda effortlessly frees the X-Wing from the bog]*
Luke: *I don't, I don't believe it.*
Yoda: *That is why you fail.*

- Star Wars: Episode V - The Empire Strikes Back

The classic scene from The Empire Strikes Back sees Yoda being brutally honest with Luke, who breathlessly says, "I don't believe it," after his Master raises an X-wing from the Dagobah swamp. Ultimately, this is Yoda showing him his downfall. It's a definitive statement that comes from Yoda's years and years of experience in connecting to the Force which now makes him a Master Jedi teacher, and it cuts through both Luke and the audience. The scene shows what is possible when we suspend our disbelief and have faith in the power of the Force to create unexpected miracles in our life.

THE POWER OF BELIEF

"The Force is what gives a Jedi his power."

- Obi-Wan Kenobi, Star Wars: Episode IV - A New Hope

Albert Einstein believed that the most important decision we needed to make is whether we believe that we live in a friendly universe or a hostile one. Basically, the way that the world is for us boils down to our beliefs. If you believe that the universe is friendly and that things come to you quickly and effortlessly, then you will be receptive; allowing circumstances to take shape. Now, this is easier said than done. It takes practice; it is an art and skill. When you open yourself up to accepting all that there is, you are opening yourself up to the abundant universe. As you let go of the need to control your life, control an outcome, or arrange your life the way that you think it should be, guess what happens?

The universe has your back!

It brings you an abundance of prosperity and wealth and it lines up - not in some crazy, haphazard way, but in a way, that suits you well, and is just the way you like it! Gurus have long shared the idea that the cosmic blueprint that we are living in is a universe of 'abundance' and that it holds the building blocks to everything.

The universe is continuously expanding to cater to our every whim and that we should not fear, as there is enough abundance for all of us and more. (109)

Ben Kenobi: Remember, a Jedi can feel the Force flowing through him.
Luke Skywalker: You mean it controls your actions?
Ben Kenobi: Partially, but it also obeys your commands.

- Star Wars Episode IV: A New Hope

The universe is manifesting our desires and thoughts according to our will, but it can only deliver that which is seen as being called into existence by us. We need to seriously filter our thoughts and emotions to project what we want to manifest in our lives.

"Man is what he believes."

- Anton Chekhov, Russian Playwright

Our perceptions are based upon the guiding principles that we call beliefs. They are recognised as internal commands to your brain as to how to understand what is going on around us. People usually feel disempowered when they lack some sort of belief system. These beliefs will come about as a result of what we learn and hear throughout our lives. Beliefs are not inherent or inherited; they are a choice. You can choose what to believe in and thus shape your own reality. They are intertwined in both our conscious and unconscious emotions. This is of particular interest in understanding why we lash out when someone challenges those beliefs.

The Biology of Belief, a ground-breaking work in the field of Biology, was published in 2008 by medical school professor Bruce H. Lipton, Ph.D. He presented his experiments, and those of other leading scientists, which examined the mechanisms by which cells receive and process information. DNA was found to be controlled by signals that came to it from outside the cell in the form of positive and negative thoughts. Genetics had very little to do with our DNA makeup in that regard.

This is fantastic news for a warrior in training as it supports his process of overcoming barriers to his strength and potential. It is no longer just a matter of hoping that some magical Force will help you, but that you can now remove the thoughts that block your connection to the Force.

*

A NEW HOPE

Hope is the idea that there will be a positive outcome, even in the face of trying circumstances. Every one of us hopes for something at one point or another. It allows us to define what we want for ourselves in future. It's part of a constant narrative that plays in our minds. It is a symbol of our desire for better things. We don't need to only have hope in a bad situation. While it's great to have the hope of getting out of a tough situation, it can also make your everyday life that much better. Just thinking about a better tomorrow can make you feel better. It can motivate you to take the steps you need to in order to make positive changes in your life.

"We Have Hope. Rebellions Are Built On Hope!"
- **Jayne Erso, Rogue One: A Star Wars Story**

Hope can give you the inspiration that you need to motivate yourself. Love can give you the compassion that you need to motivate yourself *and* to take action whenever you sense the call to do so. Improve every aspect of your life through faith, hope, and love. Faith improves the quality of your inner spiritual connection by engendering trust in the Force and helping you overcome fear.

Try to steer clear of low vibrational actions that can draw you away from faith, hope, and love. It is all too easy to be drawn back to the Dark Side by things such as materialism, lust, hedonism, envy, and egotism. Solitude will help you to develop by stripping you of false dependencies that distract you. Silence will clear your mind as you learn to recognise and trust the Force. The study will deepen you. Fasting will strengthen you as you delay gratifying your body so you can focus more on your spirit.

*

SOLITUDE AND SILENCE

Solitude will help you develop faith by stripping you of false dependencies that distract you, so you can tune in and connect more deeply with the Force. In this fast-paced world, it's easy to become distracted and taken away in the constant noise for your attention. Stillness will allow you to quieten your mind. Silence will strengthen your faith as you learn to recognise and trust the guidance that you receive from the Force.

We are a culture surrounded by noise. The psychological benefits of experiencing silence —even when it makes us uncomfortable as it can be confronting and at the time possibly intimidating — can mean more purposeful living. Silence can increase self-awareness, self-compassion, and improve decision-making skills with improved mental clarity. Use it to become more mindful and self-compassionate. The practice of silence gives you the ability to think before you act.

Silence is not just the absence of all this noise and chaos. Silence is the beginning point of your interior life. It draws you inward and encourages you to engage with your thoughts; making you mindful even with the words that you use. On a more profound level, becoming aware of the content of your thoughts, and your choices of words, is the beginning of becoming aware of the power that is contained in each word that you use.

JEDI EXERCISE: SILENCE EXERCISE

Schedule some time in your diary for you to be alone - completely alone. You may have to plan to get out of the city; somewhere that you will be undisturbed. If you cannot get away, you can create your meditation cell in your house. Turn everything off and cancel out the outside noise with a pair of headphones. Use this time to go within, but do so without expecting anything. Just be curious. Have an experience.

When you have finished, make notes and reflect on your experience in your Jedi training journal.

*

PRAYER

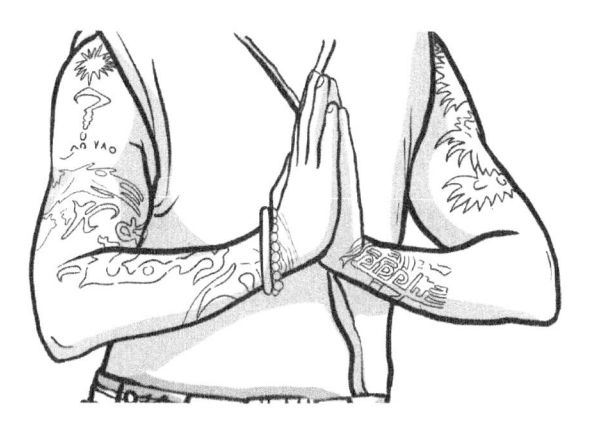

Think of power as food for the soul; spiritual nutrition if you will. Just as our physical body needs food, so does our spiritual self. It's powerful and it changes us. It is the hack into omnipotence.

Prayer will strengthen your faith as you communicate with the energy of the Force and notice more of his work in your life. Submission will increase your faith as you trust in the Force to guide you through the challenges of relationships with other people.

Strengthen me, embracing Force, that I may defend all that is in you.
Protect me, universal Force, that I always may be with you.
May the Force be with me.
Depart, O soul, out of this present world in which the name of the Force that created you, and re-join that from which you came.
From ***The Way of Jediism,*** by John Henry Phelan, Mark Barwell, and Hans Thomas Finch

HOW TO PRAY

You must make time to pray in these busy and unprecedented times that we find ourselves in – irrespective of who you pray to. Make it a part of your daily routine; praying as soon as you wake up in the morning. However, there is no right or wrong time to pray.

For this practice, go to your Jedi Sacred Space. You can pray by speaking out loud, thinking of your prayer, or even singing. Call on the Deity that you are speaking to and set the intention; such as asking for help or giving thanks.

If you have something specific to address; engage in internal dialogue, if not, then you can feel free to recite a prescribed prayer. Just make your voice heard. Whether you are asking for answers or seeking strength – for yourself or others – be authentic in your intention. You might consider requesting to be made into a better person on this journey that you have begun.

Perhaps, you would like to just show your gratitude for what you have in life, and you want to spread that message into the realm of the Higher Power. Go right ahead and do it. Whether it is brief, or you take your time, know that there is no pre-set time that should be spent on prayer.

Mention how grateful you are for everything that the Force brings into your life; clearing your mind and becoming silent. Don't feel the need to be constantly thinking, talking, or listening for messages. You may find a clearer mind that has the answers in contemplative silence. Have a look at the chapter on silence to explore this notion.

THE TEMPLE OF THE JEDI ORDER

In the Appendix, you will find several suggested prayers to get you started but you can use your own words. Create a passage that inspires you and makes you feel connected to the Force.

*

SURRENDER

The traditional thought and approach of an old-style warrior is "never retreat and never surrender" The warrior's mission was to conquer and win the battle at all costs, even if that meant losing their own life. A Kundalini Jedi Warrior is committed and focused in their approach, but understands that true surrender is actually a superpower for them. Their understanding of a greater power in the Force allows them to let go. Their battle approach is to just surrender and trust the universe; everything will unfold as it's meant to be. When we're attached to outcomes in our lives, it quickly leads to suffering and pain. We are co-creators of our lives, but we can't control what happens. The truth is, it's really not up to us to figure out. Once we can detach from trying to control and manipulate life as well as our everyday experience, we're no longer blocked, but instead open to receive life's magical moments. Take a moment to remember a time when you felt blissful, in the flow, or when you were manifesting things that you wanted. You were most likely in the space of detachment and not focused on trying to control any one thing. You were, therefore, open to receiving new possibilities. This state of being is trust and surrender in the purest form. This trust and inner position of surrender allows for something greater than ourselves to guide our lives and actions.

The universe *is* bringing you everything that you are asking for - whether you want it or not. The universe is responding to your vibration, and everything you have or do not have right now is your proof. We want hard, tangible, evidence of how we are currently connected to our higher power. If you have what you want, then your connection has been more positive than negative, but if you're seeing a lot of what you don't like, your connection to your higher power needs some work.

THE SERENITY PRAYER: JEDI EDITION

Force grant me the serenity
to accept the things I cannot change
Courage to change the things I can
and wisdom to know the difference
Living one day at a time
Enjoying one moment at a time
Accepting hardships as the pathway to peace.
Taking, as the force did, this sinful world as it is,
not as I would have it
Trusting that the force will make all things right
if I surrender to its Will
That I may be reasonably happy in this life
and supremely happy in the force
forever in the next.

From *The Way of Jediism,* by John Henry Phelan, Mark Barwell, and Hans Thomas Finch

Since we know that the universe is continually manifesting for us because we have constant manifestations - wanted or unwanted - surrendering is as easy as realising that to get what you want, you have to get yourself on the frequency of your higher power. Your higher power is not residing on the frequency of grief, resentment, anger, jealousy, fear or gossip. Your higher power is much higher than that, and until you can achieve that vibration, you will not see manifestations that you want - but you'll see a whole slew of manifestations that you do not want.

Luke uses faith when Yoda shows him how to lift out the x-wing, Luke says I don't believe it, and that is why he fails. Sometimes to surrender means giving up trying to understand the process and becoming comfortable with not knowing. Surrender literally means to stop fighting, stop controlling, and stop getting in the way of what's flowing to you and taking form. Why resist and push away the very thing that you want to create for yourself?

Now, this is where the confusion comes in for many people. If you surrender to what you have to do you just broadcast it to the universe, and 'let go' of the outcome? Does it mean that you should just sit there and wait for it to come knocking at your door?

No!

You still have to meet the universe halfway. You have to play your part in this, but you have to take action from that place of surrender-energy. Rather than forcing; running around and flapping, take it slow. Follow your heart, and follow your instincts. When you don't rush, the universe will speak to you and gently lay out the best path forward.

"You can't stop the change, any more than you can stop the suns from setting."
— **Shmi Skywalker, Star Wars: Episode I - The Phantom Menace**

Every day in this world is uncertain. Everything around us is continually changing. The recent virus has spread more fear and uncertainty about the future and as a society of control freaks, we struggle to get control of our lives. We create lists, systems, routines, schedules, comfort foods, comfortable environments, because as humans we crave comfort and safety. We create artificial comfort zones which slowly zap our energies over time. In our arrogance, we believe that we can control the uncontrollable, ever-shifting landscape of our lives. Much to our disliking, we eventually realise that control is an illusion. The Force surrounds us and works through us. It is a part of the fluidity of life. When we struggle or resist the natural flow of life, it leaves us stressed, procrastinating, depressed, or anxious. We become angry or frustrated, and we end up lashing out or constantly complaining.

The Spartans would often say return with your shield in your arms or with you on it. The only two options for them were victory or death. Surrender was not an option and it was often thought of as something totally dishonourable.

The traditional idea is that a warrior will never quit; never stop until the mission is achieved. This is one of the most distinctive and positive qualities of the warrior, and this approach can help us achieve many things. However, this new time and age require a counterintuitive strategy for the traditional warrior archetype. The Kundalini Jedi Warrior approaches life with a different perspective. They are fighting their war aided by the power of the Force. For them, the Force is their ally and guide. The Jedi Warriors understand the practice and power of surrender. The idea of letting go of some of our control, structures, and instincts in order to regain control will sound crazy to the ego. Instead of trying to make the world exactly as we like it and trying to avoid all the things that we dislike, we should surrender to the idea that these things will manifest naturally anyway. Yet, instead, we send out a message to the universal Force that we don't trust it and that we are not interested in co-creation. We are sending out vibrations that say "I can handle this life on my own", instead of, relaxing, and accepting the uncertainty and fluidity of this world. Surrendering means that we relax into the unknown. We let go of trying to control everything. We adopt a cheerful attitude; knowing that the Force is friendly and that the world is balanced as it is. It is beautiful and unique just the way it is. Surrender involves continuing to take action steps when appropriate, while giving up means shifting all your energy elsewhere. The best way to trust the universe is to learn to trust yourself. Rather than just indiscriminately repeating the mantra "let go," get curious about what specifically is preventing you from stepping up. When you can uncover that, then let go of that specific thought, belief, or assumption - whatever it is.

SURRENDER VS. CONTROL STRATEGIES

Surrender will sound crazy to us and it very well may be an approach that we have never tried before; making the concept seem silly and lame to many people. It could perhaps even sound scary. It goes against all of your evolutionary programming. Uncertainty for us is seen as the enemy that must be controlled.

We want to control our day, so we have routines, schedules, and systems. We create systems for our work; trying to get control over our days. We try to gain control of our health through new diets or exercise programs. We try to control our relationships, our future, our and our finances. While there's nothing wrong with any of this, it's a bit futile to try and control the uncontrollable. Continually trying to get control results in stress and anxiety. When we are in this mental state, not being in control means that we are mostly responding to our life and circumstances driven by our fears. We may even experience feelings of sadness over the fact that we don't have control. In the end, you keep pushing and trying harder; causing more stress and anxiety in an endless loop that leads you nowhere. Now, I'm not saying that we should never try to get control. There are ways of gaining control which can prove to be helpful, but more often than not, it's more beneficial to shift the focus from power to love. Taking care of yourself can be a loving act rather than an attempt to gain control over your health. For example, being in a surrendered state means being fully present in the moment; experiencing the sensations and being curious about it. It might look like acceptance of how things are not how we would like them to be .

WHY SURRENDER IS TRUE POWER

So, we pause our striving to control and we relax. We stop trying to change things and just become present. We tune in to how we're feeling. We notice the sensations of the moment, both in our bodies and all around us. We become present to whoever is in front of us. When we do a task, we pour ourselves thoroughly into it.

We open ourselves to the uncertainty of the moment. We see what we can learn from it – with an open mind, with curiosity and a stance of not-knowing instead of a fixed viewpoint. We start to appreciate the moment in front of us fully. There is something immensely cathartic and enthralling about being in the moment in front of us. If we stop trying to change it, trying to control it, or trying to have it conform to our idea of how things should be, we can simply *be* in it. Just as it is, it's worthy of our appreciation, gratitude, and love. We can fall in love with the moment, just as it is.

HOW TO PRACTICE SURRENDER

Look, giving up control in every sphere of your life is going to most likely lead to financial ruin, loss of relationships, and much more. That's not the purpose of surrendering. You are still required to be a person who takes action, you just have to know how and when. Simply put, you need to learn to accept things as they are; not forcing matters. You need to love people, things, and situations as they are. Coming from a place of love instead of fear of the unknown will transform you. If you would like to know how to surrender more effectively, have a look at some ideas below:

- When you're attempting to control things, pause. Feel the sensations in your body – fear, anxiety – that are making you crave control. Keep with the sensation and allow yourself to truly feel it. Surrender to it; relaxing your body.
- Notice how amazing everything is once you pause and take note. Have gratitude for the present as if you have never been here, in your skin, before. See the world through eyes of wonder.
- Find peace in the unknown; telling yourself that you do not need to know everything before it happens. You don't need to know exactly how things will play out. Find ease in the beauty of an ever-changing environment.
- Say it with me; "No matter how awesome I am, I am only human. I cannot control everything."
- Perhaps you just need a change, or are feeling frustrated. Know that it isn't the end of the world.
- Admit to yourself and to others that you don't have all the answers. Call on your Higher Power for help. Breathe and pray.
- Don't dwell on things that have gone wrong. Let it go.
- What is the universe pushing you towards trying? Get silent and look out for the signs.
- Take into account how you feel when you consider new opportunities. Keep your eyes out for them and listen to that intuition! The Force could be leading you to your next adventure. Listen.
- Cultivate an attitude of gratitude.

*

SYNCHRONICITY

Synchronicities are events that connect us to one another and to the universe. These causal relationships exist both internally and externally; acting as cross-sectional talk between the mind and matter. These synchronicities are governed by the laws of attraction.

Carl Jung believed that they mirrored our psychological processes; carrying messages to us in the same way that dreams do. They take on a meaning of their own; providing guidance around our internal experiences.

They're like little messages from the Force; directing us in what action to take next. Synchronicity can show up in the form of a song that you hear on the radio or some phrase from a song that just pops into your head. You may literally see a big sign or banner that has the message that you needed to see at that moment. I remember, just before I departed for my hero's journey to Canada, that everyday whilst I was either out or at home I would see adverts, stickers, or posters saying "Come to Canada" or "Live in Canada" or "Have you ever been to Canada?" There were adverts for holidays away, relocation services, you name it. It happened so much that I thought that it couldn't just be coincidence.

It may seem like coincidence, but it has an analogue in our psyche. It is up to us to decode these messages and use them to inform our lives. They are like little miracles; happening all around us. They connect us to the greater mysteries of life – the ones that we are all undeniably a part of.

No one has been able to fully explain synchronicity. This is the final lesson of the Jedi Warrior. One must let go of all that they have known and tap into the wisdom of the universe and its mysterious ways. (110)

"We must be willing to let go of the life we planned so as to have the life that is waiting for us."

- Joseph Campbell

Chirrut Îmwe was a blind human who happened to be a spiritual warrior-monk. Îmwe believed strongly in the power of the Force, and he was active during the days of the Galactic Empire; working as an itinerant preacher in Jedha City. In the final scenes of Rogue One: A Star Wars Story, we find our rebel heroes under attack. After learning that the master switch needed to be flipped for the Rebels to receive the Death Star plans, he made his way out onto the battlefield to activate the switch; continuing to repeat the chant, "I am one with the Force. The Force is with me." He managed to completely surrender to the Force and trust the synchronistic events as a calling for him to step up and use the Force. By managing to not be hit by any blaster bolts, Chirrut activated the switch as a fuel container was hit by Imperial blaster fire, and an explosion occurred; sending him flying backwards. He has saved his friends and completed his mission.

The same can be true for all of us. We can live in synchronicity with all that is around us and with the Force. The Force has always been there. Seek only going forward for it is not behind you. Do not be frightened or dismayed for you are one with the Force and the Force lives through us all.

JEDI EXERCISE: CONNECT WITH THE FORCE

Tune in and complete the Jedi Warm-Up set in Chapter 7. Sit in easy pose and close your eyes.

Keep your hands on your knees in Ghan Mudra. Take a deep breath in and begin chanting very slowly:

"I AM ONE WITH THE FORCE, AND THE FORCE IS WITH ME."

Listen to the sound of your own voice as you chant. Whilst doing this you will go through many different feelings and thoughts. Stay with the mantra and feel your deep connection to this truth. Start with a slow monotone voice and begin to slowly increase the speed at which you chant.

Repeat for 2, 5 or 11 minutes. (You may also practice this meditation for 40 days for 31mins and can be part of you daily Sadhana , see appendix for designing your own personal Sadhana)

"In Every Corner Of The Galaxy, The Downtrodden And Oppressed Know Your Symbol, And They Put Their Hope In It."
- **Vice Admiral Holdo, Star Wars: Episode VIII – The Last Jedi**

***

CHAPTER 20: THE PHANTOM MENACE

> *"The ego is always looking to find something – the spirit can see what's already there."*
>
> - *Marianne Williamson, Spiritual Leader and Political Activist*

THE INNER GUIDE: HIGHER SELF

We hold within us a great storehouse of wisdom and knowledge. Spiritual teachers suggest that we have a higher self that is beyond our mind, experiences, and logical thought. Your higher self is your inner spirit - the real you. It is the overseer of your life. It can see the bigger picture when you cannot, because, while your perspective is limited within the physical body, it is broadened in the spiritual body. The higher self is wise because it both figuratively and literally has a more elevated view. It is not impacted by the ups-and-downs of daily life, which stimulate emotions. It lives as a pure being in a continuously expanded state. It observes the events of our lives without judgement and provides unconditional love for us whenever we need it. The real you - your spirit - continually communicates to you through dreams, hunches, intuitive insights, and most of all, gut feelings. It guides you like an inner satellite navigation system. It shows you the easiest, fastest, and most beneficial paths for your life. There are many synonyms for Higher Self: Inner Wisdom, Spirit Self, Soul, Essence, Eternal Self, Authentic Self, Atman, and so on.

Luke Skywalker: "I've got a bad feeling about this"
Ben Kenobi: "Turn the ship around."
Han Solo: "Yeah. I think you're right"
- Star Wars Episode IV: A New Hope

Higher-selves are more like knowing. To put it simply, if something doesn't feel right then it isn't. We may also experience subtle nudges towards something. We all get those inner cues to go to a particular store, attend a specific event, or just stay at home and enjoy the family. Listen to those nudges, as your higher self is speaking to you and trying to get you to pay attention. We get downloads of information that we previously did not know; supplying us with much-needed information to make an informed decision.

Our higher-self works through our intuition. A robust, intuitive mind gives us the ability to know the unknown consequences of our actions before we act so that we can make wise choices to guide our lives. Your higher self is always with you, but if you would like a stronger connection to help you navigate the avenues of life with greater ease and enjoyment, then you may look for the ways in which intuition could be trying to signal something in your life.

This mighty Force power can be increased with practice and can become a powerful ally in your life journey as a warrior. Intuition is the ability to process information, both from the outer and inner world. It takes information from within your subconscious mind, from past experiences and knowledge, remembers all the things that you have heard and seen, and then processes all information outside and beyond your immediate environment.

It is a process of acquiring knowledge and understanding through means other than thinking, learning, or the five senses. It is a subconscious process, in which the subconscious mind brings into your consciousness information, solutions to problems, and the understanding of how to proceed in certain situations. Intuition is your guide and guardian. It is the voice of the soul. It is your inner teacher. The more attention we give to our higher self and implement its guidance, the more we are supported in our endeavours from the higher realms. This means that the communication signals become more substantial and more apparent. In order to make this connection more potent, we must become aware of the ego's distracting voice. The ego is like a phantom menace; always ready to make decisions that might not serve our higher purpose and mission.

*

EGO: THE PHANTOM MENACE

Your Ego is your conscious mind - the part of your identity that you consider your "self." If you say someone has "a big ego," then you are saying he is too full of himself. Ego is defined as the view that a person has of himself. In the prequel trilogy, we see a confident young Anakin coming into his powers and developing himself in the Jedi arts. Due to his connection with the Force and his growing abilities, Anakin begins to believe that he is above his teacher. He questions the decisions of the High Jedi council and feels that he is being held back; going on to declare that he will become the greatest Jedi ever. His inflated ego leads him towards the dark-side.

One of the biggest reasons why ego is your enemy is that it keeps you out of touch with reality. Your ego is what prevents you from hearing critical but necessary feedback from others. Ego makes you overestimate your abilities and worth, and under-estimate the effort and skill required to achieve your goals.

Research has shown that the ego can be held responsible for many negative human traits including, but not limited to, criticising and judging others, acting manipulative, being inflexible and rigid, having severe mood swings, possessing a constant need for praise and approval, as well as a need to feel superior to everyone around.

The purpose of the ego is to provide protection from psychological harm that others may do to you. See, the ego used to have an important job — **to keep us alive**, by being aware of our surroundings in case a sabre-toothed tiger or any other danger was lurking around the corner. These days, we don't run into dangers like that all that often, but our approach to life is still in survival mode. The ego does not need to be destroyed or expelled, but we do need to have it work in service of our inner spirit so that we may flow with the power of the Force. Our unaddressed ego and the idea of separation will continue to inspire fear, self-judgment, and judgment of others; causing us to create a *"them versus us"* approach to life. In spiritual paths, the work is to surrender the ego - to give up our limited experience of life, and to wake up so that we can experience the truth of who we are.

The ego is made up of thoughts and beliefs from the past - or the unreality - and it is not equipped to guide us into this new age. During significant change, the mind will advise you to separate and withdraw from others in unhealthy ways. Alternatively, it could also advise you to go into a fantasy and deny what is coming. It could even go so far as to generate thoughts of fear, so that you live in scarcity. However, human beings play a game in which we pretend that we're all isolated individuals who confront a universe that has nothing to do with us. Over the course of our psychological evolution, we've forgotten that the Universe isn't divided up into separate objects, or operations, but that it is a working functioning symbiotic whole. We imagine a psychological identity that never existed in the first place and then go around trying to negotiate each other into preserving and augmenting our identities; not realising that it is the identity itself that creates the basic sense of struggle and conflict that we try so hard to overcome. It's fighting fire with fire. Our culture and society function from the perspective that we are individual; separate from everyone else, with our individual needs outweighing the needs of others.

We live in a culture of fear and lack which leads us to believe that we must fight and war with each other; we must have victory over the other because only the strongest survive. We are operating from a strong egoistic mind. The ego-mind is limited and small. What we're talking about here is that little voice inside you that is the source of so much worry, anxiety, and suffering. The Ego is what keeps you locked away in your own little world; separated from the present moment.

The Ego is our limited perception of ourselves composed of all roles, identities, labels, comparisons, and judgments that we have created around our persona, and with which we later on identify as being who we are. It sees itself always as separate from everything else and continually filters everything through a polarity mindset of *"either/or"*; judging, labelling, analysing, and comparing in its desire to separate everything in groups of good or bad, right or wrong, white or black, and happy or unhappy. It is very intelligent and hard to identify because it is embedded in our personality and life experiences. It contains our fearful and separated thoughts, feelings, words or behaviours. We cannot get rid of our ego by repressing it or by fighting it because it will just become stronger and lash out when we least expect it.

You may be asking, *"So, how do I learn to trust my inner guidance?"*

Think about the many times you have felt that gentle nudge telling you to do something. Now, notice how many times you have chosen to ignore that nudge, and you have ended up saying, *"I knew this was not such a good idea!"* Probably, every single time.

In contrast, think about how many times you have chosen to listen to that internal suggestion and have been glad that you did. Most likely, every single time. Moreover, consider if the suggestions which you receive ever work against you and the evidence from your own life will show you that the inner guidance you receive always works to your own benefit – even if you do not understand the logic behind it at the time. If your inner guidance offers you options to your own benefit every single time, why not give its suggestions a fair chance the next time?

Most likely, you will not regret it.

So how do we separate our inner voice of wisdom and knowledge from the inner voice of the ego? This takes practice to move away from the ego voice and start following the voice of our intuitive higher self. Intuition is your very own inner guardian. Daily meditations will strengthen it and cleanse your mind. Conflicting thoughts will melt away when we listen to our intuition. You will gain the ability to know your consequences on any given action before taking it. This will allow you to make wise choices to guide your life.

CHARACTERISTICS OF THE EGO

Alexandra Moga wrote an insightful piece, on her yoga blog, about the difference between living in your ego and living from your intuition. Let's explore it now.

1. EGO IS LOGICAL - INTUITION IS CREATIVE

Often the Ego's voice will sound logical and rational. The advice is based on a past that no longer exists. It may sound like, "Of course do this because it worked for you in the past or this method worked for other people." Intuition rarely sounds logical or rational. It is the creative voice, the solution that seems to come out of left field.

2. EGO IS FEAR BASED - INTUITION IS BASED ON LOVE

Messages from the Ego will often be cloaked in fear. "You need to take that boring evening class to keep your competitive edge or other people will pass you by." "Keep that job that exhausts you, and it gives you a regular pay check. Otherwise, you will have no home; how will you survive?" The intuitive voice is rooted in love and reminds you that you have the support of the Universe every step of the way. Often with intuition, you do not receive the whole picture all at once; it is one step at a time.

3. EGO SOUNDS HARSH - INTUITION IS NEUTRAL

Ego's voice is judgmental to the point of being abusive, telling you things about yourself to make you believe that you are a terrible person and not to be trusted. This will make you treat yourself in disrespectful and unloving ways. Intuition is neutral in energy, and these messages make you treat yourself in loving and respectful ways.

4. EGO PROTECTS A MENTAL IMAGE - INTUITION PROTECTS YOUR SOUL'S JOURNEY

The Ego is invested in maintaining a mental image you have of yourself. For instance, you may be a supervisor of people in the workplace. A supervisor is a mental image (ego identification), and with this comes a lot of baggage, including all the ways the Ego thinks others should treat you. If someone doesn't play the game and surrender their Ego to your Ego, perhaps by speaking the Truth, Ego will feel threatened and lash out. Ego messages will include, "I need to put that person back in line. They need to pay for disrespecting me"—all in an effort to protect a mental image which is untrue. Intuition sees the truth that we are all spiritual beings having human experiences. We are all equal. Hierarchies are created by the Ego to keep us separate and unconscious to the truth. There is nothing to protect; our true identity can neither be harmed nor injured.

5. EGO JUMPS AROUND - INTUITION IS CONSISTENT

Often the Ego's advice will jump around from one message to the next, sometimes contradicting itself. It is like a thief that tries every way possible to get into your house. The messages you receive from your intuition are steady and consistent; you will often hear the same words or phrases over and over again. (111)

HOW DO YOU BECOME AWARE OF INTUITION?

1. It is a sort of sensation that you feel inside you.
2. It is some sort of understanding without words.>
3. You feel inner certainty.
4. You become aware of mental images that pop up into your mind.
5. You become aware of words that repeat themselves in your mind.
6. Sudden understanding of what you need to do.
7. Being aware of a solution.
8. You feel an inner urge to act in a certain way.

Once you ask to receive guidance from your higher self, it is essential to listen, accept, and allow the wisdom to saturate your consciousness. It is very easy to shrug off a nudge, impulse, or gut feeling. The more attention we give to our higher self and implement its guidance, the more we are supported in our endeavours from the higher realms of the Force, which means that the communication signals become stronger and clearer.

When you receive guidance from your higher self, it will take trust and courage to follow its advice, especially if you are just starting to become aware of the signs and signals. It is helpful to think of your connection with your higher self as any other relationship that you want to nourish and become stronger.

For example, if you want to build a stable relationship with your significant other, then you would show him or her how you care by the way that you treat them. Your words, your intentions, and most of all, your actions will support or hinder the strength of this important connection.

In an ideal relationship, the energy that you share with another person is the energy that will be reciprocated back to you. This dynamic interchange is how it works with your higher self. If you are listening, paying attention, and following the guidance, then your higher self will meet you more than half way with its consistent support and encouragement.

*

MEDITATION FOR INTUITION

In this meditation we will be working with the 4th body as we develop our neutral mind. If you are still experiencing confusion between ego and intuition, try this meditation and deeply listen afterwards. You will be shocked at how fast your intuition works. This meditation uses a four-stroke breath to stimulate the pituitary gland. It must be practiced for the full 16 minutes to open up the chakras.

Tune In:
Adi Mantra 3 times (Ong Namo Guru Dev Namo). MUDRA: Interlace your fingers except for the Jupiter Fingers (index fingers) point up. Cross the thumbs. Bring the fingers just under your nose where you can see the tip of your Jupiter fingers.

Eyes:
1/10 open.

Breath:
Inhale through 'O' mouth in 4 strokes. Exhale once through the nostrils. Use your diaphragm on the inhale.

Time:
These exercises are time-bound. Open up your chakras and open up your self-sensory system. Continue for 16 minutes.

To End:
Inhale and stretch your arms out to the sides with the palms facing up. Hold 20 seconds.
Exhale and repeat one more time. Then inhale and open the fingers and make them like steel. Squeeze all your energy and bring it to your arms. Exhale and relax. (112)

JOURNALING TO EXPLORE YOUR INTUITION

Simply think to yourself, "Higher self, please guide me. What do I need to know about this?" Then, begin writing and see what comes out.

*

DEVELOPING YOUR INTUITION

1. You can develop your intuition by being more aware of the little voice within you, which sometimes whispers to you, telling you what to do and what to avoid doing.
2. Each day, find a few moments to get quiet and listen to the small voice within you.
3. This skill gets sharper when you can calm down the endless chatter of your mind.
4. Strengthening your concentration ability helps you improve your intuition, hunches and gut feelings. This happens, because with a focused mind, you can ignore doubts, fears and distracting thoughts. In such a situation, your hunches and gut feeling gets sharper.
5. Practicing meditation can also be helpful.
6. Before making an important decision, sit down in a quiet place, think a while about the decision you need to make, and then stop thinking about it and just try to listen quietly to your intuition.

Please remember, not all inner sensations, gut feelings or sudden understandings are intuition. Think before you act and use your common sense. At the same time, do not be afraid to follow your intuition.

SILENCE TO ENGAGE YOUR INTUITION

In the previous chapter on silence and solitude we explored the power of this type of practice as a way to engage and the experience of the Force. The development of this skill lays the foundation for another powerful capacity. Another great way to engage your intuition is by spending time alone, being with yourself in silence. There is so much power in spending time in solitude. The silence gives us an excellent opportunity to learn how to quiet the mind and listen to the inner teacher. You already have the answers to what you desire, and time in silence will assist in revealing the answers. One of the characteristics of this inner guidance is that it is gentle and not forceful. Consequently, external noise and distractions, combined with our internal chatter, may distract us; thus, making it less likely for us to notice and even less listen to that inner guidance.

When you are able to quiet the busy mind and connect more with your being-ness, you'll be better able to communicate with your higher self and intuition. Answers will suddenly come to you like gifts from the Universe; instead of you trying to figure out solutions to problems alone – with your thinking mind.

*

THE GOLDEN CHAIN

Emperor Palpatine: "I am all the Sith."
Rey: "And I am all the Jedi."
- Star Wars: Episode IX – The Rise of Skywalker

In Kundalini yoga, we tune in with a mantra. Stilling the mind gives us the power to listen deeply to our inner voice and act on the guidance that we receive from within. That inner guidance is the Guru Dev - the teacher within - and its presence weaves us all together as students and teachers of life.

This mantra is the first creative action. It centres you into the higher self and reminds your lower mind that it is not your ego that will practice or teach Kundalini Yoga. The Adi Mantra connects us to the Golden Chain—the chain of teachers—your teacher, her teacher, his teacher, and so on. The Golden Chain is the channel through which the energy, the wisdom and the protection of the tradition flow to you. In the final scenes of Rise of Skywalker, we see Rey in battle with the Emperor. Almost beaten, she lays unconscious. She is able to hear the voice of all of the Jedi who came before her. Several Jedi voices call to her, lifting her up and encouraging her to win the fight, save the day, and restore balance to the Force. They channel their energy into her as they whisper to her. In this way, it is similar to the idea of Force ghosts appearing to guide both Luke and Rey. The wisdom and guidance of previous Jedi Masters has become open to the Jedi student, who has developed the stillness and silenced-mind to hear and feel said guidance.

By chanting this mantra and linking to the Golden Chain, the exercises and meditations that you practice are guided by your higher consciousness and all the teachers that have brought this opportunity to you. It makes you very receptive and sensitive to the message of your body, mind, and intuition. It is used as a link when you teach and as preparation for your personal practice. The Golden Chain is the inner spark of Kundalini that is passed from person to person; teacher to student; guru to the teacher; cosmos and God to Guru. (113)

Nota Bene:
You know you are being guided by your higher self by the way that you feel. If you are feeling positive emotion, i.e. inspired, uplifted, or motivated, then your guidance is moving you in the right direction. You don't always know the final outcome of a situation, but if your choices feel right, then they are supporting your movement forward.

Being in alignment with our higher self does not mean there won't be difficulties or challenges in our lives. Our understanding will continue to grow and evolve; allowing us to see obstacles as opportunities for growth.

***

CHAPTER 21: SACRIFICE

" *To die for one's people is a great sacrifice. To live for one's people, an even greater sacrifice."*

- Senator Riyo Chuchi, Star Wars: The Clone Wars

SERVICE TO THE GALAXY: JEDI VS. SITH

Every age has its own quality and thus affects us personally. In the opening chapter we discussed the state of the world and all the trouble and strife that we currently find ourselves facing. The yogic scriptures believe that human civilisation degenerates spiritually during the Kali Yuga. You can find more information on the ages in the Appendix. During this dark age of the empire everything turns back to front. The good are called evil. The evil become the celebrated leaders. The world of matter supersedes the world of spirit. Individually we experience spiritual bankruptcy, mindless hedonism, breakdown of all social structure, greed, materialism, unrestricted egotism, as well as afflictions and disorders of the mind and body.

The Covid-19 pandemic has crippled the world; there is no longer an accepted normal. We now fear and avoid our fellow human beings; increasing our paranoia. Climate change and unstable economy is pushing us to the limit of our fears. You can see it everywhere you look - once you actually look. Constant rage and fury are the status quo. Tired of the lies and propaganda by politicians and media, people are lashing out. Cynical scorn and bitter laughter ring out around us. Perpetual contests to gain superiority over others are commonplace. These never end, because whatever is achieved is fleeting and meaningless. Cycles of abuse and violence that churn on and on permeate our world. We have a feeling of abiding powerlessness; of absolute helplessness. There is a sense of terrible fear that's gone on so long, that it has left us numb. When we do feel something, it's just a kind of icy cold sense that nothing will ever go right for us. This frequency of fear is causing us to shrink even further into feelings of despair. Our survival instincts have kicked in and it's every man for themselves - take what you can; you must survive. We have a selfish society where *'Let's grab it while we can'* is the mantra of the day. This has led to a culture of apathy. It is unfortunate, but the fact is that many people today will not consistently help others without anticipating something tangible in return - very often that is money and money is just energy in a different form.

THE WAY OF THE SITH

"If once you start down the dark side, forever will it dominate your destiny, consume you it will, as it did Obi-Wan's apprentice."
- **Grand Master Yoda, Star Wars: Episode V - The Empire Strikes Back**

Once you make a morally questionable decision, you will start a cycle that will end in your destruction. On the other end of the spectrum, we have a different outcome when we make morally outstanding decisions.

However, as an attempt to overcome this sense of powerlessness and feelings of futility, people are creating fantasy lives focusing on emotions and thoughts that fuel a path to the dark-side. In response to this, we find a generation of narcissists, also known as the "me-me" generation or the new millennials. This is a generation of lazy, upset, selfish individuals that only care about their looks and the number of likes and follows that they receive. With an attitude of predominantly thinking about yourself and what you can get from others, the focus is on the external. This focus on oneself and thinking one is more special with an overestimation of their skills and talents is the path to the Darkside. Anakin represents many of these qualities; a whiny teenager who is overconfident, and disrespectful; believing that he will be the greatest Jedi ever. He even tries to convince Padme that they could rule the universe together. As it is, we frequently witness self-interest being placed before service in the seemingly relentless rat-race. There is often an obsession by humans to accumulate wealth, material possessions, power, fame and notoriety; all motivated entirely for individual benefit. Those on Earth who lived a life of selfishness, greed, avarice, gross materialism, and disregard for others - or worse - will find themselves in the energy of the Darkside. These outer manifestations might well be analogous to a type of "Darkside" in Star Wars terms - worlds where greed, avarice, and selfishness prevail. Eventually, however, these people will also learn their lessons and the futility of their selfish personalities.

ME-ME GENERATION: RISE OF THE SELFIE & DIGITAL NARCISSISM

"Well, I should be! Someday I will be. I will be the most powerful Jedi ever."
- **Anakin Skywalker, Star Wars: Episode II – Attack of the Clones**

What we talk about when we describe an explosion of modern narcissism is not the disorder but the rise in narcissistic traits. Examples are everywhere. The celebrity fixates on his or her appearance to meet the demands of fame. Then vanity, being the only genuinely replicable trait, becomes the thing to emulate. This has led to an increase in people wanting to be a celebrity; having cosmetic surgery coupled with a rise in depression amongst young people is soaring as they compare and compete with each other; leading to low levels of self-esteem, and high levels of anxiety and depression. Social media and camera filters continue to exacerbate vanity and an overall sense of entitlement.

The problem with narcissistic thoughts is that they're unrealistic. The belief in one's extraordinariness will soon come undone when we meet someone that we perceive as even more extraordinary. The result will be disillusionment in the best-case scenario or ever-greater fake grandeur in the worst. They are proud to be narcissistic; believing that it helps them succeed. They are all too happy to state that empathy and caring is not their thing. There's a deep belief that you've achieved everything on your own. In a narcissistic culture there is no higher power that is helping or assisting in life other than themselves. They believe in their superiority and self-sufficiency. This sense of self-importance and arrogance causes a disconnection with others. Self-promotion and individuality seem to be essential, yet in our hearts, that's not what we want. We want to be part of a community. We want to be supported when we're struggling, and we want a sense of belonging. Being extraordinary is not a necessary component to being loved.

GREEK MYTH: NARCISSUS

According to Greek Mythology, Narcissus was a figure who was so impossibly handsome that he fell in love with his own image reflected in a pool of water. Even the lovely nymph Echo could not manage to tempt him from his self-absorption. Narcissus' name lives on as the flower into which he was transformed and as a synonym for those obsessed with their own appearance.

Narcissus was born in Thespiae in Boeotia, the son of Cephissus - the personification of the Boeotian River of the same name - and the nymph Liriope. His mother was warned one day by the seer Teiresias that her son would live a long life as long as 'he never knows himself.' As he reached his teenage years, the handsome youth never found anyone that could pull his heartstrings; indeed, he left in his wake a long trail of distressed and broken-hearted maidens, and one or two young men fell by the wayside too. Then, one day, he chanced to see his own reflection in a pool of water and, thus, discovered the ultimate in unrequited love and fell in love with himself. Naturally, this one-way relationship went nowhere, and Narcissus, unable to draw himself away from the pool, pined away in despair until he finally died of thirst and starvation. (114)

We see the effects of this on those closest to us. Prominent narcissistic traits found that they do the most significant damage to those around them. Over time, this would translate to their failure to consider another person on an intimate level; seeing them only relationally. In other words, *what can they do for me,* or, in the case of their children, *how do they reflect on me, or how have they disappointed me in what they've failed to reflect?*

This narcissistic culture extends into politics, business and academics. If everyone around you is displaying narcissistic tendencies, it becomes so much easier to follow a herd mentality. Group narcissism is vast, and the worst thing our collective narcissism is doing is destroying the planet. Together, we're wiping out species after species; fuelled by consumerism and our self-importance. Our narcissism may destroy us in the end.

APATHY

The plight of the world has left us numb and feeling powerless in the face of current events. Everybody experiences apathy from time to time. You may sometimes feel unmotivated or uninterested in daily tasks. This type of situational apathy is typical, but we are now facing apathy as a primary concern for the human race.

In the words of Helen Keller, "Science may have found a cure for most evils; but it has found no remedy for the worst of them all - the apathy of human beings" (Brainy Quote, 2011). Apathy occurs when people don't care, or when they feel so helpless that they do not try to change or fix things. Apathy is the single largest problem we face today because it is the apathy that fuels the vast number of social, political, economic, and environmental issues facing society. Apathy can be seen every day by people everywhere, just by going to school, by reading the newspaper, or listening to the radio.

Apathy and passivity are spreading on an epic scale, while civilisational collapse begins in earnest. It's a kind of wilful ignorance — *I'd rather scroll through Facebook than think about how to solve the world's significant problems. What difference do I make anyways? I'm helpless, I'm powerless, I'm nobody.* Like a black tide, leaving us unable to confront, or even think about, imagine, develop, challenge, and find answers.

Despite our seemingly unlimited capacity to connect, it's very easy to feel limited in a world of dynamic change. Asking questions like *"Can I really make a difference?"* or *"How am I supposed to help?"* only serve to delay or avoid action.

THE SITH APPROACH

"Peace is a lie, there is only passion. Through passion, I gain strength. Through strength, I gain power. Through power, I gain victory. Through victory, my chains are broken. The Force shall free me."

—**The Sith Code**

One of the most compelling aspects of the Star Wars saga is the rivalry between the Sith and the Jedi. The Sith were also users of the Force energy but who utilise the dark-side of the Force. In the films we see the Darkside portrayed by Darth Vader, the emperor, and Darth maul. The Sith approach the Force from the opposite perspective of the Jedi. They view passion, anger and powerful negative emotions as necessary ingredients in them becoming more potent in their connection to the Force. They believe in conflict and battle as a way to separate the weak from the strong; seeing the weak as unworthy. This notion is part of their underlying philosophy. An attitude of "kill or be killed" and a culture of survival of the fittest is encouraged. The Sith are interested in having absolute power. Being ruthless and self-serving allows them easy access to the energy of the Force; giving them superhuman abilities and many Force powers which were used to gain material prowess through this immoral approach.

The Sith value self-centred virtues, such as pride and power, whereas the Jedi value altruistic virtues like kindness and empathy. The goal of the Sith is worldly greatness: the ability to shape and destroy the world according to one's will alone. The Jedi wish nothing for themselves and only want to protect and serve.

The Sith seem to be displaying strong narcissistic qualities and a general focus on just the needs of oneself at the expense of others. Like with anything we repeatedly do in life - be that good or bad by definition - we become the thing that we do habitually. Extended indulgence in the Darkside reshapes the user's psychology, resulting in a loss of humanity, morality, empathy, and the ability to love. This leaves every Sith - to varying degrees - amoral, cruel, sadistic and violent. However, the trade-off is the severe cost of adopting a dark triad personality that corrodes their essential capacity for empathy, kindness, and love. Severe saturation in the Dark Side may even lead to physical degradation.

Considering this dark change in personality to be a transformation into a different person altogether, they adopt another name status to reflect this transformation.

"Once you walk down the dark path it can consume you."
- **Grand Master Yoda, Star Wars: Episode V – The Empire Strikes Back**

While the Jedi were taught that fear, anger, and pain were negative emotions to be overcome, the Sith believed that these emotions helped them become more competitive. By harnessing the negative emotions rather than suppressing them, the Sith believed they could achieve real power. The Sith approach to life is one of a strong competitive mindset: to control others through manipulation and lies.

The goal of the Jedi is moral goodness: freedom from the inner, and outer turmoil and suffering. However, the Sith consider the Jedi's aspirations to be either hopeless or pathetic. To the Sith, greater power is the only authentic goal. In their narrow self-interest and focus on personal ambition, they use seductive qualities; adopting corruptive, and addictive tendencies. For the Sith robberies, betrayal, and sabotage are commonplace; murder is acceptable so long as the culprit is not caught. Whereas the Jedi encourage taking on a padawan to share what they have learnt and help develop the new padawan, the Sith encourage the overthrowing and killing of their masters – in fact, it is looked at favourably. Sith philosophy stresses that power belongs only to those with the strength, cunning, and ruthlessness to maintain it, and thus "betrayal" among the Sith is not a vice but an endorsed norm. Accordingly, the Sith reject altruism, self-abnegation, and kindness, as they regard such attitudes as founded on delusions that fetter one's perceptions and power. Sith teach their apprentices to revere the dark-side of the Force and to believe that the galaxy was theirs to rule by cosmic right.

*

SELFLESS SERVICE

"I can only protect you. I cannot fight a war for you."
- **Qui-Gon Jinn, Star Wars: Episode I - The Phantom Menace**

Selfless service also includes the progression of all humanity and life. The fortunate should, likewise, always help the less fortunate within the physical world. Such service to others can be offered in numerous, unlimited ways; ranging from financial assistance to direct physical help, all the way through to advice.

For example, telling one of your colleagues how great she or he looks in a specific colour or style might help to brighten their day. Bringing your neighbours recycling bins up to their garage doors, or sending an email of gratitude to a friend with whom you haven't spoken in a while are ways of reaching out and connecting to others on that deeper, giving level.

If all humanity would embrace these extremely important Universal principles, all of which are required for actual progression, then the greed, avarice, materialism, egocentricity, and self-gratification which are so prevalent in the world today would disappear. The world would be a vastly better place and there would be a balance in the Force. It's good for your health to engage in selfless service. It has been known to provide a reduction of emotional disturbance, greater longevity, stress reduction, improved morale, increased self-confidence as well as self-esteem, better health, pain reduction, and greater overall happiness.

"Mom, you said that the biggest problem in the universe is no one helps each other."
- **Anakin Skywalker, Star Wars: Episode I - The Phantom Menace**

Efforts need not be grandiose or even affect the whole world, as small acts of kindness to others and to ourselves will help raise our frequency. We are not aiming to change the world in one big final battle but in winning our daily battles within ourselves. Focus on the community around you, the city or town in which you live, the friendships or connections you've created, and the lives of those you're able to touch.

It can be as easy as paying the toll for the person behind you or sending a friendly email to someone you haven't spoken to in years. Stay anonymous. Give openly. The more you become comfortable with giving with no need for reward, the more you will find yourself in alignment with the Force. It is then that the Force will offer you new missions and take care of your needs at the same time.

Seva is a spiritual practice of selfless service with no thought of reward for the self. It takes you out of the limited state of the needs of the ego and puts you in the blissful, infinite space of love. We all have something to give, even if it just means a smile or a kind word to a stranger. You could even opt for a small act of random kindness anonymously. Small steps lead to great change. Seva is the karmic life preserver that keeps your spiritual head above water by helping others stay afloat.

Selfless service is an ordained philosophy in Sikh scripture. It is also known as Seva and it is the overarching theory for hermeneutics – a service performed without expectation of reward. They are merely performed for the good of humanity.

One of the most important aspects of progression in all spheres of life is the offering and provision of service to others without any thought whatsoever of reward or self-gratification. Selfless service is fundamental, both from an individual perspective and from the perspective of the entire human race, without which there can be no real progression. Selfless service should be offered and provided out of a genuine and deep desire to help and be of service to others.

It is unfortunate that many people today will not consistently help others without anticipating something tangible in return. There are of course many notable exceptions, for example, the excellent work carried out by charities as well as other volunteer workers and organizations involved in a wide range of humanitarian and selfless services. There are also those who work in service to other living creatures and the environment.

THE POWER OF SERVICE

We should all, therefore, positively live our lives, in complete peace and harmony with the world; going with the flow of energy, and always offering selfless service. We should provide service to others out of Unconditional Love whenever and wherever the need or opportunity arises, and it is appropriate to do so. Living a shallow life where token efforts are made to help others or to be less selfish only in the knowledge of the life awaiting after passing from the physical world and in the hope of enjoying a better "afterlife" will be completely futile. Relinquishing the habits and characteristics of a lifetime on Earth or "death bed confessions and conciliation" just prior to passing on mean absolutely nothing whatsoever, and will make no difference at that point.

True progression includes transcending the ego, ennoblement of Soul and Spirit, respect for all life, Unconditional Love, and living in service of others without any thought of reward.

No time should be lost in fully embracing and living life in full knowledge of the true meaning of life and being of service to others. Leading a life of non-violence, truthfulness, purity of heart, and humility contributes to the stability of mind required for fruitful meditation experiences. Selfless service provides the ingredient of grace, which helps to connect with the energy of the Force. When we help someone, our heart expands. It reaches out to embrace another as a member of one human family. This act alone opens up our connection to the Force. As our love for others flows out, the Force extends this energy of love back into us.

"Service to others is the rent you pay for your room here on earth."
— **Muhammad Ali, Heavy weight Champion of the World**

When we act in service of others, our meditative states are boosted and we, therefore, get filled with joy and peace. It can be argued that only through an act of selfless service, can we speed up our journey towards true inner peace.

Smile at the woman who serves your lunch; not because you feel bad for her, but because you see the same Force in you - flowing in her eyes. Go out of your way to return a lost credit card; not because you believe it will better your karma but because you know what it feels like to lose a credit card and it brings you joy to heal the worry of another. True service comes from the heart, not the mind. Real service is being done when no one knows what you're up to. There are no bragging rights, no rewards, and no personal benefits. Of course, people are understandably committed to their own daily needs, families, and friends; often helping each other whenever appropriate. This is of course, as it should be between families and friends. Selfless service, however, should extend far beyond family and friends. The meaning of selfless service is to unconditionally be of service whenever the need for such assistance is apparent and appropriate, and whenever it is possible to do so, without any thought whatsoever for self or gain.

*

YOUR MISSION

"Whatever you do will be insignificant, but it is very important that you do it."
— **Mohandas Gandhi**

By serving selflessly, we expand our hearts from our own self to our family, to the community, to our country, to the world, and ultimately, to the cosmos. Selfless service comes from an understanding that we are all members of one large family of God. True selfless service encompasses helping more than our own physical family; it includes all humanity. It is a noble quality to have feelings of love for all people, both those we know and those who are strangers. It is one of the goals of spirituality to help all humanity develop the quality of love and service to all. Giving has its own benefits. The joy of giving is far more exhilarating than the pleasure of getting, and it can be likened to a thrill or high.

"Reach out. Touch others. Walk tall. In every essence of life, please grow. Time is with you. Tide is with you. Tomorrow is yours and you have to build that tomorrow with the strength of compassion."
— **Yogi Bhajan, Master of Kundalini yoga**

HUMILITY

"Humility is not thinking less of yourself, it's thinking of yourself less."

— C.S. Lewis, Author

Humility allows us to grow as leaders in our communities. It should not be seen as old fashioned, but as something necessary for this day and age. It is one of the most essential attributes for growth. It allows us to build trust, and facilitates our learning. It can be seen as having a lack of harmful pride or of being of the notion that you are no more important than anyone else. It is a modesty that will take you quite far in life. The opposite of humility - as we've uncovered in previous chapters - is arrogance. For the warrior hubris can be his strongest enemy and biggest weakness. Hubris describes a personality quality of extreme or excessive pride or dangerous overconfidence, often in combination with - or synonymous with - arrogance. We see this play out with Anakin over-estimating his abilities; challenging the jedi council when he's not been given rank of master as well as when he generally ignores Obi-Wan's guidance. This is a person who thinks very highly of themselves and doesn't take other people into consideration. They cannot improve themselves because they believe that there is nothing for them to improve upon. These people have a fixed mindset as opposed to a growth mindset. When a Kundalini Jedi Warrior does not possess the ability to see their own weaknesses, they will never get to see their true potential being fulfilled. Pride will always rob you of your ability to achieve.

"Twice the pride, twice the fall."

— **Count Dooku, Star Wars: Episode III – Revenge of the Sith**

It might sound counter-intuitive, but the humbler you are, the more resilient you can be. If you can admit and recognise your part in the downfall, you can work towards changing it. If you combine humility with your passion in life, you'll rise to the top. People who have given of themselves have helped improve the quality of life on this planet. Throughout the ages, some have worked tirelessly to cure diseases or to make discoveries, invent items that will make people more comfortable and safer. Others have given their lives for the freedom and rights of others. Some have devoted their lives for the spiritual up-liftment of others. Each of us in our own sphere can use our God-given talents - our knowledge and skills - selflessly to make the world a better place for all life.

"Service creates permanent love and friendship. Self-discipline creates grace. And the neutral mind creates wisdom. These are the rules of life."

— **Yogi Bhajan**

JEDI EXERCISE: SOLUTION FOR APATHY

Let's explore the scientific musings of Dr. Leon Seltzer in accordance with his article in Psychology Today, aptly titled; *The Curse of Apathy: Sources and Solutions*. Regardless of what initially caused you to feel so unmotivated, it's your present-day outlook on it that now keeps you stuck. Your immediate task, then, is to alter this outlook. In short, you're much better off focusing on how to fix what's inside your head than what lies outside it. And no question but that you'll need to force yourself—yes, force yourself! —to uproot what's already taken residence deep inside you. So, ask yourself: "Am I willing to make a commitment to myself to give this apathy the fight of its life, even though doing so feels like it will take a lot more energy and effort than I'm now capable of?" Here are some solutions to consider:

Determine where your apathy is coming from, and contest its underlying assumptions. Since apathy is fundamentally about attitude, begin to look at yourself and your history from a different perspective. And that's one in which you offer yourself greater compassion, empathy, and understanding—and possibly forgiveness for any past insensitivities, transgressions, or shortcomings. It's time to move beyond whatever negative messages you received about yourself in the past and realise that, as long as you don't set your sights unrealistically high and are willing to apply yourself diligently to whatever is important to you, your success is virtually guaranteed.

Transition from passivity to problem-solving. What is the easiest, most do-able first step you can take to pull yourself out of the torpor you've slid into? Make a list of what isn't working for you and what could make your situation better. And if your particular circumstances aren't susceptible to change, can you accept them for what they are, get over them—and move on?

Inject some novelty into your routine. Maybe challenge yourself to initiate a conversation with someone at work you don't know very well. Or change your exercise regimen. Or make some changes in your diet, trying out new dishes or food combinations. Go on a trip, take a long walk in nature. Whatever might give you a new lease on life is well worth your consideration.

Challenge your apathy in every way you can. What turned you on before you were beset with your present malaise? Any friends you've lost track of, but always enjoyed talking to—especially if they made you laugh? Any particular music you found appealing? Places that have inspired you? The more things you try, the more likely you'll eventually be able to extricate yourself from the binding chains of your apathy.

Recall—and reawaken—happier times when you felt more enthusiastic and alive. What hobbies or leisure-time activities might you once have engaged in that you found exhilarating? It hardly matters what delighted you in the past. Anything at all will do. Taking time out to do nothing and in being aimless allows some space for us to be creative. non-doing activity serves the essential purpose of reawakening you to the simple joys that life has to offer—apart from their "practicality."

Direct your attention to a goal you might pursue right now. Considering your values, aptitudes, and preferences, choose whatever goal might best capture your attention and interest, and help you creatively re-engage with life. Even if it means arbitrarily selecting among three or four things you considered in the past, don't let yourself anguish. Choose something right now. You can always change your mind later on. What's imperative is that you lift yourself out of your current morass. Don't choose anything complex. (115)

Nota Bene:
If, after working with the above suggestions, you're still unable to escape your apathy, chances are you're suffering from a more in-depth, underlying issue that may need deeper exploration. And for this, you probably need to get yourself into counselling or therapy.

Break down your goals into smaller actions. If you want to be an honourable person, decide what actions will make you honourable—preferably ones you can practice in your day-to-day life. Helping an older person pick up items that they drop, returning lost money, and not using offensive language are all opportunities for you to be an honourable person. Consider the five principles of self-improvement: gratitude, modesty, compassion - for self and others - mindfulness and community. Some of these are obvious – humility as an antidote to self-love – and some have a practical application. You can use a meditation for humility like the one laid out on the next page.

MEDITATION: OPEN THE HEART, DEVELOP HUMILITY AND COMPASSION

Here is a great meditation practice that works on opening the heart centre and connecting you with your inner softness and love. Openness and compassion can spring forth from this space.

TUNE IN : ONG NAMO GURU DEV NAMO X 3

In Easy Pose, make a Lotus Mudra. The sides of the thumbs and the tips of the little fingers and the base of the palms touch.
The rest of the fingers spread to form the lotus petals.
Bring the hands 4 or 5 inches in front of the Heart

Center. Begin long, deep, and slow breathing. Focus your eyes down on the thumb tips. Feel the exhaled breath touch the thumbs.

Continue for 11 minutes. When finished relax on your back for 5 mins.

**

CHAPTER 22: RISE: THE FINAL CHANGES

Everyone thinks of changing the world, but no one thinks of changing himself."
— Leo Tolstoy, Russian Author

"THE ENDING: CHANGE

Most of us will have opinions on what is wrong in the world but very few will actually come up with the solutions to do anything about it. While we may feel frustrated with the status quo, many of us will stand idly by while they take place.

You must be solution oriented so that you can be part of the solution and at a place where the problems no longer affect you. Work on the parts of yourself that are at war with reality; acknowledging how and why you feel aggressive or angry towards certain situations. Life is constantly changing, so if you truly want to provide the world with solutions, provide it with a better version of yourself. Once you commit to positive change you will experience these small changes along the way. You will also realise that these small changes are something worth celebrating and you will begin to live the life that you love. Enjoy each day for what it is and don't worry about how long your journey is taking.

Instead of waiting for something to happen, make something happen. Change your situations for the better instead of waiting around for some sort of big break. They autopilot their way into their old age and if they're lucky, they might get to enjoy a bit of their lives at that point. However, by that point they're already south of 60 and they've wasted most of their lives grumbling about things they could not change and not embracing their lives for what they are. You've got to just get out of your own way and start enjoying life. Become aware of the fact that you are standing in your own way and stop holding yourself back. Go after what you want, chase your dreams and learn something new. Guide yourself towards the person that you truly want to be.

*

SPIRITUAL TEACHERS

"I need someone to show me my place in all this."
- Rey Skywalker, Star Wars: The Last Jedi

Ever since there have been human beings on this earth, there have also been spiritual teachers, saints or mystics to show us the real purpose of life. As explained earlier, the terms saint, mystic and spiritual teacher as used throughout this book apply to a person who has conquered his or her mind, elevated his or her consciousness to the highest spiritual regions, seen the reality of God face to face and merged with that reality. Life now feels like a great rushing river that seems to be gathering speed daily. The concept of time is changing and events that took place last week seemed to have happened months ago. If you rely on your ego, or your mind and its old ways during this time, life will seem overwhelming; filled with doubt, fear and anxiety. Even the greatest hero needs help and guidance in his quest. You never forget a good teacher. They help you to believe in yourself. They bring out your skills and good qualities. They bring years of wisdom; saving you time and unnecessary setbacks thanks to the path they have walked. The hero has to learn how to survive in the new world incredibly fast, so the mentor appears to give them a fighting chance. This mentor will describe how the new world operates, and instruct the hero in using any innate abilities they possess. The mentor will also gift the hero with equipment, because a level one hero never has any decent weapons or armour.

I have had the privilege to work and be tutored by great yoga teachers, martial artists, academics, and enlightened masters. I have gathered knowledge from great teachings that I have either read or watched which have made me the person that I am today. Life is also a great teacher; giving us experiences and situations that push us to grow and develop our capacities as well as to gain new understandings about life.

You don't have to be a teacher in the general sense, but you can also teach by example, which can be quite powerful. Teachers can be anyone; our neighbour, the shop assistant, and even our boss. They are people who have a prominent "presence" and generally exude humility, integrity, wisdom, light-heartedness, and strength, amongst other qualities. We can learn so much by merely observing them.

Then there are spiritual teachers and enlightened masters; opening you up to the mysteries of the Universe and the origin of our species. In Star Wars there are many great teachers and guides helping the hero and the Jedi overcome the powers of the dark-side. The fourth stage of the hero's journey is called "Meet the mentor". The adventure of our hero has finally begun, and this first encounter with their mentor will impact the rest of the story. A mentor is a figure in the story that provides the protagonist with the instruments he needs to succeed in his journey. Obi-Wan Kenobi, for example, is the one who gave Luke his lightsaber and taught him about the Force.

MENTORS

"Pass on what you have learned. Strength. Mastery. But weakness, folly, failure also. Yes, failure most of all. The greatest teacher, failure is."

- **Grand Master Yoda, Star Wars: The Last Jedi**

A good mentor will help you reach your goals. A great mentor will instil a confidence in you that will remove your need for that much help to reach those goals. Mentors can be an invaluable resource on our journey to become a Jedi. The path is long and arduous, so having someone with you who has more experience than you and who has walked the path to self-empowerment and self-discovery can guide you and save you years of toil and trouble.

When looking for a mentor, put your intention out into the Universal Force, like a request, and be specific about which type of qualities you hope they will embody. It's not about their formal qualifications, but about how you feel in the presence of their energy.

Choose a mentor that best fits your needs and connects with your particular life mission. You may find that you will have many mentors over the course of your journey. When the hero is ready, the mentor will appear. Generally, if you leave feeling empowered and having gained more clarity, you've found a great mentor. Thereafter, over time you will begin to internalise the knowledge that they have shared with you. Every great teacher, or mentor, hopes that the student will far surpass them in skills and ability - and brilliance - so that they too will pass on what they have learnt.

Not sure who to turn to? Get in touch. We offer one-on-one coaching and individual therapy sessions which can help guide you on your own hero's journey if you require the support. You will find our web address and all contact details at the back of this book

*

TIPPING POINT

"The secret of change is to focus all of your energy not on fighting the old, but on building the new."

- Socrates, Greek Philosopher

Alone, one person will not be able to singlehandedly change the world, but with the changes that you begin to implement, you can affect those closest to you. You may inspire others to create some positive changes in their own little worlds, and they may also decide to become Jedi warriors. Many individuals and groups are working in various ways to increase the amount of love, peace and cooperation to create change. Your personal development will not only help you but influence those around you. If that cycle continues, a tipping point will occur so that anger and fear no longer prevail. If that change is powerful enough, it will gather momentum to affect the whole of humanity.

REWIRING OUR HABITS

We are creatures of habit. The problems in life come from our habits. The Force dwells in the Jedi as well as in the Sith. The only difference is how people act. Our actions come from our habits. When we talk about taking on a new practice, it means that we will be taking on a new set of habits that we will repeat over time to yield our new results.

Practices are the "rituals" we perform each day that change our action or behaviour. Often, our routines are so embedded that we are not even aware of how or when we do them. They become actions and behaviours that have become automatic. Examples are brushing our teeth, kissing a loved one, typing at a computer, setting the table, driving a car, walking the dog, reading the newspaper and hundreds of other things we do automatically every day without giving them much thought.

As time passes and changes, so too do our habits. Some are more difficult to crack than others, though. Most of our behaviour is based on the habits we practice on a daily basis. It's easier to follow habit than it is to follow consciously, because habit doesn't require much thought process. It is, therefore, believed that a change in season is the best time to put your energies towards making changes in your habits and moving towards a place of consciousness. As yogis, we use the eyes, tongue and hands to rewire our brains, or Drishti, mantra, and mudras respectively.

UNLEARN WHAT YOU HAVE LEARNT
"You must unlearn what you have learned."
- **Grand Master Yoda, Star Wars: Episode V – The Empire Strikes Back**

The first step to unlearn is to be open to it. As we have seen, much of our knowledge is deeply rooted within ourselves, and it manifests through automatic behaviour. If you want to break this process, you need to be aware in order to identify the old knowledge and assimilate the new one. Let go of old ideas. As we let go of outdated beliefs and ideas, we open our consciousness up to new experiences and new realities. This approach allows us to correct our thinking and behaviour to include a larger perspective. The process allows us to gain strength in our connection to the Force. Let's explore how you can rewire your habits in accordance with the teaching of the 3HO Foundation.

Every single kriya or meditation in Kundalini Yoga changes us in very specific ways. If you practice a kriya a few times, you receive an immediate benefit. But if you want to permanently change your habits and create real change in your life - experiencing the full effects of the kriya - this is what you can do. Yogic philosophy guides us to practice a particular kriya or mantra every single day for the same amount of time. The number of days you do this creates certain neurological and physiological benefits affecting the core of our being.

Here is how it will affect your habits:

40 DAYS: Practice every day for 40 days straight. This will break any negative habits that block you from the expansion possible through the kriya or mantra.

90 DAYS: Practice every day for 90 days straight. This will establish a new habit in your conscious and subconscious minds based on the effect of the kriya or mantra. It will change you in a very profound way.

120 DAYS: Practice every day for 120 days straight. This will confirm the new habit of consciousness created by the kriya or mantra. The positive benefits of the kriya get integrated permanently into your psyche.

1000 DAYS: Practice every day for 1000 days straight. This will allow you to master the new habit of consciousness that the kriya or mantra has promised. No matter what the challenge, you can call on this new habit to serve you.

Remember, a habit is a subconscious chain reaction between the mind, the glandular system and the nervous system. We develop habits at a very young age. Some of them serve our highest Destiny. Some of them do not. By doing a 40-, 90-, 120- or 1000-day special sadhana, you can rewire that chain reaction. You can develop new, deeply ingrained habits that serve your highest good. (116)

*

Timings for meditations and postures should be followed precisely so that you may obtain the full benefit and change effect of the meditation, the following times can be used as guidelines.

EFFECTS OF DIFFERENT LENGTHS OF MEDITATION

- 3 minutes: the blood circulation starts to be affected.
- 11 minutes: The glandular system and nerves start changing.
- 22 minutes: The 3 minds get balanced (positive, neutral, negative)
- 31 minutes: cells and the mind projection are affected
- 62 minutes: The brain's grey matter changes
- 2 1/2 hours: Holds the new pattern in the subconscious mind by the surrounding universal mind.

*

MEDITATION FOR CHANGE

The law of the Universe is "change". Everything changes. However, with every change in our lives, one thing seems not to change: the attachment to our own ego. You change, but your ego does not let you see your own maturity or potential. This creates a condition of constant hassle in the mind. The difference between your reality and your perception of it through the ego creates doubts, and doubts create misery. Doubt steals three feet of your auric radiance. The ego will not let you change easily. It blocks communication. To come out of the darkness, you must assess yourself. A man fortunate enough to have a Guru can evaluate himself. Ultimately, to be happy through all change and to have the full radiance of your soul, there must be a surrender of yourself to your higher self. To aid the process of self-evaluation and to probe the ego to change and unblock subconscious communication, practice this meditation each day.

POSTURE:
Sit with a very straight spine in Easy Pose. Lift the chest.

MUDRA:
Curl the fingers in as if making a fist. Place the fingertips on the pads of the hands, just below the fingers. Then bring the two hands together at the centre of the chest. The hands touch lightly in two places only: the knuckles of the middle (Saturn) fingers and the pads of the

thumbs. The thumbs are extended toward the heart center and are pressed together. Hold this position and feel the energy across the thumbs and knuckles. Between your two thumbs, heat will start passing. You can watch it very peacefully. It is an active meditation.

EYES:
Closed.
BREATH:
Begin Long Deep Breathing. Follow the flow of the breath.
TIME:
Continue for 31 minutes.

TO END:
Inhale deeply, exhale, and relax for 5 minutes. After practicing and mastering this kriya for 31 minutes, you can extend the time to another 31 minutes after the rest period. (117)

***

THE END IS THE BEGINNING

As with all journeys, we have come to the end of ours, but really this is just the beginning of your training. We now have our foundations set. We have some tools and new skills to master. We began by acknowledging the impact that Star Wars has had on our lives and that we are attracted to the myth as well as the story of Star Wars. It calls to the hero that has always existed within ourselves. We have seen how low vibrational states can take us down the path towards the Dark Side and that by raising our vibrational frequency we can overcome fear, anger, and doubt. We can, therefore, develop a stronger connection to the flow of the Force.

Beyond all these small acts of service, the biggest thing that you can do to serve this world is doing the work.

Your work!

Devote yourself to yourself. Take the time to heal your wounds. Dedicate yourself to practice, break down your walls, invite in love, and raise your deserving power. Never take credit for your own light. Instead become so clear that divine light radiates through you. Healing yourself is the first step to healing the world. Self-care, and service to self, is the most incredible service you can do for the world.

I admit that it is difficult to focus on what is right in the world when we are governed by our internal state, which gets the better of us. The media adds to the negativity by reporting awful news to promote fear, and it becomes challenging to break the spell.

I often succumb to these disempowering states, so it would be inauthentic of me to offer advice and claim not to feel this way. Yet, through my own personal experiences, I've come to appreciate that these are fleeting states and I don't remain stuck in this condition for long. Awareness has taught me that what I focus on builds momentum and becomes integrated into my reality. Having a strong sadhana – spiritual practice – as well as choosing and practicing the meditation in this book and adopting the suggested yogic lifestyle will help you to cultivate your own awareness.

WHAT WILL YOU DO ?

This does not need to be some considerable thing like stopping climate change or ending all wars. Although these are worthy missions - and there is no reason you cannot pursue them - maybe you will go demonstrate as a way of effecting change instead. Perhaps you will develop more kindness in your work relationships. Maybe you will decide to take up a martial art. Maybe you will commit to daily meditation practice to strengthen your connection to the Force.

Do you now believe it's possible to be a Jedi in real life?
What mission will you take on?

MAY THE FORCE BE WITH YOU....ALWAYS!
JOIN US

Working together is often easier than working alone. The pandemic has made it more difficult to be together physically but we are still social beings who need connection and community to feel healthy. We have an online group to help you stay connected. I offer online training for our fellow Jedi across the world. Connect with us on Facebook, Instagram, Youtube or Pinterest. Send me an email and let me know how your training is going. Please don't hesitate to send me any questions, or even suggestions, that you may have on the journey.

***

CONCLUSION

For decades, we have been within the throws of the most heightened Kaliyuga. It marks our transition from the Piscean Age – an age of followership, where power and authority have typically been on the outside – to the Aquarian Age – an age of innate leadership, as well as of taking back our power and sovereign identity

One doesn't have to look very far to see that we are coming to the end times, but these end times don't mean the end of the world as can be expected from a religious context. On the contrary, it means the rebirth of a new world. The only thing which is ending is the world as we know it. Politicians begin to show their true nature; bloodthirsty for power and driven by personal greed. Rapists, murderers, and criminals of the lowest calibre run rampant within circles of influence; wielding unfathomable power over those beneath them.

In order for us to make this transition into the new age with as little collateral damage as possible, and with the ideals that this world so desperately needs, we must remove the armour of our defensive conditioning against the pains we have gone through and move into the higher vibrational frequency of the Kundalini Jedi Warrior. Our greatest task will be to reconnect to our essential nature; connecting with a power greater than ourselves and beginning the hero's journey to reclaim our spiritual identity. This armour isn't made from steel, bronze, silver, or gold, but it is made from our inner spiritual power, unsheathed.

We must go within; developing our nervous system, raising our frequency, and adopting the necessary attitudes through a lifestyle shift. This is the only way that we will fight the internal battles that are necessary to prepare for the coming age – and win. We must remove that which is sinister within ourselves. We must tear down the inhibitors which prevent us from experiencing our true souls and unlocking our higher sense of self. We must become one with the ever-powerful Force and tune into this life-giving source.

Once we are able to do that, and to redefine what it means to be a warrior in this age – to redirect anger and brute strength, transforming our fear into something more positive; seeing anger and fear as allies – neither good nor bad – and evolve alongside without being overcome by it, we will be able to declare ourselves as true Kundalini Jedi Warriors.

I trust that you have learned how to tune into the Force, how to centre yourself, and how to heal your chakras. It is my hope that you will have learned how to raise your vibrational frequency and strengthen the Will of the Warrior through the powerful technology of Kundalini Yoga and meditation. Ultimately, you should come away from this with knowledge of how yoga and meditative practices can be used to further tap into your Kundalini source in order to become the most centred and internally powerful warrior that you can be.

These concepts have been explored correlatively through the mythology of the Star Wars movie saga; as it has been the benchmark for my inspiration throughout my life. We see now how the films and their proposition of there being an infinite and indestructible Force that is beyond plain sight can be connected to real life. We have explored its significance in the modern world and how George Lucas banded together generations under the idea of interconnectedness to one another and to a higher power. We have come to understand the principles of good and evil in their representation of what is actually happening right here and now in this precursor to the summation of the Piscean Kaliyuga.

    This training was meant to help you circumnavigate the evils of this world; allowing you to let go of negativity, fear and a pervading feeling of apathy, so that you can begin again in the new dawn, with a new hope for tomorrow. I have faith that this guide has given you the strength to overcome the greater challenges of this current age, but also the seemingly insignificant ones which we have so wrongly come to accept as part of the status quo – the rushing, the stress, the burnout, the lack of connection to our souls, as well as a lack of connection to ourselves and the world around us.

    You are well on your way to becoming a Kundalini Jedi Warrior, so when the burden seems too heavy to bear as you navigate this new path, remember:

    You bought this book for a reason. You were guided by the Force to be here.

    To become a real-life hero; to become a Warrior; to become a Jedi.

    To fulfil your destiny.

***

AFTERWORD

EPILOGUE......BOOK 2: THE DARKSIDE

The room is stifling hot even with the window open. London is oppressive in August and the virus lockdown is adding to the feeling of suffocation in this over-crowded ancient Roman town. I am trying to move the insanity from my mind as I write these words. The centuries of stagnation are apparent and my brain is becoming rigid with disuse.

The story is ancient and still incomplete. I had reached the pinnacle of my life - having a career, a nice car, a house, and money in abundance, but then I threw it all away. Dissatisfied and bitter after so much ambition and gain; there was a darkness that still clawed inside me and ate at me like a wild animal.

My powers were at their peak, as my experience and bank balance grew. My reach was legion, my reputation unparalleled. All my decrees were obeyed, my wishes fulfilled. I became drunk with power as all bowed to my rule.

In London, the grey skies are heavy with rain. My shirt is soaked in the humidity; my lungs burning in the polluted air. My ever-present rage has stunted my creativity. I write these words with a dyslexic brain; frustrated in my capacity to express myself. As I write the chapters of the book, I reflect on my own process. The nights become longer, and what started out as a fun project has led me to dark places within myself.

This shouldn't be taking so long to write. "You're not a writer" the old familiar voice.

The days turned into weeks and the weeks into months. Then there were times of silence. Nothing creative was coming. I sat and stared at the blank screen as I entered a void of unknowing. I began to question my motives. Some days the writing and ideas would come, and I would scramble to write down and remember what I wanted to share. Then the darkness would return.

The inner voices began.

This inner voice ridiculed me and laughed at my efforts. I sat there as these demons would come to sit on my shoulder; whispering and giggling.

"This is the biggest load of shit I've ever seen."
"Other people are so much better than you."
"You know you can't construct a sentence?"

I want to throw this whole thing away. Damn, now I'm complaining and moaning - the exact thing that I've just written not to do if you're going to become a Jedi.

"What about your responsibilities?"
"You realise you're not earning any money sitting here wasting your time as the days of your life slip away?"
"You're dumb and stupid."

Kundalini Jedi Warrior

"What a loser you are."

I feel my stomach contract and the tingling of heat rise up from within me. I feel my face become hot and flushed.

Breathe, don't give in to your anger.

The energy rises, and my thinking mind is flooded with deep rage. I throw all my papers on the floor and proceed to punch and kick the wall as the anger takes over until my hands bleed and bruises appear on my knuckles. The wall took the brunt of it - another hole I will have to repair. I sat slumped with my head down; filled with sadness and shame.

Why am I writing this?
What makes me think I am a great enough Jedi Warrior to teach or lead anyone else?
I hope this book will bring me fame and fortune.
One-day people will recognise my greatness and all will bow down before me.
Finally, my mother will be proud of me.
I will become the best little boy she ever wanted.
I will have the love I always longed for.
I will become the most famous Jedi ever.

Oh dear! I sound like Anakin. Memories of past failures begin to enter my consciousness. All the times I came up short. The failures. The losses. The voices not of past Jedi but teachers and employers wondering if I would ever fulfil my raw potential. So many gifts and talents that have gone unrealised. The room is empty; there is no one here. I need love. I need to be held and told that I'm doing ok and that whatever happens she still loves me. It's okay, just stop thinking - you are loved, and you love yourself, you will be fine.

Will I ???

I slept poorly as I drifted in and out of dreams, consciousness, and sleep. That night I woke up screaming, I must have had a nightmare, but Jedi don't have nightmares. This damm book was stressing me out, not just during the day, but now the night. It was consuming me. I can't think like this. *I'm better than this*. Once again, thoughts of Anakin telling Padme the same thing.

How can I write a book when I feel the pull of the Darkside so deeply? I'm supposed to be leading the fight. I'm a servant of the light side of the Force. I'm supposed to be the teacher.

Early memories once again arose consuming my inner world. All the times that I lied and cheated to get ahead; the years that I stole money; the fights I had been involved in. But it wasn't really bullying, I was just messing about. I felt such shame and dishonour.

Flashbacks once more. I remember being beaten up by a gang of boys because of the colour of my skin. I remember the beating I endured and promising myself that I would not cry; it would not break me. I would not give him the satisfaction. I don't need to worry about all this now. This is all in the past; this is not me anymore. I reflected on the phrase 'I'm a Jedi like my father before me'. It's in my lineage. Once again, anger and rage began to rise. Growing up, my father was my enemy; my arch-rival; my nemesis. He never amounted to anything. He took the path of the Darkside and ended up doing time in prison.

Attempted murder.

Domestic abuse.

Tax fraud.

He was an alcoholic.

This was the legacy he had left me. My blood turned cold, and I froze. I could not move. It hit me. The realisation dawned on me. I could not fight the truth any longer. I was not a Jedi.......I was a fucking Sith lord...

TO BE CONTINUED............

***

AN EXPLORATIVE GUIDE INTO YOUR NEXT MISSION

KUNDALINI JEDI WARRIOR TRAINING MANUAL BOOK 2: THE DARKSIDE

Everyone has a Darkside; a part of themselves that they are not proud of. A part of themselves that they try to hide, and cover-up. We develop well-formed masks. We continue to live whilst we pretend that it doesn't exist.

Star Wars had explored the primordial battle between good and evil through the adventure of the Skywalker family. Spirituality has become polarised with a focus on good, pure righteousness, and all things positive. It has also become a place to bypass our dark and difficult histories; preferring to pretend and hide away in positive affirmations and a belief that an almighty God will take care of us and make all the bad things go away. We continue to project our own inner darkness out onto others and the world around us. We begin to realise that as humans, we have not changed much. We still rape, wage war, and pillage the earth. We always manipulate and distort truths so that we may benefit ourselves. Our hate and frustration become repressed with the only place for this energy to go being deeper within. We begin to hate ourselves. We have become masters of self-sabotage and self-betrayal.

In book 2, we continue our journeys in becoming Jedi warriors. We begin to work with our shadow aspects and reclaim as well as heal the dark energy within us. We explore all the ways in which we avoid our calling to become our greatest expressions. We explore how early life trauma and defensive strategies inhibit us and disconnect us from our connection to the source. We delve into the unconscious mind and eradicate outdated belief systems; replacing them with an updated operating system that will allow our Jedi nature to flourish. We focus on the legacy that we would like to leave behind and we build bridges that we can leave for the coming generations. We explore our relationship patterns and how they inform us of areas that still require healing and development. We enter the cave which we have avoided our whole lives. We meet our dragons and begin the work of Sith hunting. We explore the dark nature of our archetypes. Using Jung's model of the shadow, we will develop ways to transform this into the fabled golden shadow.

Are you ready to enter the Darkside?
Are you prepared to fulfil your Destiny?

***

APPENDIX

THE PRACTICE OF SADHANA

You may have had times when you felt very much in the zone, everything clicked and worked, and you felt at one with the Force. Still, you don't know how it happened and you struggle to get into that space on demand. This daily practice will begin to allow you to have greater mastery over the Force energy so that you can be in the zone more often and create change for the better.

Sadhana means daily spiritual practice. It is the foundation of all spiritual endeavours and a key component in becoming a Kundalini Jedi Warrior. Sadhana is your personal, individual, spiritual effort. It is the primary tool that you use to work on yourself to achieve the purpose of life. Sadhana is whatever you do consistently to clear your consciousness so that you can relate to the Force within you.

Before you face the world each day, you must focus and orientate yourself to the flow of the Force. Setting our intentions for the day based on the guidance from your higher self. Your personal spiritual practice can be for a few minutes or a few hours. Your practice should include some movement and exercise that tune up your nervous system and activate your Kundalini energy. Some form of devotional practice, like a prayer or a conversation with a higher power, is needed. A meditation practice is an essential part of any personal sadhana. If this is your first time developing a practice, start small. Do a few minutes of warm ups as described in the Jedi warm up set. You will find various meditation techniques in the book so you can pick one or try a combination of them. You could also adopt some of the Kundalini Jedi attitude practices and perform them during the day. Your journal practice can also make up part of your daily routine.

AMRIT VELA - FOR HARD CORE WARRIORS

What the ancient yogis called the 'Amrit Vela' - which translated means the "ambrosial hours" - was the optimal time for them to develop their spiritual powers. The two and a half hours just before sunrise, when the sun is at a sixty-degree angle to the Earth, is an energetically powerful time to achieve maximum results. Your world is still asleep. Everything is still and quieter. It's easier to meditate and concentrate before the hustle and bustle of the day begins.

Start your day gently, waking up with a few stretches and pranayama (breathing exercises focused on the flow of the breath). Then bathe, preferably with a cold shower, purifying your body and preparing it for the day ahead. Wear comfortable clothes that were not slept in and cover your head with any natural cloth scarf or head covering.

Below you will find a timetable for early morning practice. It is advisable to do your practice in a sacred physical space. Review the chapter on creating your Jedi Sacred Space in Chapter 9.

3:00 – 3:15 am: Begin wake-up /cold shower and preparation for sadhana.
3:15 4:00 am: SILENT breath meditation
4:00 – 4:20 am: Tune in with the three repetitions of Adi Mantra, Ong Namo Guru Dev Namo.
4:05 – 4:45 am: Kundalini Jedi Yoga Kriya for 25 – 45 minutes.
4:45 – 5:00 am: Deep relaxation.
5:00 – 6:00 am: reading the Jedi code, reflecting on the Jedi teachings
6:00 – 6:15 am: Contemplative Moments/Prayer.
Set intention - Begin your day

If you absolutely cannot get up early in the morning to do sadhana (due to work or family commitments not because you like to lay in), then do it some other time! Doing sadhana at any time of the day or night will benefit you. Develop a regular sadhana and you will take control of your life. Be creative, mix things up. You could add some weights to your practice and include listening to positive affirmations while you train. Commit to meeting your higher-self each morning and your decisions as well as your life will become original. Your life will bear the signature of your soul. Challenge yourself by starting and completing a 40-, 60-, or 90-day practice and experience the joy of victory that comes from discipline and completion. Enjoy and celebrate with a healthy nutritious breakfast to super power your day ahead.

*

CONTINUATION OF YOGIC PHILOSOPHY THE YAMAS AND THE NIYAMAS

Here, we'll focus on the Yamas & Niyamas, the first two practices of Yoga according to Patanjali. Yogis follow a set of ethics and observances outlined in the Yamas and yinamsa. The first two stops on the path, even before the physical postures called asana, are ethical principles that are supposed to guide how we relate to other people and how we take care of ourselves.

The idea of a yoga practice is really not just to focus and be aware and mindful and calm for the time that we're on the mat, but to carry this state of being with us when we leave class, so it can have a much deeper impact than just making us look good. Sure, we might initially come to class for the physical benefits, but the reason so many of us stay is because there's an inkling that there's some other sort of power at work here. Remember that the word 'yoga' means 'unity', 'wholeness' or 'connectedness'; of course it's essential to be mindful, gentle and present in class, but if this doesn't translate off the mat and connect into what we do in our day-to-day lives, we will never feel the real benefits of yoga.

The Yamas and Niyamas are often seen as 'moral codes', or ways of 'right living'. They really form the foundation of our whole practice, and honouring these ethics as we progress along 'the path' means we're always being mindful of each action, and therefore cultivating a more present and aware state of being. It's interesting to note that these five

Yamas and five Niyamas resemble the ten commandments, and the ten virtues of Buddhism, so we're all 'different' yet 'united' at the same time.

The word 'yama' is often translated as 'restraint', 'moral discipline' or 'moral vow', and Patanjali states that these vows are entirely universal, no matter who you are or where you come from, your current situation or where you're heading. To be 'moral' can be difficult at times, which is why this is considered an essential practice of yoga.

The Yamas traditionally guide us towards practices concerned with the world around us, but often we can take them as a guide of how to act towards ourselves too. There are five Yamas in total listed in Patanjali's Sutras:
- Ahimsa (non-harming or non-violence in thought, word and deed);
- Satya (truthfulness);
- Asteya (non-stealing);
- Brahmacharya (celibacy or 'right use of energy'); and,
- Aparigraha (non-greed or non-hoarding).

By considering these aspects in our daily practice on and off the yoga mat, all of our decisions and actions come from a more considered, aware, and 'higher' place, and this leads us towards being more authentic towards ourselves and others. The word 'Niyama' often translates as 'positive duties' or 'observances', and are thought of as recommended habits for healthy living and' spiritual existence'. They're traditionally thought of as practices concerned with ourselves, although of course we can think of them as affecting the outside world too. Patanjali lists a total of five Niyamas, but again there are other traditions and texts that list more:
- Saucha(cleanliness);
- Śantosha(contentment);
- Tapas(discipline, austerity or' burning enthusiasm');
- Svadhyaya(study of the self and of the texts); and,
- Isvara Pranidhana(surrender to a higher being, or contemplation of a higher power).

Iyengar describes both the Yamas and Niyamas as the 'golden keys to unlock the spiritual gates', as they transform each action into one that originates from a deeper and more 'connected' place within ourselves. Whether you consider yourself 'spiritual' or not though, and whether you practice yoga or not, these are all ways in which we can help ourselves and the world around us to be a better place. (158)

If we are to really benefit from a yoga practice, it has to expand beyond the mat and into life. When this happens, it's not just our bodies that get stretched, expanded and strengthened, but our minds and hearts as well. From that state of being, we move ever closer towards wholeness, connectedness and unity, and start to not just 'do' yoga, but live and breathe it in each and every moment. These principles are very important foundation steps for the aspiring warrior yogi. Let us review them here and look at how they relate to the Jedi code.

*

THE CHAKRAS

What are Chakras? The word "chakra" literally means spinning wheel. Yoga maintains that the chakras are centre points of energy, thoughts or feelings in the physical body. According to yogic teachers, chakras determine the way people experience reality through emotional reactions, desires or aversions, levels of confidence or fear, and even physical symptoms and effects.

When energy becomes blocked in a chakra, it is said to trigger physical, mental, or emotional imbalances that manifest in symptoms, such as anxiety, lethargy, or poor digestion. People can practice yoga asanas to free energy and stimulate an imbalanced chakra. (Asanas are the many physical positions in Hatha yoga.) There are seven major chakras, each with their own focus:

CROWN CHAKRA: The "thousand-petaled" or "crown" chakra represents the state of pure consciousness. This chakra is located at the crown of the head, and the colour white or violet represents it. Sahasrara involves matters of inner wisdom and physical death.

THIRD EYE: The "command" or "third-eye chakra" is a meeting point between two important energetic streams in the body. Ajna corresponds to the colours violet, indigo, or deep blue, though traditional yoga practitioners describe it as white. The ajna chakra relates to the pituitary gland, which drives growth and development.

THROAT: The color red or blue represents the "especially pure" or "throat" chakra. Practitioners consider this chakra to be the home of speech, hearing, and metabolism.

HEART: The "unstruck" or "heart" chakra relates to the colors green and pink. Key issues involving anahata include complex emotions, compassion, tenderness, unconditional love, equilibrium, rejection, and wellbeing.

SOLOR PLEXUS: Yellow represents the "jewel city" or "navel" chakra. Practitioners connect this chakra with the digestive system, as well as personal power, fear, anxiety, developing opinions, and tendencies towards an introverted personality.

SACRAL: Practitioners claim that the "one's own base" or "pelvic" chakra is the home of the reproductive organs, the genitourinary system, and the adrenal gland.

ROOT: The "root support" or "root chakra" is at the base of the spine in the coccygeal region. It is said to contain our natural urges relating to food, sleep, sex, and survival, as well as the source of avoidance and fear. (159)

*

THE 12 ARCHETYPES BY CARL GOLDEN.
1. THE INNOCENT
Motto: Free to be you and me Core desire: to get to paradise Goal: to be happy Greatest fear: to be punished for doing something bad or wrong Strategy: to do things right Weakness: boring for all their naive innocence Talent: faith and optimism Also known as the: utopian, traditionalist, naive, mystic, saint, romantic, dreamer.

2. THE ORPHAN/REGULAR GUY OR GAL
Motto: All men and women are created equal Core Desire: connecting with others Goal: to belong Greatest fear: to be left out or to stand out from the crowd Strategy: develop ordinary solid virtues, be down to Earth, the common touch Weakness: losing one's own self in an effort to blend in or for the sake of superficial relationships Talent: realism, empathy, lack of pretense Also known as the: good old boy, everyman, the person next door, the realist, the working stiff, the solid citizen, the good neighbour, the silent majority.

3. THE HERO
Motto: Where there's a will, there's a way Core desire: to prove one's worth through courageous acts Goal: expert mastery in a way that improves the world Greatest fear: weakness, vulnerability, being a "chicken" Strategy: to be as strong and competent as possible Weakness: arrogance, always needing another battle to fight Talent: competence and courage Also known as the: warrior, crusader, rescuer, superhero, the soldier, dragon slayer, the winner and the team player.

4. THE CAREGIVER
Motto: Love your neighbour as yourself Core desire: to protect and care for others Goal: to help others Greatest fear: selfishness and ingratitude Strategy: doing things for others Weakness: martyrdom and being exploited Talent: compassion, generosity Also known as the: saint, altruist, parent, helper, supporter.

5. THE EXPLORER
Motto: Don't fence me in Core desire: the freedom to find out who you are through exploring the world Goal: to experience a better, more authentic, more fulfilling life Biggest fear: getting trapped, conformity, and inner emptiness Strategy: journey, seeking out and experiencing new things, escape from boredom Weakness: aimless wandering, becoming a misfit Talent: autonomy, ambition, being true to one's soul Also known as the: seeker, iconoclast, wanderer, individualist, pilgrim.

6. THE REBEL
Motto: Rules are made to be broken Core desire: revenge or revolution Goal: to overturn what isn't working Greatest fear: to be powerless or ineffectual Strategy: disrupt, destroy, or shock Weakness: crossing over to the dark side, crime Talent: outrageousness, radical freedom Also known as the: revolutionary, wild man, the misfit, or iconoclast.

7. THE LOVER
Motto: You're the only one. Core desire: intimacy and experience Goal: being in a relationship with the people, work and surroundings they love Greatest fear: being alone, a wallflower, unwanted, unloved Strategy: to become more and more physically and emotionally attractive Weakness: outward-directed desire to please others at risk of losing own identity Talent: passion, gratitude, appreciation, and commitment Also known as the: partner, friend, intimate, enthusiast, sensualist, spouse, team-builder.

8. THE CREATOR
Motto: If you can imagine it, it can be done Core desire: to create things of enduring value Goal: to realise a vision Greatest fear: mediocre vision or execution Strategy: develop artistic control and skill Task: to create culture, express own vision Weakness: perfectionism, bad solutions Talent: creativity and imagination Also known as the: artist, inventor, innovator, musician, writer or dreamer.

9. THE JESTER
Motto: You only live once Core desire: to live in the moment with full enjoyment Goal: to have a great time and lighten up the world Greatest fear: being bored or boring others Strategy: play, make jokes, be funny Weakness: frivolity, wasting time Talent: joy Also known as the: fool, trickster, joker, practical joker or comedian.

10. THE SAGE
Motto: The truth will set you free Core desire: to find the truth. Goal: to use intelligence and analysis to understand the world. Biggest fear: being duped, misled—or ignorance. Strategy: seeking out information and knowledge; self-reflection and understanding thought processes. Weakness: can study details forever and never act. Talent: wisdom, intelligence. Also known as the: expert, scholar, detective, advisor, thinker, philosopher, academic, researcher, thinker, planner, professional, mentor, teacher, contemplative.

11. THE MAGICIAN
Motto: I make things happen. Core desire: understanding the fundamental laws of the universe Goal: to make dreams come true Greatest fear: unintended negative consequences Strategy: develop a vision and live by its Weakness: becoming manipulative Talent: finding win-win solutions Also known as the: visionary, catalyst, inventor, charismatic leader, shaman, healer, medicine man. Qui-Gon Jinn.

12. THE RULER
Motto: Power isn't everything, it's the only thing. Core desire: control Goal: create a prosperous, successful family or community Strategy: exercise power Greatest fear: chaos, being overthrown Weakness: being authoritarian, unable to delegate Talent: responsibility, leadership Also known as the: boss, leader, aristocrat, king, queen, politician, role model, manager or administrator. Chancellor Palpatine. Darth Vader. (160)

ADDITIONAL ARCHETYPES
13. THE VILLIAN
Darth Vader.

14. THRESHOLD GURADIANS
Stormtroopers

There are as many archetypes as there are characters in the Star Wars universe. Can you think of any other Star Wars characters that match with an archetype? You may also find many characters exhibiting various archetypal patterns

- The Hero: Luke Skywalker & Perseus. ...
- The Evil Adversary: Emperor & Laocoön. ...
- The Anti-hero: Han Solo & Samson. ...
- The Damsel in Distress: Princess Leia & Guinevere. ...
- The Mentor: Obi-Wan & Chiron. ...
- The Friendly Beast: Chewbacca & Argos. ...
- The Loyal Retainers: C3PO, R2D2 & Patroclos. ...
- The Threshold Guardian: Jabba the Hutt & Cerberus.

*

STAR WARS SAGA OVERVIEW
PHANTOM MENACE

The overarching story of the Star Wars film franchise begins with The Phantom Menace: under the secret instruction of Darth Sidious (soon to also be Supreme Chancellor Palpatine of the Galactic Republic), the Trade Federation deploys a blockade around the peaceful world of Naboo, setting in motion a series of events that sees Qui-Gon Jinn and Obi-Wan Kenobi escaping the planet with Queen Amidala and landing on Tatooine in search of spaceship parts. Here they meet a fatherless young slave named Anakin Skywalker, who helps the Jedi earn the money they need to fix their ship by winning an epic pod race. Qui-Gon barters for the freedom of Anakin, whose off-the-charts Midi-chlorian count could signal that Anakin is a prophesied Chosen One that will bring balance to the Force. Qui-Gon intends to train Anakin in the ways of the Jedi, but the job ends up falling to Obi-Wan after Qui-Qon is killed in combat with Sidious' apprentice, Darth Maul. There is also a space battle that Anakin plays a part in, and a land battle that Gungan comedic foil Jar Jar Binks somehow survives.

STAR WARS EPISODE II: ATTACK OF THE CLONES

Ten years later, Anakin and Obi-Wan are dispatched to aid Padme Amidala again, after an attempt is made on the queen-turned-senator's life. Anakin escorts Padme to Naboo, where the pair discover their forbidden love for one another, while Obi-Wan investigates Padme's would-be assassin and uncovers an enormous conspiracy – an army for the Republic has been created in secret, with cloners from Kamino basing a huge number of Clone Troopers on the genetic blueprint of a bounty hunter named Jango Fett, the father of Boba Fett. Obi-Wan battles Jango Fett, continues following leads, and eventually gets captured by Count Dooku, who is organizing a Separatist movement to go to war with the Republic. After taking a detour to Tatooine to discover that his mother has been killed (and promptly taking murderous revenge on a community of Sandpeople), Anakin travels with Padme to rescue Obi-Wan on the planet Geonosis, where Darth Sidious is secretly building the Death Star.

The rescue goes terribly, as Anakin and Padme are also captured, but Yoda and Mace Windu arrive with the Clone Army to save our heroes from the clutches of the Separatist's droid army. During the first battle of what will become the Clone Wars, Windu beheads Jango and Anakin gets a hand chopped off in a duel with Count Dooku. He gets a robot replacement fitted in time to secretly marry Padme.

STAR WARS EPISODE III: REVENGE OF THE SITH

Three years later, after the events of The Clone Wars TV series, Anakin and Obi-Wan rescue Supreme Chancellor Palpatine from a Separatist battleship during a battle over Republic capital city-planet Coruscant. Egged on by Palpatine, Anakin chops off Count Dooku's head. Upon his return to Coruscant, Anakin learns that Padme is pregnant and he begins to have visions of her dying in childbirth. Obi-Wan heads off on a mission to defeat General Grievous, the only Separatist general left, while Palpatine makes his move to solidify his power and turn Anakin to the dark side. Revealing his true nature as a Sith Lord, Palpatine tempts Anakin with the power to save Padme from death. Anakin gives Darth Sidious up to Mace Windu, but when it comes down to it, he stops Windu from killing Palpatine, saving the Dark Lord of the Sith. Palpatine uses his Force lightning to launch Windu out of a window to his death. Anakin agrees to become Palpatine's apprentice, earning the cool Sith name Darth Vader.

Palpatine executes Order 66, which forces the Clone Troopers to turn on the Jedi and kill them. Anakin, along with a platoon of Clone Troopers, invade the Jedi Temple and slaughter all the Jedi inside, even the younglings. Meanwhile, the attack on Palpatine has gained him more power through fear, and he anoints himself the first Emperor of the new Galactic Empire.

Yoda takes the fight to Palpatine on the Senate floor, while Obi-Wan travels to the volcano planet of Mustafar to try and sort Anakin out, but the good guys fail in both cases. Before the climactic duel between master and former apprentice, Padme tries to convince Anakin to give up his reign of terror but he Force chokes her. Obi-Wan defeats Anakin in a duel, amputating most of his limbs with one swing of his lightsaber, and the young Sith apprentice begins to burn in lava. But the Emperor is able to retrieve Vader's body before it's too late.

Having lost the will to live, Padme dies giving birth to twins – Luke and Leia. Vader, meanwhile, is told by Palpatine that he killed Padme in a rage. Palpatine, having fully turned Vader to his side, begins working on the Death Star and building up his Empire. To keep the Skywalker babies off the radar, baby Leia is sent to live with Senator Bail Organa on Alderaan while Luke is sent to the Lars homestead on Tatooine.

STAR WARS EPISODE IV: A NEW HOPE

Mere moments after Rogue One's dramatic ending, Leia puts the Death Star's plans in R2-D2 and sends the little droid off with C-3PO in an escape pod to Tatooine. The droids are instructed to take a message to Obi-Wan Kenobi, but they end up getting captured by Jawas and purchased by Owen Lars, Luke Skywalker's uncle. When Artoo escapes to complete his mission, Luke is forced to go after him, only to get caught by those pesky Sandpeople. Fortunately, Luke and his droids are saved by old Ben Kenobi, a hermit who lives out in the desert. Obi-Wan, deciding it's time to tell Luke the truth about his father, gifts the young farmer Anakin's lightsaber. Meanwhile, Uncle Owen and Aunt Beru are killed by Stormtroopers, so Luke joins Obi-Wan in his quest to bring the Death Star plans to Alderaan on Leia's instruction. They meet Han and Chewie in a Mos Eisley local cantina, but by the time they reach Alderaan, Leia's home world has been blown up by the Death Star.

The gang have no choice but to infiltrate the deadly space station, with Obi-Wan having one final rematch with Vader while everyone else rescues Leia and makes off in the Millennium Falcon. Obi-Wan is killed but continues to offer advice to Luke through the magic of the Force, even prompting him to turn off his targeting computer in the film's final action scene, a last-ditch Rebel attack on the Death Star, which enables Luke to blow up the superweapon and put a major thorn in the Emperor's side. Everyone gets a medal except Chewie. (It's revealed in a later Marvel comic that Chewie did get a medal off-screen.)

STAR WARS EPISODE V: THE EMPIRE STRIKES BACK

Three years later, Luke and the gang are hiding out in a Rebel base on Hoth, which is promptly attacked by loads of Imperial forces. Before the battle, Luke receives a ghostly message from Obi-Wan, who tells him to seek out Yoda on the planet Dagobah. Once all the Rebels escape the Imperial invasion, Luke does just that, receiving some Jedi training from the Jedi Master and having a spooky encounter with a vision of Vader in a Force cave.

Meanwhile, Han and Leia, trying to evade the Imperial forces in pursuit of the Millennium Falcon, head to Cloud City in the hope that Lando will give them some assistance. Unfortunately, The Empire got to Cloud City first, and the gang are captured by Vader and his forces. Han is frozen in carbonite and taken to his former employer Jabba the Hutt by Boba Fett because there was a big bounty on his head.

Luke skips out on Yoda to save his friends, leading to a showdown in Cloud City where Vader chops off Luke's arm and reveals that he's his dad. There's a resounding sense that the baddies have won this round, with Luke and Leia looking out glumly at the galaxy just before the credits roll

STAR WARS EPISODE VI: RETURN OF THE JEDI

Just a year after the events on Cloud City, Luke, Leia, Lando, and Chewie stage an elaborate plan to save Han from Jabba's palace, which ends with Boba Fett being eaten by the Sarlacc pit and Jabba being choked to death. Luke then returns to Dagobah, where he witnesses Yoda's death and learns that Leia is his sister. The Rebels discover that a new Death Star is under construction, so they head to the forest moon of Endor to switch off its shield generator. They team up with some native Ewoks in a skirmish with Imperial forces. The film ramps up to a third-act confrontation on the Death Star between Luke, Vader, and the Emperor, which ends with Anakin turning back to the light and chucking Palpatine into the space station's core. Before dying, Vader takes off his helmet to look at his son's face with his own eyes. With the shield generator switched off, the Rebel fleet blows up the second Death Star and the Emperor is defeated. A party is thrown around the campfires of Endor, and even the ghost of Anakin turns up (although the actor will vary depending on which version you're watching).

STAR WARS EPISODE VII: THE FORCE AWAKENS

Thirty years after the fall of the Empire at Endor, Han and Leia's Force-sensitive son, Ben Solo, has turned to the dark side under the tutelage of a new big bad named Supreme Leader Snoke. Ben becomes Kylo Ren and Snoke's revamped version of the Empire returns as the First Order. At the start of the movie the First Order already boasts a lot of firepower as well as a massive new Death Star equivalent called Starkiller Base. The First Order pretty much solidifies its power by the second act when it uses Starkiller Base to blow up the Hosnian system, taking out the capital of the New Republic in the process.

A Force-sensitive scavenger named Rey joins forces with a runaway Stormtrooper named Finn on the desert planet Jakku before bumping into Han Solo and making her way to meet Leia and join up with the Resistance in their fight against the First Order. Ultimately, Rey duels Kylo while Finn and Han infiltrate Starkiller Base to lower its shields, giving dashing pilot Poe Dameron a chance to blow up the superweapon. At the very end of the film, Rey follows a space map — the movie's McGuffin — which leads her to Ahch-To, the remote hideaway of exiled Jedi Master Luke Skywalker.

STAR WARS EPISODE VIII: THE LAST JEDI

Picking up seconds later, The Last Jedi opens with Luke receiving his lightsaber from Rey and chucking it off the edge of a cliff. Reluctantly, Luke eventually agrees to train Rey and reveals what led him into hiding – years ago, Luke sensed the pull of the dark side within Ben and felt the urge to kill his troubled nephew in his sleep. But Ben woke up and slaughtered his fellow students and burned down Luke's temple in retaliation. We also see

Kylo communicating with Rey through the Force, with Snoke encouraging this connection. At one point, Kylo is caught with his top off Meanwhile, First Order Star Destroyers are hot on the heels of the Resistance fleet. Poe and Leia have a falling out, and it is ultimately Admiral Holdo who saves the Resistance by sacrificing herself so the other can escape to the nearby planet Crait, the location of an old Rebel stronghold. During this time, Finn and Resistance engineer Rose Tico are dispatched to Canto Bight on a mission to find a tech whiz who can deactivate a tracking device, which would allow
the Resistance to jump to hyperspace without fear of being followed. They find a chap named DJ, who betrays them later on Snoke's capital ship.

The narrative strands then start coming together. There is a brief team-up between Rey and Kylo, with the latter killing Snoke before claiming control of the First Order. Eventually, a visit from Yoda's ghost spurs a reluctant Luke into action. The resurgent Jedi Master projects himself across the galaxy to confront Kylo during a battle on Crait, which buys the remaining Resistance fighters enough time to escape on the Millennium Falcon. This use of the Force drains Luke's life energy, though, killing him. Our last look at Luke is him disappearing and becoming a Force ghost as Ben and Yoda once did.

STAR WARS: EPISODE IX – THE RISE OF SKYWALKER

The Rise of Skywalker begins one year after the Battle of Crait. Kylo Ren (Adam Driver) has discovered a Sith way finder device, and uses it to head over to the planet Exegol, a secret Sith planet. Once there, he discovers Emperor Palpatine (Ian McDiarmid) still alive, and still in control of everything, but he's now physically a shell of his former self.

Palpatine reveals he created Snoke as a diversionary tactic, and to also lure Kylo to the dark side. During his time away from the limelight, Palpatine secretly built another armada of Star Destroyers. Now that everything is proceeding as he's foreseen, he orders Kylo to track down Rey (Daisy Ridley)—who's off completing her Jedi training with Kylo's mom, General Leia Organa (Carrie Fisher)—and kill her.

Meanwhile, Finn (John Boyega), Poe Dameron (Oscar Isaac), and Chewbacca (Joonas Suotamo) have learned all about Kylo's discovery from information given to them from an unknown First Order spy. Once Rey discovers Palpatine's alive, she finds Luke Skywalker (Mark Hamill)'s notes on the Sith artifact he left in the Jedi texts, including where Luke's trail went cold on the planet Passanna. Rey, Finn, Poe, Chewbacca, BB-8, and C-3PO (Anthony Daniels) head out to Passsanna to see if they can succeed where Luke failed. R2-D2 stays behind with Leia who's becoming more and more frail.

Once on Passanna, the group meets Lando Calrissian (Billy Dee Williams). Lando tells them that Leia asked for him to help them since he also helped Luke years before in the search. He informs the younger group where he and Luke's search left off years before. Unfortunately, Kylo uses his Force bond with Rey to find her location, and heads to Passanna with his Knights of Ren in tow.

By now, Rey and the others have found the remains of a Sith assassin at his ship. When Rey spots a dagger inscribed with Sith text, she asks C-3PO to translate it, but his programming forbids him from doing so.

As Kylo arrives on the planet, Rey senses his presence, and she heads out to confront him. While this takes place, the First Order captures Chewbacca, who has the dagger, and seizes the Millennium Falcon. Rey attempts to save Chewie, but her Force lightening accidentally destroys a First Order transport. As she and the rest of the group escape on the assassin's ship, they assume Chewbacca died in the transport's explosion.

With Chewie and the dagger gone, Poe suggests they head to Kijimi where they can extract the Sith text from C-3PO's memory. However, to retrieve the information from C-3PO, they have to do a factory reset and wipe the droid's memory. Reluctantly, C-3PO agrees. Meanwhile, the First Order arrives on Kijimi looking for the star warriors. Rey senses that Chewbacca is still alive and is being held on Kylo's Star Destroyer in orbit, and the group goes to rescue him.

Kylo is still out looking for Rey as she and the others get the help of Poe's old friend, Zorii Bliss (Keri Russell), to sneak into his Star Destroyer. Using their Force bond, Kylo tells Rey that Palpatine is her grandfather, and he ordered her killed as a child from the fear of her power. The Dark side is strong with Rey. Once Rey recovers the dagger, she has visions of the assassin using it to kill her parents. Soon General Hux (Domhnall Gleeson) discovers the group onboard, and he reveals himself to be the unknown First Order spy. When he allows them to escape on the Falcon, the First Order realises he's the traitor, and they quickly execute him for treason. The Star Destroyer then destroys Kijimi using a Death Star type cannon.

Now, the group follows coordinates to Endor in hopes of finding a way finder device that will reveal a way to travel safely to Palpatine's location. There, they encounter a woman named Jannah (Naomi Ackie), a former stormtrooper like Finn, who promises to help the group to
remains of the second Death Star out in the stormy ocean. Unwilling to wait, Rey goes it alone and travels to the Death Star remains. Once she possesses the way finder, Rey has a vision of herself as a Sith lord, and begins to understand her potential destiny. Once again, Kylo tracks the group to Endor, and destroys the way finder before dueling Rey. Back home, a dying Leia calls out to Kylo through the Force—distracting him during a crucial moment in his battle with Rey which enables Rey to impale Kylo with his own lightsaber.

Sensing Leia's death, Rey heals Kylo to save him. She tells Kylo that she wanted to take his hand and join him during the events of The Last Jedi, but with Ben's hand, and not Kylo's. Only now does she begin to come to terms with her Sith heritage, and she takes Kylo's ship to exile herself on Ahch-To. Rey must confront her destiny. However, Luke's Force spirit appears to her, and encourages her to confront Palpatine as he did with Darth Vader. He gives her Leia's lightsaber and his old X-wing to assist her. Rey leaves for Exegol, using the way finder from the remains of Kylo's ship.

As this goes on, Kylo has a force vision of his own of his father Han Solo (Harrison Ford). After a brief conversation, Kylo throws down his lightsaber, and embraces the light side of the Force once again as Ben Solo. The final battle begins

Once Rey arrives on Exegol, she transmits her location to the Resistance, and then heads over to confront Palpatine. Palpatine demands she strike him down so his spirit can transfer to hers.

The Resistance arrives to battle Palpatine's secret armada. Ben's there, and he takes out the Knights of Ren before helping Rey. Palpatine takes this opportunity to absorb Rey and Ben's life essence—thus rejuvenating himself.

He then uses Force lightening to attack the Resistance fleet. When it looks as if Rey's about to lose all hope, she hears the voices of past Jedi lending her their strength. Suddenly, Palpatine

attacks her with lightning, but she deflects it using the two lightsabers—killing him dead. Rey too dies from the attack, but Ben uses the Force to sacrifice himself to bring her back to life. The couple kiss just as Ben becomes one with the Force.

In the sky above, Lando leads the Resistance with some newly arrived reinforcements. Together, they destroy the remainder of Palpatine's armada.

With victory in hand, the galaxy once again celebrates. Rey visits the Lars homestead on Tatooine to bury the two Skywalker lightsabers now that she's built one of her own. As Luke and Leia's Force ghosts look on, a local shows up. When he asks her name, she replies, "Rey Skywalker," taking the name of her surrogate parents

*

THE JEDI DIET

Yogis separated food types into 3 broad categories each of which have a different energy signature and effect on the body You are what you eat. If you are free to live a quiet, contemplative life, a sattvic diet is perfect. For those who wish to maintain a meditative mind but also must live and work in the world, a diet consisting of sattvic and some rajasic foods is best.

SATTVIC:

- Clarity and lightness, purity, whiteness, clean
- Graceful, peaceful, disciplined, intuitive, sensitive.
- Most fruit and vegetables, sun foods, and ground foods. RAJASIC: Forcefulness and will-power,

FIRE, RED:

- Active, positive, demanding.
- Stimulating herbs and spices, many earth foods.

TAMASIC:
- Functioning from need and instinct
- Impulsive, dull, angry, confused.
- Meat, fish, poultry, eggs, alcohol, intoxicating drugs.

As a general observation, we generally gulp our food. It is totally unconscious and mostly just a habitual way of consuming certain food types and the time and ways we eat. We break up the food with the teeth and swallow. The problem is that digestion begins in the mouth. Your saliva breaks down starch into simple sugar. Poison becomes nectar by simply eating small bites, chewing consciously, mixing your saliva and tasting the sweetness.

"Slow eating is one of the best meditations on this Earth." Finally, he says, "Your life will be long and your power will be great if you taste every morsel of the food you eat."
—**Yogi Bhajan**

We suggest a vegetarian or plant-based diet as this allows a much easier flow of energy to be available to the body and senses. Also important is recognizing the needs of your own body and tuning into this subtle inner communication, certain times certain foods are more beneficial and at other times other types of food work better for our system. This is not about having some rigid or fixed way of eating but to development refinement for yourself and your system.

For those who practice demanding disciplines, like Kundalini Yoga or marital arts, rajasic foods are necessary, along with sattvic foods. For all these lifestyles, tamasic food is best avoided.

When adopting a new diet we begin an inner change energetically and biologically, we may notice differences in our body shape or size, we may lose weight but mostly it will make you more aware of yourself and the patterns and habits of your mind . For me, the most important result of this diet was that it opened my eyes to the joy of eating lightly and consciously. It is said to cleanse the system and revitalize the body. The first few days you may feel weak, but then gradually your strength will increase and you will start to feel light and happy. The best season for this diet is the warmer months of spring, summer and fall when fresh fruits and vegetables are readily available.

The diet will effect on in many ways:
- **Physical:** Cleansing, weight loss, clearing mucus
- **Mental:** Break negative food habits, be happy
- **Spiritual:** Transition to a more energetic and higher frequency vibration; to become more in harmony with your body and with your world.

DURATION
If thirty days sounds like too much, try two weeks. It may give you confidence that you can continue it for the full time. Once you start the diet, there may be a short period when you feel weak or low energy. This is to be expected, especially if you are coming off

a diet high in processed foods or animal products. Keep up. Allow your body to adjust to a higher frequency of energy. You will never want to go back to your old habits.

AVOID

Meat, fish, fowl, eggs, alcoholic beverages, drugs of any kind (including caffeine), dairy, grains, legumes, packaged foods, canned foods, concentrated sugars, including honey, roasted nuts, nut butter and fried foods.

EAT

Lots of salads—fresh lettuce and other greens and sprouts dressed lightly with cold-pressed oil and natural vinegar or lemon juice, with optional additions of:

- Alfalfa sprouts;
- Mung bean sprouts;
- Fresh raw vegetables;
- Avocados;
- Raw sunflower seeds;
- Sesame seeds;
- Steamed vegetables garnished with a little olive oil, a touch of sea salt and black or red pepper;
- Raw almonds soaked and peeled;
- Baked squash;
- Potatoes—yes, they are vegetables too, and very alkalizing to your system. Prepare them Punjabi style with peas and onions, with fresh cauliflower, or baked, and served with a little olive oil and soy sauce;
- Fresh fruit anytime;
- Fruit and vegetable smoothies—add a little fruit juice for sweetness;
- Herbal teas; and,
- Yogi Tea with almond milk and a little honey/

*

JEDI PRAYERS

FIND PRAYERS AT TEMPLE OF JEDI ORDER.COM

TO RESPOND TO THE CALL OF A JEDI (ONESELF OR OTHERS)

Feel the force within you, connect to its flow and shower yourself or those you bless with it.
This world is a dangerous place,
full of danger to the body, mind and soul
many seek greed, selfishness, criminality and power
they take them from others,
There are those who will fight these powerful forces

Kundalini Jedi Warrior

They are known as Jedi
armed with a strength of character, an unyielding will,
and most of all The Force,
They use the force to help those less fortunate,
To you do rise to this call,
May the Force Be with you always,
Strengthening your will, your faith and your devotion to good,
Accept this blessing and go forth knowing the Force goes with you.

PERSONAL PRAYER TO THE FORCE

My friend, my partner, the force,
I pray for strength, for there are days when I must bear the weight of the world,
I pray for wisdom, to guide my actions
I ask you to be within me always, for without the connections you bring I could not serve,
I serve life, because from life springs joy,
Where there is darkness, I will bring light,
Where there is indignity, I will bring honor,
Where there is death, I will bring preservation of life,
I seek these things in life around me,
I therefore ask them for myself as well,
So that I may be an example of duty, honor, valor, friendship to all,
allow me this confidence, I pray, so I may be better than I am today.

LUMINOUS BEINGS ARE WE

Luminous Beings are we
We Answer our call
The call of the Force
We answer our call
Without hesitation
We answer our call
While others decry us
As Freaks, weirdos or Witches
Yet we persist
For we have heard our call
& we have answered it
The call of the Force
We suffer the temptations of this Crude Matter
We suffer through bouts of Anger
We suffer through bouts of Depression
At times we feel alone
But we are never truly alone

For the Force is always with us
& it is now I say
Luminous Beings are We
May the Force be with you

(Jedi Arion Bane 28 FEB 2005. From the Jedi Sanctuary)

***

GLOSSARY

TERM	CONTEXT
1. Breath of Fire	Rapid, rhythmic, and continuous. It is equal on the inhale and the exhale, with no pause between them (approximately 2-3 cycles per second). It is always practiced through the nostrils with the mouth closed, unless stated otherwise. Breath of Fire is powered from the navel point and solar plexus. (161)
2. Cannon Breath	Cleanses and strengthens the parasympathetic nerves, and adjusts the digestion. Cannon Breath is Breath of Fire done through the mouth. Often Yogi Bhajan would call for a powerful Cannon Breath exhale to end an exercise. (162)
3. Segmented Breaths	With segmented breathing, we divide the inhalation and exhalation into several equal parts, with a slight suspension of the breath separating each part, and with a distinct beginning and end point to each segment. This stimulates the central brain and the glandular system in different ways. (163)
4. Lion Breath	Lion Breath is a powerful breath in the upper chest and throat. It cleanses out toxins, and is good for the throat chakra, and the thyroid. (164)

5.	Whistle Breath	Whistle Breath changes the circulation. The nerves in the tongue activate the higher glands such as the thyroid and parathyroid, and the lung capacity is increased. (165)
6.	Sitali Pranayam	Has a powerful cooling, relaxing effect on the body, while maintaining alertness. It is known to lower fevers, and aid digestion. (166)
7.	Vatskar Pranayam	With the Vatskar breath we sip in the air. We do not take air down as if into the stomach. Just bring it into the lungs. (167)

JAG KALEY'S BIO

If you have read the book in its entirety, you may very well no know that Jag experienced a Kundalini awakening in 2003, which changed his life journey forever. Leaving the life he knew behind to follow the call of his soul, and travelling to North America, he discovered Kundalini yoga and completed his Kundalini teacher training in the summer of 2006.

Jag is the owner and founder of the London Kundalini Centre, a Kundalini emergency and spiritual crisis Centre offering guidance and support for people experiencing Kundalini awakenings. He is creator of the Kundalini Jedi Warrior Training Academy; helping people connect to the power of the Force within them so that they may fulfil their potential. His goal is to help humanity bring in the golden Age of Aquarius.

He works as a Transpersonal Integrative Psychotherapist offering talk therapies and spiritual counselling to those on a spiritual journey of self-discovery and transformation. He is a Level 1 and Level 2 Kundalini Yoga Instructor; also having served as Director for the Great British Kundalini Yoga Festival. He is currently a trustee for the Guru Ram Das Project, a well-known yoga charity in the UK.

He is a psycho-spiritual counselor, teacher, mentor, therapist, and sound healer, who also holds a 1st Degree Blackbelt in the martial art of Taekwondo. After teaching in several countries around the globe, he has set his hopes on training a new generation of Jedi.

A lover of movies and American superhero comics, Jag has used this inspiration to touch the lives of others; providing yoga to groups within the mental health wings of the Lambeth Hospital; now operated by the South London and Maudsley NHS Foundation Trust.

***

CONTACT

I hope you have enjoyed this journey and we hope you will stay in touch with us through our website and various social media channels :
Messages and requests can be sent to
EMAIL: INFO@KUNDALINIJEDIWARRIOR.COM

For the latest news, blogs and updates on upcoming retreats and workshops please subscribe to our newsletter at our website
Website: WWW.KUNDALINIJEDITRAINING.COM

SOCIAL MEDIA :

: kundalinijediwarrior

: jag_jedi_kaley_

: KundaliniJedi

: Kundalini Jedi Warrior

: Jag Jedi Kaley

Our Youtube channel has a selection of relaxing jedi music and videos walking you through the meditations and exercises in this book.
SPIRITUAL AWAKENING :If you are experiencing a spiritual awakening or a kundalini emergency please visit our sister site London Kundalini Centre.com for guidance help and support.

LONDON KUNDALINI CENTRE
yoga • therapy • wellbeing

JEDI APPAREL :Are you looking for a new jedi robe outfit or a lightsaber for your hero's journey ,contact our friends at jedi-robe for all you jedi materials and equipment needs, you can contact via their website at jedi robe.com

INDEX

A

Abdominal Breath, 191
Adi Mantra, 142, 144, 322, 324
aggressive feelings, 214
Agni Tattva, 197, 235
Alcibiades, 115
Alderaan, 74–75, 230
Allah, 117
altruism, 112, 130, 160, 299–300, 329
Anakin, 135, 138, 181, 183, 187, 214–16, 230–31, 292, 294–95, 318, 326, 330, 333
Anakin's journey, 125
anger, 34–36, 44–45, 137–38, 214–16, 219, 221, 233–37, 240, 297, 302, 328–29, 338, 342
anxiety, 35–36, 53–54, 189, 194, 222, 226, 228, 275, 277, 297, 300, 313–14, 319
archetypal, 106–7, 111–12, 217
Arjuna, 125–26
Armit Vela, 248
Athenian warrior, 115
Attention Deficit Hyperactivity Disorder (ADHD), 108

B

Bart, 94, 102–3
Baylor University Medical Center, 35
Beowulf, 72
Bhagavad Gita, 125, 146
bija mantra, 142
Bikram Yoga, 168
Blissful vibration, 167
Boba Fett, 230
Brahma, 154, 187
Breath Awareness Meditation, 249
Breath of Fire (BOF)
Buddha, 38–39, 108, 126, 184, 241, 252, 297
Buddhism, 38–39, 49, 83, 108, 114, 126–27, 129, 231

C

Campbell, Joseph, 64–67, 70, 315
Candle Meditation, 250
Chewbacca, 56, 76
Chewie, 90
Church of Jediism, 58
Clavicular Breath, 191

Clone Troopers, 56
concentration meditation, 248–49
Creating Self-Love, 302
Creighton University, 137

D

Dagobah, 85, 152, 164, 181, 221, 230, 260, 306
Darkside, 212, 214, 217, 221, 256, 292, 326, 328–29
Dark Warrior Archetype, 215
Darth Sidious, 231
Darth Vader, 58, 76, 152, 180, 187, 221, 230, 294, 306, 328
Death Star, 76–77, 229–30, 315
depression, 44, 73, 108, 146, 190, 257–58, 275–76, 297, 326
dharana, 177
dharma, 125–26
dhyana, 177
Disney World, 79–80

E

electromagnetic, 104, 144, 155, 173, 263
endosymbionts, 165

energy, 34–35, 40–41, 133–36, 150–55, 157–60, 163–71, 173–74, 186–89, 191–94, 196–99, 209–13, 216–20, 234–35, 256–60, 263, 271–72, 276–77, 288–90, 320–22, 324–26
Eternal Tao, 119
Exegol, 293

F

Fear-Based Society, 37
fear frequency, 141
fear lurking, 187
feelings control, 239, 246
festival, 104–5
First Chakra, 197
First Order, 221
force
    absolute, 134
    galvanising, 218
    galvanizing, 113
    magical, 308
    mystical, 102
    natural, 162
    organic, 151
    spiritual, 105
    strange, 101

unifying, 168
wilful, 248
Fourth Body, 244–45

G

Galvarino, 115
Glastonbury, 164, 299
Golden Chain, 142, 324
Grand Master Yoda, 153, 158, 221, 224, 230, 233, 235, 326, 329, 337, 339
Guinness World Record, 56
Gurdwara, 89–92, 94, 102
Gyan Mudra, 144, 194, 301

H

Hari, 91–95
Hawkins, 34, 36, 38
heart chakra, 298–99
hero, 59, 62, 64–78, 107, 111–13, 118–19, 206–7, 212–13, 216–18, 297, 299, 337–38, 342
hero archetype, 118, 216
hero myth, 66
Hollywood, 29, 58, 87
Holy Warrior, 116
Hudnall, 111–12
human feelings, 213
Hydrotherapy, 269

I

Ida, 188–89
Indian Sikh people, 93
inhale and exhale, 189, 225, 301
inhale and lift, 202
inhale and relax, 171, 287
Instagram, 31, 67, 257–58, 343

J

Jag, 79, 98
Japan, 59, 115, 154, 196
Japji, 92
Jedi and Sith orders, 164
Jedi arts, 318
Jedi code, 179, 183
Jedi Code Exercise, 183
Jedi Council in Star Wars, 131
Jedi culture, 182
Jedi Diet, 272
Jedi High Council, 154
Jediism, 58, 310–11
Jedi journal, 52, 60, 68, 108, 113, 119, 139, 219, 226, 228, 236
Jedi journey, 47
Jedi Knights, 28, 136–37

Jedi Master Yoda, 85, 183, 230
Jedi Order, 38, 137, 163, 165, 182, 246–47, 310
Jedi Padawans, 47
Jedi training journal, 59, 78, 309
Jedi Way, 180
Jivamukti Yoga, 168

K

Kaliyuga, 42
kindness, 133, 147, 208, 210, 248, 255, 297, 328–30, 342
Krishna, 125–26
Kundalini Circles, 283
Kundalini energy, 150, 166, 169, 197, 199
Kundalini Jedi, 28–343
Kundalini Jedi Warrior training journey, 155
Kundalini Shakti, 151
Kundalini Yoga, 91, 141–42, 148, 168–69, 174, 193, 242, 263, 271, 283, 285
Kundalini yoga kriya, 174
Kurukshetre, 125–26
Kylo, 125, 135, 221, 293–94

L

love songs, 210
Lucas, 56, 58–59, 65–66, 131, 154, 160, 165–66, 257, 306
Luke's journey, 217
Luke's Stages, 74

M

Maa, 144, 253
Manipura Chakra, 202
mantra, 141–44, 148, 169–70, 174, 177, 208, 225, 227, 237, 246, 248, 253, 322, 324–25, 339
Mantra and sound healing, 141
Master Yoda, 153, 158–59, 181, 183, 221, 224, 230–31, 233–35, 241, 326, 329, 337, 339
Maya, 127, 147, 160
meditation practice, 95, 249, 285, 335, 342
meditation techniques, 163, 247
Mental Focus, 252
Mindfulness Meditation, 249, 279
mindless hedonism, 325
Morpheus, 30, 82–83
Mount Shaoshi, 129

Muladhara Chakra, 189
mysterious, 152, 154, 182, 315
mystical, 102–3, 133, 137, 146, 154, 164–66, 290

N
Nādīs, 188
narcissism, 173, 185, 300, 326–27
Nihang, 114
Ninjas, 114

O
One Minute Breath, 194
Ong Namo Guru Dev Namo, 142, 322
Osho, 185–86

P
Padme, 214–15, 221, 231, 235, 292, 296, 298, 326
Palpatine, 212, 229, 293, 324
Paramahansa Yogananda, 178
Patanjali, 161–63, 175–78
Patanjali's Yoga Sutras, 161
Peaceful Warrior, 82
Piscean Age, 43–44
Pisces, 41, 43–44

Plato, 48, 106, 268
Power of Service, 331
Power of Story, 61
Pratyahara, 177
Purna Yoga College, 133

R
Radiant Body, 174, 263
Rock Pose, 170, 274

S
samadhi, 162, 178
Second Body, 242
selfless service, 95, 126, 175, 329–32
service, 57, 70, 126, 135, 138–39, 175, 185, 318, 325–26, 329–33, 342
seva, 95, 330
Shambhala, 54, 126–27
Shambhala warriors, 127
Shaolin, 129–30
silence, 32, 83–84, 90, 99, 102, 105, 142, 156, 247, 308–10, 323
Sith, 161, 164–65, 179–80, 206, 212–13, 231, 234, 324–26, 328–29, 333, 338

Sivananda Yoga, 168

solar plexus chakra, 197–98, 202, 208–9

sound and mantra chapters, 148

sound Naam, 170

Special World, 75–76

Star Wars and Philosophy, 138

Star Wars Fandom, 230

Star Wars Saga, 56

Steps of Hero Pose Virasana, 207

Stoics, 137–38

Sunia Meditation, 155

Sushumna, 151, 165, 188–89

T

tantric yoga, 102–4

Taoist beliefs, 154

Tatooine, 214, 292

Third Body, 243–44

Third Chakra, 170, 197–98

Tibet, 126–27, 247

Toltecs, 127–29

True love, 294

Tzu, 116

V

Vibration & Frequency, 140

W

Wahe Guru Wahe Jio, 208

warrior archetype, 69, 109, 113, 117–18, 212–13, 215–17, 219, 312

warrior energy
  inner, 109
  negative, 220
  positive, 216, 219

Warrior Ethos, 119

Warrior Evolution, 110, 217

warrior journey, 123, 128, 155

warrior mindset, 202, 207

warrior nature, 118, 120, 211

warrior path, 198

Warrior Qualities, 130

Warrior Saint, 208

Warrior's Code, 175

warrior spirit, 118

wellbeing, 33, 142, 146, 201, 214, 268

Y

Yamas, 178–79

yoga methodology, 140

yoga movements, 260

Yoga philosophy and practice, 175

yoga positions, 134
yoga sadhana, 126
yoga studio, 102, 105

Yogi Bhajan, 171, 185, 235–36, 238, 242, 304, 332–33

CITATIONS

1. Moyers, Bill. 1999. *The Mythology of 'Star Wars' with George Lucas.* Moyers. https://billmoyers.com/content/mythology-of-star-wars-george-lucas/
2. Wachowski, Lana. Hill, Grant. 1999. *The Matrix.* Warner Brothers Pictures. Village Roadshow Pictures. Silver Pictures.
3. Hawkins, David. PhD. 1995. *Power versus. Force: An Anatomy of Consciousness.* Hay House Inc. United States of America.
4. Rappa, Peter J. MD. 2005. *Move into health.* Baylor University Medical Center. https://www.ncbi.nlm.nih.gov/pmc/articles/PMC1200705/
5. Rappa, Peter J. MD. 2005. *Move into health.* Baylor University Medical Center. https://www.ncbi.nlm.nih.gov/pmc/articles/PMC1200705/
6. Hawkins, David. PhD. 1995. *Power versus. Force: An Anatomy of Consciousness.* Hay House Inc. United States of America.
7. Dubuisson, Widmarc. 2020. *What Is The "Great Awakening"?* https://www.energyrejuvenationsolution.com/post/what-is-the-great-awakening
8. Khalsa, Santokh Singh. DC. 2021. *The Aquarian Shift: What will be Different?* 3HO. https://www.3ho.org/3ho-lifestyle/aquarian-age/aquarian-shift-what-will-be-different
9. Kumaris, Brahma. 2014. The Four Phases Or Ages Of Humanity. Confluence Media. https://confluencemedia.wordpress.com/2014/10/06/the-four-phases-or-ages-of-humanity/
10. Moving into the Acquarian Age. https://www.radiantlightyoga.be/moving-into-the-acquarian-ag/
11. The Four Phases or Ages of Humanity: http://astudypoint.blogspot.com/2019/08/contemplation-august-16-2019-winners.html
12. Babauta, Leo. 2018. *A Beginner's Mind.* http://www.spirit7moves.com/yoga-inspired/a-beginners-mind-shared-from-leo-babauta
13. Murnahan, Briana. 2010. *Stress and Anxiety Reduction Due to Writing Diaries, Journals, E-mail, and Weblogs.* Senior Honors Theses. 230. http://commons.emich.edu/honors/230)
14. Taylor, Chris. 2021. *Book Review: 'How Star Wars Conquered the Universe'.* https://www.wsj.com/articles/book-review-how-star-wars-conquered-the-universe-by-chris-taylor-1412366591
15. Choi, Charles Q. 2010. *How 'Star Wars' Changed the World.* https://www.space.com/8917-star-wars-changed-world.html
16. Wikipedia Contribution. 2021. *Star Wars sources and analogues.* https://en.wikipedia.org/wiki/Star_Wars_sources_and_analogues
17. Zehr, Dan. 2016. *STUDYING SKYWALKERS: MAY THE 4TH AND THE CULTURAL SIGNIFICANCE OF STAR WARS.* https://www.starwars.com/news/studying-skywalkers-may-the-4th-and-the-cultural-significance-of-star-wars

18. Brown, Professor. 2021. Arizona State University Film Department: *The Hero's Journey Outline, BY JOSEPH CAMPBELL.* https://www.coursehero.com/file/p5sokoo/Jung-suggested-that-these-archetypes-are-reflection-of-aspects-of-the-human/
19. Moyers, Bill. Lucas, George. 1999. *Of Myth And Men.* Time Magazine. http://content.time.com/time/magazine/article/0,9171,23298-2,00.html
20. Webster, Merriam. 2021. *Dictionary Definitions. Definition of hero (Entry 1 of 3).* Merriam Webster. https://www.merriam-webster.com/dictionary/hero
21. Twemlow, Greg. 2020. *There's A Hero In All Of Us.* Medium. https://gregtwemlow.medium.com/theres-a-hero-in-all-of-us-fb8dabaea0ed#:~:text=Giving%20himself%2C%20sacrificing%20himself%20to,that%20the%20hero%20cycle%20represents
22. Twemlow, Greg. 2020. *There's A Hero In All Of Us.* Medium. https://gregtwemlow.medium.com/theres-a-hero-in-all-of-us-fb8dabaea0ed#:~:text=Giving%20himself%2C%20sacrificing%20himself%20to,that%20the%20hero%20cycle%20represents
23. Larson, Melody. 2021. *Introduction to a 12-Part Series: The 12 Steps of the Spiritual Journey: A Map for the Seeker Going in Circles.* https://trans4mind.com/counterpoint/index-spiritual/larson6.html
24. Arianna. 2021. *Unveil your energy leaks & discover your true power.* https://www.arianna.com.au/archetypal-profiling
25. Jung, Carl. 1960. *The Structure & Dynamics of the Psyche. 2nd Edition.* The Bollingen Foundation. Routledge
26. Hudnall, Ariel. 2015. *Archetypes: Sage.* Ariel Hudnall Website. https://arielhudnall.com/2015/12/01/archetypes-sage/
27. Bessler, Robert. 2020. *The Spiritual Warrior.* Abode of the Eternal Tao. https://abodetao.com/the-spiritual-warrior/
28. Hudnall, Ariel. 2015. *Archetypes: Magician.* Ariel Hudnall Website. https://arielhudnall.com/2016/05/15/archetypes-magician/#:~:text=The%20Magician%20wishes%20to%20harness,the%20catalyst%20for%20a%20reason.&text=The%20Magician%20is%20the%20chess%2Dplayer
29. E, Hannah. 2019. *THE DEADLIEST WARRIORS THROUGHOUT HISTORY.* Daily Sport. https://www.dailysportx.com/general/deadliest-warriors
30. Hasse, Edgar S. 2014. *What So-Called Religious Wars Are Really About.* World Crunch. https://worldcrunch.com/opinion-analysis/what-so-called-religious-wars-are-really-about/jihadists-religious-warriors-isis-killing-death-muslims-christians-azidi/c7s17155
31. Pressfield, Steven. 2011. *The Warrior Ethos.* https://www.trngcmd.marines.mil/Portals/207/Docs/SOI-W/MCTB/Student-Resources/Reference-2_The_Warrior_Ethos.pdf?ver=2018-10-12-135250-303
32. Bessler, Bessler, Robert. 2020. *The Spiritual Warrior.* Abode of the Eternal Tao. https://abodetao.com/the-spiritual-warrior/

33. Ruiz, Guillermo Marín. 2021. *The Toltec Warrior.* https://mastay.info/posts/2/the-toltec-warrior/
34. Ruiz, Guillermo Marín. 2021. *The Toltec Warrior.* https://mastay.info/posts/2/the-toltec-warrior/
35. Ruiz, Don Miguel. 1997. *The Four Agreements: A Practical Guide to Personal Freedom.* http://www.toltecspirit.com/four-agreements/characteristics-of-a-spiritual-warrior/
36. Ruiz, Don Miguel. 1997. *The Four Agreements: A Practical Guide to Personal Freedom.* http://www.toltecspirit.com/four-agreements/characteristics-of-a-spiritual-warrior/
37. Ruiz, Don Miguel. 1997. *The Four Agreements: A Practical Guide to Personal Freedom.* http://www.toltecspirit.com/four-agreements/characteristics-of-a-spiritual-warrior/
38. Ruiz, Don Miguel. 1997. *The Four Agreements: A Practical Guide to Personal Freedom.* http://www.toltecspirit.com/four-agreements/characteristics-of-a-spiritual-warrior/
39. Mehta, Bina. 2015. *The War Within, Wisdom from the Bhagavad Gita – Part 1: Overview.* Bina Mehta Blog. https://binamehta.com/war-within-bhagavad-gita-part-1-overview/
40. Mehta, Bina. 2015. *The War Within, Wisdom from the Bhagavad Gita – Part 1: Overview.* Bina Mehta Blog. https://binamehta.com/war-within-bhagavad-gita-part-1-overview/
41. Mehta, Bina. 2015. *The War Within, Wisdom from the Bhagavad Gita – Part 1: Overview.* Bina Mehta Blog. https://binamehta.com/war-within-bhagavad-gita-part-1-overview/
42. Shaw, Edwina. 2017. *Embracing Our Inner Warrior to Create World Peace.* Uplift. https://brewminate.com/the-legend-of-the-shambhala-warriors/
43. Shaw, Edwina. 2017. *Embracing Our Inner Warrior to Create World Peace.* Uplift. https://brewminate.com/the-legend-of-the-shambhala-warriors/
44. Mingren, Wu. 2018. *Toltecs: Fierce Warriors Who Changed the Face of Mesoamerica for Good.* Ancient Origins. https://www.ancient-origins.net/ancient-places-americas/toltecs-warriors-mesoamerica-0010365
45. Hardman, Allan. 2021. *The Toltec Path of Transformation.* https://toltenconline.com/the-path-of-transformation/
46. Learn Shaolin Team. 2018. *How To: Shaolin Monks Training.* https://bookmartialartsinchina.medium.com/how-to-shaolin-monks-training-25b1118c49ce
47. Learn Shaolin Kung Fu Team. 2021. *What is Shaolin Kung Fu.* https://learn-shaolinkungfu.com/shaolin-monks-training/
48. Talmon, Noelle. 2018. *How Shaolin Monks Obtain Their Superpowers.* https://lethbridgenewsnow.com/2018/04/16/how-shaolin-monks-obtain-their-superpowers/

49. Toci, Mark. 2021. *7 Knightly Virtues*. Mark Toci Blog. http://marktoci.weebly.com/7-knightly-virtues.html
50. Klinker, Adam. 2021. *Stoicism and Star Wars*. Creighton University. https://www.creighton.edu/creightonmagazine/2017fallunewsstarwars/
51. Decker, Kevin. Eberl, Jason. 2000. *Star Wars and Philosophy: More Powerful Than You Can Possibly Imagine*. Open Court. https://philpapers.org/archive/STESWA.pdf
52. 3HO Team. 2021. *The Mantra Toolkit: Sat Nam*. https://www.3ho.org/kundalini-yoga/mantra/kundalini-yoga-mantras/mantra-toolkit-sat-nam
53. Snead, Ally. 2019. *This Sa Ta Na Ma Kundalini Meditation Clears Your Subconscious For A Fresh Start*. The Peaceful Dumpling. https://www.peacefuldumpling.com/sa-ta-na-ma-meditation
54. TMYC Admin. 2019. *Kundalini awakening*. https://thapovanmeditation.com/2019/11/10/kundalini-awakening/
55. Wikipedia Contribution. 2021. *The Force*. https://en.wikipedia.org/wiki/The_Force
56. Reninger, Elizabeth. 2019. *Qi (Chi): The Taoist Principle of Life Force*. Learn Religions. https://www.learnreligions.com/what-is-qi-chi-3183052
57. Spencer, Maya. 2021. *What is spirituality? A personal exploration*. RC Psych. https://www.rcpsych.ac.uk/docs/default-source/members/sigs/spirituality-spsig/what-is-spirituality-maya-spencer-x.pdf?sfvrsn=f28df052_2
58. Sat Yoga Team. 2019. *What are siddhis?* Sat Yoga. https://www.satyoga.org/blog/what-are-siddhis/
59. Wikepedia Contributor. 2021. *Siddhis*. https://en.wikipedia.org/wiki/Siddhi#:~:text=faculty%20or%20capability.-,Patanjali's%20Yoga%20Sutras,Ahi%E1%B9%83s%C4%81%3A%20a%20peaceful%20aura
60. Wikipedia Contributor. 2021. *Kundalini*. https://en.wikipedia.org/wiki/Kundalini#:~:text=The%20American%20comparative%20religions%20scholar,seven%2C%20near%20the%20base%20of
61. Caron, Matt. 2021. *10 Benefits Of Awakening Your Kundalini*. https://blog.sivanaspirit.com/md-sp-benefits-awakening-kundalini/
62. Woodyard, Catherine. 2011. *Exploring the therapeutic effects of yoga and its ability to increase quality of life*. International Journal of Yoga. https://www.ncbi.nlm.nih.gov/pmc/articles/PMC3193654/
63. Roberts, Sherry. 2021. *Patanjali's Eightfold Path of Yoga*. A Moment of Yoga. https://yoga.sherry-roberts.com/patanjali-and-his-eightfold-path-of-yoga/
64. Roberts, Sherry. 2021. *Patanjali's Eightfold Path of Yoga*. A Moment of Yoga. https://yoga.sherry-roberts.com/patanjali-and-his-eightfold-path-of-yoga/
65. Newlyn, Emma. 2021. *The Yamas and Niyamas*. Eckhart Yoga. https://www.ekhartyoga.com/articles/philosophy/the-yamas-and-niyamas

66. Osho News Team. 2020. *The rebel has no path.* Osho News. https://www.oshonews.com/2020/08/30/the-rebel-has-no-path/
67. Osho. 1987. *The Rebel, the Very Salt of the Earth.* http://www.baytallaah.com/osholibrary/reader.php?endpos=556677&page=254&book=The%20Rebel
68. Osho. 2021. *The Continuous Rebellion.* Osho.com. https://www.osho.com/read/osho/vision/the-continuous-rebellion
69. Vinuty, Akilaa. 2017. *Energy Channels and Transmitters.* http://akilaavinuty.blogspot.com/2017/11/nadis_18.html
70. 3HO Team. 2021. *Long Deep Breathing.* https://www.3ho.org/long-deep-breathing
71. 3HO Team. 2021. *Alternate Nostril Breathing.* https://www.3ho.org/alternate-nostril-breathing
72. Abate, Skya. Dr. 2021. *The Hara, the Source of Life and the Navel, the Gate of the Spirit. Southwest Acupuncture College.* https://acupuncturecollege.edu/blog/hara-source-life-and-navel-gate-spirit
73. 3HO Team. 2021. *The Agni Tattva & the 3rd Chakra.* https://www.3ho.org/3ho-lifestyle/health-and-healing/agni-tattva-3rd-chakra
74. 3HO Team. 2021. *The 3rd Chakra: The Will of the Spiritual Warrior.* https://www.3ho.org/3ho-lifestyle/men/courage-and-commitment/3rd-chakra-will-spiritual-warrior
75. Luna, Aletheia. 2020. *The Ultimate Guide to Solar Plexus Chakra Healing For Complete Beginners.* Loner Wolf. https://lonerwolf.com/solar-plexus-chakra-healing/
76. Hudnall, Ariel. 2015. *Archetypes: Magician.* Ariel Hudnall Website. https://arielhudnall.com/2016/05/15/archetypes-magician/#:~:text=The%20Magician%20wishes%20to%20harness,the%20catalyst%20for%20a%20reason.&text=The%20Magician%20is%20the%20chess%2Dplayer
77. McKay, Brett. McKay, Kate. 2011. *The Four Archetypes of the Mature Masculine: The Warrior.* The Art of Manliness. https://www.artofmanliness.com/articles/the-four-archetypes-of-the-mature-masculine-the-warrior/
78. Hillman, James. 2021. *THE WARRIOR ARCHETYPE.* Archetypal Immersion School. http://www.hillman-school.com/warrior2
79. Wookipedia Contributor. 2021. *Death.* https://starwars.fandom.com/wiki/Death
80. 3HO Team. 2021. *Anger: Find and Refine Your Power.* https://www.3ho.org/3ho-lifestyle/health-and-healing/anger-find-and-refine-your-power
81. 3HO Team. 2021. *Meditation to Transcend Individual Consciousness & Anger.* https://www.3ho.org/3ho-lifestyle/authentic-relationships/meditation-transcend-individual-consciousness-anger
82. Bessler, Robert. 2020. *The Spiritual Warrior.* Abode of the Eternal Tao. https://abodetao.com/the-spiritual-warrior/

83. Power of Positivity Team. 2015. *How To Master Your Mind: Part One.* https://www.powerofpositivity.com/master-your-mind-part-one/
84. 3HO Team. 2021. *The Three Functional Minds.* https://www.3ho.org/kundalini-yoga/ten-bodies/three-functional-minds
85. Wookipedia Contributor. 2021. *Meditation.* https://starwars.fandom.com/wiki/Meditation/Legends#:~:text=Meditation%20was%20a%20mental%20technique,state%20of%20relaxation%20or%20awareness
86. Giovanni. 2017. *Walking Meditation — The Ultimate Guide.* https://liveanddare.com/walking-meditation/
87. Back to Basics Team. 2020. *Candle Meditation.* https://www.facebook.com/BacktoBasicsWilliamstown/posts/4492489794126043/
88. Siragusa, Tullio. 2020. *How to Have a Positive Mindset During Difficult Times.* https://medium.com/radical-culture/how-to-have-a-positive-mindset-during-difficult-times-878537337ff1
89. Ramdesh, Dr. 2021. *What is the Positive Mind? (The 3rd Body).* https://blog.spiritvoyage.com/what-is-the-positive-mind-the-3rd-body/
90. 3HO Team. 2021. *Smiling Buddha Kriya - Meditation for the Positive Mind.* https://www.3ho.org/kundalini-yoga/mantra/smiling-buddha-kriya-meditation-positive-mind
91. Ho, Eric. 2013. *The Five Reasons Why Gen-Y Should Learn Martial Arts.* Elite Daily. https://www.elitedaily.com/life/five-reasons-why-gen-y-should-learn-martial-arts
92. Stevens, Eric. 2020. *5 Underrated Reasons You Should Pick Up A Martial Art.* https://breakingmuscle.com/fitness/5-underrated-reasons-you-should-pick-up-a-martial-art
93. 3HO Team. 2021. *Hydrotherapy.* https://it.3ho.org/3ho-lifestyle/daily-routine/hydrotherapy
94. 3HO Team. 2021. *Sleep.* https://www.3ho.org/3ho-lifestyle/daily-routine/sleep
95. 3HO Team. 2021. *7 Keys to Eating Wisely.* https://www.3ho.org/3ho-lifestyle/yogic-diet/7-keys-eating-wisely
96. Cuncic, Arlin. 2020. *10 Ways to Have More Confident Body Language.* https://www.verywellmind.com/ten-ways-to-have-more-confident-body-language-3024855
97. Power Smile Dental Centre Team. 2021. *What's Really Behind a Smile.* https://powersmiledentalcentre.ca/whats-really-behind-a-smile
98. Stoic Maze Team. 2018. *What is the cosmic joke?* https://www.stoicmaze.com/home/2018/8/24/what-is-the-cosmic-joke
99. Melbourne Psychology Team. 2021. *Calm Your Body and Your Mind with these Grounding Exercises.* https://www.innermelbpsychology.com.au/grounding-exercises/

100. Guru Rattan, PhD. 2021. *Lesson 13 - Befriending Your Body.* Kundalini Yoga. https://www.kundaliniyoga.org/lesson_13
101. Halliwel, Ed. 2016. *The 7 Qualities of Mindfulness Trained in the Body Scan.* Mindful. https://www.mindful.org/7-qualities-mindfulness-trained-body-scan/
102. Shilagh Mirgain, PhD. *A Body Scan Script.* UW Cultivating Well-Being: A Neuroscientific Approach. https://www.va.gov/WHOLEHEALTHLIBRARY/docs/Script-Body-Scan.pdf
103. Ivey, Madilyn. 2020. *Top 10 Romances In Star Wars, Ranked.* Screen Rant. https://screenrant.com/star-wars-romances-ranked/
104. Brown, Michael. 2020. *Desperately Seeking Unconditional Love.* http://www.creationsmagazine.com/articles/C129/Brown.html
105. 3HO Team. 2021. *Meditation to Heal a Broken Heart.* https://www.3ho.org/3ho-lifestyle/authentic-relationships/meditation-heal-broken-heart
106. Kristin. 2021. *Heart Chakra: Everything You Need to Know.* https://www.bemytravelmuse.com/heart-chakra/
107. 3HO Team. 2021. *Meditation for a Calm Heart.* https://www.3ho.org/kundalini-yoga/pranayam/pranayam-techniques/meditation-calm-heart
108. 3HO Team. 2021. *Kriya for Creating Self-Love.* https://www.3ho.org/3ho-lifestyle/authentic-relationships/yogi-bhajan-love/kundalini-yoga-creating-self-love
109. Plano, Catherine. 2017. *Surrender and Let the Universe Catch You.* https://www.catherineplano.com.au/let-the-universe-catch-you/
110. Stardust Vibes Team. 2021. *9 SIGNS OF SYNCHRONICITY - THE LANGUAGE OF THE SOUL.* https://stardustvibes.com/blogs/news/9-signs-of-synchronicity-the-language-of-the-soul
111. Moga, Alexandra. 2019. *Are you living from intuition or ego?* https://www.moga-yoga.com/inspire/intuitionorego
112. Neutrino, Michael. 2021. *The Voice of the Ego vs Intuition.* https://www.3ho.org/voice-ego-vs-intuition
113. 3HO Team. 2021. *The Adi Mantra & the Golden Chain of Kundalini Yoga.* https://www.3ho.org/kundalini-yoga/kriya/practice-guidelines/adi-mantra-golden-chain-kundalini-yoga
114. Cartwright, Mark. 2017. *Narcissus.* https://www.worldhistory.org/Narcissus/
115. Seltzer, Leon F. PhD. 2016. *The Curse of Apathy: Sources and Solutions.* https://www.psychologytoday.com/us/blog/evolution-the-self/201604/the-curse-apathy-sources-and-solutions
116. 3HO Team. 2021. *Rewiring Your Habits: 40/90/120/1000 Day Sadhanas.* https://www.3ho.org/kundalini-yoga/sadhana-daily-spiritual-practice/rewiring-your-habits-40901201000-day-sadhanas

117. 3HO Team. 1971. *Meditation on Change.* https://www.3ho.org/kundalini-yoga/pranayam/meditation-change
118. Jung, Carl. 1964. *Man and His Symbols.* Doubleday Hardcover.
119. Jung, Carl. 1969. *Archetypes and the Collective Unconscious.* Princeton University Press.
120. Jung, Carl. 1966. *The Collected Works of C.G. Jung, Volume 7: Two Essays in Analytical Psychology – The Relations Between Ego and the Unconscious.* Princeton University Press.
121. Jung, Carl. 1973. *Synchronicity: An Acausal Connecting Principle.* Princeton University Press.
122. Jung, Carl. 1933. *Modern Man in Search of a Soul.* Mariner Books Edition.
123. Pearson, Carol. 2015. *Awakening the Heroes Within: Twelve Archetypes to Help Us Find Ourselves and Transform Our World.* HarperOne.
124. Chaudhuri, Haridas. 1990. *The Essence of Spiritual Philosophy.* Harper Collins.
125. Moore, Thomas. 1994. *Care of the Soul: A Guide for Cultivating Depth and Sacredness in Everyday Life.* Harper Perennial.
126. Edinger, Edward F. 1992. *Ego and Archetype: Individuation and the Religious Function of the Psyche.* Shambala.
127. Samuel, Robert T. 2005. *The Samurai: The Philosophy of victory.* Barnes & Noble Publishing Inc.
128. Adrienne, Carol. Redfield, James. 1999. *The Purpose of Your Life: Finding Your Place In The World Using Synchronicity, Intuition, And Uncommon Sense.* William Morrow Paperbacks.
129. Campbell, Joseph. 1972. *The Hero With a Thousand Faces.* Princeton University Press.
130. Campbell, Joseph. 1988. *The Power of Myth.* Anchor.
131. Campbell, Joseph. Fairchild, Johnson E. 1993. *Myths to Live By.* Penguin Compass.
132. Campbell, Joseph. 1991. *The Masks of God, Volume 1: Primitive Mythology.* Penguin.
133. Campbell, Joseph. 2014. *The Hero's Journey: Joseph Campbell on His Life and Work (The Collected Works of Joseph Campbell).*
134. Bond, D Stephenson. 2001. *Living Myth: Personal Meaning as a Way of Life.* Shambala.
135. Rinzler, JW. Jackson, Peter. 2007. *The Making of Star Wars.* Del Rey.
136. Millman, Dan. 2006. *Way of the Peaceful Warrior: A Book That Changes Lives.* New World Library.
137. Lee, Bruce. Johnson, Gilbert. 1975. *Tao of Jeet Kune Do.* Black Belt Communications.
138. Trungpa, Chogyam. 2007. *Shambhala: The Sacred Path of the Warrior.*

139. David Stone, Joshua. 1999. *Soul Psychology: HOW TO CLEAR NEGATIVE EMOTIONS AND SPIRITUALIZE YOUR LIFE.* Wellspring/Ballantine.
140. Kipnis, Aaron. 2004. *Knights Without Armor.* Indigo Phoenix Books.
141. Yogi Bhajan. 1997. *The Master's Touch: On Being a Sacred Teacher for the New Age.* Kundalini Research Institute.
142. Wallace, Daniel. 2016. *Star Wars Year by Year: A Visual History, Updated Edition (Star Wars (DK Publishing)).* DK Publishing.
143. Leonard, George. 1992. *Mastery: The Keys to Success and Long-Term Fulfillment.* Plume.
144. Gregg, Susan. Ruiz, Miguel. 2020. *The Toltec Way: A Guide to Personal Transformation.* St. Martin's Essentials.
145. Cleary, Thomas. 2014. *Soul of the Samurai: Modern Translations of Three Classic Works of Zen & Bushido.* Tuttle Publishing.
146. Jung, Carl. Hull, RFC. 2004. *Four Archetypes.* Routledge.
147. Ruiz, Don Miguel. 1999. *The Mastery of Love: A Practical Guide to the Art of Relationship: A Toltec Wisdom Book.* Amber-Allen Publishing Inc.
148. Star Wars Blog Team. 2016. *STUDYING SKYWALKERS: MAY THE 4TH AND THE CULTURAL SIGNIFICANCE OF STAR WARS.* Star Wars Fandom. https://www.starwars.com/news/studying-skywalkers-may-the-4th-and-the-cultural-significance-of-star-wars
149. Star Wars Blog Team. 2016. *STUDYING SKYWALKERS: MAY THE 4TH AND THE CULTURAL SIGNIFICANCE OF STAR WARS.* Star Wars Fandom. https://www.starwars.com/news/studying-skywalkers-may-the-4th-and-the-cultural-significance-of-star-wars
150. Selg, Markus. Kennedy, Susanne. 2020. *Ultraworld.* VOLKSBÜHNE – Berlin. https://www.volksbuehne.berlin/de/programm/8730/ultraworld
151. Twemlow, Greg. 2020. *There's A Hero In All Of Us.* Medium. https://gregtwemlow.medium.com/theres-a-hero-in-all-of-us-fb8dabaea0ed#:~:text=Giving%20himself%2C%20sacrificing%20himself%20to,that%20the%20hero%20cycle%20represents
152. Lucas, George. 1977. *Star Wars: Episode IV – A New Hope.* Lucasfilm. 20th Century Fox.
153. Lucas, George. 1977. *Star Wars: Episode IV – A New Hope.* Lucasfilm. 20th Century Fox.
154. Johari, Harish. 1987. *Chakras: Energy Centers of Transformation.* http://www.adishakti.org/subtle_system/kundalini.htm
155. LifeCo Psychology Team. 2021. *The Chakra's.* https://www.lifeco-psychology.co.nz/chakras/
156. Woodyard, Catherine. 2011. *Exploring the therapeutic effects of yoga and its ability to increase quality of life.* International Journal of Yoga. https://www.ncbi.nlm.nih.gov/pmc/articles/PMC3193654/

157. Golden, Carl. 2020. *The 12 Common Archetypes.* Tree of Life Essays. http://www.treeoflifecounseling.life/essays/the_12_common_archetypes.html
158. Newlyn, Emma. 2021. The Yamas and Niyamas. https://www.ekhartyoga.com/articles/philosophy/the-yamas-and-niyamas
159. Silcox, Kate. 2014. How to Use the 7 Chakras in Your Yoga Practice. https://www.yogajournal.com/yoga-101/chakras-yoga-for-beginners/a-guide-to-the-chakras/
160. Golden, Carl. 2021. The 12 Common Archetypes. http://www.treeoflifecounseling.life/essays/the_12_common_archetypes.html
161. Spirit Rising Yoga Team. 2021. Breath of Fire (BOF). https://www.spiritrisingyoga.org/kundalini-info/breath-of-fire
162. The 3Ho Foundation Team. 2021. Cannon Breath. https://www.3ho.org/files/pdfs/various-breaths.pdf
163. The 3Ho Foundation Team. 2021. Segmented Breath. https://www.3ho.org/files/pdfs/various-breaths.pdf
164. The 3Ho Foundation Team. 2021. Lion Breath. https://www.3ho.org/files/pdfs/various-breaths.pdf
165. The 3Ho Foundation Team. 2021. Whistle Breath. https://www.3ho.org/files/pdfs/various-breaths.pdf
166. The 3Ho Foundation Team. 2021. Sitali Pranayam. https://www.3ho.org/files/pdfs/various-breaths.pdf
167. The 3Ho Foundation Team. 2021. Vatskar Pranayam. https://www.3ho.org/files/pdfs/various-breaths.pdf
168. The 3Ho Foundation Team. 2021. The Four Main Body Locks. https://www.3ho.org/kundalini-yoga/bandhas/four-main-body-locks
169. The 3Ho Foundation Team. 2021. The Four Main Body Locks. https://www.3ho.org/kundalini-yoga/bandhas/four-main-body-locks
170. The 3Ho Foundation Team. 2021. The Four Main Body Locks. https://www.3ho.org/kundalini-yoga/bandhas/four-main-body-locks
171. The 3Ho Foundation Team. 2021. The Four Main Body Locks. https://www.3ho.org/kundalini-yoga/bandhas/four-main-body-locks
172. The 3Ho Foundation Team. 2021. Eye Focus. https://www.3ho.org/kundalini-yoga/eye-focus
173. Dubey, Aditya. 2012. NADI'S: IDA, PINGALA AND SUSHUMNA. https://www.facebook.com/kundalichakra/posts/294014047376640:0
174. Dubey, Aditya. 2012. NADI'S: IDA, PINGALA AND SUSHUMNA. https://www.facebook.com/kundalichakra/posts/294014047376640:0
175. Dubey, Aditya. 2012. NADI'S: IDA, PINGALA AND SUSHUMNA. https://www.facebook.com/kundalichakra/posts/294014047376640:0
176. Dubey, Aditya. 2012. NADI'S: IDA, PINGALA AND SUSHUMNA. https://www.facebook.com/kundalichakra/posts/294014047376640:0